THE
POLITICAL UTILITY
OF
ISLAMOPHOBIA

How the U.S. Right used Islam
after 9/11 as a
New Field for Domestic Politics

DAVID D. BELT

About this Book

Why, in the aftermath of 9/11, did a segment of U.S. security experts, political elite, media and other institutions classify not just al-Qaeda but the entire religion of Islam as a security threat, thereby countering the prevailing professional consensus and White House policy that maintained a distinction between terrorism and Islam?

Why did this oppositional narrative about the threat of Islam expand and even degenerate into warning about the "Islamization of America" by the country's tiny population of Muslim-Americans? This Islamization threat became sufficiently convincing that conservative legislators in two dozen states introduced bills to prevent the spread of Islamic law, or sharia, and a Republican Presidential front-runner exclaimed, "I believe Shariah is a mortal threat to the survival of freedom in the United States and in the world as we know it"!

This case study of U.S. popular security discourse on Islam in the decade after 9/11 deepens the critical characterizations of this phenomenon as "Islamophobia," the "new Orientalism," the "new McCarthyism," and so on. The analysis distinctively reveals how this "threat" discourse could and did function as a deliberate strategy of the more entrepreneurial segments of the U.S. conservative movement, who—in the emotion-laden wake of 9/11—seized Islam as another opportune field of struggle to advance their ongoing project of cultural politics. The study thus challenges our basic assumption that security knowledge is inherently objective description that corresponds to reality. It instead reveals that all security issues have a much more subjective and constructed nature, with inherent political utility, and undergirded by apparatuses of political power.

About the Author

Professor David Belt, since 2008, has served as a full-time faculty member at National Intelligence University, Washington DC—the fully accredited graduate institution for the seventeen agencies in the U.S. intelligence community. There, he has led courses and supervised thesis research in the social analysis of strategic-level, security issues within Muslim communities worldwide, especially the broader Middle East. Concurrently, Dr. Belt for nearly two-years led the 23-member nation Global Futures Forum's project on Political Violence and Extremism, served two years as NIU's first Chair/Head of the Regional Issues Department, and created the university's Middle East concentration and its present six courses. Previously, David served as Assistant Professor, National Security Studies, National Defense University. Concurrently, from 2005 through 2008, he led the 400-member invitation-only global community of interest on countering violent extremism, editing its bi-weekly newsletter, "Containing al-Qaedaism," and developed and taught the university's first national security professional certified course on that topic. In a former military career, Captain Belt (ret.) also served twenty-six years on active-duty in various high-risk and combat operational and executive-level leadership positions within the U.S. Navy's non-SEAL Special Operations Officer community. He is a member of the class of 1982, U.S. Naval Academy, earned his Master's in Security Studies and Strategic Resources at the Industrial College of the Armed Forces (currently the Eisenhower School), National Defense University, and was awarded his PhD from Virginia Tech's School of Public and International Affairs, National Capital Region campus.

The Political Utility of Islamophobia

How the U.S. Right used Islam after 9/11
as a New Field for Domestic Politics

Copyright © 2019 by David Belt

Paperback ISBN 978-0-9989578-8-3

Also Available in Kindle, electronic book

First published in the United States by

David Belt
Productions

Annapolis, Maryland

CONTENTS

1

THE GREEN SCARE

U.S. Popular Security Discourse on Islam after 9/11

I believe Shariah is a mortal threat to the survival of freedom
in the United States and in the world as we know it.

—Newt Gingrich (2010)

1. The Puzzle

ON September 17th President Bush formally broke the nation's self-imposed moment of silence and rendered the official interpretation of the September 11th attack. To visually symbolize what his speech intended to convey, the chosen venue was the Islamic Center of Washington. There, the White House staff had assembled for the cameras whatever Muslim symbolic and leadership figures they could cobble together on short notice.[1]

"The face of terror is not the true faith of Islam, the president said. "That's not what Islam is all about." He then uttered these three seemingly innocuous words: *"Islam is peace"* (PBS Newshour 2001).

On the one hand, the speech was a crucial act of public diplomacy, creating distance between "terrorists" and "Islam." On the other, creating such a terror/Islam distinction must have seemed *politically safe*. Not only did it reflect a core value of Western liberalism that was enshrined in the Constitution, but it represented a historical lesson learned in the wake of a previous collective outrage over the Japanese attack on Pearl Harbor. In that *illiberal* moment, another non-white and immigrant segment of society—Japanese-

---

[1] Video of the speech is available at: http://www.youtube.com/watch?v=w0phxuzQ7sE, and the transcript is available at http://www.pbs.org/newshour/updates/terrorism/july-dec01/bush_speech_9-17.html

Americans—was collectively considered a threat and sent *en masse* to internment camps. And, only a decade later, the embarrassing anti-Communist witch hunts led by Senator Joseph McCarthy had further underscored the value's universality.

And, despite Samuel Huntington's (1993) now pervasively popularized phrase, "Islam has bloody borders," the terrorism/Islam distinction—that is, the segregation of the two concepts—prevailed amongst national security professionals and scholars across the spectrum of academic disciplines. The categories of people that security practitioners and scholars had found in Muslim societies are the same categories we had found in every society—a continuum of dynamic and diverse solidarities, groups, and agents, loosely held by ideological commitments animated by the dynamic socio-historical conditions in which they are situated (Ayoob 2007; Esposito and Mogahed 2008, for example). In the literature, "Islam" is more anthropologically "Islams"—a diverse and even dynamic continuum, with the vast majority of Muslims structured ideologically within their state's or tribal region's highly peculiar hegemony. At the historical juncture of the President's speech, this literature portrayed Muslim revolutionary movements similarly—as a complex continuum that warranted careful disaggregation of its constituent parts, and with only the more extreme fringe subscribing to an ideology that legitimizes violent jihad in contemporary contexts outside of physical occupation of Muslim territory for unequivocal hostile, self-serving purposes.

The silence in professional security writing regarding the threat of "Islam" broadly (excluding the continuing resistance of revolutionary Iran) extended back through the previous two generations of struggle to defeat Nazism and Communism. Perhaps the best symbol of this complete lack of an Islam-as-threat frame was when in 1985 President Ronald Reagan hosted the Afghanistan mujahideen who fought the Soviets at the White House. Then, a mere fifteen years before 9/11, the U.S. viewed Islam as such a benign threat that it encouraged jihadism. The *Washington Post* (March 23, 2002) captured this strategy this way:

> The United States spent millions of dollars to supply Afghan schoolchildren with textbooks filled with violent images and militant Islamic teachings.... The primers, which were filled with talk of jihad and featured drawings of guns, bullets, soldiers and mines, have served since then as the Afghan school system's core curriculum. Even the Taliban used the American-produced books.

Similarly, the U.S. clandestinely funded advertisements in newspapers and newsletters in Muslim-majority communities worldwide to induce Muslims to join the Islamic jihad (Hoodbhoy 2005).

The Counternarrative: Islam is *Not* Peace

But, 9/11 threatened to rupture that paradigmatic security frame. The attacking organization, al-Qaeda, not only identified itself as Islamic, but justified its attack within an Islamic canon, in Islamic terms. Those factors alone were sure to produce newsworthy opposition to the *"Islam is peace"* frame.

Despite President Bush's Evangelical bona fides, an early and key figure to articulate such opposition to the official "Islam is peace" storyline was Bush family friend, and prominent Evangelical leader Franklin Graham—the son of evangelist Billy Graham. "I believe it is a very evil and wicked religion," Graham said unapologetically (*USA Today* 2001, September 21). Other Evangelical leaders expressed similar opposition. Jerry Falwell, for example, in a prominent interview with CBS correspondent Bob Simon on *60 Minutes*, reflected at least some of the U.S. religious conservative consensus. "I think Mohammed was a terrorist," he said; adding that, "he was a violent man, a man of war."[2]

Dissidence also existed among the experts housed in conservative policy advocacy organizations. Typifying this heretical view of Islam as danger was William S. Lind at the conservative Free Congress Foundation, who countered the White House's official storyline about Islam. "There is no such thing as peaceful Islam," he said; adding "Islamics [sic] cannot fit into an America in which the first loyalty is to the American Constitution," and "they are a fifth column in this country" (*Washington Post* 2001, November 19).

Again, given the context, this kind of opposition from this segment of the Conservative movement should have been expected. But, such sporadic dissident and reactionary speech acts in the more immediate aftermath of 9/11 seemed destined to become relatively insignificant compared to the vast and accelerating amount of more banal information then being produced on the nexus of Islam and threat. By the post-9/11 decade's end, for instance, the number of active internet-based U.S.-only productions across the spectrum with "Islam" and "jihad" in the topic would rise to over 400 million and 50 million respectively, and English books published with "jihad" in the title in the would rise to 39,400, compared to only 4,280 published in *all previous* decades.

The popular opposition to the official, scholarly, and normative "Islam is peace" frame seemed destined to irrelevance for another reason. As distance from the 9/11 emotion-evoking dislocation was gained, we might have expected that such a *counter* narrative would be subsumed by a more rational *corrective*. One such hypothetical corrective from U.S. religious conservatives—both Christian and Jewish—reasonably might have been this: "Islam—although a false derivative of our faith—is normally peaceful, but has an ambiguous 'just war' tradition that can be readily manipulated by discontents." Another hypothetical corrective to the "religion of peace" frame from more secular conservatives might have been: "The Islamic faith is a broad continuum, part of which condones violence when other Muslims are threatened or invaded, and in those contexts celebrates self-sacrifice on behalf of the faith or other Muslims." Of course, such consensus or corrective narratives did emerge in more thoughtful and intellectually-honest venues. But, they did not supersede the early counternarrative that had emerged in popular security discourse.

By the mid-point of the post-9/11 decade, this popular (counter) narrative that Islam itself (and not Al-Qaedaism) is a threat or danger had not only persisted, but had become more pervasive, more developed, or organized, and ensconced in several organizations

---

[2] From the CBS *60 Minutes* aired 6 October 2002. https://www.cbspressexpress.com/cbs-news/releases/view?id=2199

whose mission was to warn of and resist this danger to the U.S. homeland. A more widely recognizable discourse at this point, its core tenets were summarized this way by Muslim-American journalist Stephen Schwartz (2010), under the classification of "Islamophobia:"

> The terrorism of Al-Qaida is an inevitable product of the principles of Islam; that Islam is an inexorably violent religion motivated by jihadism ("holy war"); that the radical interpretation of Islam is the only authoritative one; and that Muslims are therefore a menacing "other" inextricably linked to radical ideology.

By this juncture, this popular security discourse was beginning to have international implications. In 2006, the Organization of Islamic Cooperation (OIC) launched the *Islamophobia Observatory* to register its official protest over the discourse. In its fifth report, the OIC would use the terms "institutionalization and legitimization" to describe the more permanent structural feature of "the phenomenon of Islamophobia" in Western states (OIC 2011, 2012; *Arab News* 2012). A few signs of this institutionalization were not hard to find.

First, the counternarrative that linked Islam and danger was chiefly marked no longer by sporadic statements, but by more deliberate and apparently well-funded productions that were suitable for mass marketing and continual reproduction in various forms.

Typical was the 2006 documentary, *Islam: What the West Needs to Know*, by Quixotic Media, who uploaded the documentary to YouTube. The documentary argued from the Quran and the Sunna that violent jihad against non-Muslims, along with the subjugation of other religions and non-Islamic political systems, were unreformable, canonical tenets of Islam. The film described how these tenets had characterized mainstream Islamic thought throughout the faith's history.

Second, the discourse was increasingly undergirded by or legitimized in the mainstream media. On the 21 July 2006 and 20 August 2006 C-SPAN radio programs *Q&A*, for instance, interviewer Brian Lamb publicized the aforementioned documentary, describing how his interest in it arose from an advertisement for it in the *Washington Times*. Lamb interviewed one of the film's main spokespersons, Robert Spencer, who—as it turns out—had been a colleague with Lind at the Free Congress Foundation. When he asked Spencer what he thought of the aired statements by Presidents Bush and Clinton, along with others, that unequivocally described Islam as a religion of peace, Spencer articulated the basic elements of the counternarrative:

> I think that's all hogwash, I'm sorry to say. Islam is the only religion in the world that has a developed doctrine, theology and legal system that mandates violence against unbelievers and mandates that Muslims must wage war in order to establish the hegemony of the Islamic social order all over the world.
> Now these things are objectively verifiable facts. Anyone can look at the Koran, anyone can look at the Muslim sources, the Muslim history, Muslim legal texts and so on and find that to be true.[3]

---

[3] See http://www.q-and-a.org/Transcript/?ProgramID=1086

Third, the structured nature of this Islam-as-threat discourse could be seen in the productions of key agents like Mr. Spencer. Spencer would go on to write thirteen related books, including two best-sellers—before the decade was over, such as *Islam Unveiled: Disturbing Questions About the World's Fastest Growing Faith*, and *Religion of Peace? Why Christianity Is and Islam Isn't*.

Fourth and fifth the discourse that linked Islam and threat was also in full expansion in social media or blogosphere. Robert Spencer for example was positioned as Director of the newly created blog, *Jihad Watch*—the sole function of which was to advance the frame of Islam itself as indistinguishable from al-Qaedaism, and thus a threat.

Fifth, grassroots organizations also emerged to solely to counter the "Islam is peace" frame had emerged. One such organization, ACT! for America, would eventually become larger than even the American Israel Political Affairs Committee (AIPAC). The organization's founder, "Brigitte Gabriel"—whose real name will not be divulged here for her security—articulated the counternarrative on February 19, 2006 in Washington DC at the Intelligence Summit, for which see served on the board of directors.[4] "America and the West are doomed to failure in this war," she told the conference, "unless they stand up and identify the real enemy, Islam" (Hoyt 2008). And, according to Australian Jewish News in 2007, Gabriel characterized "Every *practicing* Muslim," as "a radical Muslim" (Hoyt 2008).

Sixth, the counternarrative's emergence as a more structural security discourse was also marked by its incorporation into the belief-structure of the U.S. populace. Prior to 9/11, the term "anti-Islam" was virtually non-existent in Western states, especially in the U.S. For instance, National Defense University's Kenneth Moss wrote just prior to 9/11, "While one can find anti-Islamic statements by American religious leaders, the characteristics of religion in the United States have insulated it some from the legacy of Islamic-Christian confrontation in Europe" (Moss 2000, 45). Yet, U.S. anti-Islam sentiments by this juncture had *increased* markedly. As early as 2006, according to an ABC poll, U.S. anti-Islam sentiments in the U.S. rivaled those in Europe: nearly six in ten Americans thought the religion was "prone to violent extremism," half regarded it "unfavorably," and one in four admitted to "prejudicial feelings against Muslims and Arabs alike" (Cohen 2006).

That a segment of the U.S. was being captured by this paradigm could also be gauged by the many bestselling books on the topic. Two of Robert Spencer's books became *New York Times* bestsellers— *The Truth About Muhammad*, and *The Politically Incorrect Guide to Islam (and the Crusades)*. And, the changing public views on Islam could be seen in the fact that both of Brigitte Gabriel's terribly-written books—including her 2008 *Because They Hate: A Survivor of Islamic Terror Warns America*—became bestsellers.

Seventh, by the end of the second administration of George Bush, Islam—the mainstream religion itself, and not its al-Qaedaist segment—also had become ensconced in rightwing Christian eschatology or apocalypicism. Unlike earlier such iconic literature, such as Hal Lindsey's *The Late Great Planet Earth*, Islam was central to the new end-times

---

[4] See http://www.actforamerica.org/index.php/learn/about-ms-gabriel July 2010.

literature. Joel Richardson, for example, attained authority status with a sizeable segment of the Church in the U.S. through his *New York Times* bestseller, *The Islamic Antichrist: The Shocking Truth About the Nature of the Beast* (2009). This work was a follow-on from his first popular book, which was also set within the counternarrative—*Antichrist: Islam's Awaited Messiah* (2006)—and was a prelude to his more recent book, *Mideast Beast: The Case for an Islamic Antichrist*.

The Green Scare: Islam-*ization*

About 2009, U.S. popular security discourse about the danger of Islam took a more irrational turn, reflecting the nature of the nation's previous "scare" discourses. In what we might call the "green" scare—following the historical colored convention for scares over perceived threats from the East—the threat was no longer an external one, Islam, but an internal one, Islam*ization*.

Of course, in the aftermath of 9/11 there had been pockets of obsession over Islam as an internal threat—that is, of a violent jihad from the privileged insider position of the nation's tiny population of Muslim-Americans. Steven Emerson's (2003) bestseller *American Jihad: The Terrorists Living Among Us*, and his highly rated 2006 *Jihad Incorporated: A Guide to Militant Islam in the US*, reflected this concern. But such concerns gradually subsided as time passed and the security apparatus had failed to produce the expected al-Qaeda-affiliated cells among Muslim Americans. In the nine-year period between September 2001 and 2010, extremism among U.S. Muslims amounted to 82 cases involving 176 mostly troubled and lone-acting young Muslim-Americans—about 20 per year, who radicalized to the point of plotting attacks (Jenkins 2011, 9; Cassidy 2013). Only four had managed to follow through with their plans and 20 Americans were killed over those nine years, or about 2 per year on average.

An average of 2 Americans killed per year by Muslim extremists 2 people killed per year hardly compared to any number of more consequential security threats, such as the 1.38 *million* Americans *each year* who—according to annual FBI violent crime statistics—were violently attacked by non-Muslims, the vast majority of whom are other at-risk youth in poorer segments of society (FBI 2008, Table 2).

Yet, according to this emerging more conspiratorial and paranoid threat narrative, Islam posed not only an open challenge to the U.S.'s hegemony, its European heartland, and its Holy Land, but also posed a more imminent and immanent subversive challenge to its Constitution and culture. Under this threat, the U.S. was now in danger of being "Islamized," or undergoing "Islamization." In other words, the Green Scare was over the irrational belief-strand that the U.S. is under the more serious threat of being toppled by the institutionalization of Islamic law, or sharia—which gradually and stealthily was being imposed upon the nation's 300 million mostly Christian and secular citizens against their collective will by a virtually invisible population of Muslim-Americans.

The threat of Islamization in the literature up until this time had been related to Muslim societies in the context of pan-Islamism, and increasingly in Europe in the context of demographic transformation associated with immigration. In the case of Europe, the well-known Islamization internal threat narrative was emblematized by Dutch politician Pim Fortuyn's (1997) book, *Against Islamicization of Our Culture: Dutch Identity as a Foundation*. It portrayed Islam as an existential internal threat to "Western civilisation"—"an extraordinary threat, as a hostile society" (quoted in Lunsing 2003, 20). Europeans since then had been bombarded with popular threat literature that warned of the gradual Islamization of European legal and cultural structures. One such work that emerged in 2007 was *Eurabia: The Euro-Arab Axis*, by Egyptian-born British political commentator, Bat Ye'or. The book's title reveals its warning of the ongoing transformation of Europe into "Eurabia"—a future continent that is a fundamentally anti-Christian, anti-Western, anti-American, and anti-Semitic cultural and political appendage of the Arab/Muslim world. The earliest major American work set within this more irrational scare was *America Alone: The End of the World as We Know It*, published in 2008 by Canadian-born conservative columnist Mark Steyn. The book earned *New York Times* bestseller status by describing the impending leftist-weakened heartland of Western Civilization overrun by barbaric "Islamists."

But the notion of an Islamization of America was particularly puzzling in that it proceeded even though the possibility of that threat had never been the subject of a respected assessment in the field of security professionals. There were two obvious reasons why not: First, there is practically no Islam *in* America; and, second, the virtually unnoticeable population of Muslim-American adults were a highly diverse, largely contented populace.

In the first case, other than the steady dribble of occasional incompetent Muslim youth extremists— 'underwear bomber', the 'Times Square bomber'—the more representative swath of Muslim-Americans is virtually invisible to the average American. Two-thirds, or sixty-two percent, of U.S. citizens admitted in an August 19, 2010 *TIME* poll taken as the height of the hype over sharia that they had *never met* a Muslim. And—as it turned out—this American minority was virtually invisible for the obvious reason. National surveys from 2000 to 2007—when this discourse was most ascendant—suggested that Muslims comprised only 0.2 to 0.6 percent of the U.S. adult population, and this populace was growing only slightly (Pew Research Center 2007, 9-10). Unlike Europe—where Muslims in 2010 would account for a much higher 3.8 percent of the 425 million E.U. inhabitants—Muslims adults comprised less than one percent of U.S. inhabitants, and since 1989 had accounted for barely *one fifteenth* of the legal immigrants who enter the country each year (Pew Research Center 2007, 2011).

In the second point, even if there had been a sizeable population of Muslim adults in the U.S., socio-economic structures of Muslim-Americans did not indicate that they were clamoring for less secularism and more Islam in their daily lives. For example, several social analyses at the height of the Islamization discourse suggested that America's tiny Muslim population were generally 'middle-class and mostly mainstream,' according to the Pew Research Center's 2007 report by that name. In stark contrast to the largely unassimilated average European Muslim (Sen 2006; Mansur 2008), Pew Research Center (2007, 1) found

Muslim Americans are "largely assimilated, happy with their lives, and moderate with respect to many of the issues that have divided Muslims and Westerners around the world." A major Gallup study corroborated this, finding that—more than Christians, Jews or any other faith group—sixty percent of Muslim-Americans were found to be "thriving" (Abu Dhabi Gallup Center 2011).

Contrary to the counternarrative's lazy groupism, which portrayed "Muslims" and "Islam" as homogenous entities, Pew Research Center (2007, 1) found America's Muslims to be "a highly diverse population … decidedly American in their outlook, values, and attitudes," and found that their political ideology (the first of the following two figures) roughly mirrored that of the general U.S. population (the latter figure): very liberal (6 vs. 5 percent); liberal (23 vs. 17 percent); moderate (38 vs. 32 percent); conservative (21 vs. 32 percent); and very conservative (4 vs. 7 percent). In other words—unlike the counternarrative's caricature of them as surreptitious cultural jihadis—Muslim-American liberals were more liberal than other liberal segments of the populace, and less conservative than the conservative segments.

The Islamization popular threat discourse also rendered completely invisible important ideational and social-psychological contexts that might help us more accurately estimate the threat component within this minority. Although a high level or religious commitment is necessary for radicalization and revolutionary development in this subculture, Pew estimated that a mere 23 percent of Muslim Americans over 18 years of age—or only 322,000—had enough religious commitment to attend mosque once a week and pray the five salah, with equal fraction not performing these obligations (Pew Research Center 2007, 25).

In addition, despite being by far the youngest group, with a median age of 36 (compared to 46-55 for other major faith groups), Gallup (2011) found little evidence of youthful extremism, and even found that Muslim-Americans were "the *least* likely major religious group in the U.S. to say there is ever a justification for individuals or small groups to attack civilians." Where "roughly 1 in 10" Muslim Americans agreed with the statement that "such attacks are sometimes justified," Gallup found that "in every other major religious group except Mormons, the proportion of people who say such attacks are sometimes justified is at least twice that" (Gallup 2011, 6).

The green scare's rapid expansion was also puzzling. By the mid-point of the post-9/11 decade, there were twenty-two works published in the U.S. on the topic of Islamization of other countries, but only *one* about the Islamization of America, from U.S. Jewish conservative intellectual, Dr. Daniel. Pipes, in a July 12, 2006 post at his website, www.danielpipes.org.

But only one year later, in 2007, other mainly Jewish-American and conservative cultural entrepreneurs joined Pipes in warning their constituents of the Islamization danger. One was David Horowitz, editor of *FrontPage Magazine* and sponsor of the aforementioned Robert Spencer and *Jihad Watch*. In a 2 April e-mail to that blog's subscribers, Horowitz fantastically warned of "the purposeful and systematic dismantling of all aspects of our culture" via the imposition of "Sharia law on the U.S., replacing our law with provisions such as the stoning of adulterous women and cutting off thieves' hands."

The next year, in 2008, a more finished Islamization product emerged—the documentary *The Third Jihad*. According the documentary's website, radical Islamists were engaging in a "multifaceted strategy to overcome the western world," waging a "cultural jihad" to "infiltrate and undermine our society from within." Despite the lack of support for this threat narrative within the academic or professional security communities, the documentary enjoyed full television preview on December 22, 2009 by FOX News Channel's *Hannity & Colmes*. Then, on 25 November 2009, Pipes wrote "Islamism 2.0," portraying moderate European Muslims and even Muslim-Americans as a fifth column, as his opening paragraph reveals:

> To borrow a computer term, if Ayatollah Khomeini, Osama bin Laden, and Nidal Hasan represent Islamism 1.0, Recep Tayyip Erdoğan (the prime minister of Turkey), Tariq Ramadan (a Swiss intellectual), and Keith Ellison (a U.S. congressman) represent Islamism 2.0. The former kill more people but the latter pose a greater threat to Western civilization.

These non-violent Western Muslims, Pipes added, "threaten civilized life" even more than the violent ones like bin Laden, as they gradually "move the country toward Shari'a." In Pipes's estimate, America's destruction by its tiny population of half-black, half-immigrant adult Muslims supposedly already had begun, surreptitiously, in a form of lawful Islamism by Muslim movements that would prefer direct violence, but must settle with a more Gramscian culture war. He noted correctly that "Other once-violent Islamist organizations in Algeria, Egypt, and Syria have recognized the potential of lawful Islamism and largely renounced violence," but then added without specific empirical support the notion that "One also sees a parallel shift in Western countries; Ramadan and Ellison represent a burgeoning trend."

By 2010, the Green Scare was in full expansion, as works with "Islamization" in the title shifted from steady dribble to deluge, rising from a mere handful to nearly 1700. Viewing the visibly emerging sharia scare from Europe, *The Guardian's* Sarah Posner in early 2011 identified its main themes, with the last three being most significant:

> The conspiracy theory about sharia law is fivefold: that the goal of Islam is totalitarianism; that the mastermind of bringing this totalitarianism to the world is the Muslim Brotherhood, the grandfather of all Islamic groups from Hamas to the Islamic Society of North America; that these organizations within the US are traitors in league with the American left and are bent on acts of sedition against America; that the majority of mosques in the US are run by imams who promote such sedition; and that through this fifth column sharia law has already infiltrated the US and could result in a complete takeover if not stopped (Posner 2011).

By this juncture, conservative legislators in nearly two dozen states had introduced bills to restrict the use of Islamic law—a completely baffling feature of American politics. Voters in the solidly red state of Oklahoma seemed so persuaded that Islam itself was a significant internal threat that seventy percent voted for the "Save Our State" amendment to contain the nefarious attempt by Muslims to Islamize the nation through the spread of sharia (Armbruster 2010).

And, among the conservative elite, many of the GOP or Republican Party candidates for president had at least suggested that Islamization was a credible threat to the nation. The apogee of the Islamization discourse seemed to be when GOP Presidential front-runner Newt Gingrich, speaking in 2010 to conservatives at the American Enterprise Institute (AEI), exclaimed, "I believe Shariah is a mortal threat to the survival of freedom in the United States and in the world as we know it" (Shane 2011). Gingrich's staff seemed bent on ignoring the aforementioned facts regarding the Muslim-American demographic, which the former Speaker of the House described as threatening "to *impose* an extraordinarily different system on us"—to "replace American freedom with Sharia" (Gingrich and Gingrich 2010).

Strategic Implications. So What?

Since this Islam-as-threat and Islamization bridged security discourse was *popular*—that is, outside the circle of security professionals—then we might tend to brush it off as insignificant. After all, across any society, there are segments of the populace who are animated over one kind of perceived threat or another. But, in the era of globalization and the social media, any significant sub-national discourse about any sensitive topic has the potential to become internationalized and morph into a strategic security threat.

We saw this long before the social media in the fallout from Salman Rushdie's *Satanic Verses* in September 1988. We saw it again in the era of the social media with the cases of the Muhammad cartoons and the "Innocence of Muslims" movie trailer, where large segments of the increasingly connected Muslims around the world were manipulated by religious elite, and even some Muslim majority state governments were forced to show solidarity as a regime security or legitimacy measure.

The more strategic implications of this popular security discourse began to emerge as early as the five-year anniversary of 9/11 in the form of anti-Americanism among a quarter of the world's population that was Muslim. At this juncture, citizens of eight Muslim-majority countries had cited "American negative perceptions of Islam" as the greatest threat to Muslims worldwide (Martin 2010).[5]

The discourse also produced strategic efforts to contain it through regulation. In view of their own restive population of underemployed and increasingly online young Muslim males, some Muslim leaders sought to rein in this rhetoric at the UN via their collective vehicle, the Organization of Islamic Cooperation (OIC). In March 2010, the UN Human Rights Council agreed with the OIC and passed the historically unprecedented resolution, "combating defamation of religions." If unchecked, the resolution warned, this security discourse would "fuel discrimination, extremism and misperception leading to polarization

---

[5] Research from American University professor Akbar Ahmed's 2006 world tour to produce *Journey into Islam: The Crisis of Globalization* (2007)

and fragmentation with dangerous unintended and unforeseen consequences" (Middle East Online, 2010).

Discourse that categorized Islam as the enemy was also arguably catalyzing the "war on Islam" master narrative, which had been conceptualized by modern Islamic thinkers, and had become pervasive in Muslim communities worldwide, especially by the end of the Bush administration's post-9/11 "War on Terror" (e.g. Jan 2002, Fatany 2004). There seemed to be a plethora of anecdotal evidence in this regard. By 2009, the main page of *Islamophobia Watch*, for instance, would describe its mission as "Documenting the War against Islam"—a function which amounted to archiving the statements of U.S. intellectuals who popularized the notion of Islam as anything but a religion of peace. Even the Secretary-General of the OIC, Ekmeleddin Ihsanoglu, was using the "war on Islam" frame for the discourse, saying that "Islamophobia, insulting Islamic values and sparking and spreading hatred for Islam are high on the agenda of the West," and urged the entire Muslim states to take established, and institutionalized collective measures to confront "the Western plots against Islam" (Fars News Agency 2010). The agitation of senior Muslim leaders over this discourse continued. In the historic July 2011 meeting between the OIC members and Western states—hosted by Ihsanoglu and Secretary of State Hillary Clinton—Ihsanoglu said that "we continue to be particularly disturbed by attitudes of certain individuals or groups exploiting the freedom of expression to incite hatred by demonizing purposefully the religions and their followers" (Arab News 2011).

The aforementioned Rushdie affair had created a similar anti-Western solidarity among Muslims worldwide (Reuters 2009). That highly publicized event, along with this highly public discourse, functioned within the category of a political grievance structure—a structure that by this point was cited widely in sociological literature as a key factor leading to radicalization (Moghaddam and Marsella 2003; Quilliam 2010; Lynch 2010; Borum 2011; Ali et al. 2011; Halverson, Goodall and Corman 2011; Speckhard 2012). Ali et al. (2011), for example, wrote that, "One of Al Qaeda's greatest recruitment and propaganda tool is the assertion that the West is at war with Islam and Muslims—an argument that is strengthened every day by those who suggest all Muslims are terrorists and all those practicing Islam are jeopardizing U.S. security."

In a slightly different frame, the much more systematic securitization of Islam by this popular threat discourse was apparently creating something of a civilizational "security dilemma," fueling ever-increasing mutual hostility that leads to more physical violence or broader conflict (Posen 1993). By the tenth anniversary of 9/11, a global poll by the Pew Research Center (2011) empirically established that such a mutually destructive mutual hostility structure had indeed emerged.

It was in this context that the *first* foreign policy initiatives of the newly-elected Obama administration were historic speeches to Muslims worldwide from both Turkey and Egypt, where the President expressly used the phrase "war on Islam" several times in attempts to contain this destructive master narrative.

Perhaps, for the first time in history, a nation's popular *discourse about a threat* was becoming recognized by that nation's leaders as a hazard to national security in its own right. *How could this be?* Given this Islam(ization) threat discourse's weak empirical grounding, the obvious question seemed to be why did it emerge in the first place and then rise to this apparent level of influence at its zenith?

2. Conceptualizing the Green Scare

Before we attempt to answer those questions empirically, we would be remiss if we did not first examine part of the explanation and broader insights offered in the literature.

Holy Land Geopolitics

Initial attempts to make sense of this discourse were dominated by the late controversial critical theorist and political activist, Edward Said. Said's prolific writing on the subject—*Orientalism* (1978, 2003) and *Covering Islam* (1981, 1997)—the original and updated works—spanned more than a quarter of a century, with his updated works addressing this more contentious U.S. discourse on Islam, both before and after 9/11. Because much of the literature's conceptualizations of this discourse (apparently unknowingly) built upon Said's earlier thinking, it seems worthwhile here to briefly illuminate some of his more salient insights into what some have referred to as the "new Orientalism" (Crooke 2006; Rowe 2012).

In his earliest work, Said's (1978) object was mainly European colonial era discourse regarding Islam. Mobilizing the early Lacanian psychoanalytical and now mainstream political and discourse theory's approach to radical alterity, he concluded that "European culture gained strength and identity by setting itself off against the Orient as a sort of surrogate and even underground self" (1978, 3). Ensuing literature observed how discourse on Islam played a role in this form of national and even civilizational-level identity politics (Bhabha 1996, 87; Castells 1997; Shryock 2013). In this vein, Said's integration of Gramsci's more political perspective was also intriguing. The vast production of knowledge on Islam by Westerners, Said argued, was never disinterested, but was a function of a broader hegemonic competition between civilizations—"the West" and "Islam"—with the ultimate intent "to control, manipulate even to incorporate, what is a manifestly different..." (1978, 12). In this sense, Western knowledge produced about the Easterner, he said, was not *pure* subject matter, but *geopolitical* subject matter; it was knowledge inextricably connected with power. In other words, knowledge produced about Islam was the handmaiden of empire. Under this paradigm, he added, the U.S. historical infatuation with that region and religion "has less to do with the Orient than it does with 'our' world" (1978, 12).

Said would continue to emphasize the role of politics or—more specifically—*geo*politics. Nearly twenty years later, in his 1997 update to his 1981 work, *Covering Islam: How the Media and the Experts Determine How We See the Rest of the World*, he retained Foucault's paradigm of "affiliation of knowledge with power," asserting that "it is not too much of an exaggeration to say that all discourse on Islam has an interest in some authority or power," and that "truth about such matters as 'Islam' is relative to who produces it" (1997, xlix, lviii).

But, strategic interest and politics inherently involves the role of political agents—both individuals and groups. For this reason, Said's (1997) emphasis turned from structure to agency—from a macro-level or civilizational form of identity politics, to a more micro-level *strategy* of Holy Land geopolitics enacted by intellectuals organic to a particular political interest. Said's claim was characteristically bold: although the knowledge produced by this advocacy network was ostensibly about Islam, he said, its unspoken aims or purposes in producing that knowledge were geopolitical—specifically, about Israel. He had broached this geopolitical notion as much as twelve years earlier, characterizing modern Orientalism as having the same neo-colonial political objective as its forebear. "The Israeli occupation of the West Bank and Gaza, the destruction of Palestinian society and the sustained Zionist assault upon Palestinian nationalism," he said in 1985, have "been led and staffed by Orientalists" (Said 1985, 8). He continued, "Whereas in the past, it was European Christian Orientalists who supplied European culture with arguments for colonizing and suppressing Islam, as well as for despising Jews, it is now the Jewish national movement that produces a cadre of colonial functionaries whose ideological theses about the Islamic or Arab mind are implemented in the administration of the Palestinian Arabs, an oppressed minority within the white-European-democracy that is Israel."

In Said's (1997, xxii) other words, this new Orientalism's function was so that "more Americans and Europeans will see Israel as a victim of Islamic violence" and to "obscure what it is that Israel and the United States…have been doing." The agency at the center of this steady portrayal of Islam as threat had two non-state components: the individual experts and intellectuals, and the media enablers. In other words, in this strategy to use Islam as a geopolitical smokescreen, Said (1997, xi) emphasized a "corps of 'experts'" on Islam, as well as the Jewish-controlled elements of the mainstream media—both of whom produced Islam as threat in effort to spoil any peace process that might demobilize Israel from its present occupation of its Biblical homeland of Judea and Samaria. This notion was strengthened a decade later by Mearsheimer and Walt's (2007) *The Israel Lobby*.

In the category of the media, the enablers included the owners of the *New Republic* and *The Atlantic*, Martin Peretz and Morton Zuckerman, whom Said (1997, xxii) asserted, were "great supporters of Israel, and therefore biased against Islam." It was in *The Atlantic*, for instance, that Bernard Lewis's "Roots of Muslim Rage" had appeared in September 1990. The editorial focus of these media magnates, he added, was "the relentless drive to defend Israel at all costs" (Said 1997, xxiv).

Beyond the Jewish-controlled media, Said (1997, xvi) reserved his keenest criticism for "vociferously polemical Orientalists." As for the individual polemicists who were advancing this discourse of Islam as a menace, he noted that they were *all* pro-Israel (1997, 13). In the frame of "The East is a career" from Disraeli's novel *Tancred* (1847, II xiv), Said (1997, xxxv) charged: "What matters to 'experts' like Miller, Huntington, Martin Kramer, Daniel Pipes, and Barry Rubin, plus a whole battery of Israeli academics is to make sure that the 'threat' is kept before our eyes," and to "excoriate Islam for its terror, despotism and violence, while asserting themselves profitable consultancies, frequent television appearances, and book contracts." Typifying this, Israel advocate Steven Emerson's PBS film *Jihad in America* was in Said's (1997, xxvi) words, "cynically designed and promoted to exploit just this fear," which was part of the overall strategy by these well-funded non-state actors to "exaggerate and inflate Muslim extremism within the Muslim world." Said characterized these polemicists as "The worst offenders in the cultural war against Islam," and cited Jewish and Zionist academic Bernard Lewis's essay "The Roots of Muslim Rage" as typical of products that characterized Muslims "as one terrifyingly collective person enraged at an outside world."

After 9/11 and just before his death, Said began to grapple with a new feature beyond Holy Land geopolitics: the obsession-like *volume* of U.S. discourse about Islam. Because this exponential increase in the production of knowledge about Islam now clearly involved much more of American society than the Israel lobby and its organic polemicists, Said (2003) seemed to be forced back to the macro-level of ideational structure, and—specifically—civilizational identity politics. America's current obsession with its perennial Eastern other, he asserted, was rooted in "fear of a monotheistic, culturally and militarily formidable competitor to Christianity" (2003, 336, 344).

Clash of Civilizations Ideology

Said's notion of a civilizational "clash"—the highest level of identity politics—was also the subject of some literature. A work that at least implied that civilizational-level identity politics was a factor in post-9/11 U.S. foreign policy and discourse related to Islam was *False Prophets: The 'Clash of Civilizations' and the Global War on Terror*, by Richard Bonney (2008), Professor of Modern History at the University of Leicester from 1984 to 2006. The book was part of an Oxford series under the conceptual framework "the past in the present." The "past" is conceptualized as a culturally-situated pretext, or cognitive schema—a relevant ideational structure that provides the unconscious underpinnings of a discourse by guiding our processing of information (Entman 1993, 53). The role of such ideational structures in influencing discourse and social practice broadly is well-informed by the more conceptual literature, which views these cognitive blueprints for the way things naturally are (or should be) as key guidelines for behavior. According to discourse theorist Van Dijk (2006, 115, 117, 120), for example, ideologies "are the ultimate basis of the discourses" and play a key role in identity politics, with the polarization between in-groups and out-groups being a prominent feature of these ideological structures.

In this context, Professor Bonney examined mainly the *ideological antecedents* of the Bush administration's "global war on terror." And, he also described the role of politically-interested intellectuals and other elite in advancing that ideology in foreign policy and security discourse during a moment of crisis after the terrorist attacks of 2001.

The specific ideology that Bonney illuminated as having a role in the securitization of Islam was a derivative of the "clash of civilizations" conflict theory popularized by the aforementioned Princeton University's professor-emeritus of Middle East history, Bernard Lewis's (1990) "The Roots of Muslim Rage," and again in Samuel Huntington's (1993, 1996) *The Clash of Civilizations*. The post-9/11's counternarrative to the "Islam is peace" frame was a derivative of the earlier clash of civilizations narrative, and similarly tended to reduce social complexity to a bi-polar cosmic struggle between the West on the one civilizational pole and its ineradicable enemy, Islam, on the other.

Bonney's *False Prophets* demonstrated how this particular paradigmatic cognitive structure was either unconsciously mobilized or deliberately "hijacked" by intellectuals and other elite agents to serve (geo)political interests. The cases he examined were "neoconservatives" tied to the Bush administration, "the American Jewish Lobby" and the "Christian Right"—all of which seemed to speak immediately and naturally in the frame of a clash of civilizations.

Tellingly, the "false prophets" whom Bonney profiled as the clash-of-civilization ideology's intellectual proponents—like Bernard Lewis and Daniel Pipes—were also the ones Said (1997) implicated in the context of Holy Land geopolitics.

Bonney demonstrated how pro-Israel and neoconservative thinkers set to work after 9/11 to frame the new threat not as a limited transnational threat—a small fringe of revolutionary extremist Muslim groups to be contained with a modest police and intelligence resources, but in the more familiar terms of an global and ubiquitous enemy that posed an existential threat to Western Civilization, and thus was worthy of a superpower's full mobilization. The titles produced by these pro-Israel polemicists were performative in this way; there were, for example, Eliot Cohen's (2001) "World War IV: Let's Call this Conflict What it is," published in the *Wall Street Journal* on 20 November, and Norman Podhoretz's (2002) "How to Win World War IV," published in *Commentary* two months later in February. Plainly, the World War IV frame conflated al-Qaeda—then a small and relatively unarmed non-state organization who had declared unilateral war on the U.S.—with Islam broadly, leading to statements from influential neoconservatives like Podhoretz, who wrote: "the stakes are nothing less than the survival of Western civilization" (Kessler 2007).

Jumping into this clash of civilizations paradigm, key thinkers in the U.S. Christian Right—both Catholic and Evangelical—played a significant role in framing Islam (global and mainstream) and not al-Qaedaism (local and fringe) as the main threat. In geopolitical terms that recall Said's (2003) description of Islam functioning within identity politics as a necessary civilizational competitor to Christianity, Catholic intellectual George Weigel described "a Europe increasingly influenced, and perhaps even dominated, by radicalized Islamic populations, convinced that their long-delayed triumph in the European heartland is at hand" (Bonney 2008, 130). Another prominent Catholic intellectual, Father Richard Neuhaus, similarly viewed Huntington's thesis of an impending clash of civilizations as America's surest guide to the post-9/11 strategic security paradigm. He framed the conflict as "a war of religion," and who described bin Laden and his ilk as "faithful Muslims" (Bonney 2008, 132).

Again, the obvious context in which these cultural elite were involved in articulating that ideology remained largely geopolitical, or in the justification for power-politics in relation to advocating for resources for the "Global War on Terror," the purportedly linked invasion of Iraq, and other foreign policy that either benefited Israel, or the Church broadly.

"Islamophobia"

About the time that *False Prophets* was going to press, most of the analyses that attempted to address the broader questions surrounding the post-9/11 securitization of Islam self-organized under the neologism of "Islamophobia." Much of this literature approvingly cited the first major report to use the neologism, *Islamophobia: A Challenge for Us All*, by Runnymede Trust in 1997, which framed the problem in terms of "the dread, hatred and hostility towards Islam and Muslims...." The popularity of the term grew exponentially in the latter half of the post-9/11 decade, roughly mirroring the emergence of more negative writing on Islam broadly. More professional literature produced *in the U.S. alone* that contained "Islamophobia" *in the title only* numbered only 21 in 1997—the year of Runnymede Trust's report on the topic.[6]

After 9/11, use of the term in titles in the more professional and exclusively U.S. literature remained fairly flat until the mid-point of the decade, when it jumped precipitously, doubling every year or two, and reaching 32,000 by 2013. A new discourse and social structure had been born.

By the tenth anniversary of 9/11, the term had taken on a reflexive element, and was used as the cover titles for the internationally-read periodicals. *The Nation*'s cover headline, for instance, was "Islamophobia: Anatomy of an American Panic," and *TIME's* was "Is America Islamophobic?"

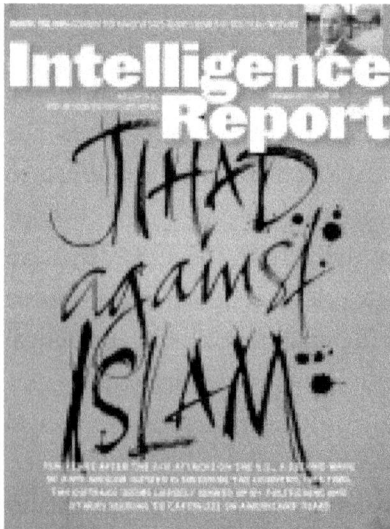

At the end of the post-9/11 decade, two more scholarly and empirical works emerged self-classified under this Islamophobia paradigm. But, like Said's books before them, these two books suggested that this form of xenophobia was less pure than political.

The first major work self-categorizing under the frame of Islamophobia was the 130 page report, *Fear, Inc.: The Roots of the Islamophobia Network in America*, published by a team of researchers—Wajahat Ali, Eli Clifton, Matthew Duss, Lee Fang, Scott Keyes, and Faiz Shakir—at the more leftist Center for American Progress, in Washington DC.[7] The report was groundbreaking in that it revealed a loose social network comprised of five principal "misinformation experts;" the philanthropic or "funders" base of primarily seven foundations; and the discourse's "echo-chamber"—a much larger set of figures and organizations across the spectrum of religious, political, media and grassroots organizers.

A pattern started to emerge. What the report called "the central nervous system of the Islamophobia network" included some of the same key figures emphasized by Said

---

[6] .pdf files containing the word "Islamophobia"
[7] Available at www.americanprogress.org/issues/2011/08/pdf/islamophobia.pdf

(1997, 2003) and even Bonney (2008), such as Daniel Pipes of the Philadelphia-based Middle East Forum (MEF), and Steven Emerson of the Investigative Project on Terrorism. The report also implicated three others: the aforementioned Robert Spencer of Stop Islamization of America (SIOA) and *Jihad Watch*, Frank Gaffney of the Center for Security Policy (CSP), and David Yerushalmi of the Society of Americans for National Existence.

A corroborating report in 2013—*Legislating Fear: Islamophobia and its Impact in the United States* by the Council on American-Islamic Relations (CAIR)—identified these same agents along with a much expanded "inner core" of around forty principal polemicists, including Pamela Geller's blog, *Atlas Shrugs*. The report stated that, "Together, this core group of deeply intertwined individuals and organizations manufacture and exaggerate threats of 'creeping Sharia,' Islamic domination of the West, and purported obligatory calls to violence against all non-Muslims by the Koran" (CAIR 2011, 2).

Fear, Inc. also pointed to the role of political activists or grassroots organizations, especially those in the religious right, including Brigitte Gabriel's ACT! for America, and that of a "loosely aligned, ideologically-akin group of right-wing blogs, magazines, radio stations, newspapers, and television news shows," such as FOX News Channel, Christian Broadcasting Network, *National Review*, and *The Washington Times* (Ali et al. 2011, 85).

The main research focus of the *Fear, Inc.* report was another element of the discourse's apparatus of power—its narrow philanthropic base. It revealed how just seven non-aligned private foundations gave $42.6 million in the decade after 9/11 to a few of the discourse's aforementioned principal agents (Ali et al. 2011).

Emphasizing the role of this social network, the report in its executive summary characterized the discourse as a narrow project—one emerging not from "a vast right-wing conspiracy," but "rather a small, tightly networked group" of polemicists who were "sustained by funding from a clutch of key foundations," and who also received support from "effective advocates, media partners, and grassroots organizing" (Ali et al. 2011).

The otherwise empirically-tethered report made an unsubstantiated leap, however, when one of its key authors and the vice president of its publishing think tank, Faiz Shakir, shifting from the title frame, *Fear, Inc.*, to a storyline of hatred. "We know it's driven primarily by hatred against Muslims," he said (Lobe 2011).

The other key work that self-organized under the "Islamophobia" frame was *The Islamophobia Industry: How the Right Manufactures Fear of Muslims*, by Nathan Lean. Published in 2012, the book was based on research from the author's academic research at Georgetown University's Center for Contemporary Arab Studies (CCAS), and its Forward was written by that institution's authority on U.S.-Muslim relations, Professor John Esposito. *The Islamophobia Industry's* chief characterization of this popular U.S. discourse was almost captured in its title and subtitle. Aligning with the findings of the aforementioned literature—including Said (1997), Bonney (2008), Davidson (2011) and the *Fear, Inc* report (2011)—Lean (2012, 133) implicated a cottage industry signified by inflammatory terms, such a "industry of hate" and a "fear industry," comprised of what he called "bigoted bloggers, racist politicians, fundamentalist religious leaders, FOX News pundits, and religious Zionists."

In Lean's other words, "the decade-long spasm of Islamophobia that rattled through the American public," rather than any detached individual agency, "is the product of a tight-knit and interconnected confederation of right-wing fear merchants" comprised of Christian fundamentalists, Zionists of all persuasions, and far right-wing Republicans (2012, 10). In this frame, Lean approvingly cited, for instance, UNC Professor Carl Ernst's description of the discourse as "a type of bigotry similar to anti-Semitism and racial prejudice" that is supported by a coalition of right-wing organizations (2012, 62). And, in public comments at Georgetown University on June 1, 2012 promoting his book, Lean characterized the discourse as "the racism du jour," but then seemed to contradict himself, adding that "the large portion of Islamophobic propaganda has actually come from people and organizations that are connected in some ways to the occupied territories" (Saif 2013).

Emphasizing the Christian element of this discourse, the book blamed another ideology closely related to Zionism: Christian apocalypticism, which casts Islam as the end-times antagonist in Israel's cosmic struggle to return and occupy all of its Promised Land, as a prelude to the Messiah's coming or return. "Behind individuals like David Horowitz and Robert Spencer," he said, "are far more nebulous and ideological figures that see the promotion of anti-Muslim sentiment as a necessary method for gaining the upper hand in a cosmic war playing out thousands of miles away in the West Bank" (2012, 11).

The Elephant in the Living Room: Domestic Politics

In any new complex social phenomenon, including this latest U.S. conspiracy about infiltrating barbarians from the East, it seems that our first inclination is to try and interpret it in familiar terms—to pour the new wine into old wine skins, as the old adage goes. The literature's various characterizations of this discourse—"new" Orientalism, "new" racism, "new" anti-Semitism, and "new" McCarthyism"—reflected this tendency. Yet, there was much sociological literature to suggest that that we might add yet another "new" variant to a very old category of practice: *politics*—especially domestic or cultural politics.

A wide consensus exists across various sociological sub-disciplines that views discourse as fundamentally political, or driven significantly by political interest.

That discourse was inherently interested was the conclusion of the philosopher of language Bakhtin (1981); all language or discourse was—in his words—"inhabited by intentions." Other discourse psychologists, discourse theorists, critical theorists, and social movement theorists have concluded similarly. Across all of these sub-disciplines there is a consensus that our descriptions of the world do not neutrally reflect that world, but play an active role in creating it, changing it, or maintaining it—always in pursuit of interests (e.g. Gergen 2009, 14; Jørgensen and Phillips 2002, 1). The very terms we use to describe agencies reflect this axiom: the "advocacy network" that defends a cause (Keck and Sikkink 1998,1); the "epistemic community" that seek change in a specific area of policy (McGann 2011, 71); the "discourse coalition" that coalesces around and advances a set of storylines to achieve its interests (Hajer 1993, 47).

The notion that a cultural production like an area of knowledge could be politicized aligns with Michel Foucault's (1979) view of discourse as plays for the "truth"—the dominant "knowledge" about the world that is sustained by the going "systems of power which produce and sustain it," or the "regime of truth." That pessimistic view of discourse flowed from his ontology of the social broadly. With key insights into culture war, and turning Clausewitz's famous phrase on its head, Foucault saw political struggle as "war" by other means, and viewed it as a permanent feature of social relations (Foucault 1997, 110). The main drama of history, he contended, was "the endlessly repeated play of dominations" (Dreyfus and Rabinow 1982, 109-10). Consequently, discourses "need to be analyzed, not in terms of types of consciousness, modes of perception and forms of ideology," he argued, "but in terms of tactics and strategies of power" (1980, 77). In this vein, power and knowledge (a discursive structure) "directly imply one another" (Foucault 1977, 27-28). Not only does knowledge in the form of ideology undergird a particular hegemony or political order, but that every political power structure capitalizes or reproduces that knowledge which is advantageous to its survival. This was what Edward Said (2003, 336) meant when he characterized Western discourse on Islam as "power using knowledge to advance itself."

But, can we go as far to say that threats to society—our "knowledge of them"—are opportunistic conditions that certain groups seize upon through "security discourse" to advance their interests? The classic case that Foucault used to underscore that argument was set forth in his *Discipline and Punish: The Birth of the Prison*. There, Foucault (1977, 25) observed that the systems of punishment in our society were "situated in a certain 'political economy' " that incentivized the prison to "participate in the fabrication of a delinquency that it is supposed to combat." In his other words, prisons did not *eradicate* delinquency in society; rather "prisons *manufactured* delinquents" (Foucault 1980, 40). Why? Because they "turned out to be useful," both in economic domain and in the political. It was in this vein that he famously quipped, "criminals come in handy."

We might extend this axiom into the security realm broadly.   If there were—as Foucault concluded—a "number of advantages" or utility of the criminal threat to society, then is it also not likely that all threats come in handy to at least some segment of society? Does not each *purported* or so-called 'threat' have an associated political economy? Can we not quickly list several so-called threats that have obvious political utility for this group or that one? Did not Khomeinism or the Revolutionary Islamic State of Iran need an American "Great Satan," for example? And, does not the U.S. military industrial complex need a perpetual clear and present danger?

Widely-cited sociological literature substantiates this notion. In their 1978 study of Britain's moral panics, for instance, Hall and colleagues observed that the media and other 'agencies of control' that benefited from the panic were problematically central to its propagation. Rather than educate the public about in order to solve the problem, they *institutionalized* it—both creating it, and then blowing it out of all proportion to the actual threat offered. In terms nearly identical to Foucault's, they characterized these so called "agents of control" as power nodes that "advertently and inadvertently amplify the

19

deviancy they seem so absolutely committed to controlling" (See Hall et al., 1978, 52).

This notion that even the media would manipulate knowledge for ideological gain was not in any way a narrow segment of the literature, as evidenced even in titles like Gans's (1979) *Deciding What's News*, in Herman and Chomsky's (1988) *Manufacturing Consent*, and in Cook's (1998/2005) *Governing with the News: The News Media as a Political Institution.*

Other prominent social philosophers hold this same view of discourse as fundamentally political. For the late French social philosopher Pierre Bourdieu (1990, 122; Bourdieu and Wacquant 1992), such interestedness was the core "logic" and "energy" in all social practice, even if it masqueraded as disinterestedness. The aim of all discursive or—as Bourdieu (1991, 167) termed it—"symbolic" struggle was to advance a group's ideology, or naturalized vision of a particular hierarchical social order "that is best suited to their interest." In his other terms, such discursive struggle aims to "transform the social world in accordance with their interests—by producing, reproducing or destroying the representations that make groups visible for themselves and for others" (Bourdieu 1991, 127). It is out of this ontology of discourse that Edward Said (1997, lviii) would assert that "all discourse on Islam has an interest in some authority or power."

Social movement theorists similarly emphasize the political nature discourse by conceptualizing Bourdieu's concept of symbolic struggle in the distinctive phrase, *"framing" strategies*. "Framing," in Entman's (1993, 52) words, means "to select some aspects of a perceived reality and make them more salient in a communicating text, in such a way as to promote a particular problem definition, causal interpretation, moral evaluation, and/or treatment recommendation for the item described." The frames advanced in this discursive process, as social movement theorists Benford and Snow (2000, 625-26) put it, are "deliberative, utilitarian and goal directed"; they are developed "to achieve a specific purpose – to recruit new members, mobilize adherents, acquire resources, and so forth."

Whether we call this process "framing," as did Entman (1993), Benford and Snow (2000), and others, "framing processes" as did McAdam, Tarrow, and Tilly (1997), or "cultural framing," as did Romano (2006), the concept implied is not meaningfully distinct from what Bourdieu (1991) described as the "labour of categorization," what Laclau and Mouffe (1985) described as "the process of identification," or what Hall (1982) termed "the politics of signification." It is by this discursive practice that individuals and groups systematically *represent* the world to shape the perceptions of those that they are trying to influence. Thus, this discourse is intensely political.

The notion that all public discourse is fundamentally political is also informed by the range of poststructuralist sub-disciplines, including critical (media and culture) theory, critical discourse analysis (van Dijk 1993), and critical geopolitics (Ó Tuathail 1996). The "critical turn" of geopolitics, for instance, emerged in recognition that the discursive practice of geopolitics was a non-neutral, social construct, reflecting both ideological or normative underpinnings and the (social) Darwinist struggle for primacy or dominance (Kearns 2003, 173). In other words, this more critical approach to geopolitics views it not as a disinterested analysis or description of the geographical world, but as a fundamentally ideological and politicized practice (Ó Tuathail and Agnew 1992).

All of this literature, therefore, posits that all public discourse—including those related to threats—is inherently interested, political, or prone to politicization. In Foucauldian terms, the discourses of the world are knowledge structures that are erected *by* power, and *for* power.

But, this paradigm of power-knowledge seems overly limiting. After all, security discourse is ostensibly a discourse about some externalized and securitized "other." For this reason, it is also helpful to conceptualize it within the *politics of identity*. Identity politics is a practice central to *all* political groups. Because the boundary between inside and outside, self and other, is in constant flux—especially in the era of globalization (Castells 1997)—constant work is required to secure the collectivity's boundaries, which are always conceptualized as at the interface between the good self and the dangerous threatening outside (Campbell 1998, 114). In other words, this inherent instability of all political identity translates to more visible identity-instituting practices or *identification*—the kind of practices that Schmitt (1932) called "the political," wherein any group can exist as an identifiable entity only through radical alterity, in juxtaposition to the other, or the constant articulation of the essentializing and dichotomizing friend/enemy distinction.

Subsequent theorizing has led to a wide consensus that all political identities are constituted "in relation to a series of differences" (Connolly 2002 [1991], 64); they are performatively constituted "through the inscription of boundaries that serve to demarcate an 'inside' from an 'outside,' a 'self' from an 'other,' a 'domestic' from a foreign" (Campbell 1998, 9). In Schmittian frames, an *other*-identity is necessary for the stable existence of any *self*-identity. And it was in this context that Edward Said (1978, 3) would assert that "European culture gained strength and identity by setting itself off against the Orient as a sort of surrogate and even underground self."

And it is in this sense that security discourses—whether on the threat of Islam, or of economic or environmental collapse—are not merely discourses that identify the evil, threatening other; they are discourses that also perform the crucial function of identifying the good self. This was Campbell's (1998) [1992] conclusion in his analysis of Cold War security texts, *Writing Security: United States Foreign Policy and the Politics of Identity*. The study revealed that there was much more going on in these strategic security and policy texts than attempts to understand and contain the Soviet threat. These security productions also functioned politically, or—in the terms of the book's subtitle—in the "politics of identity," and did so not merely in narrating or identifying the political outside, but in narrating the political inside, or "scripting the self" and the more hegemonic struggle to impose a particular order or vision of the world that served the interests of those who wrote these texts (1998, 30). Campbell (1998, 31-32) added that:

> While one might have expected few if any references to national values or purposes in confidential documents prepared for the inner sanctum of national security policy… the texts of foreign policy are replete with statements about fulfillment of the republic, the fundamental purpose of the nation, God-given rights, moral codes, the principles of European civilization, the fear of cultural and spiritual loss, and the responsibilities and duties thrust upon the gleaming example of America. In this sense, the texts that

21

guided national security policy did more than simply offer strategic analyses of the 'reality' they confronted: they actively concerned themselves with the scripting of a particular American identity.

Similarly, deconstruction of National Security Strategy (NSS) documents from the post-war Truman era to the post-9/11 War on Terror suggested that "national security" or "security discourse" was—in Schubiner's (2006) words—"a tool for identity construction of 'us' and 'them,' which works through narrations and speech acts that disguise the actual goals of the discourse." In this sense, "war is not only waged on the battlefield, but also through the dominant telling of historical narratives, through discourses that conceal the use of force and relations of power." Schubiner adds, "National security discourse—including the rhetoric of democracy, American values and free markets—functions as a polemical device that is employed increasingly to achieve political ends...."

In this vein, security discourses—in Alvarez's (2006, 77) words—are part of the collectivity's "official culture" and "provide definitions of patriotism, loyalty, boundaries and belonging." For example, in his announcement that the U.S. was sending military forces to Saudi Arabia in the second Gulf War in 1990, President Bush performatively said, "In the life of a nation, we're called upon to define who we are and what we believe." By manifestly linking American identity to present danger, the president had highlighted how—in Campbell's (1998, 3) words—"the boundaries of a state's identity are secured by the representation of danger...."

It is in this context that states of *in*security—the standing or recurrent discourses of danger, or its various assertions about its threats—are the necessary condition and means for a secure political identity. Security threats, are—again in Campbell's (1998, 13) words— "thus not a threat to the state's identity or existence; it is its condition of possibility" Paradoxically, therefore, a collectivity's identity is not as much threatened by danger as it is "secured" by it (Campbell 1998, 50).

Security Discourse as Identity or Cultural Politics

Recall that the response to the "Islam is peace" narrative was not a *corrective*, but a *counter* narrative, set in polar opposition to the identity of Islam maintained by academic security studies, by the mainstream media, and by other more progressive societal institutions. In this way, the stark counternarrative had all of the marks not of *mere* domestic political struggle that engages a proximate political enemy, such as the Democrats, or President Obama, but of *counterhegemonic* struggle. By "counterhegemonic," of course, we mean the Gramscian conceptualization of opposition to the established hegemony, or dominant ideology, or doxa—a common struggle known variously as counterculture, cultural struggle, culture war, cultural politics, and so on.

For the cultural theorist Gramsci (1971, 189), political struggle in the modern era rarely involved direct, violent engagement of the dominant and naturalized political order; instead, it usually proceeded by indirect, non-violent and largely discursive "counter-hegemonic" struggle. In every society, popular culture, or the popular realm, functioned as a form of counterhegemonic resistance; it was, in Gramsci's terms, a "conception of the world and life" that stood in opposition to the "official" one (Gramsci 1985, 189).

The practice of counternarrative—or "countermemory," in Foucault's (1977, 144) terms—is a form of power-knowledge; it is a discursive practice that opposes, challenges, undermines, and resists the dominant, normative memory, which itself effectively disqualifies, excludes, or silences alternative accounts of the world. All such "insurrection of knowledges," Foucault (1980, 87) said, were set "against the institutions" where the more legitimate, formal, or scientific discourses were housed. The practice of cultural resistance was so fundamental and pervasive that it constituted what is arguably one of Foucault's (1978, 95) most basic social axioms: "where there is power, there is resistance." In Manuel Castells's (1997) terms, it is "resistance" to the legitimizing identity and institutions.

And, the very odd emergence of such polar oppositional counternarrative (rather than a corrective) to the Islam is peace storyline suggests that it functions as a strategy in the broader cultural struggle.

The notion that the post-9/11 oppositional discourse about Islam functioned as a strategy within the GOP's broader culture war against the more progressive outside would not have surprised Bourdieu, who—like Gramsci and Foucault—viewed countercultural struggle as central to the understanding of discourse and social practice broadly. Borrowing from Gramsci, Bourdieu (1991, 129) viewed the purpose of such "heretical discourse" as counterhegemonic, aiming to "produce a new common sense." Such cultural resistance, he observed, not only rejects the dominant culture, but rejects it "in a movement of pure negation" (Garnham and Williams 1986, 126).

Counternarratives (rather than corrective narratives) emerge in society, Bourdieu observed, as marginalized or *dominated* producers "have to resort to subversive strategies" (1986, 139), or—as he said elsewhere—the imposition of rival "schemes of classification" (1991, 127-128). The purpose of such "distinction strategies" is to destroy the dominant, official, "ordinary order," either by severing adherence to the legitimate knowledge, or subverting that system by challenging it with "the politically unthinkable," "taboo," or, in the popular vernacular, the *politically-incorrect* (1993, 51, 115).

In this vein, Bourdieu made frequent references to "the establishment" on the one hand, and to its challengers on the other. The challengers were positioned outside the establishment and use as their discursive weapons "strategies of heresy" (Bourdieu 1993, 73). Theirs is the practice of "counterculture," or "the cult of everything that is outside 'legitimate' culture," or "outside the 'establishment', external to official culture," and "defined negatively by what it defines itself against" (Bourdieu 1993, 2-3). Whether it is the opposition between right and left, or orthodoxy and heterodoxy, Bourdieu (1993, 135) observed, the struggle is structurally identical, with unorthodox entrants able to unseat the establishment through cultural productions that are distinct, or distinctly unorthodox. These are the markers of highly interested or political speech, in the broader context of culture war.

Security Discourse as a "Platform" or "Field" for Politics

A report by CAIR (2013, 42) at the end of the post-9/11 decade described how Muslim-American leadership—in response to the group's survey in 2011—believed they were "being used as a political tool." There was a consensus among Muslim-American that "We are no longer considered a community as much as a *platform*." This notion that a discourse could function as a *platform*, *site*, or *field* for politic is also the subject of much literature. But, first, we should delineate a subtle distinction between the concept that a discourse can function *in* the field of politics, and the concept that it can function *as* a field of politics.

In Hajer's (1995, 1996, 2005) examination of European environmental security discourse in the 1990s, he revealed how this discourse—more than merely a discourse *about* the environment—functioned as a platform, or "stage" upon which cultural struggle could take place. In his other words, such discourse functioned *as* "a field of profound 'cultural politics'" (Hajer 2005, 297).[8] Just as Edward Said (1978, 12) had observed that discourse about the Easterner functioned not as *pure* subject matter, but *political* subject matter, so Hajer observed how discourse about protecting nature from the effects of acid rain was not merely advocating certain *policies*, but also a certain *kind of society*. Again, this is the marker of culture war.

In this way, discourse is not narrowly restricted to the linguistic tool that is used *in* a social struggle; but, rather, it can function as the cognitive space or site upon which a more fundamental, pre-existing political competition takes place, albeit in a new context. In war (and its less obvious form by other means, politics), the meeting of battling forces takes place on fields of opportunity, often "shaped" or "prepared" expressly for that purpose. New topical fields are sites of opportunity which can be seized or exploited for political struggle. Even forms of scientific discourse, such as climate change, can be appropriated by cultural entrepreneurs as a field of politics.

That security discourse can function as a field for cultural politics would have seemed axiomatic for Bourdieu. The social realm, in his view, was "the site of continual struggles to define what the social world is" (Bourdieu and Wacquant 1992, 70). He saw the broad array of social fields functioning as "a space of play and competition in which the social agents and institutions which all possess the determinate quantity of specific capital (economic and cultural capital in particular) sufficient to occupy the dominant positions within their respective fields confront one another in strategies aimed at preserving or transforming this balance of forces" (Bourdieu and Wacquant 1992, 76). In his view, scientific discourses—widely perceived as *a*political systems of knowledge—had become part of "the social mechanisms which ensure the maintenance of the established order" (Bourdieu and Wacquant, 1992, 51) and were "conducted in the name of specific interests" (Bourdieu 1993, 9). To make this point, Bourdieu noted that the sociology of rightwing intellectuals is "almost always done by left-wing intellectuals and vice versa" (Bourdieu 1993, 50).

---

[8] This notion that contemporary discourses are sites of cultural contestation appears in the literature broadly; see, for example, Shi-Xu's (2007) edited critical sociolinguistic book, *Discourse as Cultural Struggle*.

Foucault had come to similar conclusions; discourses were "strategical" *sites of struggle* upon which agents advance their interests (Foucault 1979, 101-2). In his series on *The History of Sexuality* (1978-1986), for example, he demonstrated how even the human body functioned as an opportune field of cultural struggle where ideologies were contested.

Various discourse theorists have offered similar conceptualizations of discourses as fields or sites of political struggle. Laclau (1990), for example, noted how discursive constructs like myths can function as opportunistic "surfaces of inscription" upon which social needs and projects can be sited. In a related concept, Laclau and Mouffe (2001, 112–113) observed that a discourse tends to be formed around nodal points. These identifiable nodes carry little meaning on their own—hence their term for them as "empty signifiers" (Laclau 1996, 44) or "floating signifiers" (Laclau 1990, 28). An empty signifier functions to provide structure to the discourse, the same way as a sports field provides structure for the competition; it functions as a *topic of contestation* in the underlying political project; it is an "empty" shell, populated with contending meanings by framing agents vying to advance their positions (Laclau 1996, 69).

Thus, when America's Muslim leadership expressed in a survey their belief that Islam was "being used as a political tool," and that Muslims were "no longer considered a community as much as a platform," they were revealing part of the puzzle as to why this discourse could be so irrational, and yet not only remain stubbornly persistent, but even grow and enjoy the support of a sizeable apparatus of power. Islam, it seems, had become a field of cultural struggle.

3. The Lingering Question and How to Approach It

At this point, we've seen how there is a significant consensus in the literature from across various disciplines that all public discourse and even security discourse is inherently political, and even functions as a battlefield upon which cultural struggle is waged. Our question, then, is this: *What about domestic politics?* The explanations of U.S. anti-Islam discourse to date comprise a blend of Holy Land geopolitics, clash of civilizations ideology, and even a new anti-Muslim racism and xenophobia. But, given the foregoing more theoretical literature, to what extent does this particular U.S. popular security discourse on Islam in the decade after 9/11 also have a significant basis in domestic politics or culture war? And, if so, then how does it function as a platform for cultural politics?

These questions were central to my quest; they formed a kind of hypothesis. Recall Said's (1997, lvii) only axiom related to "all discourse on Islam;" namely, that it "*has an interest in some authority or power.*" My notion was based on analogous reasoning in light of the above literature: If Zionist interests *within* the U.S. conservative movement had found the threat of Islam useful in the geopolitical struggle for the biblical homeland, then is it not also likely that key elements within the broader U.S. conservative movement would find it similarly useful in their political struggle for the culture at home?

To explore this hunch, I took a broadly interpretive approach to discourse analysis—a syncretic one that blended Foucauldian genealogy, Bourdieuian relational sociology,

Emirbayer and Goodwin's (1996) and Sewell's (2005) distinctive reformulations of interpretive sociology, and McAdam and colleagues' (1996, 1997) synthetic social movement analytic.

In the first part of this analysis I examined the discourse in terms of its apparatus of power, including its "tactics and strategies of power" (Foucault 1980, 77), and *how* the knowledge produced in this threat discourse is "enmeshed in a network of power" (Dreyfus and Rabinow 1982, 105-106, 109, 114). The questions are genealogical and functionalist in the Foucauldian sense; it asks "how is this discourse used" and "what role does it play in society"? (Dreyfus and Rabinow 1982, 17). In this vein, I examined the discourse's apparatus of power, in terms of its agency at the level of various media-political institutions and their organic polemicists, as well as its philanthropic network. I then more rigorously examined three of the organic intellectuals widely viewed by Muslim Americans and engaged Muslims abroad as the principal agents of this peculiar green scare over Islam and Islamization.

Adding range and depth and the anthropomorphism that Foucault's genealogy lacked, my approach was also an interpretive or "relational" sociology in the Bourdieuian (1977, 1988, 1990, 1991) sense—that is, placing the text in context, or placing the micro-level strategies of the agents involved in the broader macro-level conditions of emergence that rendered that practice meaningful, materially enabled it, and otherwise incentivized it or made it possible. Here I examined this popular security discourse's broader conditions of emergence—its culturally-resident political framing structure that rendered it both meaningful and credible, and its more historically contingent or eventful political openings or opportunity "structure" that otherwise enabled, supported, or incentivized it.

What became evident after the mid-point of the post-9/11 decade, was that this discourse was lodged in a narrow *political place*; it was lodged *entirely within* the U.S. conservative movement, including most (if not all) of its central, identifying institutions. Chapter 2—The Apparatus for Security Politics—examines part of this apparatus of power and how they attempted to advanced their long-standing cultural agenda on an opportune site for such security politics: Islam.

But, why was this obvious strategy of security politics—of seizing Islam as an opportunistic platform for cultural politics—rendered politically-feasible and credible among a sufficient segment of U.S. conservatives? In Chapter 3—Political Opportunities and Resources—examined this question in terms of this political strategy's set of opportunities and resources. Here, I revealed the more cultural resources it mobilized in addition to its more visible social structural apparatus of power outlined in the previous chapter. Here the inquiry turned to how—like in every political strategy—opportunities were created or seized, and resources mobilized.

More specifically, this chapter explained the U.S. conservative movement's post-9/11 strategy of security politics related to Islam in terms of three elements of its broader opportunities-resource set. First, it examined the opening for politics that U.S. conservatives created in their strategy to build a parallel society of media and other knowledge institutions for the express purpose of cultural politics, or culture war—and that conservative enclave's rapid expansion into the emerging alternative media over the first half of the post-9/11 decade. Secondly, it explored two prevailing mass-level conservative moods or emotions that these agents of security politics opportunistically seized—the identity insecurity or crises of the U.S. conservative movement, and the broader mood of civilizational fundamentalism. Thirdly, it mapped the select U.S cultural schemas, narratives, and ideologies—the building blocks of all political identity—that this discourse's elite mobilized or manipulated to render their securitization and politicization of Islam meaningful and credible within a significant segment of U.S. conservatives.

Following the more structural and eventful contexts of this form of security politics, Chapters 4, 5, and 6 more rigorously examined the strategies of three of the individual organic intellectuals within the U.S. conservative apparatus, revealing how these polemicists used the topic of Islam as a platform for cultural politics. Considering their prominence in the literature just reviewed, the three polemicists of this threat discourse selected for analysis are Daniel Pipes, Robert Spencer, and Brigitte Gabriel, along with their organizations. They and their organizations are meaningfully diverse, and offer an expanded window into how organic intellectuals of various stripes function politically, or within a political collectivity's culture war. Whereas Daniel Pipes had been at the fore of Islam criticism since the Islamic revolution in Iran, and whereas he was for years after 9/11 the lone prophet of the Islamization of the U.S., Robert Spencer had emerged only in the latter half of the post-9/11 decade, rapidly publishing eight books on Islam, two of which were *New York Times* bestsellers, and leading the most popular blog in the field, *Jihad Watch*. The selection of the also aforementioned Lebanese-American and Evangelical Christian Brigitte Gabriel took into consideration her two bestselling books set within the counternarrative, as well as her distinctive position in the field as a more activist knowledge producer and leader of ACT! for America. ACT! For America, at the time, was in Gabriel's terms, "the largest grassroots citizen action network" in the U.S., dedicated to "preserving national security and combating Islamic supremacy." The group's stated membership of 240,000 was nearly twice that of the powerful AIPAC (Fichtner 2011).

Chapter 7—Conclusions—shifts from the empirical to the theoretical, and offers a model or conceptual framework for how—based on this case—popular security discourse functions as a platform for cultural politics.

2

THE APPARATUS

for

Security Politics

Truth is something which is supported materially by a whole range of practices and institutions: universities, government departments, publishing houses, scientific bodies and so on.

—Michel Foucault (1972, 224)

THE most cursory inquiry into this peculiar post-9/11 Islam-as-threat discourse revealed that it emerged not merely from certain statements by individual proponents, but by a range of organizations and even philanthropic concerns.

To practitioners in the social sciences, this comes as no surprise. Anything that emerges as a subject of much debate is, as Foucault pointed out, largely a function of what he called an apparatus of power. This apparatus, he observed, included both discursive and non-discursive elements—that is, not only the "strategies and relations of forces supporting certain types of knowledge," but the harder forces such as institutions and financing or philanthropy (Foucault 1980, 194; Dreyfus and Rabinow 1982, 184). In his other words, an item of discourse is "supported materially by a whole range of *practices and institutions*" (Foucault 1972, 224; 1980, 194). Similarly, working from the Marxist frame, Althusser (1971) had noted how ideological beliefs were "materialized" in specific types of institutions and organizations in civil society, such as religious and political organizations (Howarth 2000, 94).

This notion that subjects of much public debate are a function of much more than mere talk was both Hall's (1972) and Cohen's (1972) conclusion in their analysis of Britain's moral panics. They discovered it was the institution of the mass media broadly that was implicated in the construction of the panic's cognitive and psychological basis.

In the United States in the decade after 9/11, much of discourse surrounding the green scare over Islam and Islamization seemed to emerge from three categories within the broader conservative apparatus of power: First, the movement's parallel knowledge society, and its institutions; second, cultural and political elite; and, third, philanthropic institutions.

Here, we will see how this form of security politics was—in Foucault's words—"supported materially by a whole range of *practices* and *institutions*."

1. The Conservative Parallel Knowledge Society and Its Institutions

In the United States in the aftermath of 9/11, much of discourse surrounding the green scare over Islam and Islamization seemed to emerge from the broader Zionism or Holy Land geopolitical institutional base—what Mearsheimer and Walt (2007, 112-117) described "the Israel lobby." The Israel Lobby, they noted, is the "loose coalition of individuals and organizations" in the U.S. that "actively work to shape U.S. foreign policy in a pro-Israel direction." This would include security policy advocacy organizations such as Jewish Institute for National Security Affairs, Washington Institute for Near East Policy, and Middle East Forum.[9]

But, as the discourse progressed, it became apparent that many of the institutions leading this green scare over Islam and Islamization of America, were more of the main identifying institutions of the U.S. conservative movement. As such, their discourse relative to the green scare reflected more interest in local, domestic politics, or the culture war against the broader progressive outside. This should not have come as a surprise. Most of these institutions' mission statements and histories suggest that they were formed for the express purpose of U.S. domestic counterhegemonic struggle, and that have continued to operate in that overarching context of the domestic culture war (Pierson and Skocpol 2007; Diamond 1995). And, as the following analysis reveals, the more identifying institutions of this parallel polis were created to politicize *everything*—that is, every topic of any national importance—including every security topic—was to be seized as a platform for cultural struggle against the progressive outside.

National Review

Recall from the introduction that, by the end of the Bush administration, the "war on Islam" master narrative seemed to be becoming a more structural hostile myth, with the potential to fuel a destructive cycle of fear and hostility between Muslim and Western societies (Lynch 2010, Pew 2011). This realization had led the new Obama administration to make this the subject of its first foreign policy initiative, resulting in the President's historic speeches directly to the world's Muslims from two traditionally aligned Muslim-majority states that had become highly anti-American. In these two speeches, President

---

[9] The authors note that, to be part of the lobby, an organization's pursuit of shaping foreign policy in support of Israel "must be an important part of its mission and consume a substantial percentage of its resources and agenda," and for an individual, "this means devoting some portion of one's professional or personal life (or in some cases, substantial amounts of money to influencing U.S. Middle East policy (2007, 114).

Obama explicitly used that phrase—"war on Islam"—in an attempt to contain this emerging master narrative. Specifically, the President tried to contain this strategically-important threat narrative by saying, "The United States is not, and will never be, at *war* with *Islam*."

Such a manifest strategic security issue and such a necessary statement, it might seem, would be immune from politicization, and would receive support from across the political spectrum.

Yet, on the day after President Obama's 4 June 2009 address from Cairo to Muslims worldwide, the iconic conservative magazine, *National Review*, published a puzzling article— "Making Believe: Obama's speech was deep in fable, short on fact." Not only did it further antagonize Muslims worldwide by explicitly countering the normative "Islam is peace" frame, but it engaged the new President's much anticipated foreign policy speech with something akin to an official GOP rebuttal to a State of the Union address—an institutionalized occasion for domestic politics. The article antagonized both of the conservative movement's enemies—foreign and domestic, religious and political— describing the speech as "warmed-over leftist dogma sprinkled with a fictional accounting of Islam and its history." Islam, it countered "isn't a religion of peace with a legacy so overflowing with achievement in science, philosophy, and the arts," as President Obama claimed. It went on:

> Though Obama portrayed Islam as having a "proud tradition of tolerance," it has a far more consequential legacy of intolerance. Islam strives for hegemony, seeking not to co-exist but to make all the world the realm of the Muslims (*dar al-Islam*) while regarding those parts not under its dominion as the realm of war (*dar al-Harb*).

The selection of the spokesperson for this deliberately subversive speech act was itself counterhegemonic in function; it was meant to resist and delegitimize the prevailing more progressive security narrative, and otherwise advance the conservative movement's culture war. Thus, this flagship of U.S. conservatism need not and chose not to tap an established scholar of Islamic affairs with a solid reputation in the Muslim-American community who could have cited the reasons why the U.S. (and especially the GOP, after the two GOP-led invasions) was not at war with Islam, and who could have articulated a more Kennan-like grand strategy for both U.S.-Muslim relations and the containment of violent extremism ideology within the Islamic continuum. Instead, it opted for counterhegemonic symbolism and published an article by someone whom it had shaped into its own columnist, Andrew McCarthy.

The key cultural capital which McCarthy possessed, and for which his rebuttal article was chosen for publishing, was that he had an established track-record (including hundreds of articles and posts in *National* Review) of practicing *security politics*; that is, of using the topic of Islam as a threat to engage in domestic politics. This was evidenced by his other *National Review* articles, such as "The President Stands with Sharia," and by the titles and subtitles of the *three* books that he managed to publish in 2010: *How the Obama Administration has Politicized Justice, The Grand Jihad: How Islam and the Left Sabotage America,* and *How Obama Embraces Islam's Sharia Agenda*.[10] In other words, this iconic conservative commentary disregarded the highly radicalizing and threatening "war on Islam" master narrative and published McCarthy's rebuttal not because of his knowledge of Islam in terms of a security issue, but because of his reliable habitus of using the topic of Islam as a platform in the delegitimizing of the conservative movement's domestic political opponents.

But, should we be surprised at this? Described by some as "the Bible of American conservatism" (Hari 2007, 31), *National Review's* advertising kit describes itself as "America's most widely read and influential magazine and web site for conservative news, commentary, and opinion" and its media-kit describes itself as "America's leading conservative voice for news and opinion" for over 58 years.[11] But, *National Review* functions not first and foremost a "news" institution, or even an "American" institution; it is a "conservative" instrument, or conservative "voice" with an overarching mission of advancing the conservative worldview.

Russell Kirk's (1953) *The Conservative Mind* was the philosophical cornerstone of the nascent U.S. conservative movement, and *National Review* was its first identifying institution (Goldberg 2005; Edwards 2003; Rusher 2002).   The purpose of its organization in 1955 by conservative intellectual and icon William F. Buckley Jr. was political knowledge, not pure knowledge. Conservative victories, Buckley wrote, suffered because of bias in the universities and in the media, prompting him to call for a new conservative journal to compete with liberals, to compensate for "Conservative weakness" in the academy, and to "focus the energies" of the movement (Edwards, 2003).

And, since its founding, *National Review* has been a counterhegemonic instrument, advocating for the conservative causes, and—correspondingly—writing against liberal or progressive causes.[12] After the Brown v. Board of Education (1954) Supreme Court decision, for example, *National Review* columnists such as former Yale political philosopher Willmoore Kendall argued against forced desegregation (Gross et al. 2011, 334). In the 1960s it advocated for Barry Goldwater; in the 1990s it advocated against Bill Clinton, and so on. In the decade after 9/11—as McCarthy's rebuttal demonstrates—the *Review* continued to function *not* as a neutral source of information and political commentary, but as a source of highly positioned adversarial advocacy to advance conservative interests on the wide range of topics.

National Review, therefore, according to Edwards (2003), was "not simply a journal of opinion but a political act…"

On the topic of Islam broadly in the decade after 9/11, the threat from Islamic extremism (let alone Islam itself) was being downplayed by even the Director of National

---

[10] McCarthy's only recognized credential was that he, when a former federal prosecutor after the first World Trade Center bombing in 1993, had prosecuted the extremist "blind sheikh," Omar Abdul Rahman, who had given the theological justification for the attack.   McCarthy himself knew that he was not an authority and in his article, he referred to Robert Spencer twice for such authority.

[11] http://mediakit.nationalreview.com/

[12] The entire history of the institution, in Hart's (2005, ix) words, "represents a Quest Narrative: the quest for a politically viable and thoughtful American conservatism."

Intelligence. But, on the pages of *National Review,* its cadre of experts on the topic—Frank Gaffney, Andrew McCarthy, Daniel Pipes, Mark Steyn, and lesser-known others—reliably kept the dual threat of Islam and progressives before us. Their articles—all readily available (listed by author and by year) on its website—typically began with the topic *du jour,* and then reliably took the counternarrative position, in opposition to the mainstream. And, then—almost in the same breath—just as reliably shifted to more performative domestic cultural politics, describing the ineptness, political correctness, or other ideological failure of some part of the more progressive outside, especially the Obama administration.

Again, in all of these articles, Islam—like so many other topics of the day—served as a useful platform for the main event: domestic politics.

The Washington Times

After President Obama's aforementioned speech in Cairo to the world's Muslim communities, another iconic conservative institution, the *Washington Times,* on June 9, 2009, carried this non-sequitur headline: "Gaffney: America's first Muslim president?: Obama aligns with the policies of Shariah-adherents." Bypassing the strategic importance of the foreign policy initiative and even rational criticism of the new administration's approach, this central identifying newspaper of the conservative movement delved into crude tabloid-like politics, noting that "there is mounting evidence that the president not only identifies with Muslims, but actually may still be one himself." It not only insinuated that the new president was deceptively practicing Christianity while actually being a Muslim, but it implied that all practicing Muslims are also practicing *taqiyya* so as to hide their subversive designs to destroy America from within.

Washington Times' chosen author for this opportunity, Frank Gaffney, was the newspaper's signature security expert. The newspaper had singularly produced Mr. Gaffney as an authority, commissioning him to publish some 1400 articles, in what has been described as "the longest-running weekly column in the history of the *Washington Times.*"[13] In the latter half of the post-9/11 decade alone, the *Times* contains 570 citations for Gaffney's articles and others that favorable cite him. In other words, the editors of the newspaper knew precisely what Gaffney would write; that is why he was in that position in the first place.

In the lead-up to the president's first foreign policy initiative regarding the "war on Islam" master narrative, the *Times* on February 3, 2009 published Gaffney's "S-U-B-M-I-S-S-I-O-N"—a reference the new Democratic president's compliance with the very meaning of the word, "Islam." And, the day after the President's first speech to Muslims worldwide from Ankara Turkey on April 6, 2009, the *Times* published its own rebuttal-like article from Gaffney, "Reality checks abroad: Obama initiatives confront unpleasant facts." Still another occasion for politicization of the topic presented itself after a seemingly innocuous statement by John Brennan—the assistant to President Obama for homeland

---

[13] See http://www.breitbart.com/Big-Peace/2014/02/25/FRANK-GAFFNEYS-WEEKLY-COLUMN-COMES-TO-BREITBART

security and counterterrorism—in early August 2009 at the Center for Strategic and International Studies (CSIS). Mr. Brennan referred to the President's statement to Muslims worldwide in Cairo in June, that "America is not and never will be at war with Islam." The *Times* predictably responded on August 12th with a rebuttal article by Gaffney titled, "But is 'Islam' at war with us," in which Gaffney reliably made the case that some undifferentiated "Islam" was at war with the U.S.

Again, none of this comes as any surprise to anyone who has ever read the *Washington Times*. The *Times* (on its website) claims itself to be "a full-service, general interest" newspaper. It mentions nothing about its being founded as a counterhegemonic institution to offset the more progressive influence of the *Washington Post*. The *Times* was read daily and endorsed as such a conservative counterhegemonic institution by President Reagan (Clarkson 1987). It is a distinctly oppositional conservative political position that progressives widely acknowledge (Blumenthal 2006; Mantyla 2007), that conservatives frequently tout. Conservapedia's article on "The Washington Times," for example, describes it as "a conservative daily newspaper in Washington, D.C. which strives to counterbalance the liberal slant of the Washington Post." And, the *Times* promotes itself, with such identifiers as the "vanguard of a media insurgency" and the centerpiece of a "news counterestablishment" (*Washington Times* 2007, May 17).

The newspaper was founded in 1982 and owned and operated until 2010 by the Unification Church of Sun Myung Moon to be the newspaper for the nation's religious conservatives. At its 20th anniversary, in 2002, Moon said that the newspaper "is responsible to let the American people know about God" and that it would "become the instrument in spreading the truth about God to the world" (Ahrens 2002). But, for the newspaper's managing editor after 9/11, Francis Coombs, the mission was political and not religious; "journalism is war," was his oft-repeated motto in the newsroom (Blumenthal 2006).

By mid-point of the post-9/11 decade, the newspaper nearly went bankrupt, with its editorial position having devolved to what was described by Blumenthal (2006) in a cover story in *The Nation* as "hard right" and "characterized by extreme racial animus and connections to nativist and neo-Confederate organizations." Southern Poverty Law Center Intelligence Project executive director Mark Potok described the institution as a "key part of the radical right's apparatus in the United States," significantly responsible for fueling the nativism that emerged within the GOP, and as being "in bed with bigots and white supremacists" (Blumenthal 2006).

As was the case with its editorial position on Islam(ization), it was arguably politics, and not bigotry or opposition to immigration that was foremost in the *Times's* editorial position. For example, Arkansas "Justice" Jim Johnson—a leader of the segregationist Capital Citizens Council chapter of Little Rock—curiously published two anti-Clinton op-ed articles in the newspaper in 1995. It was later learned that the aforementioned Richard Mellon Scaife had provided $2.4 million in a scheme in which "sources" were paid to concoct anti-Clinton stories, and that Johnson and *The Washington Times* editor-in-chief at the time, Wesley Pruden, were linked to this project (Blumenthal 2006).

And, as was the case with *National Review*, the newspaper's editorial position has been to politicize the topics that it selects for news. In the case of Islam broadly after 9/11—as the above examples begin to suggest—the newspaper's editorial mode was for its columnist experts—Gaffney, for example—to make some weak, uncontextualized reference to a purported threat related to that topic of great general interest, then to delegitimize the Obama administration in the discussion, and then to capture this politically performative speech act in the title and subtitle. For example, Gaffney's article on the 11th anniversary of 9/11 was: "GAFFNEY: Islamists' tipping point: Obama impotence signals opportunity for Shariah." His article at the 10th anniversary of 9/11 was similar: "GAFFNEY: Obama's 9/11 delusion."

In all of the *Washington Times'* security commentary, the security topic was politicized, containing politically-performative speech acts that delegitimized the Democrats, the president, his administration, or the broader more progressive "establishment." This politicization was especially evident since the beginning of the Obama administration. During the campaign, the newspaper published apparently everything Gaffney could manage to write on the topics of Islam and the Left, with titles such as: "Obama's Islamist problem" (August 19, 2008). After conservatives lost the White House, the threat commentary became even more politically antagonistic, with articles like "Embracing of Shariah? 'Respect' should be a two-way street" (March 17, 2009); "GAFFNEY: Courting Shariah: Kagan supported Islam at Harvard but not the U.S. military" (June 2009); and "Security compromised: White House policies embolden our enemies" (November 24, 2009).

And in the lead up to the mid-term elections in 2010, it was dubiously "Obama" that was centered in all "security" commentary, with articles like: "GAFFNEY: A Shrine to Sharia" (June 28, 2010); "GAFFNEY: Obama's 'teachable' Shariah moment" (August 17, 2010); "GAFFNEY: Obama's sneak attack on U.S. defense" (November 15, 2010); GAFFNEY: Obama's next war: President's ill-considered Islamist backing puts Israel in the cross hairs (May 23, 2011); GAFFNEY: The post-constitutional president: Obama shows contempt for his oath of office (Oct 8, 2012).

The Washington Times—and not merely Gaffney, McCarthy, Pipes, and rest of its cadre of experts—was so fully central to the sharia scare strategy that on September 29, 2009, the newspaper's editors published their own article, "The threat of 'stealth jihad': West responds to pressure with accommodation."

Even in titles that weren't more explicit in this regard, all articles advancing the Ialam(ization) threat narrative functioned counterhegemonically—that is, within the realm of the conservative movement's domestic cultural struggle—to somehow delegitimize the more progressive outside. For example, at the ninth anniversary of 9/11, on September 14 2010, *The Washington Times* ran the article by the aforementioned Andrew McCarthy and colleagues, "WOOLSEY & MCCARTHY & SOYSTER: Second Opinion Needed on Sharia: Our Political Establishment Wears Blinders and Ignores the Threat." The article followed the same pattern as that of McCarthy's in the *National Review* (and expressed clearly in titles or subtitles of each of McCarthy's books) to raise the specter of a great threat from

Islam(ization), and then to use that platform of fear to go on and delegitimize the progressive outside broadly, signified variously in code words such as "political establishment," or "politically-correct," and often more explicitly referring directly to "Obama."

This pattern or strategy of action extended across all possible events remotely related to Islam, and across all of the newspaper's cadre of experts—whose clear role was not only to obscure key contextualizing facts related to Islam and Islamization that would reveal the absurdity of this threat discourse, but to antagonistically delegitimize some view or policy of the Left broadly and the president and his administration specifically. In the articles by its riable Islam-politicizing agent, Daniel Pipes, just as those written by Gaffney and McCarthy, as we've seen, even the article titles accomplish the same purpose. For example, we find: "PIPES: Obama: My Muslim Faith" (September 11, 2012); "PIPES: Obama: 'I have never been a Muslim'" (September 7, 2012); "PIPES: 'Rushdie rules' reach Florida: Obama endorses privileged status for Islam" (September 20, 2010), and so on.

Again, within this strategy of security politics, any event broadly related to Islam, no matter how trivial, constituted opportunity for domestic cultural politics, and the newspaper's cadre of Islam politicizers were expected to rise to the occasion. In the case of the latter mentioned article by Pipes, the security event selected for politics was Florida Pastor Terry Jones's planned burning of the Quran, and the fact that the President, the Secretary of State, Hillary Clinton, and others had all urged him not to, for fear of Muslim violence against Americans if he proceeded. Had *The Washington Times* responsibly and apolitically sought to inform debate, its editors could have asked Pipes to inject some context with his criticism. Pipes might have at least acknowledged that in the era of global-connectedness, such an act by an obscure pastor of a tiny church of twenty persons in rural Florida might be viewed by those in less free societies as tacit U.S. government approval and another pillar in their "war on Islam" master narrative, and sure to spark some to call for retributive justice in their Friday sermons, thereby putting U.S. citizens working in Muslim majority countries at much greater risk. No such context was to be found. Instead, Pipes reliably politicized the event, saying, "Mr. Obama, in effect, enforced Islamic law, a precedent that could lead to other forms of compulsory Sharia compliance."

FOX News Channel

At the 11th anniversary of 9/11, the FOX News anchor pulled her viewers' attention from the hundreds of other important national and international issues, and introduced a "controversial" "anti-jihad" subway advertisement going up in ten subway stations across New York City. As the FOX News cameras displayed the ad, she read it: "In any war between the civilized man and the savage, support the civilized man. Support Israel. Defeat Jihad." "And here's *the woman* behind the ads...," she added, insinuating that she was introducing a total stranger. Another FOX co-anchor also remained coy about the relationship between FOX and the woman, saying only that, "Actually, we've reported some other controversies having to do with *this particular woman*." She added:

"We have; Pamela Geller *is her name*—a very outspoken blogger who's been in *the headlines* before. She headed a campaign some two years ago to block construction of a mosque near ground zero...."[14]

Neither co-anchor let on that it was FOX News that had put Geller in the headlines before—both on the Mike Huckabee show, and many other FOX programs in 2010 on the subject of "the 911 mosque at ground zero." And neither FOX co-anchor let on that Geller since had been an institution in FOX programming, appearing regularly across many of its programs to speak as this institution's authority on matters related to Islam broadly.

Just ten days earlier, for example—during the violent protests over the purposively provocative "Innocence of Muslims" movie trailer—Geller had been a guest expert on FOX, appearing with former ambassador John Bolton. Then, FOX's anchor Patti Ann Browne introduced Geller a little differently, saying, "let's bring in blogger, author, and executive director for Stop the Islamization of America."[15] Browne said nothing about the fact that Geller's organization was listed as a hate group by the Southern Poverty Law Center. And although the topic this time was how the strategically-important relationship between Egypt and the US has changed, Browne made no mention that Geller was not a foreign policy expert but a college drop-out whose only bona fides for the interview seemed to be that she was prone to politically-antagonistic rhetoric, having regularly referred to President Obama as "Hussein," describing him as "the love-child of Malcolm X," and so on.

Only nine days before, on the September 15 edition of *FOX & Friends*, FOX had created yet another "news" opportunity for Geller to appear and speak on the Islam-insulting Innocence of Muslim YouTube trailer that had started protests in Muslim communities worldwide. FOX prefaced their introduction of Geller with their cameras slowly panning across her book, *Stop the Islamization of America*. The following thrust of her interview, predictably, was not informative commentary on the security issue, but on attacking the President, saying that president Obama is "sanctioning these murderous rages that these Muslim mobs have been going on" and that the President—"by condemning the movie" is adhering "to the blasphemy laws under sharia" which state that you "cannot criticize or offend Islam" (MediaMatters 2012).[16] During Geller's speech, FOX's foot screen banners were also hard at work politicizing the topic, reading "Respecting religious freedom: President Obama's stance under scrutiny," and "Avoiding confrontation: Geller: President sanctions blasphemy laws," and so on.

By featuring Geller regularly and across the spectrum of its programming, FOX News Channel singlehandedly transformed both her, her books, and her rancorous politics into nationally-known commodities, just as the *Washington Times* had done with McCarthy, Pipes, and Gaffney.

---

[14] See video "FOX News report on Pamela Geller and anti-jihad subway ads" at http://www.youtube.com/watch?v=a2QPQCmOlfk.

[15] See video "Pamela Geller on FOX News on Libyan Embassy Attack and the Violent Muslim Protests across the world" at http://www.youtube.com/watch?v=XjRCJKlb4og.

[16] See video at http://mediamatters.org/video/2012/09/15/FOX-guest-pamela-geller-obama-is-sanctioning-th/189919

Beyond this, FOX went out of its way to promote Geller's politically-antagonistic books that were only superficially related to Islam(ization). When Geller appeared on FOX's September 21, 2011 edition of the Sean Hannity show, Hannity introduced Geller—while the camera pans to across her new book—as "the author of the BRAND-NEW-BOOK—in bookstores everywhere—Stop the Islamization of America—conservative blogger and our friend, Pam Geller...."[17] Earlier, on the March 13, 2011 edition of *FOX & Friends*, the hostess rhetorically asked whether the *New York Times* was being insensitive by running a full page ad "It's time to quit the Catholic Church," but refused an almost identical ad "It's time to quit Islam." The host then said, "And here is the creator of the ad, author of the book, *Stop the Islamization of America*. As was FOX's usual mode, its cameras at this point slowly panned across Geller's book.

Similarly, on the July 29, 2010 edition of *FOX & Friends*, the topic delivered via the main FOX banner was "Honor killings on the rise: Group launches campaign to end Muslim murders." The show's hostess Gretchen Carlson shifted to the non-sequitur, introducing Geller as "a blogger for AtlasShrugs.com and the executive director of Stop the Islamization of America; and she's co-authored a new book *The Post-American Presidency: The Obama Administration's War on America*." After the camera slowly pans across Geller's book, Carlson then asks Geller, "Alright, what are the issues that you are tackling, not only in this book, but also in this billboard campaign?" Two days later, on July 31st edition of FOX Business, FOX produced Geller again to discuss yet another wide-ranging topic; this time, the British Prime Minister's description of Gaza as a "prison camp," and—before the interview, in what would otherwise be a non-sequitur on this topic of Gaza's siege—the host introduced her new book, *The Post-American Presidency*.

The pattern was always the same; FOX produced Geller as an authority on opportune events related to Islam not because of any authoritative credentials, for which she had none whatsoever; but because she and her books was useful politically at the domestic level, in delegitimizing President Obama and/or the Left broadly. This working relationship for purposes of Islam-related politics continued well beyond the tenth anniversary of 9/11. On the July 1 2013 edition of FOX News's *Hannity*, for example, Geller was hard at work, describing President Obama as "consistently on the side of jihadic Islamic supremacist regimes" (MediaMatters 2013).

FOX News Channel during this time was the highest rated cable news network during this time, attracting more viewers than all other cable-news outlets combined (Gillette 2008). According to Nielsen Media Research, the cable giant was reaching 98 million households in America—virtually the entire country. And, it was also the most profitable component of Rupert Murdoch's News Corp, reaping an estimated profit of $816 million, rivaling the earnings of News Corp.'s entire film division, which includes 20th Century FOX (Dickinson 2011). But, with its bare-bones newsgathering operation—with only one-

---

[17] Geller provides all of her FOX News Channel appearances on her own YouTube site. This video can be viewed at http://www.youtube.com/watch?v=5BSI9yq9oFs.

third of the staff and 30 fewer bureaus than even CNN, which is not a serious news source—FOX was hardly in the business of professional journalism (Dickinson 2011).

Given FOX News Channel's reliable propensity to politicize all topics of national security, it comes as no surprise that the viewing public, in a Pew Research Center 2009 poll, identified FOX News as the "most ideological network." This came as no surprise to the FOX News Channel employees. A former deputy of FOX's Chairman Roger Ailes also described the network in terms of political machine disguised as news: "It's a political campaign – a 24/7 political campaign" (Dickinson 2011). And, based his extensive interviews of several hundred FOX employees, past and present, Dickinson (2011) summarize their views of FOX as "a giant soundstage created to mimic the look and feel of a news operation, cleverly camouflaging political propaganda as independent journalism." Sean Wilentz, a Princeton historian and author of *The Age of Reagan*, also characterized the entire network "devoted 24 hours a day" to entirely politics …" (Dickinson 2011). Jones (2012) similarly noted that "The genre of news offered important and necessary 'cover' for the [FOX] network, helping to thwart charges of propaganda or partisanship" (Jones 2012, 178).

And, all components of the FOX News programming function as vehicles for politics (Jones 2012, 179). FOX Chairman Roger Ailes, for example uses *FOX & Friends*—what appears to be merely a morning talk show—as one of his primary vehicles for politics. Dickinson (2011) notes that "According to insiders, the morning show's anchors, who appear to be chatting ad-lib, are actually working from daily, structured talking points that come straight from the top. A former FOX deputy said that "Prior to broadcast, Steve Doocy, Gretchen Carlson – that gang – they meet with Roger…. And Roger gives them the spin." *FOX &* Friends, Dickinson (2011) points out, was the program where the smear about Obama having attended a madrassa emerged, with Doocy stating that Obama was "raised as a Muslim" (Dickinson 2011).

In his analysis of FOX News Channel, Jones (2012, 179) states: "That FOX News is, consistently and across all of its programs, offering a conservative ideological voice and doing so under the heading of 'news' is, at this date, an undeniable point. Scholars and media-watchdog groups have provided detailed evidence of FOX's overtly ideological narratives in both its news and its opinion programs." He revealed how this niche media institution used the format of "news" stories surrounding the Islamization of America to conduct political work:

> FOX News's speech acts may name something—say, for instance, branding an Islamic community center in the Manhattan neighborhood near the former World Trade Center a "Ground Zero mosque"—but the utterance also warns citizens of a supposed threat to American values and honor, perhaps even mobilizing people to vote in the midterm congressional elections for candidates voicing opposition to such a "mosque." Thus, the repeated iteration of such utterances across programming day parts not only creates realities—"mosque," not community center, becomes the standard usage, even outside of FOX's utterances—but also has the potential to mobilize actions through its performative power (Jones 2012, 184).

Jones adds, "FOX has successfully shown how TV news need not be *about* politics but can *be* politics instead. FOX has demonstrated that news production is aimed not at representing truth but at representing audiences it can assemble around its ideological renderings of 'truth'."

FOX's strategy is also counterhegemonic, in terms of the broader conservative cultural struggle. In the words of FOX News host Chris Wallace, FOX was the counter-weight [to NBC News] ... they have a liberal agenda, and we tell the other side of the story" (Corn 2011).

It is in this strategy that we begin to understand how Geller's distinct *lack* of authoritative credentials was actually her main form of cultural capital, as it aligned with FOX's unabashed anti-intellectualism and anti-elitism, and was performative in that it tacitly denigrated or resisted the scholarly and security professional communities, which FOX systematically excluded from its programming.

In this vein—following the aforementioned move by *National Review* in selecting Andrew McCarthy for its rebuttal to the president's historic address to Muslims worldwide—FOX News rarely (if ever) invited highly-credentialed scholars or security professionals to provide apolitical analyses that reflect the complexities reliably found in security threats. Instead, FOX's editorial policy sought out polemicists like Geller who were organic to the conservative movement, and with the propensity to engage in politics, but possessing few if any of the credentials normative for the status of authority in the dominant societal institutions.

Along this line, Geller and Spencer's grassroots organization, Stop Islamization of America, was itself a form of taboo or counterhegemonic resistance. The fact that Geller's organization was listed as an "anti-Muslim hate group" by the Southern Poverty Law Center, for example, seems less a problem for FOX than it was a deliberate criterion for her selection. In this, FOX's production of Geller—again, much like the *National Review's* and *Washington Times's* production of McCarthy during this time—can be viewed as a function of her ability to serve as a symbol of resistance to the dominant and more progressive societal order.

This was FOX's broader mode of operation. For example, when National Public Radio fired its popular host Juan Williams for admitting to Bill O'Reilly on an October 18, 2010 show that he felt fear when he saw people in traditional Muslim dress when flying, FOX immediately hired him in a three contract worth $2 million. Obviously, FOX hired Williams not for what might have been its new strategy to provide more substantive, nuanced discussion of newsworthy events and trends, but merely as a symbolic counterhegemonic statement of FOX's position opposite to that of the more progressive outside.

Conservative Publishing Houses: Regnery and Encounter Books

In 2006, the official and societally-dominant "Islam is peace" frame was represented in Karen Armstrong's glowing biography of Islam's prophet, *Muhammad: A Prophet for Our*

Time, by the mainstream publisher Harper-Collins. But, that same year, another book—distinctively oppositional in the title—*The Truth about Muhammad: Founder of the World's Most Intolerant Religion*, emerged from the niche conservative publisher, Regnery. What the farther Left and former Catholic nun author, Karen Armstrong, had excluded from view in her work on Muhammad, the farther Right and Catholic deacon author, Robert Spencer—an employee of David Horowitz—used for his entire text on the faith's founder. In this rebuttal-like, counternarrative, Regnery was continuing its strategic habitus of counterhegemonic publishing—that is, publishing against the prevailing progressive cultural ethos.

In this strategy, Regnery productions subvert the more progressive and dominant outside by excluding from view all texts and authors housed within the more legitimate knowledge society, and selecting for the entire realm of visibility those topics or objects that dominant societal norms and legitimizing institutions viewed as taboo or considered illegitimate knowledge. To facilitate this mode of struggle, Regnery developed its trademarked "politically incorrect" series, exemplified by Spencer's *New York Times* bestseller, *The Politically Incorrect Guide to Islam (and the Crusades)* (2005).

On the topic of Islam broadly, all of Regnery's productions could be categorized within this realm of politically-incorrect—counter cultural, that is, supporting the conservative opposing or counternarrative. It produced titles like Michelle Malkin's *In Defense of Internment* [of Muslim-Americans], Robert Spencer's *Onward Muslim Soldiers* , his *Religion of Peace? Why Christianity Is and Islam Isn't*, his *Stealth Jihad*, and his *The Complete Infidel's Guide to the Koran*, Erik Stakelbeck's *The [Muslim-American] Terrorist Next Door*, Tony Blankley's *The West's Last Chance* [in the face of Islam's takeover], Geert Wilders's *Marked for Death: Islam's War Against the West and Me*, and so on.

Regnery more explicitly institutionalized its strategy of security politics via the platform of Islam with titles like David Horowitz's *Unholy Alliance: Radical Islam and the American Left* (2006), all the while continuing to struggle in works not related to Islam, such as Horowitz's McCarthyesque works, *The Professors* (2007), and *Radicals* (2012)—both of which denigrated and securitized progressive elite in academic and politics.

The obvious politicization evident in Regnery's publishing should surprise no one. Up until this point, Regnery Publishing had been the country's leading publisher of distinctively conservative books. Founded by Henry Regnery in 1947 with counterhegemonic struggle in mind, the publisher openly touted its position as "central to the conservative movement."[18] Regnery helped establish and sustain the postwar U.S. conservative intellectual movement with works such as Russell Kirk's *The Conservative Mind* (1953) and William F. Buckley Jr.'s *God and Man at Yale* (1951). Its website states:

> Since Regnery opened its doors back in 1947, the conservative movement has grown from a few intellectuals, economists, editorial writers, and authors to become the most vibrant political and intellectual movement in the country. Regnery Publishing has

---

[18] See http://www.regnery.com/about/

grown with the movement and is as central to the conservative movement today as it was more than 65 years ago.

Owned by the Washington DC-based Eagle Publishing, Regnery's stated ideological position is opaque compared to its sister institution, *Human Events*, which was also co-founded by Henry Regnery, and whose website touts itself as "the nation's leading conservative voice since we were established in 1944." Its editor, David Harsanyi is senior editor at *The Federalist*, and was author of *Obama's Four Horsemen: The Disasters Unleashed by Obama's Reelection*, as well as the well-read *Nanny State: How Food Fascists, Teetotaling Do-Gooders, Priggish Moralists, and other Boneheaded Bureaucrats are Turning America into a Nation of Children*. Harsanyi also contributed to Glenn Beck's *Arguing With Idiots* and is a major partner for Beck's website, *The Blaze* (Roberts 2011). Regnery's short list of eight contributors include Raymond Ibrahim, who was functioned more as the more politically-incorrect "bad cop" at both Spencer's *Jihad Watch* and Pipes's *Middle East Forum*, as outlined in the later profiles.

Given this ideological orientation, it is not surprising that Regnery touts its counterhegemonic purpose of publishing books that "challenge the status quo."[19] As was the case with its books related to the topic of Islam, Regnery's mode is often explicit delegitimizing of the progressive outside, seen in titles like these from its website, beginning with just the first three letters of the alphabet:

A Slobbering Love Affair, Bernard Goldberg
In the New York Times bestseller, A Slobbering Love Affair, author Bernard Goldberg shows how the mainstream media's hopelessly one-sided coverage of President Obama has shredded America's trust in journalism and endangered our free society.

After America, Mark Steyn
Just in time for the presidential election, the New York Times bestseller comes to paperback! Featuring a new introduction, this edition takes on Obama's disastrous plan for our nation, and reveals what a post-American world could look like.

Bad News, Russ Braley
The New York Times is the most enterprising American newspaper in the field of foreign policy. It maintains more foreign correspondents–at enormous expense–and publishes more foreign news than any other American news organization. This combined

Bankrupt, David Limbaugh
The intellectual and moral bankruptcy of the Democratic Party, by a lawyer and syndicated columnist.
Beating Obamacare, Betsy McCaughey

Betrayal, Bill Gertz
Gertz tells the alarming story of how the Clinton administration has weakened our military and jeopardized our national security.

---

[19] See http://www.regnery.com/about/

41

Boy Clinton, R. Emmett Tyrrell, Jr.

Tyrrell draws all the known facts about Clinton–plus many never before revealed–into the most comprehensive and illuminating biography ever written about a sitting U.S. president.

Breakdown, Bill Gertz

Extensive material on how Clinton administration mismanagement of both our military and our intelligence agencies made us sitting ducks for this kind of attack.

Conduct Unbecoming, Buzz Patterson

Conduct Unbecoming reveals how Obama's disregard for our military and a strong foreign policy is exposing us to unprecedented risks in the 21st century.

Control Freaks, Terry Jeffrey

Provocative and compelling, Control Freaks sounds the alarm that Barack Obama and the liberal establishment are stealing our liberties–and shows why we need to wake up and do something about it while they can still be stopped.

Courting Disaster, Marc Thiessen

Courting Disaster shows how America's dedicated intelligence professionals went head-to-head with the world's most dangerous terrorists, and won–only to have Barack Obama expose America's secrets to the enemy, endorse smears against our intelligence officers, and put them at risk of prosecution for defending our country.

Crimes Against Liberty, David Limbaugh

Skillfully unraveling the tangled web of Obama's broken promises and blatant fabrications, bestselling author David Limbaugh constructs an air-tight indictment of Obama, charging him with ambitiously unraveling the Constitution and ultimately stripping of us our God-given freedoms.

Culture of Corruption, Michelle Malkin

In her devastating expose, Culture of Corruption, bestselling author and investigative reporter Michelle Malkin cites example after example of Team Obama's corrupt dealings and abuses of power. Malkin shows how Obama has hand-picked a team that will do his dirty work for him and exposes dozens of corrupt dealings–all of which the liberal media would rather keep hidden.

But Regnery was not alone in the realm of counterhegemonic publishing. Andrew McCarthy's (2010) aforementioned *The Grand Jihad: How Islam and the Left Sabotage America*—the repackaging of Horowitz's book by Regnery—was published by another conservative heavyweight, Encounter Books, with praise on its book cover from the more polarizing conservative elite, such as Rush Limbaugh. That the book was written not to assess the threat from this faction's newest foreign enemy, but the threat from its old domestic one, is evident in Encounter's book summary also printed on its cover. It notes how the global jihad movement "has found the ideal partner in President Barack Obama, whose Islamist sympathies run deep."

That yet another publisher could advance the Islamization scare strategy, and even implicate the U.S. president as being part of the Islamo-Leftist alliance out to "shred the fabric" of the Constitution, is understandable when we learn that Encounter was founded by Peter Collier, who wrote such works as *The Anti-Chomsky Reader*, with David Horowitz, and who chose to name the publishing house after the neo-conservative icon Irving Kristol's magazine, *Encounter*.

Encounter's strategic habitus and function in the conservative cultural struggle is also evident in the books published by its editor since 2005, Roger Kimball. These include resistance works such as *Tenured Radicals: How Politics Has Corrupted Our Higher Education* (1990, 2008); *The Rape of the Masters: How Political Correctness Sabotages Art* (2004); *Experiments Against Reality: The Fate of Culture in the Postmodern Era* (2000); and *The Long March: How the Cultural Revolution of the 1960s Changed America* (2000).

Encounter's counterhegemonic strategy is also evident in its list of authors—which includes all of the Right's chief ideologues, such as William F. Buckley, David Horowitz, William Kristol, Norman Podhoretz (the neo-conservative *Commentary's* editor-in-chief for 35 years), David Pryce-Jones (a senior editor at *National Review* since 1999. It can be seen in their politically antagonistic titles, such as Horowitz's *Indoctrination U.: The Left's War Against Academic Freedom*, John Bolton's *How Barack Obama is Endangering our National Sovereignty* and Ronald Radosh's (of PJ Media) *Commies: A Journey Through the Old Left, the New Left and the Leftover Left*). Encounter's list of politically-incorrect titles related to Islam— Spencer's *Islam Unveiled*, Melanie Phillips's (who also works for Horowitz) *Londonistan*, and Ibn Warraq's *What the Koran Really Says*, and so on—function similarly to delegitimize the more progressive regime of truth.

Encounter Books's function as a key pillar in the conservative culture war was rendered possible by the underwriting by key conservative philanthropic institutions who directly funded its Encounter for Culture Foundation. The aforementioned conservative patron, the Lynde and Harry Bradley Foundation, for example, invested $3.5 million to start up Encounter as its own publishing arm, and then contributed around $1 million annually to Encounter Books from its "Intellectual Infrastructure" project. By 9/11, before underwriting much of the principal polemicists of the Islam(ization) threat strategy, the Bradley Foundation had supported over 400 books in the previous fourteen years. Its president, Michael Joyce, explained that "if you want to have an influence on the world of ideas, books are where you want to put your money. It is what we are most proud of, of all the things we've done here" (Alterman 1999).

Policy Advocacy Organizations:

Frank Gaffney's Center for Security Policy

The title of the 90-minute speech advertised at the National Press Club on August 8th, 2012 was not that odd given the U.S. discourse over the previous decade: "Muslim Brotherhood Influence Operations." The organizer of this event was the conservative security policy advocacy organization, the Center for Security Policy. Although no credible security professional ever even hypothesized that the U.S. remnant of the Muslim Brotherhood posed any threat of Islamization of America, the Center helped spread the green scare over Islamization by implicating Secretary of State Hillary Clinton's aid, Huma Abedin, as an infiltrating agent of the Muslim Brotherhood. But, dubiously, this conspiracy excluded from view—as the *Washington Post* had pointed out—that Abedin was anything but Islamist, as she had not only posed for provocatively for *Vogue*, but had married and had the child of a Jewish congressman, New York Democratic rep. Anthony Weiner, who was imprisoned for multiple sexting scandals, such as sending out a photo of his genitals on Twitter (Milibank 2012).

In the Press Club brief, the Center's agent, the now familiar Andrew McCarthy, reliably used the opportunity for politics, lamenting the present time "when government policy"—a euphemism for the Obama administration—"is being radically harmonized with the agenda of the Muslim Brotherhood," and when "policy has shifted in the direction of avowed enemies of the United States."

The Center for Security Policy, of course, was not alone in its unabashed politicization of Islam. Analyses of think tanks in America have revealed how they have—in Medvetz's (2012, 6) words—"become indispensable to the practice of 'politics as a vocation.'" But this particular "security policy" organization exemplifies how some of these institutions carry on such a political vocation under the guise of impartial security analysis.

Founded in 1988 by the aforementioned Frank Gaffney, who remained active as its president throughout the post-9/11 decade, the Center's place in the broader conservative apparatus and culture war is well-known. According to its website, the Center "has been nationally and internationally recognized as a resource for timely, informed and penetrating analyses of foreign and defense policy matters." Few would agree with that self-characterization. A political appointee of Ronald Reagan, Gaffney's credentials are political, not substantive in security terms. His Center follows this mode of political knowledge, rather than pure knowledge. Rather than being nationally or international recognized as a source for insightful analysis, Gaffney's institution, like Gaffney himself, is merely an instrument for narrowly advancing the U.S. conservative movement on the platform of security.

In the decade after 9/11, Gaffney and his Center opportunistically shifted the vast bulk of its security platform to Islam, becoming sufficiently adept in that topic to use it as a platform for political struggle. During the mid-term elections in 2010, for example, the Center released the report "Shariah: The Threat to America," by an assembled group of that described themselves as "Team 'B' II"—following the earlier Team 'B' of the Committee for the Present Danger (which—much to the satisfaction of military industrial complex—overblew the Soviet threat).

The original Team B—a group of non-intelligence community realists including Rumsfeld, Cheney and Wolfowitz— was chaired by Daniel Pipes's father, Richard in 1976; it was formed to provide an alternative assessment of the Soviet military and political threat (Sandbrook 2011, 99).

Those conservative bona fides notwithstanding, it seemed odd that Gaffney's team would identify with such a failed project. Kaplan (2004) pointed out that the Team B report had "been wrong on nearly every point." In a BBC documentary about Team B's estimate, Anne Cahn of the Arms Control Disarmament Agency said that "all of it was fantasy," adding that "if you go through most of Team B's specific allegations about weapons systems, and you just examine them one by one, they were all wrong" (Paine 2005, 23). And Peter Kenez, one of Richard Pipes's own graduate students at Harvard, contends that the elder Pipes approached the Soviets as an adversary advocate prosecutor intent only on proving the worst, and excluding other information from view (Kenez 1991, 1995).

The "Team 'B' II" report on the Sharia threat was proceeding in the same paradigm as the earlier failed project—that is, in Pipes's own graduate student's words—"intent only on proving the worst, and excluding other information from view."

The subtle nature of the conservative use of security topics for purposes of cultural struggle against the more progressive security thinking was evident in Part II of the "Team 'B' II" sharia report, on page 134:

> As we have discussed above, such unwillingness to recognize and acknowledge the enemy's battle doctrine emanates directly from the proclivity of Americans, both in and out of public office, to accommodate even troubling conduct in the name of religious tolerance, multiculturalism and political correctness. This blindness, however it is rationalized, has a predictable effect: It translates into an inability even to gauge accurately how far advanced is the assault, let alone to execute an effective strategy for countering it.
>
> Former Joint Chiefs of Staff analyst Stephen Coughlin wrote his seminal master's thesis for the National Defense Intelligence College on the U.S. refusal to study and internalize *what the enemy himself says* about why he fights jihad. Coughlin concluded that the failure to investigate these sources has left U.S. national security leadership "disarmed in the war of ideas."[410]

CSP's sharia report also contained this more direct denigration of the Obama administration on page 135:

> Of particular concern are the 2010 versions of the Pentagon's Quadrennial Defense Review, the Homeland Security Department's Quadrennial Review413 and the White House-issued National Security Strategy.414 All hew to the same troubling language guidelines promulgated by DHS,415 the FBI's Counterterrorism Analytical Lexicon416 and the National Counterterrorism Center's vocabulary regulations417 – to the effect that no reference to Islam, jihad or shariah may be made when discussing the threat. This is not simply incompetence. It amounts to malfeasance and it places the U.S. government demonstrably and officially in compliance with Islamic law on slander – a posture that puts the nation in grave peril.

After citing the U.S. oath of office and the duty of government officials to protect the U.S. Constitution against all enemies, foreign and domestic, the report then more directly attempted to delegitimize the Obama administration, saying, "There is, arguably, no more dramatic example of a senior U.S. government official failing to perform his duty to know – and, seemingly, to fulfill his oath of office – than that of John Brennan, Homeland Security Advisor and Counter-terrorism Advisor to President Obama."

It was politically performative productions like this that earned the Center for Security Policy the endorsement of Republican Vice President Dick Cheney for its "contributions to the national debate about security policy."[20]

Gaffney's Center for Security Policy seems poised to continue this form of security politics. Only a month after the brief by McCarthy that it had organized at the National Press Club—a full eleven years after 9/11—Gaffney himself was at the Family Research

---

[20] See http://www.centerforsecuritypolicy.org/about-us/what-others-have-said-about-the-center/

Council's September 2012 Values Voter Summit. He flashed a Power Point slide of Muslim organizations in the United States, and charged that "all" of the U.S. major Muslim organizations are offshoots of the Brotherhood, and committed to "civilizational jihad." And, true to form—lest anyone think that this was an ordinary security brief— Gaffney then flashed the photos of eight prominent Muslims who serve in or are close to the Obama administration, and charged that they—obviously with the administration's complicity— are "working to subvert our nation from within" (Jilani 2012).

More Explicitly Counterhegemonic Organizations:

David Horowitz Freedom Center

Following the pattern of the aforementioned identifying institutions of the conservative movement, another segment of threat discourse related to Islam after 9/11 was published or sponsored by institutions that abandoned all presentations of disinterestedness and had long functioned in the open as recognizable counterhegemonic nodes in the conservative domestic culture war. The David Horowitz Freedom Center provides a useful window into this component of the Islam(ization) threat discourse's apparatus.

The role of using the platform of security to engage in domestic cultural politics is implied in the Freedom Center's stated mission—"the defense of free societies whose moral, cultural and economic foundations are under attack by enemies both secular and religious, *at home* and abroad." With Horowitz's aforementioned book *Unholy Alliance: Radical Islam and the American Left* already in view, we could have readily concluded that the ambiguous language of *enemies at home* and abroad, secular and religious, is obviously highly euphemized code for the Left and Islam. The next statement on its website removes all doubt:

> The David Horowitz Freedom Center combats the efforts of the radical left and its Islamist allies to destroy American values and disarm this country as it attempts to defend itself in a time of terror. The leftist offensive is most obvious on our nation's campuses, where the Freedom Center protects students from indoctrination and intimidation and works to give conservative students a place in the marketplace of ideas from which they are otherwise excluded.

Horowitz was never known for his contributions to the nation broadly through the production of apolitical knowledge, or knowledge beneficial to all segments of society. He always has been and remains known for being a more extreme culture warrior. A member of the radical Left in his youth, Horowitz explained on Al-Jazeera's August 21, 2008 *Riz Khan Show* that he had "spent 25 years in the American Left," whose agendas, he asserted, "are definitely to destroy this country." His Saul of Tarsus-like conversion to the radical Right in the 1980s led to the 1988 establishment of his counterhegemonic Center for the Study of Popular Culture, and its mission for the next eighteen years (until renamed in 2006) was to establish a conservative presence in Hollywood and show how popular culture had become a political battleground. Horowitz's new mission was emblematized by his pamphlets, "The Art of Political War" that exhorted the GOP to more adversarial politics, and "Hating Whitey," which confronted the progressives for blaming whites for the relatively deprived state of minorities.

Beyond his recent counterhegemonic books, including *The Professors: The 101 Most Dangerous Academics in America* (2007), Horowitz's primary mouthpiece is his Center's *FrontPage Magazine*, which boasts 1.5 million visitors and over 870,000 unique visitors a month (DHFC website 2014). In terms of counterhegemonic content, style and regulations concerning authoritative knowledge, *FrontPage* boasts hundreds of columnists who are largely non-institutionalized conservatives who—outside of their own blogs—lack larger access and credibility.[21]

The openly counterhegemonic nature of Horowitz's Center is also seen in its component projects. Since 2003, the Freedom Center has promoted an Academic Bill of Rights to—in its words—"free the American university from political indoctrination and renew its commitment to true intellectual diversity." Since 2005, its DiscoverTheNetworks.com has in another McCarthyesque mode mapped the Left and its apparatus of power, and bills itself as "the largest publicly accessible database defining the chief groups and individuals of the Left and their organizational interlocks."

In the same vein, the Horowitz Center's Israel Security Project functions to counter the more progressive movement's dual support for both an Israeli and a Palestinian state's right to exist side by side, and its TruthRevolt project works—in its words—"to unmask leftists in the media for who they are, destroy their credibility with the American Public, and devastate their funding bases."[22]

But, the Center's web-based self-description of counterhegemonic activity also contains two apparent non-sequitur projects related to Islam. The first was its 2003 launch of JihadWatch, and the second was its 2007 launch of the national "Islamo-Fascism Awareness Week," which was a program on college campuses in affiliation with conservative student groups.

But, why would a conservative institution of such long-standing and openly touted counterhegemonic bona fides bring the topic of Islam broadly—of watching jihad and making the nation aware of "Islamo-fascism"—into its tent? One answer might seem obvious from the Freedom Center's text above. It is because Jihad Watch's radical counternarrative on Islam (along with the national broadcasting of the politically-incorrect term "Islamo-Fascism") functions like terrorism; that is, it is so egregious and transgressive of societal norms that it at once draws the attention of the more progressive national media, and counters its security narrative in a kind of complete negation.

Thus, as the Horowitz's book *Unholy Alliance: Radical Islam and the American Left* suggests, the threat of Islam presented yet another angle or platform from which U.S. conservatives might delegitimize the more progressive culture or doxa.

---

[21] See the DHFC's list of columnists at http://www.frontpagemag.com/columnists/
[22] See the DHFC's self description "About DHFC" at http://www.horowitzfreedomcenter.org/about

2. The Cultural and Political Elite Base

In addition to the Islam-as-threat discourse's institutional apparatus, there was another social structural element to this emerging discourse that was also crucial to its rapid emergence, persistence, and anachronistic expansion throughout the post-9/11 decade: its base of solidarity among the U.S. conservative religious and political elite.

Security Politics by Some Religious Conservatives

For U.S. religious conservatives, Islam after 9/11 was much less a threat to their existence than a resource for their movement's survival. The topic of Islam offered key elite within the religious Right the necessary platform to delegitimize the broader progressive, secular worldview of the Left.

When Christian evangelist Billy Graham, for example, talked about Islam in terms of "barbarians beating at our gates from without," he did not stop there. In that same sentence he went on to link that threat of barbarians without to the "moral termites from within"—a phrase that his audience understood as denoting progressivism broadly (Chafe 2003, 26-27).

The political utility of Islam for the U.S. religious Right emerged in Pat Robertson 28 April 2006 Christian Broadcasting Network's *The 700 Club*. When he countered the dominant consensus about Islam, saying "It is not a religion of peace," he then used that segue to engage the more familiar enemies domestic, "the American left"—as he described them—who needed to "wake up" to the danger that Islam presents (MediaMatters 2006). These subtle non-sequitur political content would not be noteworthy were they not so pervasive, accompanying nearly every conservative statement or production on the topic of Islam, as just indicated.

By the tenth anniversary of 9/11, the political utility of the Islamic threat for the Right's culture war against the Left was capitalized by nearly every conservative culture warrior. In March 2011, popular FOX News Channel host Glenn Beck linked his domestic enemies to his newest foreign enemy, warning that America and other Western states are "being divvied up" by the "uber left" and the "Islamicists" (Mirkinson 2011). In March 2011, Beck hosted a program to advance the bridged frame of Islam and the Left as the dual threat to America; he spoke of "history's failed revolutions and what they can teach us today," and contended that "radicals, Islamists, communists, socialists, labor unions from all over the world are working together, even though they don't agree with each other on everything … (Theel, 2011).

In this same frame, Erick Stakelbeck, the Christian Broadcasting Network's "terrorism analyst"—in a June 2011 event hosted by ACT! for America's Brigitte Gabriel—explained that "the Left sees Islam as an ally and Western Civilization and the Judeo-Christian tradition is the enemy" and they (Islam and the Left) "have a shared hatred for this country" (Ingersoll 2011).

There were several key religious conservative elite whose statements advancing the Islamization scare were broadcast by the conservative apparatus. Frank Gaffney's aforementioned 2011 project, *Sharia: The Threat To America*, touted its lead author, who was the former Deputy Under Secretary of Defense for Intelligence, General "Jerry" Boykin. Boykin had gravitas on the subject of Islam among key evangelical elite because he was the symbol for the movement's politically-incorrect counternarrative regarding Islam. For example, The Oak Initiative—a coalition of evangelical and Pentecostal clergy founded to be "salt and light" in the time of America's crisis and "greatest threat to its continued existence,"[23]—featured Boykin in a video on its website, giving tacit approval to his charge in the video that ostensibly all Muslims—"those following the dictates of the Qur'an"—are "under an obligation to destroy our Constitution and replace it with shari'ah law" (Mantyla 2010).[24]

And, James Dobson—well-respected among evangelicals and Christians broadly as founder and host of *Focus on the Family*, was also infatuated with Boykin, hosting him *ten* times on his daily radio show. On the February 17th and 18th 2011 programs, and then again on the January 3rd and 4th 2012 programs, Dobson took his audience's eyes off of real family and spiritual issues to let Boykin—whom he described as his personal hero and a long-time "personal friend"—explain how the Muslim Brotherhood is currently entering "phase four" of a five-phase plan to take over America (DrJamesDobson.org 2011; Mantyla 2011). On the second of the last two programs, when asked by Dobson "what do you see in store of us in this tired old world?" Boykin advanced the green scare this way, with an implicit criticism of the more progressive establishment that was allowing if not enabling this threat: "Let me say I have six grandchildren and three of them are females and I must tell you, I am greatly concerned about the day coming when they will be wearing burqas. That's how serious I consider this threat."[25]

The politicization of the topic was evident not so much in what was said in response as in what was erased from view. Neither Dobson, nor his son, nor co-host LuAnne Crane attempted to challenge General Boykin's wildly untethered Islamization threat frame. Instead of an empirical check on reality, Dobson and *Focus on the Family's* leadership team tacitly approved Boykin's assessments, saying that "we cannot stick our heads in the sand" pretending that this threat doesn't exist.

Yet, sticking their heads in the sand is what the three *Focus on the Family* hosts did overnight, between the first and second interviews, and between when the interviews were recorded and broadcast. Widely publicized and recurrent scientific studies reveal how the population of Muslims in the U.S. is expected to increase from only 2.6 million U.S. Muslims (adults and children) in 2010 to 6.2 million in 2030, or from a mere 0.8 percent of the U.S. population to 1.7 percent (Pew Research Center 2011). And, it is likely that a mere 4 percent of that tiny population of Muslims (about 230,000) will be classified as "very conservative" (Pew Research Center 2007). In other words, only 1 in every 1500 Americans

---

[23] See https://www.theoakinitiative.org/our-purpose#.VA2TgBZuX2k

[24] The video is available at http://www.rightwingwatch.org/content/boykin-islam-should-not-be-protected-under-first-amendment

[25] All of the programs are listed at http://www.drjamesdobson.org/search-results?indexCatalogue=default&searchQuery=boykin&wordsMode=0

in 2030 *might* believe that a woman's wearing of a burqa is a religious obligation.

Instead of doing the most cursory of analysis of Boykin's wildly irrational, hyperbolic, and unloving, unChristlike Muslim-bashing statements, Dobson and the *Focus on the Family* leadership team—having long touted their 501(c)(3) tax exemption on the basis of refraining from any political activity—raised domestic political themes of liberal, activist judges, anti-immigration, the need to mobilize conservative voters, and so on.

Conservative talk radio is another important element of the conservative apparatus of power that advanced this strategy of security politics. Typical was Bryan Fischer and his *Focal Point* radio show of the evangelical American Family Association—an organization self-describes as on "the frontlines of America's culture war," and boasting over 2 million subscribers and owning 200 radio stations.[26] In mid-May 2011, Fischer first captured his audience's attention with a statement on how, following Mohammed's example, "Muslims have been [inbreeding] for fourteen hundred years" at "an enormous cost in intellectual capacity." Then, using that platform for politics, he went on to denigrate the more progressive regime of truth that would exclude such statements from the realm of authoritative knowledge, saying, "And you get hammered for saying it, but that's because the truth has now become hate speech, the truth has now become bigotry." Rather than censuring the popular conservative figure for this kind of speech, the Republican leadership tacitly condoned it; evangelical presidential contenders Michele Bachmann, Mike Huckabee, and Tim Pawlenty appeared on Fischer's show (Rayfield 2011).

Security Politics by Most Conservative Political Elite

Despite the broad diversity or heterogeneity within the U.S. conservative movement, as noted by Factor (2014, 93, 215, 362, 375), solidarity for the Islam(ization) threat discourse was also strong among a surprisingly large segment of the conservative political elite, and especially among every front-running GOP presidential candidate except one during the latter half of the post-9/11 decade. Just as conspicuous, was the fact that this discourse was *absent entirely* from speech acts by Democrat political elite (Summers 2011). The radical politicization of the Islam-as-threat discourse could thus be seen in the mere fact that there was such a polarity on the discourse depending upon which political party one identified with.

For right-wing political elite, the often unspecified "threat" of Islam provided the crucial opportunity to showcase their *conservative* national security bona fides and at the same time engage in security politics—that is, the familiar practice of political frame bridging, or the linking the movement's foreign and domestic enemies, Islam and the Left.

For example, after his second place in the Iowa primary in 2008, GOP presidential hopeful Senator Rick Santorum uttered the counternarrative's more apocalyptic elements. In a speech organized by David Horowitz, Santorum first targeted the progressive culture of Europe, which—in his words—was "creating an opportunity for the creation of Eurabia, or Euristan." For this reason, he said, "there will be no Europe left to fight [Islam,

---

[26] http://www.afa.net/Detail.aspx?id=31

with us]." Santorum then incoherently shifted the threat axis from the Left to Islam, and from Sunni extremists to the Shi'ite sect as a whole, because they want "to bring back the Mahdi." He added more egregious incoherence and error, saying: "And do you know when the Mahdi returns? At the Apocalypse at the end of the world. You see, they are not interested in conquering the world; they [all Shia Muslims] are interested in destroying the world." What we need to do to prevent this apocalypse, he concluded (with great ambiguity and huge debits to U.S. moral capital, or soft-power), is "eradicate." In a post-script, he added, "this is going to be a long war" (Santorum 2007).

In his next bid for the presidency to unseat Barak Obama, Santorum demonstrated complete solidarity with the Islamization threat narrative, parroting without explaining the unsubstantiated, untethered, irrational security frame that "creeping sharia" is a "huge issue" and "an existential threat to America" (Summers 2011).

Santorum perceived "Islam" as so useful that it was often woven into his political speech as a non-sequitur, out of place ingredient. In January 2012 during the South Carolina caucus, Santorum juxtaposed enemies foreign and domestic. He centered "the people on the left" and their push for equality, asking "where do you think this concept of equality comes from?" "It doesn't come from Islam" he said, "It comes from the God of Abraham, Isaac and Jacob" (Walshe 2012).

Similarly, in a July 2010 speech at the *American Enterprise Institute*, as the mid-term elections loomed, Presidential hopeful Newt Gingrich shifted the threat axis from multiple strategic crises in American manufacturing, energy insecurity, healthcare costs, urban education, crumbling infrastructure, structural deficit, the blooming national debt, cybersecurity, and other critical topics, to the nonsensical sharia, which he characterized as a "mortal threat to the survival of freedom in the United States and in the world as we know it" (Shane 2011, Miller 2010). "Stealth jihadis," he added, "use political, cultural, societal, religious, intellectual tools…to replace Western civilization with a radical imposition of Shariah" (Shane 2011).

The same year, at the 2010 Values Voters Summit, Gingrich called for a federal ban on sharia, and on the ninth anniversary of 9/11, went as far as to produce a film with his third wife on the existential threat of Islamization, *America at Risk: The War With No Name*. In it, he warned Americans about unspecified and ambiguous "radical Islamists" inside America, who were threatening "to impose an extraordinarily different system on us"—to "replace American freedom with Sharia" (Gingrich and Gingrich 2010).

But, Gingrich found the conspiracy about the left's involvement in this Islamization too useful to pass up. In his July 2010 speech to AEI, he said that "The left's refusal to tell the truth about the Islamist threat is a natural parallel to the 70-year pattern of left-wing intellectuals refusing to tell the truth about communism and the Soviet Union" (Shane 2011).[27]

---

[27] Continuing that paranoid theme of infiltration into the Republican New Hampshire primary presidential debate, Gingrich tacitly securitized all Muslim-Americans, citing a case where one had lied about his loyalty to the nation in order to attack it, and then compared the situation of America's current 5th column in this minority community to that of the Nazis and Communists (Khan & Bingham, 2011).

Then, at Christian Zionist leader John Hagee's Cornerstone Church in Texas, Gingrich spoke in highly euphemistic terms that his audience understood well. "If we do not decisively win the struggle over the nature of America," he said, the nation will be "a secular atheist country, potentially one dominated by radical Islamists and with no understanding of what it once meant to be an American" (Mantyla 2011).

And continuing this form of frame bridging, at the First Redeemer Church in Cumming Georgia in late February 2012, he said, "We have a secular elitist wing that deeply, deeply disbelieves in America, that wants to create a different country based on a different set of principles," he said. "And we have a radical Islamist one which legitimately and authentically hates us and should" (Lin 2012).

In a similar strategy of identity politics, Gingrich told religious conservatives at the American Family Association's pastors' policy briefing in Iowa that "until you replace this president and until you have the Congress and the new president replace large parts of our bureaucracies, we're going to continue to be dominated by secular, anti-Christian and anti-Jewish elite." He then pointed to "our secular elites" who "do everything they can to prove they are not anti-Muslim" (Marr, 2011).

Not to be outdone by Gingrich, Minnesota Republican Congresswoman and founder of the House Tea Party caucus, Michele Bachmann, during her run for President, also maintained strong solidarity with the Islam(ization) threat discourse. During mid-term elections in 2010, Bachmann, in an interview on conservative radio's popular *The Mike Gallagher Show*, asserted that the GOP's opposing domestic political party had allied with their ideological foreign enemy to destroy the nation. "It seems like there is this common cause that is occurring with the left and with radical Islam…" she said, adding that "It's frightening to think how the left in this country, just as you've correctly stated, Michael, is throwing in with common cause with these radical elements of Islamic extremism" (MN Progressive Project 2010).

On the threat of Islamization, in July 2012, Bachmann issued a 16-page letter defending her McCarthyesque jihad to root out "deep penetration" by the Muslim Brotherhood into the U.S. government. The highly-publicized letter obviously had ulterior motives than protecting the nation from subversion. Had the Congresswoman really had credible, actionable intelligence that terrorist supporters had infiltrated the U.S. government, the letter would have been classified secret, and we would have not learned about it until after the investigation, thereby not tipping off the purported infiltrators. But, Bachmann sent her letter to the media and then in July appeared on the American Family Association's *Sandy Rios in the Morning* to broadcast it (Tashman 2012). And, when challenged, she hinted that she has access to secret information as a member of the House Select Committee on Intelligence supporting her claims (Seitz-Wald 2012).

GOP presidential frontrunner Herman Cain also maintained solidarity with the counterhegemonic Islam-as-threat threat narrative (Patten, 2010). In a 21 March 2011 interview with *Christianity Today*, Cain wildly departed from the more progressive official and formal consensus on the topic and set down the basic counternarrative: "Based upon the little knowledge that I have of the Muslim religion," he said, "they have an objective to convert all infidels or kill them," and then went on to parrot Bachman's McCarthyesque tacit critique of the progressive administration by framing Islam as forcing Muslim into the subversive "attempt to gradually ease sharia law and the Muslim faith into our government" (Persaud 2011; Sullivan 2011). *Christianity Today's* interviewer, Trevor Persaud, did not challenge Cain's characterization of Islam, or the perceived threat of Islamization, but tacitly affirmed it, responding with the closer, "Is there anything else you'd like to say?" (Persaud 2011).

With that oppositional frame present in his reasoning, Cain later made headlines when tacitly criticized the Obama Administration, saying that "I wouldn't have Muslims in my administration" (Tashman 2011).

At the level of the US Congress, the Islam(ization) threat narrative also enjoyed broad solidarity. Gaffney's 2010 report "Sharia: The Threat to America" was praised by Republican members of Congress, such as Trent Franks (AZ), Michele Bachmann (MN), and Pete Hoekstra (MI). When the major conservative alternative media site *WorldNetDaily* published *Muslim Mafia: Inside the Secret Underworld That's Conspiring to Islamize America*, Republican North Carolina congresswoman Sue Myrick wrote its forward and led Representatives John Shadegg (AZ), Paul Broun (GA), and Trent Franks (AZ) in calling for an investigation. Similarly, Florida congressman Allen West on Frank Gaffney's radio program in late December 2010 said that he hoped that Congress would focus on the "infiltration of the Sharia practice into all of our operating systems in our country as well as across Western civilization" (Fang 2011).

On the House floor, Texas congressman Louie Gohmert suggested that President Obama's allegiances were with Islamic states instead of the U.S. "I know the president made the mistake one day of saying he had visited all 57 states, and I'm well aware that there are not 57 states in this country, although there are 57 members of OIC, the Islamic states in the world." "Perhaps there was some confusion whether he'd been to all 57 Islamic states as opposed to all 50 U.S. states. But nonetheless, we have an obligation to the 50 American states, not the 57 Muslim, Islamic states.... This administration [has been] complicit in helping people who wants [sic] to destroy our country" (Zafar 2011).

On CSPAN's *Washington Journal* after the Benghazi embassy incident and the rise of the Muslim Brotherhood President Morsi in Egypt, Gohmert said that "the only way you could explain the horrendous decisions that were complete wrong-headed was if this administration had a bunch of Muslim Brotherhood members giving them advice."[28]

As the decade wore on, it was *only* Republicans who were supportive of the contentious Islam(ization) threat discourse, and—with one sole apparent exception—only Democrats expressing opposition to it.[29] For example, based on the dozen or so news reports on the topic, when Republican New York Representative Peter King chaired House Homeland Security Committee hearings on Muslim-American radicalization in the first half

---

[28] See https://www.youtube.com/watch?v=WzBxJjmNYqw
[29] The literature suggested otherwise. Sheehi (2011, 43), for example, contended that "Islamophobia" "cuts across party lines." It didn't in the latter half of the post-9/11 decade, when Democrats lined up in juxtaposition to Republicans in relation to this discourse.

of 2011, only the Democrats at the hearings were criticizing them, and only Republicans were defending them. And, during King's second hearing on Muslim radicalization in U.S. prisons on 15 June 2011, for example, King's GOP colleague Mike McCaul praised the hearings as a way to "end the era of political correctness" (Kane 2012), while his other Republican colleagues Dan Lungren and Jeff Duncan noted how "the political correctness" among Democrats in the room was "astounding," and complained that the mere discussion about the threat of radical Islam appeared to be "off limits" for Democrats (Piraneo 2011).

Similarly, it was only House Republicans and not one Democrat who on December 15, 2011, signed a letter sent to Defense Secretary Leon Panetta and Attorney General Eric Holder objecting in principle to considering changes to training programs regarding Muslims or Islam in some defense and intelligence institutions that had been identified as anti-Islamic and anti-Muslim in nature.[30] And, over half of the members of Congress active in the Christian organization House Capitol Ministries[31]—all 23 of them in the Republican Party—had made anti-Muslim statements, supported the Islam(ization) of America conspiracy theory, or supported anti-Muslim groups (Musaji 2012).[32]

Among the nationally-recognized GOP elite vying for president, it was only former Massachusetts Governor Mitt Romney, Congressman Ron Paul, and New Jersey Governor Chris Christie who did not demonstrate solidarity with the Islam(ization) threat narrative. Christie warned in mid-August 2010 against politicizing the planned lower-Manhattan Park 51 community center and mosque initiative, adding "What offends me the most about all this is that it's being used as a political football by both parties" (Hook and Hamburger 2010).

Lastly, it was virtually only Republican state legislators who introduced nearly eighty bills to safeguard the Constitution from sharia. In states prone to racism across the political spectrum, only four Democrats (Alabama, South Carolina, South Dakota and Kansas) joined the widely publicized conservative-led legislative initiative to restrict judges from consulting sharia in their rulings (despite the fact that state judges are already prohibited from overriding U.S. law, and despite the fact that the vast majority of voters in their states personally did not even know a Muslim) (Langer 2009).[33] These bills selectively obscured the fact that the issue had no relevance in their own states, and pointed dubiously to cases of judges in faraway Dearborn Michigan, who purportedly privileged sharia over the U.S. Constitution. Countering these charges, Dearborn's mayor Jack O'Reilly (D) said, "These people know nothing of Dearborn," adding that this stereotype continually hounds

---

[30] See http://myrick.house.gov/uploads/12152011_Letter%20to%20DOJ%20and%20DOD%20re%20CT%20training%20changes.pdf

[31] http://www.capmin.org/site/

[32] According to Musaji (2012), these include Michele Bachmann, Paul Broun, Trent Franks, Louie Gohmert, Ralph Hall, Pete Hoekstra, Steve King, Doug Lamborn, Gary Miller, Sue Myrick, Mike Pence, Tom Price, Lamar Smith, Allen West, and Lynn Westmoreland, among others. Similarly, among the nation's other Christian elite, it was only conservatives who expressed opposition to the "religion of peace" storyline.

[33] According to an ABC News-Washington Post poll in 2009, over half of all Americans concede that they personally don't even know a Muslim (Langer 2009).

the city. The mayor then stated that these conservative legislators "just seek to provoke and enflame their base for political gain" (Press and Guide 2011).

The evidence for Governor Christie's and Mayor O'Reilly's categorization of this scare as more about domestic politics than national security seemed overwhelming. When pressed, the sponsors of the wave of anti-sharia legislation in 2010 and 2011 could not cite any empirical evidence to justify the legislation that they were introducing with much fanfare. When asked for examples of the threat that had so animated them to take leave of the many pressing economic, health, education, and other needs to introduce legislation to prevent the Islamization of their state, none of them could produce a single case in which Islamic law posed a threat (Murphy 2011). At the time, the legislators—many of whom were lawyers—collectively obscured the obvious, relevant, material facts that were readily available.

The anti-rationalist nature of this solidarity began at its source. When Gaffney's Center for Security Policy released its follow-on June 21, 2011 report, "Shariah Law and American State Courts: An Assessment of State Appellate Court Cases," it pinpointed 50 rulings from courts in 23 states that ostensibly proved the "creeping sharia" conspiracy. Yet, in his analysis of the report, Brayton (2011) wrote: "Let me make this as clear as I possibly can: This report is not merely badly researched and badly prepared, it is an outright fraud. No one who actually reads the rulings could reach anything but the opposite conclusion from the one they intend to foster. Nearly every single case they offer argues *against* their conclusion. Now let me prove that assertion." Brayton then went on to show how the first five cases actually demonstrated the opposite of Gaffney's claims. In the Michigan case, Brayton observed: "Not only did the court not apply Sharia law, they explicitly rejected any such application and did so precisely on the grounds that doing so would violate the rights of the woman who filed the suit. And this is offered as evidence of creeping Sharia." That alone, he said, "should give you some idea of the intellectual honesty of those who put out the report."

Similarly, in its counter report, "Nothing to Fear: Debunking the Mythical 'Sharia Threat' to Our Judicial System," The American Civil Liberties Union (2011), characterized the claims of sharia infiltration as "wrong" and "based both on misinformation and misunderstanding of how our judicial system works." The ACLU added that "There is no evidence that Islamic law is encroaching on our courts." On the contrary, it went on, the court cases cited as purportedly illustrative of this problem "actually show the opposite: Courts treat lawsuits that are brought by Muslims or that address the Islamic faith in the same way that they deal with similar claims brought by people of other faiths or that involve no religion at all" (ACLU 2011).

The conservative power apparatus as the state level was just as complicit in advancing this anti-rationalist security narrative. Typical of state legislators clearly involved in security politics was Republican Texas state representative Leo Berman, who justified his anti-sharia bill by mentioning the far-removed city of Dearborn Michigan six times, but giving no examples from his own demographically-unique state. Without any empirical evidence, Berman said that "the judges in Dearborn are using and allowing to be used sharia law."

When pressed for details, the lawmaker managed only to say that "I heard it on a radio station here on my way in to the Capitol one day," adding, *"Isn't that true?"* (Somanader 2011).

Similarly, when pressed by curious reporters at the state capital, the sponsor of Alabama's anti-sharia legislation, Republican Senator Gerald Allen, could neither offer examples of Muslims trying to have Islamic law recognized in Alabama courts, nor even define sharia in an interview, embarrassingly saying "I don't have my file in front of me" (Buckner 2011). In light of such otherwise anti-rationalist statements, one begins to imagine the marching orders that this state legislator received by influential elements of the broader conservative apparatus.

The first indication that the conservative apparatus of power had politicized Islam—as we began to see in the introduction—was when all context and empirical rigor was systematically erased from view. This is precisely the strategic habitus of conservative elite. Conservative elite like Gingrich, Bachmann, Boykin, Dobson and others excluded from view this the vast amount of relevant open source literature on the topic that would contextualize "Islam's" threat to the homeland. None of these right-wing religious and political elite, for example, bothered to perform any degree of serious analysis on the issue. None dared mention, for example, that of the 150,000 murders in the United States in the post-9/11 decade, eleven Muslim Americans were responsible for only 11 of these deaths, or that virtually no Muslims were involved in the 1.4 million violent crimes or almost 100,000 forcible rapes in the U.S. that took place *each year.*[34]

Observing this odd solidarity of the Islam-as-threat counternarrative among some of the more prominent Republican political and conservative religious elite, and their propensity to erase from view the realm of facts that did not fit their counternarrative, Sheila Musaji—editor of the *American Muslim*—concluded that "The GOP has declared war on American Muslims" (Musaji 2011). But, there was much more to this discourse than hatred of Islam and Muslims. The GOP was merely embellishing the threat from America's half-immigrant, half-black Muslim community in order to create another opportune platform from which to advance against their domestic political rivals. In other words, like the Muslim-American leadership had surmised in the aforementioned poll, Islam was being used as a platform for politics.

3. The Philanthropic Base of Security Politics

Recall that another element of the apparatus of power that undergirded a discourse, according to Foucault (1980), was its philanthropic base. This should come as no surprise to conservatives; the U.S. conservative movement owes its current force to philanthropic support. The activities of 350 public policy-oriented think tanks at the federal, state, and local levels were supported largely by the strategies of only 79 conservative philanthropic foundations (Krehely et al. 2004).

---

[34] See http://sites.duke.edu/tcths/research/ and https://www2.fbi.gov/ucr/cius2008/data/table_01.html

One conservative philanthropic institution, the John M. Olin Foundation, for example, spent hundreds of millions of dollars to construct what its president William E. Simon called the "counterintelligentsia" to offset the dominance of liberals in universities and the mainstream media, and to otherwise advance the conservative cultural struggle (Miller 2006; O' Connor 2008; Stefancic and Delgado 1996). Miller (2006) described the role of the Olin foundation in assisting Irving Kristol and others as they moved ideologically from left to right to found the neoconservative movement, and in building institutions such as the Federalist Society and the Heritage Foundation.

And, post-9/11 U.S., the popular security counternarrative on Islam and the more explicit politicization of that security topic, proceeded because the conservative philanthropic base was eager to seize this security issue as a battlefield for the more profound security politics. Based on their annual reports and tax form 990s in the first nine years after 9/11, just seven philanthropic organizations—Donors Capital Fund, Richard Mellon Scaife Foundation, Lynde and Harry Bradley Foundation, Newton and Rochelle Becker Foundation and Newton and Rochelle Becker Charitable Trust, Russell Berrie Foundation, Anchorage Charitable Fund and William Rosenwald Family Fund, and the Fairbrook Foundation—gave $42.6 million to the main proponents of this popular security discourse that seized the opportune platform of Islam to engage in security politics. These recipients were David Horowitz's Freedom Center (including Jihad Watch), Daniel Pipes's Middle East Forum, Frank Gaffney's Center for Security Policy, and Brigitte Gabriel's ACT! for America, Steven Emerson's Investigative Project for Terrorism, along with the Clarion Fund (Ali et al. 2011,13-15).

Apparently, several conservative philanthropists were attracted to the Islam(ization) threat discourse because of the perception that it benefited the Zionist movement directly—that is, using the topic of a threatening Islam as a platform for Holy Land geopolitics. Ali et al. (2011) and then Bulkin and Nevel (2012) revealed how some of the philanthropic institutions that had funded these proponents of the Islam(ization) scare were the main patrons of the U.S. Zionist movement, and had also funded organizations associated with the Israeli settler movement. The main patrons for this security discourse who also had track records of giving to Zionist causes included the Newton D. and Rochelle F. Becker Foundations, the Anchorage Charitable Fund and the William Rosenwald Family Fund, the Russell Berrie Foundation, and the Fairbrook Foundation (Ali et al. 2011, Blumenthal 2012, Bulkin and Nevel 2012).

Per its publicly available IRS tax form 990s, the Fairbrook Foundation was apparently motivated by Zionism, funding the Zionist American Friends of Ateret Cohanim, which funneled money to the more radical Yitzhar settlement in the Northern West Bank and which funds Jewish settlement in East Jerusalem through "appropriation" of Arab homes—as well as the Central Fund for Israel, a New York-based tax-exempt non-profit, which has been described as a clearinghouse for funding part of Israel's settler movement (Blumenthal 2010; Rozen 2010). Chernick, through the Central Fund of Israel and Ateret Cohenim, has reportedly funded the Yitzar settlement, as well as to the messianic settlers dedicated to "Judaizing" East Jerusalem (Blumenthal, 2010). Yitzar's rabbi, Yitzhak

Shapira, in his book *Torat HaMelech*, or *The King's Torah*, cited rabbinical texts to declare that gentiles, including their babies, could be killed in order to "curb their evil inclinations." In 2006, the rabbi was briefly held by Israeli police for urging his supporters to murder all Palestinians over the age of 13 (Blumenthal, 2010).

And, in addition to giving $619,000 to the Zionist Organization of America, the Foundation's patrons— Aubrey Chernik, a Los Angeles-area software security entrepreneur, and his wife—funded other less extreme components of what Mearsheimer and Walt (2007) described as U.S. Zionist apparatus, or "Israel lobby," such as the Hudson Institute, Foundation for Defense of Democracies, Middle East Media Research Institute (MEMRI), the Anti-Defamation League, and CAMERA, which polices anti-Israel bias in the media (See also Bulkin and Nevel 2012).

Yet, some key patrons with a Zionist emphasis displayed much stronger conservative interests. The giving record of the less Zionist Anchorage Fund, for example, included many conservative institutions that could be classified as more conservative than Zionist, such as the Hoover Institution. And, like the other organizations here that are categorized as U.S. Zionism's patrons, the Fairbrook Foundation's ideological criterion for giving includes broader conservative interests. Aubrey Chernick in 2005, for example, helped provide the first round of the $3.5 million venture capital funding to the conservative e-commentary Pajamas (now PJ) Media (Pajamas Media 2005).

The largess of conservative patrons with significant Zionist ideological motivations notwithstanding, the largest donors to the more prominent agents of Islam politics had been the central patrons of the U.S. conservative movement broadly, with comparatively little or no Zionist sympathies in their giving records. The established conservative foundations of Richard Mellon Scaife, and Lynde and Harry Bradley gave far more than did foundations sympathetic to Zionism to two of the Islam(ization) threat discourse's principal agents, Frank Gaffney's Center for Security Policy ($3.7M non-Zionist vs. $0.9M Zionist) and David Horowitz's Freedom Center ($7.7M non-Zionist vs. 0.7M Zionist).

The major funding sources for Gaffney's center, for example, were, in order of amount given, the archconservative philanthropist Richard Mellon Scaife ($3 million); the Lynde and Harry Bradley Foundation ($800,000), the Newton and Rochelle Becker Foundation (and Charitable Trust) (about $375,000) and the Anchorage Charitable Fund and William Rosenwald Family Fund (about $437,000), and with the Fairbrook Foundation contributing smaller amounts (Ali et al. 2011). This can be gleaned from the table in the Fear Inc., report by Ali and colleagues (2011, 13-15).

In the case of the trio of foundations controlled by Richard Mellon Scaife and his family members, they gave $7.9 million dollars between 2001 to 2009 to just eight of the principal agents involved in politicizing Islam. This included $2.9 million to Gaffney's Center for Security Policy and $3.4 million to the Horowitz's Freedom Center (Ali et al. 2011).

The criterion for all funding from the Scaife foundation was solidly conservative, rather than Zionist. With annual giving at the launch of the post-9/11 decade ranging around $26 million, the Scaife foundations were described by the *Washington Post* in its May

2, 1999 edition with the headline "Funding Father of the Right."[35] The patronage of the Scaife foundations—in contrast to that of Chernick—centered on the conservative movement's main institutions, including the Heritage Foundation, American Enterprise Institute, the Federalist Society, the Free Congress Foundation, the Cato Institute, Grover Norquist's Americans for Tax Reform, and many others. The Scaife funds provided comparatively minor funding to a few components of the conservative apparatus that could be classified as neoconservative with Zionist interests, such as the flagship magazine *Commentary* and the Foundation for Defense of Democracies (Bulkin and Nevel 2012).

And, in the case of the Lynde and Harry Bradley foundation and its aligned donors, it gave a total of $5.4 million to those agents advancing the counternarrative on Islam in the strategy of security politics, including $3.4 million to Horowitz and $815,000 to Gaffney, and $300,000 to Pipes (Ali et al. 2011). Similarly, the Bradley Foundation similarly had little apparent Zionist interest. Founded by a cofounder of the far-right John Birch Society, the Bradley Foundation's ideologically-tied giving made the Bradley Foundation—in the words of Media Transparency—"the country's largest and most influential right-wing organization,"[36] with assets at over $650 million and annual giving at $45 million at the beginning of the decade.

The Bradley Foundation's conservative motivation can be found in its annual reports reveal that it intends to fund those U.S. organizations deemed by its Board (which includes the popular conservative commentator George F. Will) to be important in the strengthening of the central institutions of the conservative movement. The Bradley foundation's "current program interests," for example, constitute a restatement of the main grievance against the Left that animates U.S. conservatism: "This expansive understanding of citizenship is being challenged today, however, by contemporary forces and ideas that regard individuals more as passive and helpless victims of powerful external forces than as personally responsible, self-governing citizens, and that foster a deep skepticism about citizenly values and mediating structures. Consequently, authority and accountability tend to flow away from citizens toward centralized, bureaucratic, "service-providing" institutions that claim to be peculiarly equipped to cope with those external forces on behalf of their "clients." This systematic disenfranchisement of the citizen, and the consequent erosion of citizenly mediating structures, pose grave threats to the free society that the Bradley bothers [sic] cherished."

It is by this ideological criterion that the Bradley foundation awarded the vast majority of its grants, which in just 2010 involved $37 million directed toward many of the central,

---

[35] Available at http://www.washingtonpost.com/wp-srv/politics/special/clinton/stories/scaife050299.htm
[36] Available at http://cursor.org/about/themoney.php. This description aligns with this philosophical position in its 2010 annual report: The Bradley brothers were committed to preserving and defending the tradition of free representative government and private enterprise that has enabled the American nation and, in a larger sense, the entire Western world to flourish intellectually and economically. The Bradleys believed that the good society is a free society. The Lynde and Harry Bradley Foundation is likewise devoted to strengthening American democratic capitalism and the institutions, principles and values that sustain and nurture it.

identifying organizations of the U.S. conservative movement. Notably, the foundation did not privilege organizations sympathetic to Zionism; it gave less to the pro-Israel Foundation for the Defense of Democracies, for example, than it did to the Institute for Global Engagement—a small Washington DC-based organization, whose conservative Christian President Chris Seiple had been critical of Israeli settlement expansionism at the expense of Palestinians, calling for a more "just peace" with a state for the Palestinians.[37]

These facts somewhat problematize Said's early critique and the subsequent literature's characterization of this security discourse as funded by primarily Zionist interests. Together, the Scaife and Bradley foundations—with historical track records of giving tied directly to exclusively conservative cultural politics—gave *twice* as much as the aforementioned four patrons with Zionist interests to organizations that did little else during this decade than promote Islam(ization) as a threat (Ali et al. 2011, 13-15). This does not mean that Holy Land geopolitics was not a key factor in this security discourse; rather, it means that domestic politics or the local culture war was also a factor, and—based on amounts given and founding, identifying statements and histories—*perhaps the larger one.*

Conclusion

In conclusion, recall Said's (1997, lviii) Foucauldian axiom that "it is not too much of an exaggeration to say that all discourse on Islam has an interest in some authority or power." Analysis of the Islam-as-threat apparatus of power reveals how this basic counternarrative regarding Islam that emerged soon after 9/11 began to reliably include a non-sequitur mass at its core that was not nearly as much about the newest foreign enemy as it was about the old domestic one. As we saw, based on what was reliably removed from view, the discourse under the Islam-as-threat (counter)narrative that was being produced was much less about pure knowledge, than political performance—that is, of delegitimizing the more progressive doxa broadly, and the Obama administration particularly. The newest *foreign* enemy, it seemed—like so many other topics of national debate—had become politically useful and a form of security at the *domestic* level. Thus, rather than posing a threat to conservative America, Islam had become a chief resource for its survival.

---

[37] See Chris Seiple's article on this at http://www.glocal.net/2009/01/26/palestinian-israeli-conflict/

3

POLITICAL OPPORTUNITIES

AND

RESOURCES

The construction of identities uses building materials from history... and from personal fantasies, from power apparatuses and religious revelations. But individuals, social groups, and societies process all these materials, and rearrange their meaning, according to social determinations and cultural projects....

—Manuel Castells (1997, 7)

WHY was this obvious strategy of security politics—of seizing and securitizing Islam(ization) as an opportunistic platform for cultural politics, and thereby blowing the threat wildly out of proportion—rendered politically-feasible and credible among a sufficient segment of U.S. conservatives?

We will examine this question in terms of this political strategy's set of *opportunities* and *resources*. Both social movements and their strategic discourses are rendered possible by opportunities and resources—ideational, cultural, and mass-emotional structures which are categorically distinct from the more visible social structural apparatus of power.[38] Here we will examine how–like in every political strategy—opportunities were created or seized, and resources mobilized.

---

[38] In Emirbayer and Goodwin's (1996) widely-elaboration of the interpretive approach, they conceptualize the environmental context of social action in terms of three distinct structural realms: (1) the cultural realm of basic mental schemas, hostile myths, master narratives, political ideologies and so on; (2) the social-psychological realm of collective anxieties, insecurities, fear, hostility, hatred, resentment, grievance structures and so on, as elaborated upon by Roger Petersen (2002) and Ted Gurr (1970); and (3) the social-structural realm of material, media-institutional, social network elements, of all kinds. To these three environmental structures or contexts Emirbayer and Goodwin add agency, or the strategies of the agents involved, as the fourth category of analysis in their solidly interpretive model of collective action and revolutions.

Specifically, this post-9/11 Islam-as-threat discourse became so powerful for three reasons:

First, the discourse's proponents were able to avoid sanction by bypassing the legitimate, official, formal discourse on the topics of Islam and threat. We saw how conservatives did this with the National Review, Washington Times, FOX News Channel; "think" tanks like Center for Security Policy, and blogs like Horowitz's Freedom Center—all of which were designed for the express purpose of cultural politics, or culture war. But, after 9/11, the Islam-as-threat discourse agents seized the opportunity afforded by social media and expanded this alternative or parallel media and knowledge society, in an identifiable rightward lurch that enabled this irrational discourse to expand further and more rapidly.

Second, conservative cultural warriors capitalized on two prevailing mass-level conservative moods or emotions. These were the identity insecurity or crises of the U.S. conservative movement, and the broader mood of civilizational fundamentalism.

Thirdly, conservative movement entrepreneurs mobilized powerful, identifying U.S cultural schemas, narratives, and ideologies.

1. Creating Opportunity for Security Politics: The Conservative Parallel Society and Its Post-9/11 Expansion

Again, we said that the Islam-as-threat discourse's proponents were able to avoid sanction by bypassing the legitimate, official, formal discourse on the topics of Islam and threat. We saw in Chapter 2 how the agents of this discourse did this with the National Review, Washington Times, FOX News Channel; "think" tanks like Center for Security Policy, and blogs like Horowitz's Freedom Center—all of which were designed for the express purpose of cultural politics, or culture war.

Here, we should further examine features of this apparatus of power that enabled this irrational discourse that fused what U.S. conservatives identified as their main threats, foreign and domestic—that is, Islam and the Left— to expand so rapidly.

The Parallel Knowledge Society

We saw how the public mission statements and history of the central identifying conservative institutions that advanced the counternarrative on Islam and more explicitly politicized the topic, readily admit that they are part of a broader conservative enclave that was from the start envisaged as an apparatus of power and knowledge that would bypass the more progressive establishment. Conservative political elite admit as much. For example, in a 6 April 2011 interview with one-time Republican presidential contender, Mike Huckabee, *The Daily Show* host Jon Stewart pointed to this strategy, and Huckabee did not deny it. Rather, he justified it in view of the mainstream institutions being so heavily biased toward the liberal worldview.

The construction of a parallel society has been well-theorized and long-implemented by fundamentalist movements and other groups marginalized or stigmatized by the dominant knowledge society, who seek to create greater opportunity for political struggle. All cultural struggle is struggle over truth or legitimacy. For this reason, in every society, there is—in the words of Herman and Chomsky (1988, 298, 305)—an "elite" or "doctrinal consensus" that cultural producers must negotiate.

"In every society," Foucault said, "the production of discourse is at once controlled," adding "we all know the rules of exclusion" and that "the most obvious and familiar of these concerns what is prohibited" (1972, 216). Each society, Foucault's (1980) added, is marked by a dominant "regime of truth"—which has a material, institutional base—and its "general politics of truth."

U.S. conservatives in the decade after 9/11 constantly referred to this dominant politics of truth as "political correctness," and their strategy of "resistance" or "subversion" was not to work within that regime of truth, but to *bypass* it altogether in such a parallel society.[39]

To do so, we saw how in the decades preceding 9/11, the U.S. conservative movement embarked upon such a counterhegemonic strategy of institution-building, driven by perceptions that existing knowledge institutions were in the thrall of liberalism, and hostile to conservative values and ideology (Gross et al. 2011, 333). Conservative intellectual William F. Buckley's launch of *National Review* in 1955 was the first strategic move toward such a parallel knowledge society that, in Friedman's (2005, 224-225) words—began to enable conservatives to "compete with and triumph over the prevailing interpretations of the previous half-century."

This strategy was reinvigorated by former Supreme Court Justice Lewis F. Powell Jr's memo in the early 1970s calling for business leaders to fund the construction of a conservative "counterestablishment" to disseminate conservative ideas (Reclaim Democracy, 2014).[40] In his August 23 1971 "Confidential Memorandum: Attack of American Free Enterprise System" to his friend on the U.S. Chamber of Commerce, Powell—who was serving on the boards of 11 corporations at the time—outlined a series of modest steps for corporate funded scholars and other experts to vigorously counter the perceived "broad attack" by "Communists, New Leftists and other revolutionaries" and by liberal elites in the "college campus, the pulpit, the media, the intellectual and literary journals, [and] the arts and sciences."

The actual attempt at such a strategy came later in the 1970s, when neoconservative Irving Kristol and former Treasury Secretary William Simon spearheaded a coalition of businessmen to fund conservative think tanks, intellectuals, and commentaries that would flood the media with conservative perspectives. Conservative philanthropists were recruited to advance this strategy. Heir of much of the Mellon oil fortune, the late Richard Mellon Scaife—who (as we saw in the last chapter) was a chief source of funding for the

---

[39] In Bourdieu's (1993, 2) terms, this parallel conservative society was a strategy of "counterculture," which—if you recall—is "the cult of everything that is outside 'legitimate' culture," "outside the 'establishment,' external to official culture."

[40] Available at http://reclaimdemocracy.org/powell_memo_lewis/

principal agents who framed Islam(ization) in the post-9/11 decade—was a chief patron of this strategy to build counterhegemonic parallel society of conservative institutions, for reasons Kaiser and Chinoy (1999) describe:

> Confounded by Goldwater's devastating defeat that November, many conservatives concluded that they could only win an election in the future by matching their enemy's firepower. It was time, as a Scaife associate of that era put it, to wage "the war of ideas." Scaife enthusiastically adopted this view. "We saw what the Democrats were doing and decided to do the mirror image, but do it better," this Scaife associate said. "In those days [the early 1970s] you had the American Civil Liberties Union, the government-supported legal corporations [neighborhood legal services programs], a strong Democratic Party with strong labor support, the Brookings Institution, the New York Times and Washington Post and all these other people on the left – and nobody on the right." The idea was to correct that imbalance.

In addition to those central identifying institutions created expressly for cultural struggle, the list of lesser known conservative institutions built as part of this parallel society is extensive. To counter the progressive National Public Radio, a universe of conservative talk radio emerged, hosted by polemicists like Rush Limbaugh and Michael Savage, and those of Christian genre, such as James Dobson's *Focus on the Family*. To counter the ACLU, conservatives built alternative legal advocacy institutions, such as the American Center for Law & Justice (ACLJ), the Alliance Defense Fund, and the Thomas More Law Center. To counter the secular influence of public schools and progressive academia, the homeschooling movement and several institutions of higher learning emerged, such as Jerry Falwell's Liberty University and Bob Jones University, whose science departments advance a young-earth creationism. And, to counter the evolution-naturalizing scientific establishment, conservatives built institutions that housed the counternarrative of "intelligent design," such as the Discovery Institute, and the more young-earth Institute for Creation Research, and Creation Research Institute. The list is far more extensive in each of these categories.

This practice by marginalized elements of society is widespread. Muslim fundamentalists, for example, have long advanced a strategy to create a parallel religious or "Islamic" enclave in the areas of education, religion and culture which competed with and diminished the effective control of the state, and gradually won over the masses from the secular order (Hefner 2001, 504). In Egypt, for example, the *Ikhwan* or Muslim Brotherhood established itself in the 1970s through such a "parallel Islamic sector," as an alternative to the various cultural, religious, and service-oriented institutions of the state (Wickham 2002, 95).[41] Similarly, the marginalized Muslim population in Germany has also erected such a "parallel society" (Pötzl 2008) or "Parallelgesellschaften" (Hiscott 2005). And, under communism, dissident movements like Poland's Solidarity similarly bypassed

---

[41] According to Nawara (2013), the *Ikhwan* movement "functions as an international secret underground society operating its own totalitarian parallel state, a state-within-the-state"; it "secretly owns and/or controls businesses, political parties, militias, media institutions, schools, hospitals, charities, syndicates and even student unions…"

the centralized, official, and political society and created political space in the form of their own institutions—resistance institutions that subverted and weakened the legitimizing institutions (Kumar 1993, 386; Lagos et al. 2007). Czech dissident Vaclav Benda (1977) [1991] advanced this strategy in the tract *Parallel Polis*, published through the *samizdat*—the movement's underground publishing apparatus.

Such a strategy of bypassing the legitimizing institutions was a foreign concept to the earliest and more Marxist theorists of cultural struggle. (Counter)hegemonic struggle in Gramsci's view, for example, was *intellectual* in nature; it proceeded as a political ideology's elite and intellectuals seek through a "war of position" *within* civil society's dominant institutions—the mass media, schools, churches, etc.—to imperceptibly subvert the dominant ideology or doxa housed therein (Gramsci 1971, 125-33).[42] Writing earlier in the twentieth century, Gramsci could not have imagined how media or informational technological innovations might democratize and help build these institutions, thereby enabling a counterhegemonic project to turn from an *intellectual* movement within the legitimate society into a *secessionist* one outside of and parallel to it. In the information age, and especially in the digital age of the alternative media, marginalized political factions could simply create their own alternative sub-society, or information ghetto, thereby effectively bypassing and weakening the more official, dominant, or legitimizing knowledge society.[43]

And this is precisely what the conservative movement did.

Expansion into the Alternative Media and the Rightward Shift

Before 9/11, what could be said about Islam by conservatives was still largely determined by the conservative parallel knowledge society's more central, "big tent" institutions. But, by the mid-point of the post-9/11 decade, that had changed. The emerging "new" or alternative media significantly had eroded the "monopoly of production" long held by these central identifying institutions of the conservative movement. Just before the height of the Islamization conspiracy expanded so exponentially across much of the conservative movement, a March 2010 CNN survey had revealed that more Americans were getting news from the internet than from traditional print media or radio (Gross 2010).[44]

---

[42] Gramsci (1971) theorized that every society is in the process of non-violent but potentially destabilizing wars of position for cultural dominance in civil society's institutions. His emphasis on the war of position derived from Marx's gradual realization that modes of thought are not overdetermined by dominant material or economic relations, but by societal institutions that emerged to reproduce the ideology that serves the interests of those who want to preserve their privileged status within the unequal social order. Within this superstructure of modern Western state are a vast range of institutions—political, religious, educational, media, even athletic or sports—that comprise "civil society" (Gramsci 1971, 12). Because of this role of the cultural superstructure, Gramsci argued, revolutions in Western societies required a war of position fought over a protracted period in that realm (1971, 108).

[43] This process of culture war was described by later theorists who saw cultural struggle proceeding as the challenging movement "slowly builds up the strength of the social foundations of a new state" by "creating alternative institutions and alternative intellectual resources within existing society" (Cox 1983, 165).

[44] As early as 1996, *National Review* was forced to align with the trend, leading the way with its National Review Online, NRO, which featured separate and always more extreme editorial content from the print magazine.

To the farther right, this was a golden opportunity for a new twist on the strategy of secession that Justice Powell had advanced in the 1970s. In a fitting article for the new conservative e-daily, *WorldNetDaily*, William Lind (2007)—an aforementioned early proponent of the counternarrative and the Director of the Center for Cultural Conservatism at the Free Congress Foundation—expressed this sentiment, saying, "We can separate ourselves and our families from the institutions the cultural Marxists control and build new institutions for ourselves, institutions that reflect and will help us recover our traditional Western culture" (Lind 2007). Apparently unaware of the conservative movement's history or its then-sizeable existing institutional sub-society, Lind advocated that conservatives place more emphasis on the "movement to secede from the corrupt, dominant culture and create parallel institutions."

And, writing from his ever-popular *JihadWatch* blog, Horowitz's employee, and Lind's former colleague at the Foundation, Robert Spencer, captured the spirit of this invigorated strategy in a 9 July 2010 post. "We have the truth on our side," Spencer said confidently, "we have the alternate media—which is still very small compared to the mainstream media, but it is growing apace as the frustration of people who realize they're being lied to increases."

And, it was growing apace. Many conservative upstarts in the alternative media were now functioning as key nodes in the conservative parallel universe—alternative media institutions like *WorldNetDaily*, Horowitz's *Front Page Magazine*, *American Thinker*, and *Pajamas (now PJ) Media*. It was in this rapid expansion of these media outlets that conservative culture warriors with a modicum of cultural capital could bypass what Daniel Pipes derogatively referred to as the "stifling consensus" of the "establishment" (Pipes 2010; Pipes & Chadha 2006).

WorldNetDaily was key in this regard. Created in 1997 as a project of the more rightist evangelical, Joseph Farah, the e-daily apparently printed everything that the Islam(ization) threat discourse's principal agents managed to write. Reflecting the rightward shift in the GOP, this alternative conservative e-daily became more influential than the more identifiable legacy institutions. By 2009, in the new Obama Administration and the more forceful emergence of the green scare over sharia, the institution had become so central to the conservative movement that the Republican National Committee apparently rented access to its email list (Henke 2009; Krepel 2009).

With this kind of cultural capital, the e-daily could even branch into publishing. In 2009, *WorldNetDaily* published *Muslim Mafia: Inside the Secret Underworld That's Conspiring to Islamize America*, which had been funded by Gaffney's Center for Security Policy (Elliot 2011); and in 2011, it published *Stop the Islamization of America*, by Pamela Geller.

The Islamization conspiracy theory was but one of many that the tabloid-like institution had advanced. It was also a leader in advancing the "birther" movement related to President Obama's citizenship. When confronted on this, its editor and CEO, Farah, admitted the site knowingly published misinformation if it supports their political goals (Elliot 2011). With its track record clearly established, *WorldNetDaily* was dubbed by *Salon* as "the biggest, dumbest wingnut site on the Web" (Goode 2003, 4; Pareene 2011), and more moderate elements of the GOP had begun urging other conservatives to not support it (Henke 2009).

This changing nature of the conservative media society was bound to have concomitant effects on the subculture's political ideology, in keeping with the tenets of medium theory (Deibert 1997, ix-x; Meyrowitz 2008).[45] And, by the end of the post-9/11 decade, this ideological shift was visible; the more rightist alternative media-based nodes had clearly eclipsed the more centrist elements of the conservative enclave's legacy apparatus of power, and were dragging them farther right. Digital Director of the Romney campaign, Zac Moffat, said that websites like Breitbart and Drudge represent a major shift in how the media works, significantly eroding the influence of everything more toward the political center on the conservative electorate (O'Connor 2012).[46]

In this new episteme, truth mattered much less, as information was less pure and more politically performative—that is, meant to do or achieve something. At Andrew Breitbart's consortium of blogs (where Gaffney's column from the *Washington Times* would eventually move in 2014),[47] for example, all topics of news were politicized. It was here that Andrew McCarthy in 2010 could credibly say (without challenge) that "Islamists" and "leftists" share totalitarian goals, "totalitarian in the sense that they want to control every aspect of the individual's life, and [are] virulently opposed to capitalism and individual liberty," adding that "even though they [Obama and Saudi King Abdullah] part company on the details of what they would transform it into, they both need to topple American constitutional republicanism in order to install their utopias" (Posner 2011).

Another example of how their expanding alternative media enclave seemed to be normalizing more extreme, anti-rationalist forms of political discourse among key conservatives was the aforementioned *Pajamas* (later PJ) *Media*. Launched in November 2005, *Pajamas Media's* mission was to replace the mainstream media's professional journalists with a network of conservative and politically activist citizen-journalists. The institution's name, "Pajamas" reflected this strategy; it was a reference to the "Pajamahadeen," or those mujahideen-like bloggers, who—from home in their pajamas—could "challenge and fact-check traditional media." The website was the brainchild of activist Charles Johnson and Roger L. Simon, who—after his investigation into the Killian documents controversy—forced a retraction of *60 Minutes* criticism of President George W. Bush's service in the Air National Guard, and forced Dan Rather's resignation from CBS News. Johnson (2012)—reflecting back on *Pajamas Media's* beginnings—noted how it was "conceived as a place where left and right could meet and engage in rational debate." Its earlier centrist positioning strategy was the reason it had kept putting off *Jihad Watch's*

---

[45] Media is thought to be not simply channels for transmitting information, but are themselves distinct social-psychological environments that shape certain types of interaction and interpretation, and discourage others (Meyrowitz, 2008).

[46] Breitbart's farther Right editor John Nolte has called for a "twitter war" to harass liberal elite and media, and whose own militant tendencies is reflected by his twice sending tweets calling for liberals thought to be leading America's moral slide to be murdered (Johnson, 2012: 05.16).

[47] See http://www.breitbart.com/Big-Peace/2014/02/25/FRANK-GAFFNEYS-WEEKLY-COLUMN-COMES-TO-BREITBART

Robert Spencer who—according to Johnson—incessantly asked to have his articles published at the site. Yet, the ideological shift over the next seven years was profound enough to force Johnson to leave. And, at the end of the post-9/11 decade, on the news that Spencer had finally landed a column there, Johnson (2012) lamented, "I suppose this is another indicator of how far to the right the conservative movement has swung…."

The Farther Right Episteme

For a significant segment of conservatives, this parallel knowledge society fostered an epistemic shift; that is their approach to knowing the world shifted toward anti-rationalism—it shifted from *critically evaluating* information to *identifying with* information—that is, *selecting* or subscribing to (with a simple mouse click) those nodes of ideologically-driven knowledge that aligned with their predispositions and worldview. In this process, the alternative media allowed the unwary or uncritical to become captured by their own identification practices, and thereby become sequestered in a self-reinforcing information ghetto.

In other words, the rapid emergence of the alternative media coincident with the post-9/11 decade enabled individuals who are ideologically aligned, or who have similar needs or interests to create a "virtual community" or "internet mediated community" (Iriberri and Leroy 2009, 11; 19; Bellini and Vargas 2003, 3).

In the specific context of the conservative knowledge ghetto, Jamieson and Cappella (2008, x) argue that this structure of conservative media produces a safe haven that "reinforces the views of these outlets' like-minded audience members, helps them maintain ideological coherence, protects them from counter persuasion, reinforces conservative values and dispositions, holds Republican candidates and leaders accountable to conservative ideals, tightens their audience's ties to the Republican Party, and distances listeners, readers, and viewers from 'liberals' in general, and Democrats, in particular."

Similarly, Jones (2012, 181) concludes that FOX News Channel, in conjunction with other conservative media outlets, "provides a steady and consistent diet of such overtly ideological symbolic material to sufficiently sustain viewer interest and commitments as a community."

This notion that a politically meaningful segment of U.S conservatives had allowed themselves to become ideologically captured by and insulated within their incestuous, solipsistic media enclave was evident at the end of the post-9/11 decade. According to Public Policy Polling (PPP) in January 2014, for example, 69 percent of Republicans viewed FOX News Channel as the most trusted, with no other network polling above 7 percent for GOP viewers.[48]

By the time the Islamization scare had captured so many conservatives, this information ghetto had become a strategic issue for the GOP. Polling from various organizations from 2007 to 2011, for example, consistently revealed that FOX News's market was least knowledgeable about national and international affairs (Pew Research

---

[48] An almost equal 57 percent of Democrats deemed FOX the least trusted network.

Center, 2007; World Public Opinion, 2010; Public Religion Research Institute, 2011). A study by the University of Maryland revealed that the ignorance of FOX News Channel viewers actually *increased* (rather than decreased, as would be expected) the *longer* they watched the "news" network (Dickinson 2011). Similarly, nearly six in ten Republicans who said that they trusted FOX News believed also believed that Muslim-Americans were trying to establish sharia in the U.S., contrasted with Republicans who relied on other news sources, whose beliefs align with those of the general population (PRR and Brookings 2011).

At this point, a segment of conservative intellectuals had begun the debate surrounding the epidemic of anti-rationalism that the information ghetto was creating—an episteme that Julian Sanchez of the libertarian Cato Institute called "epistemic closure." Sanchez noted how identifying institutions like FOX News Channel and *National Review*, along with popular experts like Rush Limbaugh and Glenn Beck, had "become worryingly untethered from reality as the impetus to satisfy the demand for red meat overtakes any motivation to report accurately" (Cohen 2010).

A typical example of how political spin trumped accuracy in reporting in the conservative information ghetto could be seen during the GOP primaries on May 1, 2012, when FOX News's Sean Hannity interviewed Geert Wilders.[49] When Wilders wildly exaggerated the threat from Islamization, saying that Europe had become "almost half Islamic," Hannity never challenged him.

During the lengthy interview, FOX News's editors could have checked and notified Hannity of Eurostat's figures, which showed that Muslims comprised only 13 to 16 million, or merely 2.5 to 3.5 percent of the EU's population of 500 million in 2009. They could have even reviewed the widely publicized short excerpts of Saunders (2012, 54), which debunked the Islamization of Europe threat narrative, and pinpointed the future Muslim population of the Netherlands—Wilders' home—in 15 years at only 7.8 percent.[50] They could have pushed back further, noting that much of that very small Muslim population (almost 1/20th of the U.S. Hispanic population, for example) was fully assimilated and more European than Islamic in cultural values. And, FOX's editors could have also quickly checked that—accounting for population growth—the Muslim population across all of Europe in 2030 will be only 2 percent higher than then, according to Pew Research Center's latest estimate (Pew Research Center 2011). But, FOX's silence on this context imparted authority to Wilders. With that goal achieved, FOX News could move on in non-sequitur fashion to more blatant domestic politics: "This president [Obama] won't even recognize that there is a war on terror," Hannity blurted.

---

[49] http://www.youtube.com/watch?feature=player_embedded&v=oE0SMdKn71g
[50] In a widely publicized excerpt of his book, Saunders (2012) wrote: "More than 13 million people have now viewed the YouTube video Muslim Demographics, which claims among other things that Germany will be a "Muslim state" by 2050. Every one of the video's claims is untrue. It says that French Muslims have 8.1 children and ethnic-French families 1.8 (the figures are 2.8 and 1.9, respectively). It says that a quarter of the Belgian population is Muslim (it's 6%), that the Netherlands will be half Muslim in 15 years (it will be 7.8% Muslim in 18 years) — and so on."

Increased Authority of Popular Experts

The practice using Islam as a platform in a strategy of security politics was rendered further feasible by the increase in authority of popular experts, or organic intellectuals. The rapid expansion of the conservative enclave into the alternative media through institutions like *WorldNetDaily* and *Pajamas Media,* along with the rise of the new conservative episteme, presented the more politically-antagonistic and activist intellectuals with the kind of authority that heretofore had been reserved for those with traditional credentials and who were further accredited by their positions in recognized authoritative institutions of knowledge—that is, in the dominant regime of truth.

For example, by the end of the post-9/11 decade, Horowitz's *FrontPageMagazine* had over 870,000 unique visitors each month (65 million hits) and was linked to over 2000 other conservative websites (DHFC website 2014). This trend had grown throughout the post-9/11 decade, as the Horowitz center's Tax Form 990 for 2008 shows, before *JihadWatch's* popularity grew significantly in 2010.[51]

4b	(Code·) (Expenses $ 664,457. including grants of $) (Revenue $ 30,268.)

-FRONTPAGEMAG.COM (FPM) IS THE CENTER'S MAIN DAILY NEWS WEBSITE. WITH UP TO 10 ORIGINAL ARTICLES FEATURED DAILY, THE CENTER BRINGS NEWS AND COMMENTARY TO MILLIONS OF PEOPLE WORLDWIDE. THE MISSION OF FRONTPAGE IS TO DELIVER THE NEWS ON THE WAR AT HOME AND ABROAD. FPM HAS ABOUT 750,000 UNIQUE VISITORS EVERY MONTH.

4c	(Code·) (Expenses $ 369,213. including grants of $) (Revenue $ 3,441.)

-JIHAD WATCH IS A CENTER PROGRAM RUN BY NOTED AUTHOR ROBERT SPENCER. JIHADWATCH.ORG IS A DAILY NEWS SITE WITH NEWS AND OPINION ON THE WAR WITH RADICAL ISLAM, THE STUDY AND DISSEMINATION OF INFORMATION REGARDING THE JIHADIST WORLDVIEW, SHARIA LAW, AND THE THREATS TO WESTERN CIVILIZATION. JIHAD WATCH IS READ BY OVER 500,000 UNIQUE VISITORS EVERY MONTH. ROBERT SPENCER IS A NY TIMES BESTSELLING AUTHOR AND HIS ARTICLES ARE READ BY MILLIONS WORLDWIDE.

But it was more than impressive "circulation" that contributed to this subtle epistemic effect of the democratization of authority. Regulations for authority in the alternative media were also alternative, benefiting the popular and more dissident, countercultural producers. By 2008, Pew Research Center found that Western societies were decreasingly in a mood to rely on mainstream media and institutionalized authorities for their truth, and increasingly relying on more popular sources proliferating in the alternative media (Pew Research Center 2008). The movement's affinity for the samizdat-like alternative media can be found in McLuhan's (2005)[1967] axiom, "the medium is the message." The *alternative* media, more than anything, symbolized an alternative message, and that in itself drew U.S. conservative political entrepreneurs to it.

Traditional epistemic authority also suffered decline in relative terms; it was simply

---

[51] The entire Form 990 is available at *The Tennessean,* http://archive.tennessean.com/assets/pdf/DN1658821023.PDF

being "drowned out" as the nodes of information multiplied exponentially from 16 to 2,280 million between 1995 and 2012. The circulation figures for popular conservative experts on Islam(ization)—those of Horowitz's *FrontPageMagazine* and Spencer's *Jihad Watch*—concomitantly grew, even exceeding those experts in the traditional, professional security field, and effectively bypassing what Foucault (1972, 50-55) had called society's "enunciative modalities," and challenging the "rarefaction" of authority within academic disciplines (Foucault 1981, 60). Even celebrated institutionalized conservative scholars like Bernard Lewis watched their influence shrink relative to these popular authorities, who were housed not at places like Princeton (like Lewis) and publishing in peer-reviewed journals, but housed and publishing in their own institutions in the alternative media.

In McLuhan's terms, the alternative medium that these conservative agents spoke from was the alternative message, and it was for that tacit counterhegemonic symbolism that the counterhegemonic *FOX News* and other conservative-niche media institutions summoned agents like Pamela Geller for discussion on Islam broadly.

From this, it should not be surprising that internet posts referencing a widely-known traditional scholar like Bernard Lewis on the subjects of "Islam" or "jihad" are at least a third fewer than those referencing Daniel Pipes or Robert Spencer, for example.[52]

This same pattern of effective popular authority can be seen with other experts on Islam. The number of web entries returned from an advanced Google search of the discourse's principal agents at the end of the post-9/11 decade compared to more traditional experts on the topic of Islam begins to reveal just how much authority had been democratized:

Internet Citations	Name (as Searched)	Institution and Credentials
1,090,000	"Daniel Pipes"	Add 402,000 if "Middle East Forum" is included
929,000	"David Horowitz"	Add 1,930,000 if "FrontPage" Magazine is included
927,000	"Robert Spencer" with "Islam"	Add 8,570,000 if "Jihad Watch" is included and 1,240,000 more if "jihadwatch" is included
458,000	"Frank Gaffney"	Add 267,000 if "Center for Security Policy" is included
351,000	"Brigitte Gabriel"	Add 3,330,000 if "ACT! for America" is included.
118,000	"Marc Lynch" with Islam	George Washington University's authority on the Muslim Brotherhood; author of the blog, Abu Aardvark
20,900	"Quintan Wiktorowicz"	Scholar on Islamism on Obama's National Security Council; author of *Radical Islam Rising*.
18,100	"Peter Mandaville"	Director, Ali Vural Ak Center for Global Islamic Studies, George Mason Univ.; author of *Political Global Islam*.

---

[52] If the search is expanded to include references to Spencer's organization "JihadWatch," the comparison becomes even more lopsided.

And, Bonney's (2008) analysis of Bernard Lewis's influence on Vice President Dick Cheney and the Bush administration's invasion of Iraq notwithstanding, it was apparently not so much the traditional, formal authorities operating in the legitimate knowledge society, but the popular ones operating in the alternative media segment of the parallel conservative knowledge society, who had the most influence in shaping the early counternarrative on Islam and the later more open counterhegemonic strategy of security politics. Presidential frontrunner Newt Gingrich's emphasis on the threat of sharia and his use of the term, "stealth jihad" in 2010, for example, were borrowed not from formal authorities like Lewis, but from the popular expert, Spencer, who had published his book by that name in 2008.

2. Seizing the Mood: The Opening for Politics Created by Identity Insecurity

In addition to creating the opportunity for politics, cultural warriors within the conservative movement also seized the affective moment, particularly the general mood of identity insecurity, and the rightward shift that it shaped.

Identity Insecurity or Crisis Within the U.S. Conservative Movement

At the socio-historical level of analysis, the (counter)narrative of the present danger of Islam (ization) advanced within the conservative parallel knowledge society in the post-9/11 decade might be further explained by the accentuated crisis (of identity) that was then animating the "big tent" U.S. conservative movement.

In the conceptual framework outlined in Chapter 1, we reviewed why so much of public discourse—even security discourse—is now politicized. A key reason, we saw, is that the nature of identity in late modern Western states in particular is inherently unstable and insecure. For the big-tent U.S. conservative movement, this inherent crisis of identity extended across three of its main constituents—the neoconservatives, social conservatives, and paleoconservatives.

Crises within Neoconservatism

Per Bonney's (2008) analysis, the neoconservative role in the post-9/11 Islam(ization) threat discourse was huge. This may be partially explained by its revolutionary rightward influence on the U.S. conservative movement broadly, as described by Friedman's (2006) *The Neoconservative Revolution*, and its decidedly rightward influence on the Israel lobby more narrowly. In Mearsheimer and Walt's (2007, 128) analysis, the GOP experienced a decided "drift to the right" upon neoconservatism's emergence.

There were two distinct crises that neoconservatives were experiencing at the beginning of the 9/11 decade and towards its mid-point:

The first neoconservative crisis was at the international level, and was significantly in existence on the morning of the 9/11 attacks. U.S. neoconservatives are distinct from U.S.

social conservatives, who are more focused on declining morality and Judeo-Christian identity as a function of secularism, and U.S. paleoconservatives, who tend to emphasize the threat of diluted biological and cultural identity as a function of multiculturalism and lack of restrictions on immigration—both threats on the domestic axis. The threat that typically animated neoconservatives up to this juncture had tended to be not domestic but foreign in nature—threats to Israel, and threats from rival universalist ideologies like "Godless Communism." When translated to domestic politics, these perceive foreign threats manifested as opposition to the Carter administration, for example, who neoconservatives believed as "hostile to Israel" (Friedman 2006, 149-50), and whose policies towards the Soviet Union, especially détente and the SALT II agreements, they saw as catastrophic and influenced by the largely antiwar left (Ehrman 1995).

To establish neoconservatism's political relevance, the threats to Israel and the threats from Communism had to be exaggerated. We've already seen how the "Team B" of neoconservatives led by Daniel Pipes's father, Richard, operating first as The Committee on the Present Danger exercise in 1976, wildly over-constructed the "Soviet threat," as it had been conceptualized by the officialdom of Presidents Nixon and Ford and their foreign-policy mentor, Henry Kissinger (Saunders 1983; Kampleman 1984; Dalby 1988).

After the fall of Communist empire, and thus without a rival superpower with a competing universalist ideology, and without any remote threat to Israel from any of the two-dozen Middle East authoritarian regimes that were far more animated by the threat within of democracy than hostility to Israel, the neoconservative movement lacked the necessary "others" which it had been created in juxtaposition to. Recall Campbell's (1998) terms, that this threat was less a threat to the nation's existence than it was the condition of the neoconservative movement's existence. For its own survival as an identifying conservative ideology, neoconservatism needed a new threat—a near-peer, hegemony-bent ideology and political rival that threatened its own universalist, hegemonic self-vision of the U.S., and that threatened Israel's existence.

It is in this context that, near the end of the Soviet Union, neoconservative-oriented intellectuals like Daniel Pipes, Bernard Lewis, and Frank Gaffney began to construct Islam itself within the "clash of civilizations" paradigm (Bonney 2008, Mearsheimer and Walt 2007). Daniel Pipes began this project in 1983 with his book on fundamentalist Shi'ite Islam, or Khomeinism, *In the Path of God: Islam and Political Power*.

And, after 9/11, and in a significant advisory capacity to the Bush administration, it was these same neoconservatives, along with Norman Podhoretz and others, who—as Bonney's (2008) analysis revealed—advanced this clash of civilizations ideology. These neoconservative conspiracy theorists drew parallels between the Red Scare of the Cold War era and threat of shariaization by a superpower-like global network of Islamists. Former intelligence chief James Woolsey (who served on Gaffney's "Team 'B' II" report, said that the goals of radical Islamists are "roughly parallel to communists in the '50s and '60s... We're in a war with terrorists but that's not the end. We're at war with those who want to impose shari'ah, this is our toughest fight" (Posner 2011).

The second aspect of the neoconservative crisis was—counterintuitively—at the domestic level of politics, and it emerged at the mid-point of the post-9/11 decade. The impetus of this second and domestic crisis was the strategic, neoconservative-led failures of militarily invading Afghanistan and Iraq, and attempts at "nation-building," and the subsequent landslide defeat of the neoconservative-led GOP (Friedman 2006). The disastrous foreign policy initiative of the Iraq War—in Packer's (2005, 15) terms—"will always be linked with the term 'neoconservative.'"

The conservative electorate's reaction to neoconservatism's failure in leadership was such that, even before the end of the Bush administration, the *Times* of London heralded "the end of an ideological era in Washington," the *Toronto Globe and Mail* reported that neoconservatism had been "decisively wiped out," and even the *National Review Online*, in an article by John Derbyshire, concluded that "all the buzz is that neoconservatism is as dead as mutton." It is in this context that neocon Reagan defense official Kenneth Adelman lamented that "most everything we ever stood for now …lies in ruins" (Muravchik 2007).

It was this second and separate domestic crisis emerging at the mid-point of the post-9/11 decade rendered all exaggerated threat discourse regarding Islam as not merely politically safe, but politically necessary. And, it was at this juncture, when neoconservatism was being pronounced dead from the hands of its own conservative electorate, that the more serious neoconservative construction of Islam-as-threat began to emerge. Emblematic of this crisis was both Norman Podhoretz's (2007) bestselling *World War IV: The Long Struggle Against Islamofascism*, and Gaffney's reconstruction of the Cold-War era Committee on the Present Danger, with its new emphasis on the threat of radical Islam.

Crisis within Social and Paleoconservatism

The crises confronting U.S. social and paleoconservatives in the post-9/11 decade was the subtler threat of late modernity's ideological threat's or "—isms."

For social conservatives, the threat was described as progressivism and secularism in the dominant institutions and electorate of U.S. society, which had significantly diluted the Judeo-Christian-based moral fabric of the nation, evidenced in the increasing normalization of abortion, homosexuality, erosion of marriage and the family, and so on.

For paleoconservatives, the threat was more that of multiculturalism, which through unrestricted immigration had significantly diluted the largely white, European and Judeo-Christian identity, and which had formed the base of the GOP (Foley 2007, 318). The conjuncture of globalization, the information and communication (ICT) revolution, with its attending new, social and alternative media, had thrown the metaphysical legitimating foundation of traditional identities in the West and worldwide into even greater crisis, with many progressive identities increasing relative to more singular traditional ones (Marty and Appleby 1991, 2004; Giddens 1991, 2002; Laclau 1994; Castells 1997).

It is these elements of the broader crisis that rendered possible the wildly untethered and anti-rationalist Islamization security narrative. In Ian Buruma's (2009) words, "In a bewildering world of global economics, multinational institutions and mass migration, many people are anxious about losing their sense of place; they feel abandoned by their own elites. Right-wing [anti-Islam] populists like Geert Wilders are tapping into these fears."

Baruma seemed to have put his thumb on the broader factor. For identities in crisis, security narratives can function more implicitly and semiotically as metaphor for deeper societal problems. In European environmental security discourse in the 1990s, for instance, Hajer (2005, 298) observed how "acid rain," was "emblematic of the bigger 'problem'"; it was part of a broader critique narrative on industrial society itself. Dead trees from acid rain metaphorically signified a "structural problem" with society broadly—"a broader crisis of industrial society" (2005, 299). In other words, discourse on acid rain was really more about the prevailing culture and governmentality (Hajer 1996, 256).

Similarly, in their examination of British society's extreme overreaction to the threat of "mugging" in the 1970s, Hall and colleagues (1978) argued that this mugging crisis was not merely about crime per se. Instead, this crime of mugging, with its attending themes of race, immigration and degenerative morality of British youth, became for the social conservatives the metaphor and index for the purportedly broader, more profound crisis of hegemony, or the disintegration of the dominant social, moral order. For these conservatives, it was the symbol for the broader master narrative of declinism—that the "British way of life" was coming apart at the seams (1978, vii-viii).

From this vantage point, we might ask whether the seemingly anti-rational and empirically-challenged crisis over sharia or Islamization—like the crisis over mugging in post-war Britain, or that on the threat of acid rain later—was emblematic of the deeper structural crisis or identity insecurity that conservatives and fundamentalists in every society perceive. Social complexity and ambiguity drives the need for all such metaphorical devices, and the structural crisis of identity and hegemony facing America's conservatives was highly complex. On the one hand, in the religious and cultural realm, there was identity insecurity over the dilution of Jewish, Orthodox, Catholic and Protestant institutions in the Northern Hemisphere and Israel by ascendant populations of others in the Western heartland and its Holy Land, broadly denoted as "Islam." On the other hand, in the domestic political realm, there was the steady slide toward political progressivism and increased philosophical secularism, broadly denoted as "the left."

In reaction, Castells (1997, 97, 2) contends, conservatives dug in, with more entrenched affirmation of traditional values, and producing "the widespread surge of powerful expressions of collective identity that challenge globalization and cosmopolitanism on behalf of cultural singularity." Similarly, Balz and Brownstein (1996, 173) wrote that "Behind all these swirling, swelling movements on the Right is the fear of a world spinning out of control. "People feel they don't have control over their own lives," said Republican pollster Frank Luntz, "That they can no longer shape their future" (cited in Castells 1997).

The search for meaning in this crisis, Castells adds, took place "in the reconstruction of defensive identities around communal principles," giving way to the "new primacy of identity politics" (Castells 1997, 11).

In this milieu, Giddens (2002) observed the issues-centered "culture war" emerging between two polarized groups—the cosmopolitans, who embrace the age's cultural complexity, and traditionalists or fundamentalists, who "find it disturbing and dangerous" and "take refuge in a renewed and purified tradition" of counterhegemonic struggle.

Laclau (1994, 4) similarly explains why so much has been radically politicized in late modernity: The more the "foundation" of the social is put into question, he says, the less the sedimented social practices are able to ensure social reproduction, and the more new acts of political intervention and identification are socially required. This necessarily leads to a politicization of social identities, which we see as a main feature of social life in the societies of the end of the twentieth century. And, lest we lose focus, the identities politicized and securitized in this Islam(ization threat narrative are the conservative movement's enemies, foreign and domestic—that is, Islam and the left.

The Rightward Shift

It was in this context of more radical identity politics that a more rightist political zeitgeist gradually became normalized across the central conservative establishment in the post-9/11 decade, increasingly dichotomizing the social space.[53]

The U.S. conservative movement had always had a xenophobic urge, but in the late 1950s, the GOP had begun to shift more rightward, with the incorporation of factions like the Communist conspiracy-oriented and anti-Semitic John Birch Society (Hofstadter 1964), and the anti-Catholic sentiments (Weigel, 2008). This shift to the right was evidenced with the emergence and normalization of more radical figures like Republican Wisconsin Senator, Joseph McCarthy. In his *America's Right Turn: From Nixon to Clinton*, Berman (1998, 1-3) describes the GOP's first "rightward shift" as frustration mounted over the New Deal coalition and the liberal welfare state, when "Liberalism had become a pejorative word for millions of voters because it was a vehicle for big governmental spending programs for blacks."

When William F. Buckley Jr. founded the *National Review* in 1955, he countered this early Zeitgeist with a big tent concept of the GOP, with no room for the party's trademark bigotry. Buckley's "greater public service," said Catholic polemicist George Weigel, "was to purge the conservative movement of the anti-Semitism, racism, xenophobia and isolationism that had infested the fever swamps of the American Right in the FDR period and beyond" (Weigel, 2008). For example, Buckley in 1952 left his post as an editor at the *The American Mercury* when he sensed it was turning anti-Semitic. Yet, in his book *McCarthy and His Enemies* (1954), it was evident that the party's rightward shift had infected even him.

As a marker of this rightward shift, Goldwater's acceptance speech at the 1964 Republican National Convention accepted some extremism in the big tent. "Anyone who joins us in all sincerity, we welcome," he said, adding, "that extremism in the defense of

---

[53] This can be conceptualized as the cognitive alignment to "bimodal value structure" in which political discourse was being clustered on the pole, or on polar opposition to the perceived counter-position (Edelman 1964: 175-177; Billig 1996).

liberty is no vice" and "moderation in the pursuit of justice is no virtue" (*Washington Post* 1998).[54]

In the later 1960s the movement continued to drift right. According to Himmelstein (1983, 15-16), this "explosion of conservative activity," was largely in reaction to the counterculture of liberalism, free love student radicalism, and other "counterestablishment" movements.

These early rightward shifts notwithstanding, the party up through the Goldwater era still had a significantly moderate ideological center that was a champion of many virtues— of peace (with significant opposition to the Vietnam War), of environmental stewardship, of the civil rights movement, and of the secular order more broadly as our best guarantee of personal liberty (Kabaservice 2012).

The GOPs more noticeable shift to the right, however, came after Goldwater in the 1970s and 1980s with the addition of the New York Jewish intellectuals who became known as the neoconservatives (Friedman 2006), and with the rise of the "New Right" and the more fundamentalist and evangelical religious right; and the "New Christian Right" (Himmelstein 1983; Liebman and Wuthnow 1983). The main threat that gave rise to this latest rightward shift was not merely that of "Godless Communists" abroad but also of the New Left at home (Rusher 2002, 322; Blee and Creasap 2010, 273).

But, forty years later, with the fall of the Soviet Union and with the green scare following 9/11, key conservative elite began to so egregiously politicize the topic of Islam. Dubbed by its critics as "the New McCarthyism,"[55] this latest shift was also due in no small part to the emergence of the Tea Party movement in response to the most severe global financial crisis since the Great Depression, along with the GOP's landslide loss to the nation's first black and Democrat president (Kabaservice 2012; Skocpol and Williamson 2012).

It was in this more politically-charged atmosphere that the political center was displaced, and the crises of described widely and variously as "gridlock," "partisan politics" and so on emerged. Comprised of older, conservative white voters, Tea Party leaders had issued direct threats and ousted any centrist incumbent and candidate who might have engaged in the kind of compromising governance necessary for a democracy to function (Skocpol and Williamson 2012, 155). As a result, more polarizing figures were vetted for the party's highest posts of leadership, and charismatic, populist culture warriors like David Horowitz gained greater influence. These radical discourse agents, or "Caesars," as Gramsci called them, tended to arrive in all crises at the point in which "the old is dying and the new cannot be born," when "a great variety of morbid symptoms appear" (Gramsci 1971, 275; Jones 2006, 99-100).

And, it was within this crisis and attending rightward shift that the more entrepreneurial conservative elite began the political practice enemy frame-bridging—that

---

[54] See http://www.washingtonpost.com/wp-srv/politics/daily/may98/goldwaterspeech.htm
[55] A January 2013 Google search for the term "new McCarthyism" returned 153,000 posts to the internet with that exact term, nearly all of which were posted since 2005.

is, linking new enemies foreign and old enemies domestic—Islam and the Left—in a conspiratorial grand scheme to both Islamize and secularize the nation.

Civilizational Fundamentalist Mood among the Masses

In addition to solidarity at the elite level, the Islam(ization) threat discourse (and its principal agents) enjoyed significant support at the mass-level. The aforementioned crises among all three categories of conservatives—neo, social, and paleo—were reflected was an identity structure whose inside—like that of white nationalism in Europe—was defined primarily by its outside, which post-9/11 was increasingly the Islamic other.

As anti-Islam discourse expanded and as people read and saw more anti-Islam productions, favorable impressions of Islam among the U.S. populace sank from 50 percent just after 9/11 to 20 percent by the mid-point of the decade (Hoar 2006).[56] And, by the tenth anniversary of 9/11, nearly 6 in 10 white evangelical Protestants—the base of the conservative movement—believed that even the more basic "values of Islam" were "at odds with American values" (PRRI 2011).

This anti-Islam mood in the U.S. was still less prevalent and extreme than it was in Canada and in Europe during this juncture. In Canada, a national poll revealed that a "majority" saw an "irreconcilable" rift between (mainstream) Islam and the West (Macleans 2011).

Similarly, across the Atlantic, a May 2006 Allensbach study commissioned by the Frankfurter Allgemeine Zeitung newspaper revealed that 60 percent of Germans were "increasingly of the opinion that a lasting, peaceful coexistence with the Islamic world will not be possible" (Deutsche-Welle 2006). By 2008, Gallup's Dalia Mogahed and Ahmed Younis reported that "Clear majorities in all European countries" expressed "a perceived 'Islamic threat' to their cultural identities, driven in part by rising immigration from predominantly Muslim regions" (World Economic Forum 2008, 25).

By the end of the decade, fewer than 10 percent of Germans subscribed to the "religion of peace" storyline of Islam apologists (Kern 2011).[57] Similarly, in Britain, researchers in January 2010 found that "only a quarter of native Britons remained optimistic about the local Muslim population" (Sapsted 2010).[58] And, overall, almost 60 percent of Europeans believed Muslims were "fanatical," and 50 percent believed they were "violent" (Pew Research Center 2011).

This mass-level mood or perception of present danger from Muslim immigration and Islam broadly had by the end of the post-9/11 decade in Europe translated to the

---

[56] 29 percent of Americans told *Washington Post*-ABC News pollsters in April 2009 that *mainstream* Islam—to say nothing of the more extreme segments—advocated violence against non-Muslims (Cordesman, 2009). Similarly, by the end of the decade, 28 percent of Americans told Gallup that *Muslim Americans* are sympathetic to al Qaeda (Newport 2011).

[57] See http://www.uni-muenster.de/imperia/md/content/religion_und_politik/aktuelles/2010/12_2010/studie_wahrnehmung_u nd_akzeptanz_religioeser_vielfalt.pdf.

[58] Similarly, a YouGov poll of June 2010 that found 58 percent of Britons linked Islam with extremism (YouGov 2010).

emergence of a plethora of civilizational fundamentalist groups, amounting to a political movement. According to a study by the British think tank Demos in 2011, many of Europe's youth were animated over the same things as U.S. paleoconservatives—"worried about the erosion of their cultural and national identity" from Muslim immigration, and were "turning to populist movements, who they feel speak to these concerns." In 2010, for example, Marine Le Pen, the president of France's National Front party likened Muslim street prayers in France to the Nazi occupation, sparking widespread condemnation (Al Jazeera 2012). Matthew Goodwin, who spent four years among the farther Right in Britain, explained that "they stressed the need to take urgent and radical action to defend their families and native Britons from extinction and mass conflict" (Goodwin 2011).

In response to these sentiments, political parties with anti-Islam platforms spread to even the traditionally more liberal Netherlands and Scandinavia, and gained parliamentary blocs in eight countries (Guardian 2011). As early as 2007, the nationalist Danish People's Party had won 14 percent of the vote. In an interview, the party's leader Pia Kjærsgaard said that "the most important thing for the Danish People's Party is to maintain the Danish identity…" (Alexandru about Denmark 2007). That year, the nationalist Swiss People's Party (SVP) won 29 percent of the vote. Later, in 2012, far-right Marine Le Pen of France's Nationalist Front party won 20 percent of the presidential vote, and in Greece, the neo-Nazi Golden Dawn (Chrysi Avgi)) won almost seven per cent of the vote.

And, political movement in Europe translated to political action. Beginning with the French "headscarf" ban in 2004, the post-9/11 decade witnessed a wave of legislation that restricted visibility of Islamic symbols, including the 2009 referendum in Switzerland that banned the building of minarets. This rising resistance to Islam(ization) in Europe was noted by Daniel Pipes in the April 15, 2008 article "Europe or Eurabia?" published by *The Australian*. Pipes expressed pleasure with the progress of the Europe's emerging resistance to Islamization, which advocated "national values" against the dominant approach of multiculturalism. In a related article, Pipes went on to cite polls of the readership of six leading newspapers in France, Italy, Germany and Spain that week that were in favor of similar anti-Islamization legislation by wide majorities, ranging from 73 percent on the low side among France's *Le Figaro* readers, to 93 percent in Spain's *20 Minutos* readers (Pipes 2009, December 9).

Perhaps riding this wave of resistance, on July 20, 2011, U.S. House Resolution 306 passed, demanding restitution for the "Ottoman Empire's oppression and intentional destruction of much of its ancient Christian populations, including over 2,000,000 Armenians, Greeks, Assyrians, Pontians, and Syrics" (Smith 2011). Taking advantage of this solidarity, the French Senate followed suit and on January 23, 2012 *criminalized* any public denial of the Ottoman Empire's genocide of Armenians.

This mood of civilizational fundamentalism was also marked by a series of Malthusian jeremiads, beginning with former GOP Presidential candidate Pat Buchanan's (2001) bestseller *The Death of the West: How Dying Populations and Immigrant Invasions Imperil Our Country and Civilization*. Buchanan specifically warned that demographics is destiny, as radically secular, cultural Marxist progressives are not having enough children to replace themselves, while Europe's Muslims are. Following Buchanan, there was a procession of popular works by other Western civilizational fundamentalists in Europe, such as: Oriana Fallaci's (2002) *The Rage and the Pride*; Bat Ye'or's (2005) *Eurabia: The Euro-Arab Axis*; Bruce Bawer's (2006), *While Europe Slept: How Radical Islam is Destroying the West from Within*; Melanie Philips's (2006) *Londonistan*; Mark Steyn's (2008) *America Alone: The End of the World as We Know It*; Walter Laqueur's (2009) *The Last Days of Europe: Epitaph for an Old Continent*; Filip Dewinter's (2009) *Inch'Allah?: The Islamization of Europe*; Steyn's (2009) *Lights Out: Islam, Free Speech, and the Twilight of the West*; and Steyn's (2011) *After America: Get Ready for Armageddon*. And, in his 2006 *America Alone: The End of the World as We Know It*, the Canadian conservative Steyn earned *New York Times* bestseller status by taking advantage of this conservative mood of "civilizational exhaustion" from the combined effects of multiculturalism and progressivism—themes sure to resonate with U.S. paleo and social conservatives.

Other principal Islam(ization) threat discourse agents similarly took advantage of this civilizational fundamentalist mood. In a 2010 brief sponsored by Daniel Pipes's Middle East Forum, titled "How Islamists Turned the World Upside Down," Melanie Phillips— the author of her 2006 bestseller jeremiad, *Londonistan*—promoted her newest book on the crisis, *The World Turned Upside Down: The Global Battle over God, Truth and Power*. The brief reliably moved passed the newest enemy of Islam(ism) to target the long-time conservative domestic enemy, euphemized as "Western intelligentsia" and "secular ideologies."

This mass-level mood of civilizational fundamentalism would not stop at the end of the post-9/11 decade. It would lead to a radical shift to the right, and the rise of extreme white nationalism, symbolized by figures like Hungarian prime minister Viktor Orban, Brazilian president Jair Bolsonaro, head of the Polish Law and Justice party Jaroslaw Kaczynski, Italian interior minister Matteo Salvini, and U.S. president Donald Trump. The more radical civilizational fundamentalists within another half-decade would cause three times as many deaths as militant Islamist terrorism.

3. Political Framing: U.S. Cultural Building Blocks Manipulated for Security Politics

Every political project, or every project of identity politics—as the earlier quote from Castells articulates—uses "building materials" from history and culture so that the resulting discourse makes sense and appeals to those the project is trying to mobilize.

All knowledge is represented by these "culturally shared mental constructs," which "function automatically, outside of conscious awareness" (Brubaker, et al. 2004, 41). Ideologies work in this unconscious fashion. As Volosinov stressed in his *Marxism and the Philosophy of Language*, ideologies encompass the ways of thinking, speaking, and behaving which make the ways of that society seem "natural" or unquestioned to its members (Eagleton 1991)

This notion that cultural or ideological structures are creatively put into play by social actors—whether unconsciously as common sense, or strategically or deliberately to achieve certain interests—was first popularized by Swidler's (1986) phrases, "culture in action" and "cultural toolkit." Borrowing from David Snow and various colleagues' work on the issue, social movement theorists McAdam, McCarthy, and Zald (1996) acknowledged this function of "cultural framing" as "… conscious strategic efforts by groups of people to fashion shared understandings of the world and of themselves that legitimate and motivate collective action." Entman (1993, 52), similarly described culture as "the stock of commonly invoked frames."

To engage in a cultural practice so fundamental as a public discourse, means—in Sewell's (2005, 164) terms—"to utilize existing cultural symbols to accomplish some end." Agency, to put it Sewell's other terms, is the actor's capacity to reinterpret and mobilize an array of resources in terms of cultural schemas other than those that initially constituted the array (Sewell 2005, 143).

We will now examine the U.S. cultural political schemata, threat myths, and other ideational resources that were mobilized in the farther right's strategy of security politics. From the foregoing preliminary analysis of several of this security discourse's principal agents, we can map their semiotic work's linkage to (or usage of) more basic cultural resources—the frame categories, mental schemas, and ideologies resident in the U.S. and conservative subculture.

The use and influence of cultural antecedents such as ideologies or elemental security discourses in security writing is well established. Dalby (1988, 415), for example, documented how the U.S. Cold War Committee on the Present Danger drew on a four "security discourses," especially geopolitics, but also realism, Sovietology, and nuclear strategy "to ideologically construct the Soviet Union as a dangerous 'Other.'"

And from this vantage point of their cultural tool kit, we can ascertain this post-9/11 discourse's basic nature or motivation—the end that they were trying to achieve (Entman 1993, 52; Swidler 1986).

According to the prevailing consensus in the literature, if we were to examine the basic linguistic frames of this more tendentious post-9/11 popular U.S. conservative discourse about the threat of Islam, then we would find cultural building materials of racism, xenophobia, and Holy Land and civilizational clash ideologies. That consensus is rooted in the literature's many signifiers for this discourse—signifiers such as the "new McCarthyism" (Fekete 2009, Beinin 2004), the "new anti-Semitism" (Fotopoulos 2007), and "new face of discrimination" (Allen 2005), and so on. In each these cases, the adjective "new" is joined to something quite old and familiar, and implies that this new discourse is in essence the same old racism and xenophobia that has been reconstructed in a new skin. As Nobel laureate John Coetzee (1980) aptly put it regarding U.S. propensity for xenophobia, "In every generation, without fail, there is an episode of hysteria about the barbarians."

Again, if the political project is also racist or xenophobic in nature, then an excavation to that discourse's cultural foundations would find familiar related and transposable cognitive frames or schemas, and other mental structures, such as ideologies, scripts and so on.

U.S. culture broadly—like so many if not all others—is marked by symbolic binary codes—ultimately political—that specify good and evil (Alexander and Smith 1993). In terms of the Schmittian political binary, this translates to the good self, or friend on the one hand, and the evil other, or enemy on the other.

And, within this latter subcategory of the evil other, or enemy, there are two more distinctive schemata subcategories of enemies outside and inside, institutionalized as the familiar phrase, "enemies foreign and domestic," in the U.S. Oath of Office. And, here again, U.S. culture is congruent with that of others. Fundamentalist Muslims, for instance, distinguish between the "far enemy" and "near enemy"—terms that are so pervasive as to constitute common knowledge. And, as we've seen thus far, and as will be more persuasively demonstrated in the following three chapters which analyze this discourse's principal agents, it was these basic political binaries of the evil other—both enemies foreign and domestic—and the good self, that continually emerged and became a characterizing schema. And, as we saw and will see more clearly, these discourse agents manipulated these cultural security resources to achieve primarily domestic political interests.

Enemies Foreign: The East and Islam as "the West's" Dangerous Other

As noted in the introduction, the post-9/11 counternarrative regarding Islam and ensuing Islamization conspiracy was never *pure* description; it did not sufficiently correspond with objective, grounded reality in the broader swath of the world's Islams. The reason is quite simple: *It did not have to.* There were basic schemas within U.S. culture that pre-identified both the East and Islam as other and danger, and both of these schemas could be transposed onto the contemporary events to emphasize Islam's danger. In other words, since these early statements about Islam aligned with the more fundamental political schema within U.S. culture, they were—for many—believable *a priori*—that is, without getting off of the couch, so to speak, to check it out.

Recall how the post-9/11 threat frame so readily shifted from al-Qaeda in particular to Islam broadly—in stark opposition to the more official and academic "Islam is peace" frame and terrorist/Islam distinction. The shift in threat frames from the tiny extremist terrorist group of perhaps 300 members worldwide to the broader religion of 1.2 million Muslims occurred so naturally, as if it were something that U.S. conservatives religious and political elite somehow already knew, but had remained silent about.

There was something deep in the U.S. conservative subcultural and epistemological framework that made this shift so natural.

The East as Other

For many Western conservatives, the East has always symbolized evil. And it was because of this East as threat security frame that Islam could be omitted and replaced with the word East and even Arab. We saw this in Milton Viorst's (2007) book title, *Storm from the East*, which was all about the new threat of Islam. And recall how several conservative figures after 9/11 felt politically safe, supported, and understood when they so readily advanced these civilizationalist threat frames. In another instance, while in his military uniform among his audience at First Baptist Church of Broken Arrow, Oklahoma in June 2002, then Deputy Under Secretary of Defense for Intelligence, and Army Lieutenant General William G. "Jerry" Boykin explicitly opposed his Commander-in-Chief's public diplomacy strategy. Flashing to the audience images taken while commanding the 1993 failed mission in Mogadishu Somalia, Boykin said, "Ladies and gentleman, this is your enemy," implicating the entire town and their religion, Islam. "It is the principalities of darkness," he said, "it is a demonic presence in that city that God revealed to me as the enemy" (Arkin 2003).

Similarly, among the more apocalyptically-minded Christian audiences fixated on Israel, these frames were especially prevalent. At John Hagee's 2007 Christians United for Israel (CUFI) conference, Brigitte Gabriel told her Christian audience (to much applause): "The difference, my friends, between Israel and the Arab world is the difference between civilization and barbarism," adding that "It's the difference between good and evil."

The U.S. "enemies foreign" schema has always had predominantly Eastern orientation. The Oriental's central position in this Western cultural schema hearkens back to the Platonic era, in Aristotle's bifurcations of reality into Greeks within and Orientals outside and to the East (Dossa 1987). Dossa (1987, 343) argued that a key foundation for this practice was basic Western political philosophy dating back to the Classical period of Plato. In discovering their own political philosophy, the ancient Greeks, he contends, discovered "their Orient—an Orient radically opposed, in politics and morals, to their own Occident."

Four centuries later, John of Patmos, in the least certain canonical book of the Bible, the Book of Revelation, had a vision of hordes of invaders from lands to the East descending upon the Holy Land for the great battle of Armageddon. In one verse, for example, we read how "The sixth angel poured out his bowl on the great river Euphrates, and its water was dried up to prepare the way for the kings from the East" (Revelation 16: 12).

Given the Christian heritage of European states and the U.S, this frame is prominent in contemporary extra-biblical apocalyptic and threat literature dating back to the Industrial Revolution, when in 1895 Kaiser Wilhelm II is said to have sketched his famous "Yellow Peril." With the lebensraum tacitly framed as the new Promised Land, the sketch depicted the Archangel Michael in company with angelic-like German citizens with military shields under a heavenly cross, standing their ground as hordes from the Orient approached.

Dostoevsky advanced this frame as the East as other and threat in his supreme achievement in literary history, where he described "the crimes committed by the Turks and Circassians in all parts of Bulgaria." "They do all sorts of things you can't imagine," said one Bulgarian eyewitness, and he went on to give this account of their "bestial cruelty:" "These Turks took pleasure in torturing children, too; cutting the unborn child from the mother's womb, and tossing the babies up in the air and catching them on the points of their bayonets before their mother's eyes. Doing it before the mother's eyes was what gave zest to the amusement" (Dostoevsky 1933, 245).

Similarly, it was this "kings from the East" frame that informed the popular book *The Yellow Peril or Orient vs. Occident* in 1911, by the influential American Church of God leader and British Israelist, Greenberry Rupert. The "yellow peril" threat frame would go on to become culturally-ensconced. On September 11th, 1933, *TIME* lamented, "Again, Yellow Peril." The magazine wrote that "The Yellow Peril has for 30 years been a great circulation-getter for the Hearst papers…," attributing the scare to Hearst's "fertile mind" wherein "the stern duties of a patriot and the hot desires of a journalist are constantly interbreeding."

These frames of enemies foreign and the East-West demarcation of self and other materialized in Kennan's (1946) description of an implacable enemy in racialized terms of naturalized difference, such as "the Russian or the oriental mind." The East-West bifurcation was accentuated after World War II when the collective geopolitical construct "the West" was interpellated with greater vigor to justify the vast expenditure of funds for the reconstruction of Germany (Jackson 2006). In this discursive strategy, Western Civilization (including Germany) was set off as under threat against its civilizational other to the East, represented by the contemporary Soviet threat (Jackson, 2006).

After 9/11, threat discourse from disparate U.S. conservative intellectuals involved a similar grand geopolitical and hegemonic strategy, which can be characterized as civilizational fundamentalism or *civilizationalism*,[59] which sought to suture the "the West"— from Amsterdam to Americus Georgia—as an enduring, stable and homogenous collective identity via its juxtaposition to threats of "Islam" and "multiculturalism," which were the predominant euphemisms for the East and Easterners within (O' Hagan 2004; Cox 2002).

Islam as Other

After 9/11, among a significant segment of U.S. conservatives, the cultural schemas of both "enemies foreign" and the East-as-threat were bridged with Islam. But, although absent in official threat discourse, the frame of Islam-as-threat had deep cultural antecedents.

Western frames of Islam as both other and danger—externalized and securitized— had their origin in the wartime propaganda at the time of the First Crusade (Lyons 2011; Reeves 2000). The menace of Islam continued to figure prominently from medieval era Christian texts through the colonial period (Southern 1962, 22-24). Recall, for instance, Dante's 14th -century epic poem *Inferno*, where Muhammad was depicted in the deep recesses of Hell and sliced from chin to navel with his bowels falling out, as the fitting punishment for someone "who divided society"—an image still common in contemporary art and political cartoons (Moore, 2006). Centuries later, Rupert (1911) had identified "Mohammedans" as the "kings of the East." Even in modern European philosophical texts, such as Hegel's (1924) *Lectures on the Philosophy of Religion* and *The Philosophy of History*, Islam was framed as antithetical to Western, Christian thought and a threat. In his *Lectures* Hegel states that the "religion of Islam is essentially fanatical"—a charge that he repeats in his *History* (Schewel 2011, 11).

---

[59] Cox (2002, 163) described civilizationalism as "a conscious affirmation of belonging to *a* civilization," meaning a particular Civilization, as opposed to civilization.

In his *New York Times* bestseller, *The Politically Incorrect Guide to Islam (and the Crusades)*, Robert Spencer (2005) worked from a wealth of anti-Islamic discourse from various European elite now enshrined in Western history, for example:

Winston Churchill (1899, 249-50) wrote, Far from being moribund, Mohammedanism is a militant and proselytizing faith. It has already spread throughout Central Africa, raising fearless warriors at every step; and were it not that Christianity is sheltered in the strong arms of science, the science against which it had vainly struggled, the civilisation of modern Europe might fall, as fell the civilisation of ancient Rome (Spencer 2005, 92).

These cultural antecedents notwithstanding, the main cognitive structure that rendered credible the post-9/11 discourse on Islam was not the relatively obscure texts and quotes by Europeans during the colonial era that few Americans had read or heard.

First, the post-9/11 caricatures of Islam and Muslim were characteristic of a much more familiar and even home-grown language, reflective of the racialized grammar of representation of blacks in the U.S. prior to the civil rights movement (see Leab's (1976) *From Sambo to Superspade*, or Bogle's (1973) *Toms, coons, Mulattos, Mammies and bucks: an interpretive history of blacks in American films*. It is these features that prompted the substantive literature's characterizations of the discourse as "new face of discrimination" (Allen 2005).

Second, the securitization of Islam was also enhanced by events in more recent history, as the "Arab terrorist" and threat frame that emerged from the attack on Israeli athletes at the 1972 Munich Olympics morphed into the "Islamic terrorists" frame during the 1979 Iranian revolution, when US embassy personnel were taken hostage in Iran for 444 days (Kumar 2012).

Third, and as was the case with Rupert's (1911) *Yellow Peril* over Russia and "the Mohammedans," the cultural antecedents that informed the threat axis shift from al-Qaeda to Islam by key U.S. conservatives after 9/11 were *scriptural*. In the first book of the Christian New Testament, six hundred years before the advent of Islam, Jesus had warned that "false messiahs and false prophets will appear" after him, and that God's elect should not go after them (Matthew 24: 24). The widely-held Christian classification of Muhammad as such a false prophet is enhanced by a story set down two thousand years earlier in Genesis, the first book of the Jewish Pentateuch and Christian Old Testament. There, the angel of the Lord in metaphorical terms described the nature and position of Ishmael, who is held by both the Quran and the Bible to be the father of the nation of the Arabs. This text positions Ishmael as "a wild donkey" whose "hand will be against everyone" and who would "live in hostility" toward his brother Isaac, later renamed as "Israel," who in this context is a metaphor for the nation of Israel (Genesis 16:12; 32: 28). After Jesus, the Apostle Paul positioned Ishmael and Isaac in a metaphorical binary schema of the flesh (our evil, carnal nature) and the spirit, with the former warring against the latter (Galatians 4: 21-30). It was in this Judeo-Christian scriptural context that Republican Congressman Allen West from south Florida felt free to express his conviction that Arabs are naturally "wild" because God cursed Ishmael and his descendants (Tashman 2010).

And, in the last book of the New Testament, there are other antecedents to the "kings of the East" mentioned in Rupert's text regarding the final battle of Armageddon. The "four angels who are bound at the great river Euphrates"— who had been "kept ready for this very hour" were "released to kill a third of mankind" (Revelation 9: 13-15). The obvious contemporary application is that of four countries among those there—Iran, Iraq, Turkey, and Pakistan, perhaps—who would cross the Euphrates on land in route to Jerusalem. Then in Revelation 17 we read how Babylon the Great—whose ancient seat is in modern day Iraq—is "the mother of all prostitutes and of the abominations of the earth," and how this woman "was drunk with the blood of God's holy people, the blood of those who bore testimony to Jesus."

Still other biblical antecedents that inform the ideology of Christian Zionism also undergird post-9/11 U.S. threat discourse regarding Islam. Works such as John Hagee's (2007) bestseller, *In Defense of Israel: The Bible's Mandate for Supporting the Jewish State*, mobilize scripture such as where the Lord said to Abram, "To your offspring I give this land, from the river of Egypt to the great river—the river Euphrates" (Genesis 15: 18). A much larger set of scriptural passages like this informs the widespread affinity for Israel among Christians worldwide and especially Americans. For many U.S. religious conservatives, the only entities blocking the way of Israel's rightful and certain expansion into the fullness of the lands promised it by God are the Philistines who still inhabit those lands, along with their faith, Islam. This sentiment was evident in Christian Zionist and Armageddon hawk Joel Rosenberg's (2006) bestselling novel, *The Ezekiel Option*, by the Christian publisher Tyndale House. In this plot, the head of the Mossad, Dr. Mordechai, sees an emerging axis of Russia, Iran Syria, Lebanon, Turkey, Sudan and Saudi Arabia as forming against Israel, but proposes not a military or "Samson Option," but instead "The Ezekiel Option," in which Israel allows God to wage war against its enemies.

With these frames operative in many of the post-9/11 bestsellers—both non-fiction and fiction—we can begin to understand the vast influence of Samuel Huntington's (1996) clash of civilizations thesis, as noted by Bonney (2008). When Huntington (1996, 217) warned that the "fundamental problem for the West is not Islamic fundamentalism. It is Islam, a different civilization," he was merely stating what many—somehow—already knew. Five years later, in 2001, this frame of Islam as threat was more fully ensconced in the American psyche, and ready for mobilization after al-Qaeda's attacks, providing a key element of resistance to the more dominant terrorist/Islam and emerging good Muslim/bad Islamist distinctions (Belt 2009). With their market sensitized to these subcultural resources, some conservative elite could credibly shift the threat axis from al-Qaeda—the newly-emerging small transnational, non-state actor organization armed only with small arms—and could readily call into remembrance the West's eternal civilizational Other to the East, and that they heretofore had ignored to the nation's peril.

Enemies Domestic: Infiltrators and Traitors

As we saw from the security discourse in the first four chapters, the main threat axis in U.S. conservative discourse about Islam shifted from enemies foreign to enemies domestic—to both infiltrators and traitors.

Infiltrators

About the time that the threat from elements of Islam as a foreign enemy outside was assessed to be minor in the grand, strategic sense, the threat axis in U.S. conservative discourse shifted inward: the foreign enemy was now within; it had infiltrated the homeland. Markers of this shift in the threat axis frame emerged in force. In the realm of book titles, there was, for instance, Sperry's (2005) book *Infiltration: How Muslim Spies and Subversives Have Penetrated Washington*, published by world's largest Christian publisher, Thomas Nelson. Then there was Gaubatz and Sperry's (2009) *Muslim Mafia: Inside the Secret Underworld that's Conspiring to Islamize America*, published by evangelical Joseph Farah's conspiratorial *WorldNetDaily*. Among political elite, former-GOP presidential frontrunner Michele Bachmann garnered headlines in at the end of the post-9/11 decade by claiming that key government institutions had been infiltrated by disloyal Muslim-Americans who were agents of the nation's enemies. Bachmann told the American Family Association's Sandy Rios that "there has been deep penetration in the halls of our United States government by the Muslim Brotherhood," and that "it appears that there are individuals who are associated with the Muslim Brotherhood who have positions, very sensitive positions, in our Department of Justice, our Department of Homeland Security, potentially even in the National Intelligence Agency [sic]" (Tashman 2012).

The infiltration schema was also shaping the discourse of some prominent religious figures. In a March 2011 interview with *Newsmax*, Franklin Graham said that President Barack Obama had allowed the Muslim Brotherhood to infiltrate the US government and influence administration decisions. "The Muslim Brotherhood is very strong and active here in our country," Graham told Newsmax. "We have these people advising our military and State Department. We've brought in Muslims to tell us how to make policy toward Muslim countries. He added, "It's like a farmer asking a fox, 'How do I protect my hen house?'" (Gonsalves and Walter 2011). Similarly, on July 4, 2011, in an interview with the increasingly right security pundit Frank Gaffney, the aforementioned former Deputy Under Secretary of Defense for Intelligence, Army general and popular Christian speaker Jerry Boykin implicated as an agent of a Muslim Brotherhood plot "to penetrate our government" the young Muslim woman, Huma Abedin— a longtime logistics (not policy) aide to the Obama administration's Secretary of State, and highly-likely future presidential candidate, Hillary Rodham Clinton (Tashman 2011).

Conservative media institutions also were eager to advance the infiltration frame. In a series of articles in 2008, *Washington Times* reporter Bill Gertz hounded Muslim-American Hesham Islam—a former naval officer and then senior advisor to the Secretary of the Navy—implicating him as an agent of the enemy. Gertz alleged that Hesham had persuaded Pentagon officials to not renew the contract for J2 intelligence analyst, Stephen Coughlin. At the time, Coughlin's unclassified Power Point brief—based on his 2006

Master's unclassified thesis from National Intelligence University (then Joint Military Intelligence College)—was enjoying far-reaching access at the Pentagon and defense strategy offices broadly. Coughlin's brief/thesis framed "true" Islam within the jihadist interpretation, in opposition to the Commander-in-Chief's "Islam is peace" frame, thereby tacitly framing Muslim-Americans who had any past or present association with the predominant Muslim-American civic associations as infiltrating agents of the Muslim Brotherhood.[60]

The frame of infiltration was advanced even among some active and former military officer faculty at government institutions of higher learning within the defense and interagency arena. At National Defense University's Joint Forces Staff College in Norfolk Virginia, for example, the curriculum text and outside speaker presentations for a course on Islam made nation-wide headlines when it was learned that it framed the American government bureaucracies, the White House, and even Capitol Hill as co-opted by subversive Muslim elements (Rushing 2012).

Traitors

As we saw in the discourse of many U.S. conservative elite, this pervasive post-9/11 frame of the infiltrating foreign enemy was almost always tethered that of the traitor. The traitor, or disloyal citizen, is some trusted part of the self, who, from their position on the inside, functions as an accomplice by unlocking the gate, aiding and abetting. In the case of the purported Islamization of America, the infiltration of foreign religious competitors—euphemized variously as a "stealth jihad"—was being made possible by the farther Right's duty traitors—the more radical Left.

Judging by how prevalent this practice became in their discourse, this practice of linking the conservative movement's newest foreign enemy with its traditional domestic enemy was deemed to have political utility. Recall how Republican candidates for president, Michele Bachmann and Newt Gingrich had repeatedly asserted that the opposing political party had allied with America's ideological foe to destroy the nation. And recall how the texts that housed this latest episode of paranoia did not stop with disloyal Muslim-Americans, but always bridged that infiltrator frame by linking enemies foreign and domestic. We saw this in titles such as David Horowitz's (2006) *Unholy Alliance: Radical Islam and the American Left,* along with Andrew McCarthy's *The Grand Jihad: How Islam and the Left Sabotage America,* and his *How Obama Embraces Islam's Sharia Agenda.*

Known as "frame bridging political movement theory (Benford and Snow 2000, 624), this practice of linking one's more progressive domestic political rivals to foreign enemies is a subculturally-ensconced strategy of action among the farther right everywhere. Fundamentalist Islamic movements, for example, link the local regime judged to be insufficiently Islamic—"the near enemy"—with secular Western states who are thought to be surreptitiously Westernizing and destroying their culture—"the far enemy"—in the

---

[60] Based on the author's professional meetings with Mr. Coughlin at the time, and the unclassified version of his thesis he voluntarily gave me.

effort to delegitimize the former (Gerges 2005). In the eyes of Iran's clerics, says Qom-trained Shiite theologian Mehdi Khalaji, the enemy's armies are innumerable and include everyone who adheres to modern liberal values and cultural institutions. In the view of Ayatollah Ali Khamenei, he explains, "Western cultural colonizers are trying to destroy the cultural 'authenticity' of Muslims and deprive it of its 'originality' and there are colonized minds within Muslim community who are knowingly or unknowingly the West's agents…such as intellectuals, scholars, artists and writers…" (Khalaji 2012).

In nearly all of the recurring episodes of hysteria about the far enemy among the more rightist conservatives, there are corresponding frames of that foreign enemy having infiltrated with the aid of a domestic one. This is exacerbated in the more heterogeneous and pluralistic Western societies, where the question of who is part of self and who is not engenders perennial identity insecurity. This insecurity of self—in turn—generates antagonistic identity politics to secure self-identity through the ideological demarcation of those inside—often signified as "the patriots"—and those outside—"the traitors," "infiltrators," the "fifth column," and so on. This may explain why many American conservatives are said to be not so much nationalistic as they are patriotic (Lievan 2004).

For the patriot subject position to figure so prominently in U.S. conservative subculture, its opposite the traitor must be prominently juxtaposed—co-constituting each other in what Foucault (2003 [1975], 109) termed as a "schematic dichotomy" of patriot/traitor, which was also a "binary schema" in the sense that it divides society in two. Just as there can be no heroes without villains—and no great heroes without great villains—the frame of the patriot has no meaning apart from that of the traitor, or the enemy within; the presence of one evokes the other; the one has no meaning and cannot exist apart from the other (Hall 1997, 236; Derrida, 1978, 1981).

For this reason, perhaps, it should have come as no surprise that when the threat frame of Islam as a foreign enemy was losing its political utility, some influential conservative intellectuals and elite shifted the threat axis once again to religio-political enemies that dwelled within the nation's borders—both the infiltrators, or the tiny half-immigrant, half-black minority group of Muslim-Americans, and the traitors, or the more hegemonic domestic political rivals, the Left. For Bourdieu (1991, 130, 167), this would have come as no surprise; this construction of the self and other through the imposition of a binary or hierarchical schema was inherently interested, and what he called the "political labor of representation," which advances a group's ideology and interests.

Every (sub)society has its folk devils—groups or archetypes that occupy this position, and who are useful as boundary markers, or visible reminders of what we should not be. As Cohen (1972, 2) in his work on Britain's moral panics notes, "the identities of such social types are public property;" they are culturally fixed subject positions.

This subject position of the traitor, or enemy within, can be traced to the beginning of Western Civilization, beginning most famously with Nero's persecution of the Church in the first century, and Pliny's inquisition of the Christians in the early second century Roman Empire. After the Christianization of that empire by Constantine, the enemy within mentality turned to heretics. In 390, Rome's Theodosian Code established a state religion, thereby implicating anyone who did not submit to it as "demented and insane" with "depraved desires and beliefs." By 1163, Englishmen William of Newburgh wrote that heretics "as the prophet says," seem to have "multiplied beyond number," and characterized them in so many medical tropes, such as "pest," "cancer," "leper," and "germ" (Bosmajian 1999, 20-21). The twelfth and thirteenth century witnessed more Nero-like persecution of the disloyal elements within in Pope Innocent III and Gregory IV's inquisitions.

In U.S. history in particular, the frame of the foreign enemy within—the traitorous elements, impurities or infectious elements on the inside that were vectors of outside diseases—what Hofstadter (1964) pejoratively called the "paranoid style"—has been pervasive and has permeated all genre of discourse.

In the American Revolution, the link was manifest in the form of coercive loyalty oaths, which served to demarcate the friend-enemy boundary—those inside who sided with the Revolution from those outside who were "secret enemies" or "traitor[s] in thought, but not in deed," in Jefferson's words (Levy 1963, 30; Bosmajian 1999, 50). By 1778, each of the colonial states had a loyalty test that it imposed upon all citizens, with New York law having empowered the Commissioners for Detecting and Defeating Conspiracies to tender such an oath (Bosmajian 1990, 50).

In language identical to that of today's Islamization conspiracy proponents, Scottish physicist Dr. John Robison in 1797 wrote *Proofs of a Conspiracy against all the Religions and Governments of Europe, carried on in the Secret Meetings of the Free Masons, Illuminati, and Reading Societies* (Edinburgh), and thus began an influential scare in Europe. He framed the Masons on continental Europe as formed "for the express purpose of rooting out all religious establishments, and overturning all the existing governments of Europe" (Robison 1798, 12).[61] On the morning of May 9, 1798, on the day of that John Adams had proclaimed for "solemn humiliation, fasting, and prayer," Connecticut-born Reverend Jedidiah Morse—at both the New North Church in Boston and the other from his home pulpit in Charlestown—announced that the secret European society which was believed to have caused the French Revolution, the Illuminati, had infiltrated the U.S. and was now actively working to overthrow the nation's civil and religious institutions (Stauffer 1918, 10-11). Morse, who had just read Robison's (1797) *Proofs of a Conspiracy*, which had been reprinted in the U.S. in 1798, was armed with all he needed. "As a faithful watchmen," he said, "I would give you warning of your present danger." The context, according to Stauffer (1918), was the rapid disintegration of puritanism after the Revolution, and ominous discontent with the standing order.

Lyman Beecher's (1835) "Plea for the West" claimed that "Protestantism was engaged in a life-or-death struggle with Catholicism" (1835, 47). Beecher, a Presbyterian minister from New Haven, fancied that "A corps of men acting systematically and perseveringly for their own ends," may "inflame and divide the nation…and throw down our free institutions" (Beecher 1835, 63). The Catholicization narrative began to take root that

---

[61] Can be read electronically at https://archive.org/details/proofsofconspira00r

same year, 1835, when Samuel F.B. Morse—the inventor of the telegraph—wrote *Foreign Conspiracy Against the Liberties of the United States: The Numbers of Brutus*, attempting to prove that a plot by the Catholics was afoot. Austria is "now acting in this country" said Morse; "She has devised a grand scheme. … She has her Jesuit missionaries traveling through the land.…" He added "This society having ostensibly a religious object, has been for nearly four years at work in the United States, without attracting, out of the religious world, much attention to its operations" (Morse 1835, 17-18). Twenty years later, the Catholicization threat-narrative was still dominant; the *Texas State Times*, on September 15, 1855 wrote that:

> It is a notorious fact that the Monarchs of Europe and the Pope of Rome are at this very moment plotting our destruction and threatening the extinction of our political, civil, and religious institutions. We have the best reasons for believing that corruption has found its way into our Executive Chamber, and that our Executive head is tainted with the infectious venom of Catholicism… (Hofstadter 1964, 78).

In the nineteenth century, the U.S. experienced still more conspiracies about resistance elements inside linked to the nation's foreign enemies. The emergence of trade unions in the nineteenth century were similarly framed in terms of the enemy within linked to foreign elements. Outlawing a tailor's union in 1830, the judge wrote of them "they are of foreign origin and I am led to believe mainly upheld by foreigners" (Zinn 1980, 218, 235).

After World War I, the conspiracies linking domestic traitors with foreign enemies resumed. The Bolshevik Revolution in 1917 gave new life to this conspiracy frame, and underscored the primacy that the U.S. gave to enemies domestic. The threat writing at the time of this "First Red Scare"—as it became known—revealed that "most Americans were more concerned with Bolshevism at home than Bolshevism abroad" (Leffler 1994, 14-15). The Bolsheviks—like all (inflated) security threats—turned out to be politically useful, as politicians on both sides discovered this "new rhetorical resource" and framed their domestic opponents as closet sympathizers with this foreign ideological other (Jackson 2006, 57). Moves of self-purification followed, such as the Palmer raids of 1919 which deported suspected communist sympathizers, and the institutionalization of the "House Un-American Activities Committee" during the Interwar period (Kovel 1994, 17-21; Leffler 1994, 15-16).

Primed in this way, the attacks on Pearl Harbor set off a second and well-known episode of hysteria about the enemy within. On the mere suspicion of mass loyalty of Japanese-Americans to the Japanese emperor, President Roosevelt signed an executive order in February 1942 ordering to concentration camps in the interior of the United States 127,000 Americans of known Japanese ancestry—two-thirds of whom were born in the U.S., most of whom had never been to Japan to visit relatives, and many of whom were World War I veterans (Library of Congress 2014).

Notwithstanding these historical resources, the dual infiltration-traitor frame that pervades post-9/11 discourse had its clearest antecedents in the Second Red Scare, between the mid-1940s to the mid-1960s. By 1947, the House Committee on Un-American Activities, led by the newly-elected representative Richard M. Nixon, was re-enacting this age-old fundamentalist mentality to root out the enemy, the godless, the heretic within.

American students of the Jehovah's Witnesses faith who could not pledge allegiance to the flag were deemed treacherous and threatened with incarceration (Bosmajian 1999, 4). And, when women fought for the retention of day-care programs after the war, the *New York World Telegram* in 1947 charged that "the entire program of child care was conceived by leftists operating out of communist work cells" (Chafe 1991, 165).

That same year, the Sovietization of America frame emerged at the more popular level in the comic-book classic, *Is This Tomorrow: America Under Communism.* Published by the Catechetical Guild Educational Society under the leadership of Father Louis Gales, it told the over-the-top story of a Red sleeper cell that takes over America through agents in the media, Congress, and public schools. It begins, saying:

> Today, there are approximately 85,000 official members of the Communist Party in the United States. There are hundreds of additional members whose names are not carried on the Party roles because acting as disciplined fifth columnists of the Kremlin, they have wormed their way into key positions in government offices, and other positions of public trust.

> Communists themselves claim that for every official Party member, there are ten others ready, willing and able to do the Party's bidding.

> These people are working day and night—laying the groundwork to overthrow YOUR GOVERNMENT!

The next year, in 1948, this deep subcultural threat frame emerged even at the official level in U.S. strategic document, NSC-17. Appropriately titled "The Internal Security of the United States," this national security strategy warned of the unofficial members of the Communist conspiracy: the "convinced communist," who hid membership; the "fellow traveler" who was not a member; the "sympathizer" who was not in total agreement but entertained "friendly feelings"; the "opportunist" who furthered his own interest through the party; the "confused liberal" who believed cooperation was possible; and, finally, other "well-meaning, socially minded, charitable people" who were deceived by Communist slogans or fronts (Peck 2006, 264).

It was in this paranoid milieu that the era's more emblematic framer of "enemies domestic" emerged. Wisconsin Senator "Joe" McCarthy had advanced the Red Scare by framing the nation's foreign ideological enemy as infiltrating the homeland at the highest levels of government, with the aid of traitorous domestic rivals. The aforementioned charge by former GOP presidential frontrunner Michele Bachmann that agents of the Muslim Brotherhood had infiltrated key government and intelligence positions unwittingly had mobilized the classic frames and from the patriot subject position of Senator Joe McCarthy who in February 1950 told the Senate that he had a list of 57 "card-carrying Communists" (members of the Communist Party of the United States of America, CPUSA), yet were working in the State Department (Reeves 1997, 224).

Speaking in the Senate on June 14, 1951, McCarthy incredulously implicated U.S. Secretary of State George Marshall as the leader of "a great conspiracy" involving the alliance of the nation's foreign and domestic enemies. "How can we account for our present situation," he began his speech, "unless we believe that men high in this government are concerting to deliver us to disaster?" (Congress 1951). He added:

> It is the great crime of the Truman administration that it has refused to undertake the job of ferreting the enemy from its ranks. I once puzzled over that refusal. The President, I said, is a loyal American; why does he not lead in this enterprise? I think that I know why he does not. The President is not master in his own house. Those who are master there not only have a desire to protect the sappers and miners - they could not do otherwise. They themselves are not free. They belong to a larger conspiracy, the world-wide web of which has been spun from Moscow.

As the progenitor of the anti-elitism strategy of action that would soon come to characterize the GOP, McCarthy went on to frame "the traitorous actions" of the nation's elite, "born with silver spoons in their mouths," who have lived in "the finest homes" and had "the finest college educations."

And as an antecedent to the aforementioned post-9/11 conspiracies about Islamist-Leftists alliance infiltrating key government agencies, McCarthy He framed as "elitists" the federal workers at the U.S. Department of State and linked that frame to that of the traitor, saying "I have here in my hand a list of 205" who are "members of the Communist Party and who are nevertheless all still working and shaping policy in the State Department" (Lately 1973, 94).

The McCarthyesque frame of high-level traitors—the foreign enemy within *and in control*—was propagated well into the 1960s by political advocacy groups in civil society. The influential John Birch Society, established in 1958, was notorious in this regard. Its founder, Robert Welch—implicated even President Eisenhower of being a Communist agent—an enemy-infiltration frame repeatedly reconstructed by Daniel Pipes with regard to President Obama. Of Eisenhower, Welch wrote in a widely publicized piece that began the society's demise, "it is difficult to avoid raising the question of deliberate treason" (Berlet and Lyons 2000, 179). In 1964, the society had broadened its infiltration frame, imagining that the United Nations (an initiative of President Franklin D. Roosevelt) was—in the words of that organization's John Rousselot—"an instrument of the Soviet Communist conspiracy" (San Francisco Chronicle 1964, July 31). The John Birch Society has since extended its conspiratorial and infiltration frames, and is currently active throughout the U.S., part of the broader anti-government "Patriot" movement, according to the Southern Poverty Law Center (SPLC 2012).

The frame of enemies within next became politically useful during the civil rights era. A classic case was when the House Un-American Activities Committee met in October 1967 to determine the extent and manner to which various troubles the country was experiencing—race riots, lootings, arsons, and so on—had been "planned, instigated, incited, or supported by Communist and other subversive organizations and individuals" (Congress, 1967). Yet, these hearings were dubiously led by white southern segregationists like Virginia's Representative William Tuck, who supported the "massive resistance" policy introduced by Virginia Senator Harry Byrd to resist the Supreme Court's 1954 Brown vs.

Board of Education ruling, which mandated public school desegregation (Woods 2004, 227-228).

After 9/11, an almost identical set of hearings on the threat of radicalization among Muslim-Americans was led in the first half of 2011 by Republican New York Representative Peter King, who chaired House Homeland Security Committee. The genuine intent to determine the facts was dubious, given that much of the Republican members' focus was on scoring political points against the Democrats.

For example, during King's second hearing on Muslim radicalization in U.S. prisons on 15 June 2011, Republican representatives Dan Lungren and Jeff Duncan found the platform useful to point out how "the political correctness" among Democrats in the room was "astounding," and to complain that the mere discussion about the threat of radical Islam appeared to be "off limits" for Democrats (Piraneo 2011).

After such a reliable history of this practice, we might have predicted the post-9/11 emergence of this bridged threat frame that linked the newest foreign enemy to the old domestic one. And, predictably, once the Green Scare is largely discredited and is no longer mentioned by conservative political and religious elite, then a still newer variant of the old threat frame will emerge. In early stages of the post-Great Recession era, the more popular and rightist element in the U.S was already engaging in characteristic hyperbole by remobilizing the "Sovietization of America" frame in the domestic political struggles from gun control to the Affordable Care Act.

The Patriot Self in Decline: Disciplining the Vulnerabilities

Recall from the conceptual framework how all identity is constituted in relation to difference, and—therefore—how a collective's security discourse about its others also and necessarily is an act of self-identification, (re)constituting itself. In Campbell's (1998, 9) words, identity is performatively constituted "through the inscription of boundaries that serve to demarcate an 'inside' from an 'outside,' a 'self' from an 'other,' a 'domestic' from a foreign." In still other words, threat discourses not only politically identify the collective's outside—those events, structures and agencies that are not us, and that through this process of externalization and securitization constitute danger—they identify the We, the self, the inside, the realm of security. It is in this context that *in*security—or identity insecurity—is the necessary condition and means of a secure identity.

In the case at hand, post-9/11 threat discourse that was ostensibly about America's newest dangerous other was shot-through with frames of self and practices of self. Much more than merely a practice that identified the movement's others—its enemies foreign and domestic, religious and political, Islam and the Left—it was also what Foucault (1982, 208) described as a "dividing practice" that not only separated these others from the self, but also *separated the healthy and diseased tissue* within the body politic. This latter dividing practice functioned as a form of self-identification by way of self-discipline.

Historically, this self-identifying and self-disciplinary feature of identity or cultural politics has permeated U.S. threat or security discourse. Texts identifying foreign and domestic *threats outside* of the movement were replete with identification of *vulnerabilities inside*. The concept of security in these texts, therefore—rather than entailing eradicating dangers outside the movement—involved reducing insecurity inside. It was in this vein that Buzan (1991, 112) had noted that "Insecurity reflects a combination of threats and vulnerabilities, and the two cannot meaningfully be separated."

And, this is what we find; post-9/11 conservative threat discourse warned of a nation and broader civilization in dissolution or decay, and especially in terms of loss of cultural identity (Bowman 1994, 144). Civilizational fundamentalists on both sides of the Atlantic bridged the frame of Islam as evil with the frame of the Western self in decline, or the crisis of traditional identity.

Such post-9/11 declinism was characterized in a dual threat frame of the progressive culture (the Left) and its destructive policy of multiculturalism, which was responsible for the reverse colonization of the Western heartland and Holy Land (by Islam). In this dual-threat frame, the battle is established along both religious and political, and foreign and domestic lines, against the "Islamo-Leftist axis."

One of the first to give credence to this dual threat frame of the "Islamo-Leftist" axis was Samuel Huntington (2004, 171), who broadened this threat conception of Islam as the fundamental problem for the West to include the ideology of multiculturalism (2004, 171). In his *Who Are We? The Challenges to America's National Identity*, Huntington (2004) asserted that the advance of both progressive ideology and its offspring multiculturalism had meant that few people in the West—whether more progressive natives or immigrants—identified with Western Civilization, and few of America's more progressive cultural and business elites still identified with America's once dominant Anglo-Protestant culture (see also, Kurth 2009).

Similarly, in 2006, a cartoon by *Studi Cattolici*—an Italian magazine with links to the conservative Roman Catholic group, Opus Dei—featured a photo of Dante's Muhammad. "Isn't that man there, split in two from head to navel, Mohammed?" Dante asks Virgil in the cartoon's caption. "Yes and he is cut in two because he has divided society," Virgil replies, adding that. "While that woman there, with the burning coals, represents the politics of Italy towards Islam." In this frame of self-decline, Cesare Cavalleri, the editor of the magazine, said "This is not a cartoon against Mohammed. It is a cartoon which addresses the loss of the West's identity" (Moore 2006).

Attending these prominent frames of civilizational declinism at the hands of these religio-political others, were frames of self-exceptionalism. Together, the two bridged frames interpellated the reader into a dual strategy of self-purification and patriotic action to save the good self from certain death by the dual threats of enemies foreign and domestic. Recall Canadian-born conservative columnist Mark Steyn's (2008) *America Alone: The end of the world as we know it*—a *New York Times* bestseller, which similarly portrayed a leftist-weakened heartland of Western Civilization overrun by another civilization, as captured in the book's cover introduction:

> Someday soon you might wake up to the call to prayer from a muezzin. Europeans already are. And the liberals will still tell you that "diversity is our strength"—while

Talibanic enforcers cruse Greenwich Village burning books and barber shops, the Supreme Court decides sharia law doesn't violate the "separation of church and state," and the Hollywood Left decides to give up on gay rights in favor of the much safer charms of [Islamic] polygamy.

In themes of self-discipline in the face of self-decline, Steyn then notes that the future, belongs to the fecund and the confident. The Islamists, he says, are both, while the West is looking ever more like the ruins of a civilization. In still clearer self-disciplinary moves, Steyn adds, "But America can survive, prosper, and defend its freedom only if it continues to believe in itself, in the sturdier virtues of self-reliance (not government), in the centrality of family, and in the conviction that our country really is the world's last best hope."

The farther right's self-disciplinary themes figured prominently in Catholic intellectual Roger Scruton's (2009) "Islam and the West: Lines of Demarcation," published in the Jewish quarterly, *Azure*. The article quickly made its way onto Brigitte Gabriel's *ACT! for America's* education page, where it gained wider, Evangelical readership. Despite the title's implied threat axis of the "Christian West's" newest chief foreign enemy, the article's obvious purpose was to identity the West's internal vulnerabilities, such as the "enormous cultural shift" since the Vietnam War, by which the author need not mention to his audience the twin ideological culprits of progressivism and multiculturalism. In a classic jeremiad style self-discipline, this conservative Catholic thought-leader laments how that (more progressive) citizens of Western states "have lost their appetite for foreign wars" and "lost confidence in their way of life," and how self-criticism by his rivals on the Left, such as Edward Said and Noam Chomsky, "alerts your enemy to the possibility of destroying you." Scruton then adds, "We should therefore be prepared to affirm what we have, and to express our determination to hold on to it."

Another work typical of this self-disciplinary strategy of action was the article "Fearing for Freedom in a Post-Christian Europe," which appeared in Daniel Pipes's *Islamist Watch* on January 31, 2010. The project's director David Rusin—a U.S. professor of astrophysics and cosmology—chastised European Christian leaders for failing to defend "their faith and the civilization built around it." Since self-discipline must always proceed in juxtaposition to the threatening outside—enemies foreign and domestic—Rusin cited retiring Czech Cardinal Miloslav Vlk, who warned of the "fall of Europe" as "the spiritual vacuum" created by Europe's radical secularization was being filled by Islam.

A similar article sponsored by Pipes's *Islamist Watch* that typifies this feature of self-discipline in post-9/11 threat discourse was Kathy Shaidle's article, "Toronto's Love of Diversity Is Tested by Islamists." Published by the farther Right e-daily *Pajamas Media* (now *PJ Media*) on June 9, 2010, this Canadian blogger—who wrote the blog *Relapsed Catholic*—similarly focused not on Islamists, as the title suggests, but on the progressive elite and culture. For this task, Shaidle approvingly cited dissident intellectual Salim Mansur:

> The elite in this country has abandoned its own history out of any number of reasons — too tired to procreate, too despondent about the future, too concerned about the immediate present, too many guilty feelings about the past, too little pride in the achievements of those who built this country — and decided that the better way of

securing 'peace, order, and good government' [Canada's official motto] is to appease the demands of immigrants rather than demand of them an acceptance of the country's history which they have chosen to make their home.

Such frames in post-9/11 conservative discourse on Islam lends credence to Said's (2003, 344) last formulation regarding U.S. discourse on Islam, which characterized it as "fear of a monotheistic, culturally and militarily formidable competitor to Christianity."

The Islamo-Leftist threat to the Christian Western Civilization, in the farther right's post-9/11 self-disciplinary discourse, shaded to Holy Land politics. Fearful of collectively losing God's blessing as a nation, the more Zionist segment of evangelicals often fused the two nation's identities. With America's identity conflated with Israel's, threats to Israel were threats to America. Moreover, loyalty to Israel means not only loyalty to America, but the very *existence* of America, as the Christians United for Israel (CUFI) slogan "Defend America, Vote Israel" suggests. For example, at a Republican Jewish Coalition in Los Angeles in 2010, then presidential candidate Michele Bachmann said that "I am convinced in my heart and in my mind that if the United States fails to stand with Israel, that is the end of the United States" (Birkey 2010).

Similarly, on June 7, 2011, bestselling Holy Land thriller novelist and Armageddon hawk, Joel Rosenberg, marked the anniversary of Israel's Six Day War by sending his subscribers an e-mail celebrating the fulfillment of the Biblical prophecy about how God would bring the Jewish Diaspora home from the nations, and how this miraculous event marked the "dramatic retaking of the Biblical heartland known as Judea and Samaria by the prophetically reborn Jewish State." But, the more practical self-disciplinary utility of the bridged Israel-self frame was evident in Rosenberg's e-mail to his subscribers two weeks later, on August 10, 2011, when he announced the event in Washington DC titled in jeremiad style: "The gathering storm: An urgent call to prayer, fasting and repentance for America, Israel and the Church."

But, such self-disciplinary and self-identifying strategies of action related to the Holy Land also shaded to domestic politics. The Washington DC event's underlying political purpose was evident in its two framing questions that centered Islam and the Left: "How serious is the threat of Radical Islam to America, Israel and the Church?" and "How serious is the threat of Rampant Secularism to America, Israel and the Church?"

Still another key feature of this segment of U.S. conservative politics of self identity is how frames of self-decline—from which the self-disciplinary or self-normalizing strategy is based—are also tethered to frames of self-exceptionalism and even universalism (Kagen 2008). Of course, the ideology of American exceptionalism permeates across the political spectrum, but the conservative threat discourse was unique in its bridging of frames of exceptionalism and decline, evidenced in the Tea Party's post-Obama-election battle cry of "we want our country back." Another typical instance of the articulation of exceptionalism amidst decline and loss; it was Andrew McCarthy's book jacket endorsement for Stop Islamization of America's director Pamela Geller's latest book, *The Post-American Presidency: The Obama Administration's War on America*. There, McCarthy characterized the book as must read for those who want to know "where we're headed if we don't take our exceptional country back."

The self-disciplinary pattern of framing security from outside threats in terms of purity and health on the inside had its U.S. antecedents in the jeremiad literary device common in early colonial security discourse. Deriving its name and style from the biblical Old Testament books of Jeremiah and Lamentations, the earliest jeremiads in Puritan discourse lamented the backslidden state of morality or sinfulness of society, and prophesied its downfall if meaningful repentance did not emerge (Bercovitch 1978). The jeremiad as a literary device, in this regard, forms a conjuncture with the broader Western emergence of another biblical frame or archetype of pastor (and of pastoral writing or pastoral power) which Foucault (1982, 218) traced as spreading throughout the social body in non-religious institutions and settings.

The U.S. jeremiad is not merely a literary device; it is a culturally-ensconced mindset or predisposition of fundamentalists in which self-identity is wrapped in adversity, and is therefore prone to dissonance or identity insecurity during episodes of victory, before the normal state of adversity is recreated (Perry 1953, 33). Perhaps, it was this cultural schema that predisposed some prominent conservatives to imagine the enemy of Islamization inside when the nation was obviously no longer existentially threatened by Islam outside.

The jeremiad's attempt to discipline the societal self into a homogenous unity, while punishing those perceived to be the source of impurity derives from the Puritanical, fundamentalist *ideal*. In the U.S. colonial era, for instance, the Massachusetts Bay Colony punished Thomas Morton for his book, *The New English Canaan* (1637), wherein Morton had denounced the Colony's policy of land enclosure and near genocide of the native population, whom he found "more full of humanity than the Christians…" (Drinnon 1997, 19). For his moral challenge to Puritan identity and to their di-vision of the world into civilized/barbarian, the Colony governor speculated that Morton might be the agent of a foreign power sent to undermine the Puritan colony. "It is most likely the Jesuits… have sent him over to do us mischief," he said (Drinnon 1997, 33).

Historically, in the identification of the more fundamentalist U.S. self, identity—like identity everywhere—has been acquired relationally in an economy of sameness and difference. Strength at the center is set off against weakness at the center—purity against impurity, civilization against barbarism, the healthy body against diseased tissue, and so on (Campbell 1998, 88-89).

In addition to those resistance elements on the inside like Morton who challenged the frames of self, the sources of impurity in Colonial America were usually those who were the weakest. In the sixteenth and seventeenth centuries, this translated to women, who constituted over eighty percent of the witch trials. In Massachusetts alone, beginning around 1694, up to several hundred thousand women functioned as this necessary source of difference—the weak and impure elements of the body politic—and were executed on spurious charges of sorcery, witchcraft, and black magic.

Other minorities similarly filled the "heretic" subject position. In this category were the Quakers, or "Friends," who had under William Penn's leadership signed the unbreakable peace treaty with the Indians. Others deemed to be "fifth columnists" in Satan's army were the Catholics in Virginia who refused to attend Church of England services (Slotkin 1973, 128-45; Boyer 1974, 6).

Jeremiad-like frames of societal decline have also infused more contemporary and prominent Western discourse. The geopolitician H.J. Mackinder (1902, 358) wrote that Britain's own resources had been exhausted and that it needed those of its "daughter nations" to stave off further decline (Toal 1989). The fantastic sales across Europe and the U.S. of Spengler's two-volume series *The Decline of the West*, which appeared in Germany at the end of World War I in 1918, hinted at a broader Western market that was predisposed or perennially obsessed with the loss of self.

As we have seen throughout Western threat discourse during the Cold War the process of self-identification in these texts depended on the ability to persuasively link elements of identity insecurity on the nation's inside to threats on the outside (Campbell 1998, 140). Ostensibly about dangerous others, these texts also served as a platform for self-identity politics, advancing the seemingly incoherent dual frames of self-exceptionalism and self-vulnerability.

And, like the earlier jeremiads, the Cold War texts were not merely descriptive of threats on the outside, but politically performative, disciplining the vulnerabilities on the inside. In Campbell's (1998, 31) words, they were "replete with statements about the fulfillment of the republic, the fundamental purpose of the nation, God-given rights, moral codes, the principles of European civilization, the fear of cultural and spiritual loss…." For example, the Cold War's overarching top secret policy document, National Security Council Paper (NSC-68), conceptualized containing the Soviets as a function of "the creation and maintenance of strength at the center" (Campbell 1998, 24; Foreign Economic Policy 1977, 406).

This document's pretext, the 1946 "Moscow Embassy Telegram #511"—contained similar frames of self-discipline in the face of decline. Here Kennan argued that "World communism is like a malignant parasite which feeds only on diseased tissue" (Etzold and Gaddis 1978, 63). Four years later in 1950, Kennan advanced this self-disciplinary frame, writing that Communism "had to be viewed as a crisis of our own civilization and the principal antidote lay in overcoming the weaknesses of our own institutions."[62]

Frames of self-discipline were often positive in tone; rather than a strategy of delineating the negative developments or sinfulness of society, they recalled the nation's exceptionalism as if to hold out the standard for which we must reenergize ourselves toward to gain security. For instance, in the NSC-17 series (1948), which dealt with internal security, Communism was "directed generally against the inherent dignity, freedom, and sacredness of the individual; against all God-given rights and values; against the Judeo-Christian code of morals on which our western civilization rests…" (Campbell 1998, 27).[63]

---

[62] "Draft Memorandum by the Counsellor (Iennan) to the Secretary of State," February 17, 1950, in FRUS 1950, Volume 1, p. 164.

[63] Source: NSC-17, "The Internal-Security of the United States," June 28, 1948, Records Group 273, National Archives of the United States. See page 6-7, 9, 20.

Immediately after the Cold War, U.S. self-identifying and self-disciplinary discourses that bridged frames of danger abroad and decline at home, and security outside by purity inside, were redeployed in new contexts. In the late 1980s and early 1990s, for example, a revisionist discourse emerged in which the nation's staunchest Cold War ally, Japan, was re-cast into enemies-foreign category, but not so much as a civilizational or cultural threat as economic one (Ó Tuathail 1992, 976). The fear then was not Sovietization, but Japanization of America, and the attending discourses posited the need to reclaim the American dream by adopting new practices of social discipline (Luke 1990, 35). Ostensibly a threat discourse about a foreign other at the economic gates, it featured a significant self-identifying or self-disciplinary element, with politically useful "policy prescriptions for reinvigorating American society and industry" (Ó Tuathail 1993, 191).

Conclusion

The question that this part of the inquiry continued to explore is how post-9/11 conservative discourse agents could so readily construct and expand an empirically-challenged and seemingly anti-rationalist counternarrative regarding Islam, a related panic over Islamization of the stalwartly Christian and secular nation, and a conspiracy linking their traditional political rivals to this plot, and still remain credible leaders and authorities among a sufficient segment of their market.

In addition to the rich political resources found in the discourse's cultural frames and its philanthropic and media-institutional base, we find that the threat discourse's agents enjoyed a significant "structure" of opportunities that cross-cut the information-technological, social-structural realms, and political-cultural-ideological realms.

First, at the informational-technological level, the ICT revolution and especially the advent of the alternative media enabled U.S. conservatives to increasingly break away from the mainstream knowledge society and expand their own competing "cultural commune" (Castells 1997, 67) or parallel society knowledge institutions. It is in this samizdat-like ungoverned virtual space that the conservative threat discourse's agents gained a measure of distance from the sanctions of society's more progressive legitimatizing institutions, and were able to capture a conservative niche market that increasingly identified with information and sources that aligned with their ideological predispositions.

Second, in the category of broader and even external contexts, there were two related moods that incentivized and enabled this strategy of security politics. There were accentuated crises within three of the U.S. conservative movement's central and relevant constituencies—neo, social, and paleo—in which the entire practice was housed. These crises, in addition to causing a lurch rightward, normalized more extreme discourse (and its agents) that opposed the perceived sources of the threats to Western civilizational hegemony and domestic cultural identity, which they signified variously as multiculturalism and secularism, Islamism and progressivism—or the metaphor that captured them both, Islam(ization). In addition, there was a related and politically-supportive general mood of anti-Islam, civilizational fundamentalism that gradually emerged in greater force across the post-9/11 decade in the U.S., Canada, and Europe, reflecting and trailing the much greater resistance to Islam that had developed in Europe by the end of the decade.

Thirdly, the key frames and ideologies selected to produce this latest little scare over the Eastern barbarians at the gate were not merely those that the literature led us to anticipate—those of racism, xenophobia on the one hand, and those of struggle for the Holy Land on the other. They were also *political* frames—that is, the historically-shaped and enacted mental structures that encompass both dyads of the political—the identification of the enemies foreign and domestic—with the latter in terms of infiltrators and traitors—and identification of the exceptional yet vulnerable self. In other words, this latest conspiracy of foreign agents infiltrating the homeland with the assistance of familiar traitors, was incentivized and rendered credible to no small degree by the rich culturally and subculturally-resident *political* schemas, cognitive frames, recurring strategies of action, and ideologies that a few more entrepreneurial conservative actors could and did transpose onto current contexts, with an expectation of gaining political advantage.

In the next three chapters we will rigorously examine how three of conservative polemicists mobilized these political resources in their strategy of security politics.

4

DR. DANIEL PIPES

No Ordinary Scholar

The costumes of revolt are woven from a blend of inherited and invented fibers into collective action frames in confrontation with opponents and elites.

—Clarence Tarrow (1998, 118)

WHEN President George W. Bush nominated Dr. Daniel Pipes to the board of the U.S. Institute of Peace in 2003, a congressional filibuster immediately ensued. Paradoxically, the filibuster was led by two of Pipes's fellow Harvard alumnus—Democratic Senators Ted Kennedy and Tom Harkin. Harkin based his opposition upon Pipes's remarks from October 21, 2001 speech to the American Jewish Congress Convention, where he implicitly had securitized all Muslims and Islam broadly, saying that the "increased stature, and affluence, and enfranchisement of American Muslims...will present true dangers to American Jews." "Some people call [Pipes] a scholar," Harkin concluded, "but this is not the kind of person you want on the USIP" (Baltimore Chronicle 2003, July 23). In a subsequent press conference seeking to undo some of the damage over Pipes's nomination, White House spokesman Ari Fleisher assured the nation that "Mr. Bush disagrees with Mr. Pipes about whether Islam is a peaceful religion" (Stevenson 2003).

Obviously, had Dr. Pipes been an *ordinary* Harvard intellectual—one whose scholarship on the topics of the Middle East and Islam had been more widely recognized as useful to society broadly—then such a filibuster would not have ensued. But, as Senator Harkin astutely noted, Pipes is no ordinary scholar. As the following analysis demonstrates, the knowledge that Daniel Pipes produces on topics related to threats in the Middle East and Islam broadly reliably functions less to describe the world accurately than it does to advance the conservative culture war against the Democratic Party, the political Left in general, and the broader more progressive order.

1. The Political Function of Intellectuals

At this point—before examining the nature of Dr. Pipes's discourse on Islam broadly—a short parenthetical aside is in order. The question of how U.S. post-9/11 discourse on the threat of Islam functioned politically at the domestic level obviously implies that the discourse's principal polemicists were *not* disinterested security professionals, but political apparatchiks—even cultural warriors. But, such an implication aligns with the Gramsci's (1971) classic conceptualization of the nature of public intellectuals, experts, pundits, polemicists, or specialists in modern, Western society.[64] Gramsci provided an epistemological break from the structuralist preoccupation with the text alone, and embraced a more interpretive understanding that texts or discourses emerge from culturally and historically specific social struggles, produced by agents who are not disinterested, but who are strategically engaged in the struggle for power (Jones 2006, 5).

One category of agency in Gramsci's framework is the more specialized and political intellectual—one who is organic to the non-elite, or working class and who functions in support of that political block's social struggle. These organic intellectuals were in no way rare. In the modern Western state, Gramsci observed that *every* political, economic and/or cultural interest had its own particular specialized category of intellectuals who served its interests. "Every social group coming into existence," he said, "creates together with itself, organically, one or more strata of intellectuals which give it homogeneity and an awareness of its own function not only in the economic but also in the social and political fields" (Gramsci 1971, 5). The bourgeoisie, he added, created their organic intellectuals; and, similarly, the capitalist entrepreneur, he said, "creates alongside himself the industrial technician, the specialist in political economy, the organizers of a new culture, of a new legal system, etc."

Gramsci (1971, 3) observed that society's intellectuals were not in any way apolitical—as we might imagine—but were "the thinking and organizing element of a particular fundamental social class," and should be characterized "by their function in directing the ideas and aspirations of the class to which they organically belong."

It was precisely this view of intellectuals that Senator's Kennedy and Harkin had in mind in their characterization of Pipes as no ordinary scholar.

Looking beyond the classic texts on the topic, we readily observe how Gramsci's insights were generalizable. In the U.S., the liberation of blacks, women, gays and other marginalized identities in various civil rights movements were largely a function of their own intellectuals, and not led from the outside. Even capitalism emerged lock-step with new types of intellectuals—to include accountants, lawyers, economists and finance experts, industrial engineers, and so on. Outside of the U.S., every social movement coming into existence had its strata of intellectuals. This is true in the case of Pipes's new

---

[64] See Gramsci's eighth of his ten *Prison Notebooks* (1971). His earlier 1926 essay, *Some aspects of the southern question*, written before his arrest by Fascist forces, also deals with the production and function of public intellectuals. Under the Marxist paradigm, intellectuals were expected to be political; many of his cohorts were public leaders and organizers of a more communist counter-hegemonic project toward proletarian self-government within a civil society then dominated by Fascist bourgeois interests (Herrera-Zgaib 2009, 148).

post-9/11 nemesis, the Muslim Brotherhood, which had its cadre of intellectuals, as did Pan-Islamism broadly.

The pervasiveness of these more practical, non-elite intellectuals across the world's political movements owes to their unique efficacy in counterhegemonic struggle: they are the only ones capable of speaking the language of their constituents, and thereby gradually breaking the masses away from the existing consensus or "common sense" regarding the social order, and producing a new revolutionary mass consciousness—what Gramsci referred to as the "national popular" ideology, or "new modes of thought" that better served the interests of their faction. Achieving that break simply could not be done by out-of-touch formal scholars who sat in ivory towers writing erudite and scholarly arguments for obscure academic journals, or by the more traditional elite intellectuals who saw themselves independent of any political group—the kind of intellectuals who would not have caused a filibuster had the Bush administration appointed them.

Gramsci (1971, 334) added that "there is no organization without intellectuals, that is without organizers and leaders," for they provide the necessary "theoretical aspect of the theory-practice nexus essential to all effective organizations." For this reason, Gramsci (1971, 10) saw the intellectual mode less one immersed in "eloquence" then "in active participation in practical life, as constructor, organiser, 'permanent persuader' and not just a simple orator...." For Gramsci, the notion of a non-interested intellectual—one independent from a political group—"is a myth" (1971, 3).

The interestedness of discourse agents goes beyond that organic to any particular political faction. Even geopolitical discourse from Ratzel to Mackinder, Haushofer to Bowman, Spykman to Kissinger—in the words of Ó Tuathail and Agnew (1998, 79)—was never an objective and disinterested activity but "an organic part of the political philosophy and ambitions of these very public intellectuals." Their geopolitics has not been a disinterested explanation of the world, but rather a production of knowledge to aid nationalistic pursuit of primacy over the other.

With this feature of the social in view, President Bush's appointment of a political apparatchik in intellectual's cap and gown should not have been a surprise. And, as the following case suggests, Dr. Pipes's politically-interested knowledge production related to Islam was at the service of several political projects: first West-Islam civilizational politics, then Holy Land geopolitics, and finally U.S. conservative domestic cultural politics.

2. Dr. Pipes's Early Years: From Civilizational to Holy Land Geopolitics

It was Daniel Pipes's nemesis, Edward Said, who—on the subject of politically interested intellectuals—reminded us that "no one has ever devised a method for detaching the scholar from the circumstances of life, from the fact of his involvement (conscious or unconscious) with a class, a set of beliefs, a social position..." and that "these continue to bear on what he does professionally" (Said 1978, 10).[65] In Dr. Pipes's case, such positionality seemed to be especially influential in his Islam-related productions—his books, articles, blog posts, and so on. In 1979, when Islamic revolutionaries in Iran were dynamically rupturing the subservient relationship of Islam to the West and its puppets, Daniel Pipes was anachronistically focused on medieval Islamic history as a student at Harvard. Pipes's couldn't have been more irrelevant.

Yet, Daniel Pipes was no stranger to utopian revolutionaries; his father Richard—still a professor in Harvard's History Department—had narrowly escaped from the Nazi invasion of Poland and the Holocaust, and dedicated his life to containing the next world-changing political movement, pledging in his memoirs to teach the world "how evil ideas lead to evil consequences" (Pipes, 2004). From that position, Richard Pipes crafted his path to the aforementioned Washington-based Soviet-focused Committee on the Present Danger (CPD), and to Chairman of "Team B." As mentioned earlier, this Team B was a group of non-establishment experts brought in by Donald Rumsfeld, Dick Cheney and George H.W. Bush of the Ford administration to challenge the CIA's orthodoxy regarding the Soviet military threat. An ideologue himself, Richard Pipes's more Manichean mode of knowing and its dichotomy of the world into white and black, good and evil, powerfully shaped his characterization of America's Cold War geopolitical rival. In other words, it was Pipes's ideological straitjacket that shaped Team B's assessment of the Soviet threat, producing a counternarrative that not only departed from the professional consensus of the CIA, but departed from reality and distorted Soviet threat (Dalby 1988, 423).

Richard Pipes's propensity for the dissident security writing—the threat *counter*narrative—would come to run in the family. A quarter century later, when the events of 9/11 would present for U.S. conservatives a new ideological foe, the Committee on the Present Danger was reinvigorated under the "present danger" of Islam, or—euphemistically—"terrorism and the ideologies that drive it." And, in a contemporary reenactment of the Biblical story in 2nd Kings of the younger Elisha inheriting the prophetic mantle from his elder, Elijah, Daniel replaced Richard at the CPD to advance the counternarrative regarding Islam.[66] Observing the same "against the flow" disposition of his father in Daniel's own security writing, *Harvard Magazine* would later describe him as a "chip off the old block" (Tassel 2005).

Daniel Pipes's Own Ideological Struggle: Civilizational Geopolitics

Back when the new cold war with Khomeini's fundamentalist, revolutionary Islamic regime in Iran emerged, Daniel realized the opportunity presented by America's newfound interest in Islam by writing *In the Path of God: Islam and Political Power*. Completed in 1983,

---

[65] This was also Bourdieu's essential concept regarding cultural productions—that one's habitus is *structured* by one's class, upbringing, worldview, experience, forms of capital, and position in the field, but also *structuring* of one's dispositions, thinking, and practice.

[66] See
http://www.committeeonthepresentdanger.org/index.php?option=com_content&view=article&id=1744&Itemid=89

the book was reliably a counternarrative regarding Islam, and thus earned criticism by Edward Said (1985) in his "Orientalism Reconsidered."

Edward Said characterized Daniel Pipes as part of an emerging field of "uncritical" and "younger ideologues and Orientalists." According to Said, Pipes's book was marked by "intellectually scandalous generalizing;" it "makes its assertions and affirmations with little regard for logic or argument;" and uses "rumor, hearsay, and other wisps of evidence" as "the only proof." The work, Said concluded, "is magic quite unworthy even of high Orientalism," in that it "masters neither its genuine learning nor its pretense at disinterestedness." Said (1985, 96) further characterized Pipes's work as politically motivated, "wholly at the service not of knowledge but of an aggressive and interventionary State—the U.S.—whose interests Pipes helps to define."

Pipes's first book, therefore, seemed to foreshadow the kind of scholarship that Senators Kennedy and Harkin were deriding. In it, Pipes (1983, 333) departed from the kind of context-based assessment that professional security writing would demand. Instead of calculated empirical analysis, Pipes felt at ease to simply and confidently predict the certain "collapse of Khomeini's government," asserting that its "wealth and power will vanish as rapidly as they appeared," "as oil revenues subside," and that the "Islamic alternative will lose its appeal." Like his father's Team B assessment of the Soviet threat, Pipes's estimate of the newest threat could not have been more wrong.

These criticisms and weaknesses aside, the experience writing it evidently transformed Pipes's interests and he abandoned his foundational expertise in the increasingly anachronistic and even non-sequitur realm of medieval Islam, and moved into the policy realm. After brief stints teaching history in his father's department at Harvard in parts of 1983 and 1984, in the policy-planning bureaucracy at State Department, and in the policy department at the U.S. Naval War College, Pipes in 1986 found a more ideologically-aligned home at the dissident Cold-War institute, Foreign Policy Research Institute (FPRI), which had by that time been marginalized by academia. There, Pipes would eventually lead that institution and serve as the editor of its quarterly journal of world affairs, *Orbis*. But, he would also continue his trajectory in intellectual dissidence regarding the containment of the West's newest ideological foe, Islam, publishing in 1989 *The Long Shadow: Culture and Politics in the Middle East*.

The Long Shadow foreshadowed Pipes's trajectory as no ordinary scholar. On the scholar side of the phrase, the book contained rich and rare (if not unique) veins of insight. But, on the "no ordinary" side of the phrase, these insights were buried in a broader mountain of empirically unconfirmed generalization and opinion. The book contained a more dubious political edge, replete with crude political binary schemas—caricatures of political enemies like "foreign policy liberals" and "pro-Arab" sympathizers—all juxtaposed to their equally caricatured political opposites. In that early work, Pipes alluded to two principles that he would quickly abandon: that of "placing current events within their larger context" (1989, xi), and avoiding the practice of America's media and thought leaders, whose (over)"emphasis on Israel fundamentally distorts the way Americans perceive the Middle East…"(1989, 273).

In 1988, a second and largely manufactured-for-media event—"the Rushdie affair"—provided Pipes with yet another emotion-heightened opportunity to engage in civilizational geopolitics—this time with a book that took advantage of the event's popular name. His *The Rushdie Affair: The Novel, The Ayatollah, and the West*—although admittedly rushed to the publisher in 1990—was brilliant. Years ahead of Samuel Huntington's popularized thesis and again foreshadowing his own propensity, Pipes provided and insightful account of "a confrontation of civilizations"—between the West and Islam—where freedom to criticize another's religion in the former is interpreted as a hostile act of blasphemy in the latter. Unlike the abysmal predictions of his first book, here Pipes provided the context to understand how globalization would foster an increasingly antagonizing form of identity politics, seen in familiar headlines such as the Muslim politics over the Mohammed cartoons and the "Innocence of Muslims" movie trailer.

The book also contained two topics and themes that would permeate all of Pipes's work. It broached the basic conservative concern regarding freedom of speech in the secular state in the era of globalization—a topic that he presciently knew would impact his own propensity to speak conservative truth to more progressive power. And, it tacitly advanced the more paleoconservative threat frame of loyalty of Western immigrants and Israeli Muslims, or—in his words—"the many millions of Muslims now living in the West and their relationship to the civilization around them" (1990, 16). In a backhanded slap at U.S. conservative "enemies foreign and domestic"—Islam and the Left—Pipes identified Rushdie "a man of the Left" whose work was emblematic of much of the Muslim diaspora's anti-Western and third wordlist anti-Americanism.

The Shift to Holy Land Geopolitics

As America's interest in Islam waned throughout the 1990s, Pipes abandoned his interest in the clash of civilizations between the West and Islam for another rising ideological struggle—this time as far-right Zionism's advocate, providing the counternarrative to the Oslo peace process by defending Israel's continuing expansion into the Biblical Jewish homeland of Judea and Samaria in the West Bank. Like any handmaiden to empire, Pipes's geopolitical advocacy required a lesser of two evils approach; it meant framing Israel's infraction of international law in terms of self-defense against an entire neighborhood that was evil naturally, or perennially, *because it was Islamic.*

To erect such a racialized regime of representation—of naturalized difference between the Jews in Israel and the Muslims surrounding and resisting Zionism—Pipes had to mobilized every opportune event. When in 1991 the U.S. military had ousted Saddam Hussein from Kuwait and was in a position to prevent his post-war revenge on the Kurds, Pipes provided the counternarrative. In his "Why America Can't Save the Kurds," in the April 11th edition of *The Wall Street Journal,* Pipes offered little objective justification, but merely warned idealist-leaning policymakers against false hopes, citing the immutable "realities" of Muslim culture and the "inhumanity" inherent to Middle East politics.

Similarly, in 1993, as the Oslo peace process was raising hopes of a two-state solution for Israel and Palestine, Pipes again provided the counternarrative by assembling eighteen unaltered, previously published articles into the book, *Sandstorm: Middle East Conflicts and America*. Here, again, Pipes justified far-right Zionism's advancing occupation and control of Palestine by framing Islamic culture as a primordial, unchanging, and dysfunctional, and thus framed Muslim elites shaped by that culture as unreliable partners in the peace process. Tearing a page from his father's and the Committee on the Present Danger's structurally deterministic and realist discourse on the Soviet Union, Pipes's assured his readers that "Little really changes in the Middle East," and advised that we abandon all idealism (that the Oslo peace process represented) and leave the region to its determined primordial identity, because—as he put it—"neither American power nor the strength of its example can push away deeply grounded perceptions and habits."

In 1994, Pipes institutionalized his function as a geopolitical advocate for Zionism by founding the Middle East Forum. The institution's new journal, *Middle East Quarterly*, immediately began to function within its design parameters: providing the counternarrative to the rising tide of largely unchallenged criticism of Israel's expansionist illegal settlements and stifling control of Palestinian lives from the academy and global public opinion. For this subversive mission, the Quarterly's board of editors is comprised of dissident non-Muslim and farther right Zionist academics that Pipes would later describe as the "five percent" who are not part of the Middle East Studies Association. This five-percent club included fellows from the conservative American Enterprise Institute, and the AIPAC-affiliated Washington Institute for Near East Policy (WINEP)—both identified by Mearsheimer and Walt (2006) as key pillars in the "Israel Lobby."

But, by 1995, Pipes had grown more preoccupied with the domestic critics of Israel's expansion than with its Muslim neighbors. In the Fall 1995 edition of the *National Interest*, in the article "There are no moderates," his shift in emphasis from the far enemy to the near was evident, describing the peace process as "the misguided U.S. policy" and blaming "the usual suspects" in the U.S. usually critical of Israel's policies: the "academic specialists."

Pipes received precisely the response from these domestic rivals that he had hoped for. Edward Said (1997, xviii) responded by describing Pipes as a "perfervid anti-Muslim" for advancing the counternarrative that moderate Islamists necessary for peaceful interstate relations in the Middle East simply don't exist. Said wrote in *The Nation* on August 12th, 1996 that Pipes's function within the pro-Israel apparatus was to "make sure that the '[Islamic] threat' is kept before our eyes, the better to excoriate Islam for terror, despotism and violence, while assuring themselves profitable consultancies, frequent TV appearances and book contracts." These characterizations became more widespread after 9/11. Georgetown University Professor John Esposito described Pipes as a political activist with "a right wing Zionist agenda" (Parry and Abunimah 2002). And even the more conservative *Wall Street Journal* (2002: 09.18) identified Pipes's Middle East Forum as a "pro-Israel think tank."

As an apparatus for Holy Land geopolitics, *Middle East Forum*'s productions—like those of Pipes's father Richard in the CPD—entailed ideological moves of exclusion that removed from view Islamism's complex causal basis in the realm of human (in)security. Pipes swept from view the fact that—for hundreds of millions of working-age Muslim males with no hope of achieving culturally-important social, political or economic aspirations—a more socially-just and less corrupt Islamist-led regime was preferable to the U.S.-supported "status quo," which Pipes advocated for. Since there are no moderate Islamists, Pipes (1995) reasoned, "we should stand by the non-fundamentalists, even when that means accepting, within limits, strong-arm tactics (Egypt, the PLO), the aborting of elections (in Algeria), and deportations (Israel)."

Pipes was silent on how the regimes that made up that status quo not only plundered the billions annually in U.S. largess in exchange for looking the other way as Israel accelerated its move into Palestinian territory, but that they were otherwise brutal, inept, and more broadly corrupt—having under the guise of Western-mandated neo-liberal reforms plundered their economy with crony capitalism and other forms of regime corruption, and otherwise prevented the emergence of both a normal civil society and private sector economy.

Pipes's security discourse erased from view the fact that this status quo that he was advocating for, under which most Muslims were suffering, was protected from external threats by Western powers, especially the U.S., and protected from internal threats by their oppressive *mukhabarat*, or the undemocratic, authoritarian deep-state police and intelligence power centers. Compounding this intractable structure of thwarted human needs, the spread of satellite television was at last revealing the stark differences between their lives under that status quo and the lives of Westerners whose governments' policies were helping to maintain it. The absolute lack at the local level, and relative deprivation at the global level, fueled frustration and resistance from the only bastion of political opportunity remaining: the mosque. Yet, for Pipes's threat analysis of Islamic activism and anti-Western sentiments, all of this social context would be systematically obscured from view.

Given that propensity to produce security knowledge in the service of far-right Zionist interests, it was no surprise that Pipes in 1996 landed a position as a visiting fellow and adjunct scholar at the Washington Institute for Near East Policy (WINEP)—a think tank spun-off by AIPAC. The institute, according to John Mearsheimer of University of Chicago and Stephen Walt, academic dean at Harvard University's Kennedy School of Government, played a crucial function within the Israel lobby. In their book, *The Israel Lobby and US Foreign Policy* (2007), they note that "Although WINEP plays down its links to Israel and claims that it provides a 'balanced and realistic' perspective on Middle East issues, this is not the case." Instead, they noted, "WINEP is funded and run by individuals who are deeply committed to advancing Israel's agenda," concluding that "they are hardly neutral observers" (Mearsheimer and Walt 2007, 175-176). Martin Indyk—AIPAC's deputy director for research—was frustrated that his security writing not taken seriously *because* of his position in AIPAC, and so WINEP was spun off as its own organization to foster the appearance of political neutrality (Ottaway 1989). Beinin (1993) noted the nexus of knowledge and power in this part of the broader apparatus:

> WINEP built its success on ample funding; an extensive network of relations with the media, policymakers and academics; and dogged focus on its central policy objective-keeping the strategic relationship with Israel at the center of US Middle East policy, a goal that resonates with the anti-Arab and Islamophobic premises of the conventional wisdom on Middle East affairs. During the Persian Gulf war, WINEP associates were frequent sources of the sound bites, op-eds and canned quotes featured by the mass media. They reinforced the Bush administration's framing of the issues, legitimized the war, affirmed the authority of the media, and provided color commentary once the shooting began (MER 180).

It was at WINEP that Pipes reliably published a policy advocacy paper, *Syria Beyond the Peace Process*, which—like his other politically performative threat writing—functioned as part of the broader argument to derail U.S. support for the ongoing Oslo peace process. Facing significant momentum towards a final settlement that would share the Jewish biblical homeland and its capital with the native peoples, as well as make some restitution for the half million refugees displaced in Israel's 1948 land-grab, the greater Zionist project simply needed unreliable partners for peace. And, Pipes produced them. Under his pessimistic and conspiratorial lens, Assad's overtures were placed within the prism of George Kennan in the last great ideological struggle— namely, *the Eastern mind's deceptiveness*. In this racialized frame, Assad's pursuit of a peace process with Israel was merely a farce to—in Pipes's assessment—"improve his standing in Washington" (1996, 92-93).

And, because the proponents of Israel's expansion needed spoilers such as Assad leading the adjacent states, Pipes also advocated that we keep them there. To this end, he parroted the well-worn tactic by the authoritarian regimes of the status-quo, which was—in Pipes's terms—the argument that "fundamentalist Islam has become the region's greatest problem," and that—like the other devils we know—Assad's potential to "help resist the surge of fundamentalism" have made him "less of an opponent and more of an ally" (1996, 101-2). Here, Pipes seems vindicated. Almost twenty years later, as the emergence of *takfiri* ideology and the Islamic State group revealed, the regime of al-Assad and other authoritarians indeed seemed to be the lesser of two evils in the minds of many more traditionalist and secular Sunnis in Syria and beyond. But, any security professional with a Middle East portfolio and worth their salt will identify the looming youth bulge and lack of diversified, competitive private-sector economy as the legacies the status quo that will prove to be of far more importance than (and the cause of) al-Qaeda and Islamic State movements.

Continuing his role as framing Muslims as unreliable peace partners during the Oslo process, Pipes in 1996 published *The Hidden Hand Middle East Fears of Conspiracy*. In frames of civilization and barbarism, reason and its lack, Pipes again attempted to naturalize difference between the Western and Islamic culture; the book framed the Arab mind's primordial predisposition for conspiracy thinking, with the effect (and apparent intent) to convey the determined, unchanging nature of political and economic life of the region, including the propensity to political extremism, violence, and lack of modernization.

It was in this strategy that the topic of Islam increasingly became a useful tool in the hands of those contemporary Joshuas in the U.S. and Israel, and their irredentist strategy of reenacting the more than 3,000-year-old conquest of Canaan, taking it from its modern-day Philistines. In view of this obvious function, Edward Said pinpointed the political economy of "the menace theory of Islam." He characterized the entire project as pro-Israeli special interests hoping convince the public that Israel is "a victim of Islamic violence" and to obscure what it is that Israel and the United States have been doing (1997, xxi). Said's characterization of Pipes as an organic polemicist for the farther-right Zionist political apparatus would be vindicated after his death, when Pipes was recognized by Bar-Ilan University's Ingeborg Rennert Center for Jerusalem Studies, with their annual "Guardian of Zion" award.

As we've already seen, Pipes's geopolitical advocacy translated to discrediting the chief source of criticism of Israeli and U.S. policies *outside of the Middle East*: the Middle East studies organizations and regional departments in American universities. Toward this effort, Pipes (and a co-author De Atkine) in 1995 wrote the McCarthyesque "Middle Eastern Studies: What Went Wrong?" which questioned the loyalty of American scholars who were critical of U.S. or Likud-led Israeli policy in the region. In response to the many letters to the editor that their work predictably provoked, their reply marked the point in Pipes's discourse in which themes of countercultural struggle became a pervasive feature:

> The Middle Eastern specialist class has had its holy writs questioned! How dare one challenge the conventions of those gurus? Our article aspired to serve notice on an academic community that too often has abrogated its scholarly standards in the quest of political correctness and an elitist countercultural stance (De Atkine and Pipes 1997).

Such counterhegemonic themes became central to Pipes's more-advocacy focused security discourse. In the January 2000 edition of the neoconservative journal *Commentary*, Pipes reviewed Efraim Karsh's *Empires of the Sand*. Positioning himself more completely as a dissident academic, Pipes selected this revisionist work for review *because* it was revisionist—a counternarrative to postcolonial studies and the Third-Worldism in particular. In his terms, it "upends the conventional narrative" constructed in academia—that Middle Easterners were "hapless victims of predatory imperial powers." He concluded on a counterhegemonic and politically antagonistic note of satisfaction, saying that already this "radical rejection of prevailing wisdom has prompted strong reactions from the scholarly community."

Given this dissidence, it is no surprise that Pipes found himself increasing marginalized—a marginalization that would end when a well-trained cell of al-Qaeda operatives produced the next major opportunistic event in West-Islam relations.

3. 9/11 as Political Opportunity: The Shift to Domestic Cultural Politics

9/11—in addition to its rupture of the U.S. security narrative—constituted perhaps modernity's greatest opportunity for what we have already identified as "security politics"—the use of an emergent security topic to advance one's domestic, cultural struggle. As he had done in the two earlier events in West-Islam relations, Daniel Pipes quickly moved to capitalize on the vast resource of emotion that emanated from this national trauma and security rupture. With the nation mobilizing for retribution and hungry for knowledge about their newest and shadowy enemy, Pipes rushed to obscure that enemy by republishing his 1983 book about Iran's revolution. That it was an insignificant revision to the earlier edition undoubtedly reflected Pipes's own primordialist vision outlined earlier—that nothing really changes in the Middle East, and that all Islamic fundamentalist movements are the same.

With Islam centered in national debate, Pipes's trademark realism and his propensity to counternarrative functioned as a dissident conservative *subject position*—a necessary commodity in the realm of media-sponsored cultural politics. He readily occupied the identifiable conservative pole-position that was opposed to the more progressive consensus. In that symbolic role, Pipes appeared on 110 television and 450 radio shows—an average of ten a week in the twelve-month period following the 9/11 attacks (Press 2004), and played a key role in convincing the neoconservative elite of the Bush Administration to invade Iraq. It was for this reason that Harvard University by October 2006 had ranked him 84th on its "Harvard 100" list of its most influential living alumni.

Subversion of More Progressive Institutions

But, Daniel Pipes's impressive rise in influence was not merely a factor of his self-positioning into the niche role of a counterhegemonic commodity for purposes of debates in the media. Like Robert Spencer, it was also due to his threat-writing's increasingly counterhegemonic function within the U.S. conservative movement's broader culture war.

By the mid-point of the post-9/11 decade, Pipes's threat writing related to Islam increasingly contained a curious element of counterhegemonic resistance or subversion aimed at not merely at the Middle East academia and broader criticism of Likud-led Israel's apartheid-like policies with regard to the Holy Land, but at the enduring rivals of the U.S. conservative movement—that is, the Democrats, the more progressive dominant institutions of academia, government and the media, and the broader, more progressive and secular culture.

For example, just weeks after the 9/11 attacks, when the nation was trying to interpret the rationality and contexts of al-Qaeda's horrific and symbolic attacks on innocent American civilians and icons of power, four master narratives on Islam began to emerge from the Bush Administration and the broader government institutions—namely, that "there is no clash of civilizations"; that "terrorism is not Islamic"; that "Islam is compatible with American ideals and adds to American life"; and that "Americans must learn to appreciate Islam." But, Pipes, in his new subject position, reliably provided the counternarrative to these master security narratives of "officialdom," as he called it, publishing in his *Middle East Quarterly*, "The United States Government – Islam's Patron?" In the piece, Pipes delegitimized the more progressive outside, sarcastically charging that U.S. officials "are at pains to distance themselves from the great unwashed, those everyday people who watch the news and associate Islam with violence."

Also in 2002, despite the conservative movement's increasing demands on him as their star organic polemicist on the topic of the movement's newfound existential threat, Pipes managed to publish *Militant Islam Reaches America*. The book was not only unscholarly in tone or approach, but was obviously rushed and unenlightening, even at this early juncture of knowledge production related to the threats within the Islamic continuum. The production was, however, politically performative; it was yet another milestone along the way in Pipes's strategic turn from the far enemy to the near—that is, from the containment of over-the-horizon revolutionary Islamic resistance to U.S. hegemony, to the war of position at home against domestic political rivals. Buried beneath the title and focus on the newest foreign enemy, the book's chapter titles—"Jihad and the professors," "A monument of apologetics," and so on—revealed the production's underlying focus on the U.S. conservative movement's domestic enemies by securitizing the more progressive academic and government institutions, which were framed as serving as militant Islam's "apologists" and "patrons."

Even in the book's Preface, Pipes began its gaze not on enemies foreign, or "militant Islam"—as the title suggested—but enemies domestic, and specifically Pipes's own more progressive rivals in the academy. Setting the tone for what would follow, Pipes cited Georgetown University professor John Esposito's four-volume *Oxford Encyclopedia of the Modern Islamic World*, sarcastically describing it as "the best that current scholarship has to offer on the subject of Islam." He added that "I found that, in an age when objective knowledge has faded as a goal, scholarship readily turns into partisanship…" (Pipes 2002, xvi). Pipes (2002, 89) continued this tack of cultural politics, describing Esposito's book, *The Islamic Threat: Myth or Reality* (1992), as emblematic of the threat-obscuring straightjacket worn by the exclusively Leftist Middle East Studies Association and the American academy broadly. And, addressing the dominant "political correctness" that was continually sanctioning all of his own production, Pipes (2002, 108) rhetorically imagined an institution without such stifling "political constraints," but then lamenting: "that would be asking for a very different academy." He concluded in counterhegemonic lamentation over the "stifling consensus" and "intellectual scandal" in the academy over the meaning of "jihad" in Islam and the associated "religion of peace" storyline (2002, 258-268), and noted with dismay that "anyone seeking guidance on the all-important Islamic concept of *jihad* would get almost identical instruction from members of the professoriate across the United States" (2002, 259).

Within this same counterhegemonic strategy of action, Pipes in the June 25, 2002 edition of the reliably conservative *New York Sun*, published "Extremists on Campus." With the nation's hunger for knowledge related to foreign extremists, Pipes was instead on the frontlines at home, fighting the domestic ones. "For three decades," he wrote, "left-wing extremists have dominated American academics, spouting odd but seemingly harmless theories about 'deconstruction,' 'post-modernism,' 'race, gender and class,' while venting against the United States, its government and its *allies*"—a euphemized reference to Israel (Pipes and Schanzer 2002). He concluded the article with a Frantz Fanon-like call to decolonize: "the time has come," he wrote, "to take back the universities as institutions of civilized discourse."

In this vein, in the December 31, 2002 column in the more-dissident conservative outlet, *New York Post*, under the headline "What is Jihad," Pipes began by advancing the threat counternarrative regarding the newest foreign enemy. But, the piece's title notwithstanding, "jihad" merely served as a platform to politically engage the more idealistic progressive academy. Pipes charged the academy with being unrealistic about Islam, and used as his case three American professors of Islamic studies who "colorfully" reinterpret jihad away from its historical martial signification. In his niche subject position as the lone sober realist and adult in the face of broadening trend of immature idealism, Pipes concluded: "It would be wonderful were jihad to evolve into nothing more aggressive than controlling one's anger, but that will not happen simply by wishing away a gruesome reality." Of course, Pipes carefully obscured from view the more authoritative contemporary *fiqh* of jihad, such as that published by Sheikh Yousef al-Qaradawi in 2009, and which most Muslims see as their authority on the matter, which reserves jihad's martial variant as a kind of defensive just war doctrine, and jihad's near and non-violent variants as means to win the world to Islam—a dual frame of "struggle" that many Christian soldiers have similarly naturalized.

Pipes would continue this early counterhegemonic strategy. On November 15, 2009, Cinnamon Stillwell of *Campus Watch*—an organization that Pipes created after 9/11 expressly for waging the conservative movement's culture war against the more progressive academe—wrote "Fort Hood and the Academic Apologists," using the murder of 13 soldiers by a radicalized Muslim Army major, Nidal Hasan, as a platform for domestic politics. Reliably publishing the piece in the conservative platform for this culture war, the *American Thinker*, Stillwell lamented that for interpretation the Muslim army officer's attack, "the media has turned to Middle East studies 'experts' for enlightenment." In an implicit framing of an alliance between the Left and Islamists, she noted that writing for the *Washington Post's* 'On Faith' blog, John Esposito, professor and founding director of the Saudi-funded Prince Alwaleed bin Talal Center for Muslim-Christian Understanding at Georgetown University, "extends his long tradition of issuing apologias for radical Islam by conflating Hasan's actions with 'extremists' of all religions." Stillwell's article continued its counterhegemonic function, describing "the culture of political correctness and willful blindness towards Islamist ideology that has infected the U.S. military, intelligence agencies, and so many other institutions" as a condition fostered by "the denizens of the Ivory Tower."

Similar to what we will see in Spencer's threat writing, Pipes's subversion of the dominant, more progressive regime of truth involved more than merely delegitimizing institutionalized scholars and the rest of "officialdom"; it also included rendering visible the tabooed topics or things typically regulated out of professional security writing, academic security studies, and mainstream journalism. For example, using his reliable neoconservative outlet, *Commentary*, Pipes in October 2002 resurrected the long-tabooed subject of race as an object of security, making visible the "well-established tradition of American blacks who convert to Islam turning against their country" (Pipes 2002). In his similarly reliable conservative outlet, the *New York Sun*, Pipes subverted societal norms again by raising for visibility the connection of America's non-whites with danger, this time championing the more rightist Michelle Malkin's (2004) *In Defense of Internment: The Case for Racial Profiling in World War II and the War on Terror*. Pipes wrote on December 28th that "Ms. Malkin has done the singular service of breaking the academic single-note scholarship on a critical subject, cutting through a shabby, stultifying consensus…" (Pipes 2004).

By making visible the tabooed things that the more progressive institutions *normally* exclude, Pipes's analyses defiantly stood juxtaposed to the hegemonic order. The almost puritanical, oppositional nature of all of Pipes's threat assessments by this time functioned as an ever-present reactionary power that undermined the legitimacy of those institutions, and—by perceived connection—the Left broadly.

Dissident Mode of Production

Daniel Pipes's emerging practice of counterhegemonic struggle or subversion at this juncture was not merely *discursive* in nature; that is, it did not merely produce threat analyses that were subversive in terms of their counternarratives and more explicit political statements. It was also subversive in a *non-discursive* way; that is, in its mode of production or publishing. Pipes's productions always bypassed or excluded altogether the more formal, mainstream, dominant, societal regime of truth. In this non-discursive strategy, Pipes was merely aligning with the aforementioned conservative counterhegemonic strategy of subversion of the more progressive societal institutions, as manifested in the construction of a samizdat-like alternative society of dissident institutions, increasingly based in the alternative media.

To this end, Pipes created his own dissident set of Middle East Forum institutions, including the *Middle East Quarterly*, Campus Watch, Islamist Watch, and his blog "Lion's Den."

At this point, Pipes openly identified his Middle East Forum as a counterhegemonic institution. In response to Edward Said's reference to him in his post-9/11 *Culture and Resistance* as "a second-rate, unemployed scholar" (2002, 177), Pipes wore the characterization as a badge of honor, boasting that "think tanks (like the Middle East Forum) have emerged in the last couple of decades as leading actors in the making of public policy, much to the frustration of the academic thought police" (Pipes 2003), sarcastically turning the more leftist Orwellian and Foucauldian phrase on its head.

In this newest mode of subversion, Pipes enacted a kind of epistemic solipsism, wherein he published solely from within the conservative enclave or knowledge sub-society. For example, Middle East Forum had its sponsored articles in 2010 and 2011 (until 9/11) published exclusively in one of two places: in its own *Middle East Quarterly* (70 articles), or in one of the knowledge institutions within the conservative enclave created expressly for counterhegemonic struggle—*Pajamas Media* (33 articles), *FrontPageMagazine* (33 articles), *American Thinker* (31 articles), *Hudson New York* (19 articles), *Jerusalem Post* (7 articles), *National Review Online* (6 articles), and *Jihad Watch* (4 articles), *National Interest* (3 articles), and *Foreign Policy*.com (8 articles).

In other words, it was *because* these institutions were dissident or subversive by intent that Pipes sought them out for publishing, and that his threat assessments were published there. In the case of *Foreign Policy*, for example, its founding purpose and mission—according to its website—"was to question commonplace views and groupthink and to give a voice to alternative views about American foreign policy."[67] And, since its establishment, Pipes's *Middle East Quarterly* similarly had been functioning as such a dissident institution within the conservative power-knowledge apparatus; its samizdat, subversive nature was part of its branding, or niche market strategy.

All of Pipes's threat writing by the midpoint of the post-9/11 decade seemed to be not only against the flow of professional consensus regarding Islam, but operating in another realm altogether. When so many security and intelligence professionals focused on al-Qaeda and the potential nexus of al-Qaedaism and weapons of mass destruction, Pipes, for example, was launching the political surveillance apparatus, *Campus Watch*, which in McCarthyesque style began to compile blacklists and dossiers of faculty at US campuses whom it considers unpatriotic, America-hating leftists. Inspired in part by a 2001 work from the Israel lobby's Washington Institute for Near East Policy (WINEP)—*Ivory Towers on Sand: The failure of Middle Eastern studies in America*, by Martin Kramer—Campus Watch's counterhegemonic mission—in Pipes's terms—was that of "condemning and curbing the leftist activism that too often passes for Middle East scholarship" (Pipes and Schanzer 2002). Reflecting a central frame in the U.S. conservative cultural struggle, the website's introduction, "About Campus Watch," reconstructs the McCarthyite charge that "academics seem generally to dislike their own country and think even less of American allies abroad."

In April 2006, Pipes again extended the enclave of conservative institutions—its political apparatus—with the launch of Islamist Watch. Created ostensibly for the front lines of a Kennan-inspired containment of America's newest Cold War enemy *within*, Islamist Watch's actual function was that of citizen soldiering—of subversively enacting a kind of self-governance and popular security. "The war," its website proclaimed—and in which it meant not merely the war against Islamists, but against the Left—"needs to be understood to involve scholarship, think tank research, textbooks, campus activities, the media, press relations, philanthropy, corporate decisions, political lobbying, lawsuits, feature movies, toys, computer games, and much else." This is not the domain of "government," it explained, because "the demands of political correctness" prevent government authorities from doing and saying what is needed. Like Spencer's Jihad Watch,

---

[67] See http://fpgroup.foreignpolicy.com/about/history/

Pipes's Islamist Watch was not primarily a technology for surveillance of the 0.6 percent of the U.S. population that was Muslim adults, but for the disciplinary surveillance of the majority of non-Islamist and more progressive Americans.

By this juncture, *all* of Pipes's organizations related to the Middle East or Islam functioned as platforms for the conservative culture war. Writing "Five Years of Campus Watch" in the *Jerusalem Post* on September 20 2007, Pipes externalized the legitimizing or dominant societal knowledge institutions, referring to those in them as "the anti-Americans," and stating that they "do not have a monopoly on intelligence or skills, just a near-monopoly on power." He noted with satisfaction the early success of the cultural struggle, and particularly the contribution of Campus Watch as a dissident institution. Campus Watch, he boasted, had already overturned the "once insular world" of Middle East specialists. Yet, Pipes lamented, "the field's basic problems remain in place," namely "analytical failures, the mixing of politics with scholarship, intolerance of alternative views, apologetics, and the abuse of power over students." Pipes added that the function of Campus Watch was to retake American universities from the illiberal left. The meant that "pro-American scholars"—who he estimated as comprising as much as five percent of Middle East specialists—would need to grow and to "reach parity with the anti-Americans."

In summary, Daniel Pipes followed McLuhan's (1967) argument related to the media that "the medium is the message." In his increasingly puritanical resistance to the established, orthodox mode of security analysis, the alternative medium advanced the alternative, counterhegemonic message. Pipes—the consummate dissident culture warrior—lodged all of his work in this ungoverned virtual realm of the conservative enclave in the alternative media—a dissident or protest realm of knowledge, outside the circle of professionals, avoiding almost certain sanction by university officials or journal or major publisher editors and any meaningful peer review process.

The strategy was as pragmatic as it was principled. His signature website, DanielPipes.org, emerged as one of the more accessed internet sources of politically dissident knowledge about Islam and the Middle East, attracting by 2011 sixty million page visits, and garnering 112,000 comments.[68] From there, his blog—"Lion's Den"—a play that links him to his heroic namesake Daniel in the Bible—could be accessed to capture his even less regulated (and more political) threat writing.

4. Barak Hussein Obama, the Neoconservative Crisis, and More Aggressive Domestic Politics

At the end of the post-9/11 decade, Middle East Forum and its journal, *Middle East Quarterly,* had a track record—in the July 1st 2010 words its editor, Efraim Karsh—of "questioning established wisdom, debunking popular myths, and providing an alternative

---

[68]   According to the counter on his website in August 2012, there had been 63 million visits to his personal website, DanielPipes.org. The website's popularity in the US according to traffic is ranked at 67, 646 in August 2012 (See http://www.alexa.com/siteinfo/danielpipes.org#)

perspective on the region's history and current affairs" (Middle East Forum 2010). This flaunting of the strategy of counter-cultural struggle does not begin to adequately describe the broader elements of cultural politics that Pipes and his institution had quietly embarked upon.

Daniel Pipes's increasing propensity to use his threat writing and his Middle East Forum as platforms for counterhegemonic struggle had taken a markedly more earnest and explicit turn in November 2008, after the landslide defeat of the neoconservative political bloc, from which he had derived much of his capital. Dr. Pipes's threat writing at this juncture began to reflect four more counterhegemonic features: (1) a much more diligent strategy of linking the newest foreign enemy, Islam, to the new Obama administration; (2) a more aggressive struggle against progressive elite; (3) a more popular and politically-antagonistic style of threat writing, and (4) more blatant, explicit form of cultural struggle against domestic political enemies.

Linking Domestic Rivals to the Newest Foreign Enemy

As Jewish scholar, it might seem that Pipes would have been sensitive to any modern-day reenactment of the anti-Semitic conspiracy, *Protocols of the Elders of Zion*. Yet, Pipes played the leading role in constructing its modern-day variant: the purported conspiracy by an allied Islamists and Leftist bloc to destroy the U.S. Constitution. The strategy projected the conspiratorial and racist frames that were historically directed at the Jews onto the conservative movement's primary enemies, foreign and domestic, religious and political—Islam and the Left.

By 2008, this strategy to construct an Islamo-Leftist conspiracy had become a strategic pillar of Pipes's Middle East Forum, reflected in its expanded mission statement clause—to "protect the Constitutional order"[69]—a mission statement clause that otherwise logically could not be coherent to an organization named "Middle East" anything.

Here, Pipes's strategy of action was also nearly identical to that of Kennan and his notion of a grand conspiracy called the "concealed Comintern"—an "inner central core," who "may also appear and act in unrelated public capacities," but "are in reality working closely together as an underground operating directorate of world communism." For Kennan, this conspiracy involved a Gramscian-style war of position to penetrate and control what he called "a wide variety of national associations or bodies," and Pipes was now framing Islamists and Leftists as allied in such a conspiracy.

In this strategy, when political pundits and polls were beginning to predict a sound defeat of the McCain-Palin platform, Pipes did his part by publishing "Allied Menace" in the July 14 2008 *National Review*. The article described "the burgeoning alliance of Western leftists and Islamists" as one that "impedes the West's efforts to protect itself." The origin of this alliance, he explained, goes back to Foucault's visit to Iran during the revolution to overthrow the popularly illegitimate and U.S.-backed Shah dynasty. Pipes gave four reasons for this seemingly oxymoronic alliance. First among them was the one given by

---

[69] See www.meforum.org, accessed 31 October 2011.

British politician George Galloway: they have the same enemies, namely, "Western civilization in general and the United States, Great Britain, and Israel in particular, plus Jews, believing Christians, and international capitalists …."

The components of Pipes's Middle East Forum during this time functioned as part of the broader ultraconservative apparatus to link the conservative movement's newest foreign enemy with its traditional domestic one. The Winter 2010 edition of *Middle East Quarterly*, for example, promoted Jamie Glazov's (David Horowitz's editor of *FrontPageMagazine*) recent productions, *United in Hate: The Left's Romance with Tyranny and Terror*. The absurdly short, one-page "book review" by Pipes's former co-author and acolyte described how Michel Foucault, Edward Said, and other more leftist academics had lauded early Islamic revolutionary movements, by which he meant the Iranian Revolution. In the next two sentences in this one-page review Glazov resurrected McCarthyesque and early John Birch Society frames to charge politically progressive journalists, members of the film industry, and even former Democratic president Jimmy Carter with having colluded with this newest foreign enemy within. Such one-page book reviews can suffice if you are merely stating what your readership already knows and expects to see reaffirmed in their subscription.

In all of his threat writing at this point—rather than substantive knowledge that might inform the policymaker or strategic planners—Daniel Pipes's focus was glaringly domestic cultural politics.

This same strategy to seize the topic of Islam's threat as an opportune platform for cultural politics was on display when President Obama and his entire security team, including General David Petraeus, had chastised Terry Jones—the self-obsessed and arguably mentally-deranged pastor of a tiny Florida church—for burning the Quran. Pipes reliably departed from any reasonable, empirically-tethered professional security discourse and used the occasion for a kind of discursive domestic political terrorism. Writing in his reliable mouthpiece, *Washington Times*, he advanced the Islamo-Leftist alliance frame, asserting that the President had "enforced Islamic law," and described it as "a precedent that could lead to other forms of compulsory Shariah compliance" (*Washington Times* 2010).

By the mid-term elections, such overt domestic cultural politics permeated nearly everything Pipes was writing broadly related to the threat of Islam. Nearly everything he wrote on the topic of Islam or the Middle East broadly contained non-sequitur statements that denigrated the U.S. conservative movement's domestic political rivals, particularly the nation's black president with Muslim ancestry, who had defeated America's conservative hero, John McCain, in a landslide victory.

This move was typified by his December 10, 2010 interview with the new conservative *Pajamas* (now PJ) *Media*, titled "Israel, Iran, Barack Obama's presidency…" (Mitzner and Solomon 2010). And, on the pages of *Commentary* in late April 2010, for example, the topic was Israel, but the emphasis was on the silver lining as the "permanent damage these fights have inflicted on Obama," who in the eyes of many "Zionist Americans" according to an April 22, 2010 Qunnipiac poll—"is seen as "insufficiently supportive of Israel (Pipes 2010: 06; Israel Project 2010).

Even when fundraising, Pipes's function of producing knowledge about the threat from Islam was inseparable from combating the conservative movement's domestic political enemy. In a June, 7, 2011 fundraising e-mail to his subscriber list, Pipes sought financial support by framing enemies foreign and domestic in the same breath, thereby bridging these threats in the minds of his conservative audience:

> Barack Obama is demanding that Israel make concessions to its sworn enemies—or, in Newt Gingrich's words, demanding that Israel 'commit suicide'—even as the president's director of national intelligence absurdly praises Egypt's Muslim Brotherhood as 'a very heterogeneous group, largely secular, which has eschewed violence.'

More Aggressive Struggle against the Liberal Elite

Although Pipes had often centered the Obama Administration in his framing of this new conspiratorial allied menace, Pipes's threat writing continued to be marked by his earlier habitus of counterhegemonic struggle against progressives on both sides of the Atlantic. Pipes did this, for example, in his July 20, 2009 "Europe's Future, Newsweek's Fantasy"—a response to the Italian newspaper *Il Foglio's* request to react to an optimistic analysis in *Newsweek* titled, "Why Fears of a Muslim Takeover Are All Wrong." In this piece, Pipes securitized Europe's liberal "elite," criticizing their idealistic paradigm that "symbiosis, assimilation, good feeling, compromise, and muddling through will prevail."

Similarly, in his counterhegemonic "Why I stand with Geert Wilders," published in January 2010 in the reliable *National Review*, Pipes subtly securitized the Left and its political correctness, or "conventional wisdom"—the "view of most politicians, journalists, and academics"—and their "idealistic approach" of multiculturalism. Evoking medical tropes of the sick and weakened host being consumed by the stronger parasite, he noted the lack of virility of the Leftist culture, especially secularism, and its impact on even its Christian women, whose fertility rate is about one third less than the replenishment level, compared to that of the Muslims who enjoy "a dramatically higher, if falling, fertility rate."

In a more aggressive civilizationalist self-disciplinary move, Pipes framed the sick man of Europe as no longer the Islamic Ottomans but the Left-stricken Western Europe. Europeans, he lamented, "no longer cherish their history, mores, and customs." Leftist ideology, he said, produces "self-disdain;" it naturalizes "guilt about fascism, racism, and imperialism" and thus devalues Judeo-Christian culture, forming a barrier to assimilation." In the unlikely event that the nationalist "anti-immigrant parties" gain power, Pipes imagined a healthy civilization in which the progressive slide to Eurabia is stopped. "They will likely seek to reject multiculturalism, cut back on immigration, encourage repatriation of immigrants, support Christian institutions, increase indigenous European birthrates, and broadly attempt to re-establish traditional ways," he said.

Also typical of this more aggressive anti-left strategy of action was *Middle East Forum's* May 10, 2010 presentation by Melanie Phillips. Phillips was selected *because* she was the author of *Londonistan*, which was a critique of the more progressive governmentality of multiculturalism. Her topic, predictably, was her latest subversive and apocalyptic book,

The World Turned Upside Down: The Global Battle over God, Truth and Power. Although Phillips began by talking about the religious rival, Islam, she quickly shifted to cultural politics, delegitimizing the more progressive social order, euphemized as "Western intelligentsia." The Forum's summary of the brief amounted to only 348 words of text, with its function more politically performative than informational— delegitimizing "secular ideologies" the postmodern "decline in reason" that allows Islam "to fill the vacuum left behind."

As was now his habitus with the Obama administration more directly, Pipes used every possible opportunity to link the conservatives' newest foreign enemy with the more progressive elite. On the occasion of "The Ninth 9/11," for instance, Pipes in the *National Review Online* gave the equivalent of the Republican state of the union address. To the nation's credit, he said, the conservative half of the population "has made substantial progress;" it has "read the Koran" and volunteered for combat. But to its discredit, "the liberal half and the establishment it inevitably controls, from government to media to the academy to the arts, has become ever more determined to ignore the religious aspect of the war and instead reduce it to counterterrorism and economics."

The next year, at the tenth anniversary of 9/11, Pipes answered the question put to him by Frank Gaffney's farther Right *Center for Security Policy*: "Are we safer?" Instead of an objective assessment of the threat of al-Qaeda to the homeland, the center of Pipes's response was reliably the domestic enemy. He noted that "a White House policy document dares not even refer to terrorism in the title," and that "politicians, journalists, and academics" obscure "the nature of the threat and the proper response to it (Pipes 2011).

In this strategy to use the topic of Islam's threat as an opportunity for cultural politics, Pipes made sure that no potential political opportunity in any bit of news broadly related to Islam was lost. On the eve of Turkey's elections, for example, in a June 9, 2011 "Lion's Den" blog post, he provocatively reclassified the longtime but complex NATO member and U.S. ally as a "hostile state." He then suggested that this new Islamist enemy is being aided and abetted by America's Leftist elites. His analysis did not contain the expected empirical engagement with the kind of factors that we might expect for such a security analysis; but instead merely produced a photo of President Obama's Secretary of State, Hillary Clinton, caught "high-fiving" Turkey's Foreign Minister Ahmet Davutoğlu.[70]

Pipes's strategy of security politics—particularly that of linking enemies foreign to enemies domestic—both the progressive elites broadly and the Obama administration more narrowly—showed no sign of abating after President Obama's reelection. The July 27, 2012 article in Campus Watch, "Professors and Politicos Fooled by the Muslim Brotherhood," achieved both aims, combining the older, subtler counterhegemonic strategy of delegitimizing the progressive academy to the newer, more blatant one centered on the Obama administration.

The piece began saying, "Engagement with Egypt's Muslim Brotherhood is the consensus among elite opinion and certainly among the ranks of North American Middle East studies academics, the 'experts' tasked with informing the public and, often, policy-

---

[70] See http://www.danielpipes.org/blog/2011/06/on-the-eve-of-turkey-elections

makers on foreign policy in the region." It then shifted, noting that "these academics have whitewashed the Muslim Brotherhood, downplayed its Islamist agenda, and urged U.S. cooperation—a policy suggestion the Obama administration has clearly taken to heart," and then added, "Many have been shocked by the speed with which the Obama administration has pursued this policy of outreach."

More Popular and Politically-Antagonistic Style of Threat Writing

Out of the neoconservative crisis which effectively exiled Pipes from Washington, there was another manifest shift in his security writing; it became increasingly marked by a distinctly more popular, unprofessional, and politically-antagonistic style. From his blog, Lion's Den, on June 4, 2009, in a post titled "Islam in Obama's Cairo Speech," any vestiges of Dr. Pipes the strategic intellectual was gone, and the new trivial, partisan, conspiracy-minded, and FOX News-like commentator had emerged. Rather than provide politically-incorrect insights regarding U.S.-Islam relations, as he was once prone to do, Pipes now displayed a more anti-rationalist mode of understanding that must have been designed to appeal to that like-minded segment of U.S. religious conservatives. This time, Pipes advanced a conspiracy over the new president's greeting in his speech; namely "a greeting of peace from Muslim communities in my country: Assalaamu alaykum." "This Islamic greeting, here written 'Assalaamu alaykum,'" Pipes claimed, "is for one Muslim to address to another" and that "By saying these words, Obama hints at his being a Muslim." Thus, in his trademark ideological move of exclusion, Pipes renders invisible the universal tradition to use whatever common vernacular cultural greeting as a matter of respect. Most security professionals, diplomats and business people who routinely travel to Muslim majority countries or who regularly address Muslim groups or even individuals on American streets use this greeting as a voluntary sign of respect. The old adage, "when in Rome…" applies.

To help him spearhead his strategic shift to more politically-antagonistic, low-brow threat writing, Pipes embraced the very "anti-Islam bloggers" that he was beginning to deride (Boorstein 2010), hiring Raymond Ibrahim from Robert Spencer's Jihad Watch team as the Forum's Associate Director and then Associate Fellow. Ibrahim, of Egyptian Coptic Christian descent, also provided commentary on the president's speech in Cairo in his "Islamist Perfidy and Western Naivety: Which is More Lethal?" in *Pajamas Media*, which was—as everything this field of security polemicist wrote—reliably republished at Middle East Forum. After showing how the Leftist elite systematically obscure the true meaning of "jihad," Ibrahim then carefully used Barack Obama's middle name, "Hussein," to advance the Islamo-Leftist conspiracy. Ibrahim noted how Obama had selected for his coded speech a passage from Sura 9, "the most violent and intolerant exhortations in all the Koran," thereby implying that the President's true identity was that of a closet stealth jihadist.

Part of Pipes's shift to a cruder form of threat writing entailed a more diligent move of exclusion with regard to anyone or anything published outside of the more rightist end of the conservative knowledge enclave. Many of the experts that Pipes now cited in his threat writing were those who he had formerly classified as anti-Islam bloggers. In his "Uncovering Early Islam" in the May 16, 2012 edition of *National Review Online*, for example, Daniel Pipes favorably reviewed Robert Spencer's new provocative book, *Did Muhammad Exist?* As with his other book reviews, Pipes chose the book to review *because* it was revisionist—in his words—"demonstrating the inconsistencies and mysteries in the conventional account concerning Muhammad's life, the Koran, and early Islam."

Dr. Pipes's more popular, dissident, even heretical form of threat writing abandoned the unwritten rules of the security profession broadly, and instead operated in the realm of emotion-evoking political antagonism. Typifying these features was the article "Life Under Sharia," published by his project, Islamist Watch, on June 21, 2012. Here, professionally-normative, in-depth, rationally-based analyses—what Khaneman (2011) called the "System 2" mode of thought, with rigorous empirical confirmation and contextualization—was absent. In its place was the more emotional and stereotypical "System 1" mode. The piece first evoked a fear of extinction over Islamization, reminding its anticipated conservative market that this "project of the Middle East Forum, defends the freedoms and liberties of Western society against 'stealth jihad,' a campaign by Islamists to slowly and methodically implement a Sharia-compliant theocracy in the West."

As an implied example of the America to come, the article contained links to eight graphic videos of extreme violence or cruelty that took place in Muslim societies: women beaten in Sudan and Saudi Arabia, a stoning to death in the Afghanistan-Pakistan border, long imprisonments for men in Turkey and Kuwait for atheist and anti-Muhammad tweets, executions of homosexuals in Iran, and the slaughtering of a convert to Christianity in Tunisia.

In the latter case, there was a link to the June 4, 2012 article, "Graphic Video: Muslims Slaughter 'Apostate" in Tunisia," wherein Pipes continued to subvert the establishment's Islam-is-peace frame in another piece by his protégé, Raymond Ibrahim. Ibrahim described how the masked Muslim perpetrator in the video "begins to slice away," and how after about a minute "of graphic knife-carving," the young Christian "drowns in blood" while the head is held aloft to "more Islamic slogans of victory." Pipes by this time had encouraged Ibrahim's System 1 mode of production, typified by his July 12, 2012 "Sodomy 'For the Sake of Islam"—the title of which accurately denoted the dissident, politically-incorrect content. By this point, Pipes had so fully embraced the cruder popular style that he was routinely citing or other promoting Ibrahim by cross-posting his anti-Islam blogger-style productions at Gatestone and *Pajamas Media* to the Middle East Forum, sometimes under a slightly different title.

Pipes's affinity for the Gatestone Institute, where Ibrahim was lodged, stemmed in part from the 2.3 million dollars of his funding from Sears Roebuck heiress Nina Rosenwald, founder and director of the Gatestone Institute, and former board member of the Israel lobby's AIPAC (Blumenthal 2012). In addition to funding Pipes, Rosenwald had given millions to similar Islam-as-threat polemicists like David Horowitz, Brigitte Gabriel, and Frank Gaffney (Ali 2011).

More Explicit Mode of Cultural Politics

In addition to Daniel Pipes's implicit mode of counterhegemonic struggle—again, through counternarrative about Islam and through non-discursive dissident strategies of production, some of his productions exhibited a more blatant, explicit element of domestic political struggle.

For instance, although Pipes's key interview role in the low-brow anti-Islam documentary production, *Obsession: Radical Islam's War Against the West*, remained centered on the newest foreign enemy, Islam, the production itself by Clarion Fund, where both Pipes and Gaffney served on the board, was aimed at the old domestic enemy (Goldberg 2008; Kindy 2008). $17 million given for the film's marketing—a pass through gift from an anonymous donor via Donors Capital Fund marked for the Clarion Fund to distribute the film—paid for some 28 million DVD copies of the film to be distributed in household newspapers in key swing states just before the 2008 presidential elections, in an obvious effort to sway voters towards the more hawkish GOP McCain-Palin ticket and against the Democratic one of Obama-Biden (Elliot 2008). And, at his blog, "Lion's Den," Pipes frequently relaxed and took a more explicit approach to the conservative culture war, typified by the cross-post from his piece in the *National Review Online* on the eve of the general election, "Why I Am Voting Republican."

5. More Indirect and Puritanical Modes of Culture War

In addition to the more diligent and even cruder political engagement of domestic political rivals—both the Obama administration and more progressive elite—Daniel Pipes's counterhegemonic strategy included a still more indirect and even puritanical element of culture war that was aimed at the subversion of the broader, more progressive culture, including its societal regulations concerning authority, along with its politics of truth.

Subversion of Societal Regulations Concerning Authority

To advance his aforementioned notion of conservative power-knowledge reaching parity with that of the "anti-Americans," or "the establishment," as he was prone to refer to the political outside (Pipes and Chadha 2006), Dr. Pipes seemed ever-more determined to subvert the more progressive political order indirectly—by subverting its societal norms surrounding the production of truth, especially its regulations regarding authority, or credentials in security writing.

Pipes's basic assumption was correct, of course; every society has a dominant system or regime for producing "truth," or authoritative statements, along with largely unwritten but well-understood regulations concerning the authorities that produce them—what his nemesis Foucault referred to as the "authorities of delimitation" (Foucault 1972, 46-49, 55). And, to be clear, Pipes had long enacted such a counterhegemonic strategy regarding the *content* or narratives of his threat assessments. For example, when considering whether to publish an article, *Middle East Quarterly's* editors had to answer "no" to the question, "Is this an article other quarterlies would publish?"(Getz 2000). That regulatory structure that other journals were constrained by was openly derided in Pipes's journal, *Middle East Quarterly*, by selecting or commissioning threat writers with few or none of the credentials normative of the more dominant societal regime of truth.

In the *Quarterly's* Winter 2008 edition, for example, Melvin E. Lee—identified as "a sea captain and a nuclear engineer in the United States Navy"—fills the dissident journal's pages with "The Fallacy of Grievance-based Terrorism." In a move that tacitly delegitimized all of the authoritative literature on the topic, the article defiantly negated any role of political grievances in radicalization. In a mocking, sarcastic tone, that was steeped in anti-intellectualism, this "sea captain" and "nuclear engineer" scornfully dismissed decades of empirical research across a broad swath of international scholarship that underscored the role of political grievances in revolutionary movements that use terrorism as a means of struggle. For example, Europe's main think tank manned by former extremists—the Quilliam Foundation—in 2010 published a case study of radicalization in British Universities which validated a conceptual framework that gives political grievances a central role in the process towards participating personally in terrorism (Quilliam, 2010).

But Pipes's expert in this article wiped all of that scholarship from view and asserted without empirical confirmation that those researchers forming broader sociological and psychological consensus "misunderstand the enemy and its nature" (Lee 2008).

Similarly, the Winter 2011 edition of Pipes's journal mocked the academy with an article appropriately described as "the "alternate perspective," by a graduate student at Catholic University. The review attempted to delegitimize the book *Anti-Terror Lessons of Muslim-Americans* (2010), by David Schanzer and Charles Kurzman of Duke University, and Ebrahim Moosa of University of North Carolina. This more extreme counterhegemonic move of pure negation was that of having a student—not another professor of the more conservative persuasion—delegitimize these established scholars' attempt to answer the question "do Muslim-Americans support terror?" by characterizing their study as a "complete methodological failure."

In a similar strategy, Pipes's Campus Watch recruited a Jewish student who had just graduated from New York University with a degree in Middle East and Islam to criticize prominent scholars on those topics, like Georgetown University's John Esposito. Campus Watch functioned as the agent to get the student's criticism of the establishment faculty published in the conservative magazine, *American Thinker* (Goldman 2010).

In another instance, Campus Watch sponsored an article to—in classic McCarthy-esque form—delegitimize fifteen established professors guilty of "whitewashing the Muslim Brotherhood." The credentials of the author sponsored for this task were openly flaunted as "a writer whose interests include public affairs and foreign policy," thereby deliberately mocking the orthodox rules for authority (Doerflinger 2011). Campus Watch helped that unorthodox author publish her work in Horowitz's blatant instrument of culture war, *FrontPageMagazine*.

This more indirect counterhegemonic strategy of *pure negation* of the societal regulations concerning authority was also on display in the Summer 2011 edition of *Middle East Quarterly*, in the article "Shari'a and Violence in American Mosques." First, the report's findings were reliably transgressive of societal norms regarding speech that impugned the broader Muslim-American community; it described how it surveyed 114 randomly selected mosques, finding that "fully 81 percent of the mosques featured Islamic texts that advocate violence" and "in nearly 85 percent of the mosques, the leadership (usually an imam or prayer leader) favorably recommended this literature for study by congregants." In that vein, the report's authors added that "58 percent of the mosques invited guest lecturers known for promoting violent jihad" (Kedar and Yerushalmi 2011).

Second, it was not merely the content that was transgressive of the societal taboos; the authors themselves were heretical, and tacitly functioned to delegitimize the going regulations on authority related to security knowledge. One author, David Yerushalmi, was not merely an Orthodox Jewish lawyer in Brooklyn who had no recognized credentials on the security topic; he was the legal counsel of record for the political apparatchiks Frank Gaffney, Robert Spencer and Pamela Geller, and had authored the model legislation to contain the sharia-ization or Islamization of America that was introduced in two dozen conservative states (Summers 2011). In other words, the very author of the legislation to prevent the Islamization of the nation was the author whom Gaffney had commissioned (and Pipes had published) on the topic of the degree to which U.S. mosques used the harsher interpretations of sharia and other doctrines. The other author, Mordechai Kedar, similarly had no pretense of scholarly disinterestedness, and his presence gives some credence to much of the literature's characterization of this discourse as motivated primarily by hatred for Muslims; love for Israel. Kedar had founded the McCarthy-esque Israel Academia Monitor—the Israeli equivalent of Pipes's Campus Watch—for purposes of fighting left-leaning "extremist Israeli academics who exploit academic freedom in order to take steps to deny Israel's right to exist as a Jewish state," according to its website.[71]

Increasing Transgression of Threat Taboos and Strategies of Euphemization

A celebrity after 9/11 for being about the only conservative writer on the threat topic of Islam, Daniel Pipes was by the end of the post-9/11 decade effectively marginalized by the thousands of high-quality, professional security products on the topic that had emerged each year. His more complete marginalization during the neoconservatives' exodus from Washington marked the point in Dr. Pipes's security writing in which he began to openly reflect and even revel in that marginalization as a form of counter-cultural distinction. His writing at this juncture became much more heretical, transgressing societal norms, specifically regarding the norm of political disinterestedness in professional security writing, and norms regarding the classification of all of Islam as a threat.

Pipes's main challenge in this mode of counterhegemonic struggle remained familiar: it was to transgress these norms while continuing to attract his long-time, more centrist

---

[71] See http://www.israel-academia-monitor.com/

philanthropic patrons, avoiding being classified as an anti-Islam blogger himself. To do this, Pipes crafted a sanction-avoidance strategy that carefully and intermittently transgressed the societal taboos regarding speech on Islam. Pipes's earlier mode of production has already revealed how this strategy is commonly advanced by counter-cultural producers—one that Bourdieu (1991, 20, 84) described as "strategies of euphemization,"[72] and one that Shuy (1997, 121) described as coded language.[73] Practically, this merely meant that Pipes's writing on the topic of Islam's threat was increasingly marked by highly-euphemized, implicit, coded, messages designed to delegitimize the dominant, more progressive culture.[74]

For example, in his November 20, 2009 article "Major Hasan's Islamist Life," the title implies that Islamism by itself explains his terrorist actions, and that the political correctness in the increasingly progressive military ignored the warning signs. The piece avoids sanction by societal norms that politely avoid linking Islam with violence by adding the safely ambiguous suffix, "ist." Beyond the title, in the text, however, the necessary euphemization was relaxed either intermittently or entirely—using the intended signifier "Islam" and its euphemized, more acceptable codeword "Islamist" interchangeably. Engaging the broader more-progressive culture's political correctness, Dr. Pipes wondered rhetorically about the establishment's investigations into the Fort Hood incident: "will they confront the hard truth of the Islamic angle?" The euphemization or coded language is again dropped as Pipes expects that—given the Left's hegemony in academia, government and the media—there will be "a whitewash of the massacre," rendering invisible the "hostile ideology nearly *exclusive to Muslims*." Continuing to subvert the more progressive outside and relaxing this strategy of euphemization, Pipes laments that "initial responses from the U.S. Army, law enforcement, politicians, and journalists broadly agreed that Maj. Nidal Hasan's murderous rampage had nothing to do with Islam." As a final subversion of the more progressive societal regime of truth, Pipes readily published the piece not in a legitimate journal or more mainstream magazine, but in David Horowitz's radically counter-cultural and anti-Left *FrontPageMagazine*.

In another example, in the Fall 2009 edition of the *Middle East Quarterly*, its editor (not Pipes) reviewed Jon Davies' 2009 book, *In Search of the Moderate Muslim*. The implicit message was in the title, which the reader readily recognized as adapted from the television show "In Search of Bigfoot"—the perennial fuzzy monster who everyone knew didn't

---

[72] See Bourdieu's essay "Censorship and the Imposition of Form," pp 137-162. All such strategies of subversion, Bourdieu observed, enact a style that is "highly sublimated and euphemized" (Bourdieu 1986, 147). The productions subvert the legitimate culture by circumventing its regulatory framework—what Bourdieu called its "system of specific sanctions and censorships"; and this occurs through forms of "self-censorship," including the manner of saying, "code switching" or "bilingualism" (Bourdieu 1991, 37-38, 77, 129).

[73] Shuy (1997, 123) describes a "partial and disguised codes" as those when "the substituted or coded words are carefully selected to make it appear to anyone who should happen to intercept the conversation that the participants are talking about one thing when, in reality, they are talking about something quite different."

[74] Baklouti (2007) first noted this operation of implicit messaging or "degrees of implicitness," or a "secondary meaning" in anti-Islam discourse, where the signifier has obvious meaning to the subcultural market beyond the explicit or obvious meaning.

exist. The review concludes that the author performs an important service by dispensing with the establishment's trite references to "moderate Muslims." The article marked a milestone in Pipes's own journey. In only 14 years, he had gone from "there are no moderates" referring to the Islamist-leaning political class in the Middle East, to the frame that no Muslim could be moderate.

To his subscribers, Daniel Pipes openly touted this form of subversion in a December 16, 2010 private fund-raising e-mail. He described the new strategy as the *Forum's* "careful anti-Islamism," and noted with satisfaction that it was finding wider market appreciation "as anti-Islam sentiments gain traction."

Another way in which Pipes could subvert the political outside and avoid its sanction was to use much if not most of the *Forum's* annual budget to sponsor dissident threat writers to produce articles for publishing in other magazines or e-dailies within the conservative knowledge enclave. As we saw in the case of Pipes's adroit use of anti-Islam blogger Raymond Ibrahim, he increasingly commissioned authors for articles *because* of their propensity for a radical counternarrative regarding the threat of Islam, and for their propensity to otherwise subvert the broader politics of truth. Again, technically, this strategy was less new than it was more advanced. Pipes had begun this particular distancing or sanction-avoidance strategy a couple years earlier. In 2006, for example, Middle East Forum sponsored David Yerushalmi—the aforementioned co-author of "Shari'a and Violence in American Mosques"—to conduct a self-disciplining review of a piece, *Knowing the Enemy,* by even a Bush political appointee who would become a resident at both FPRI and AEI, Mary Habeck. Pipes commissioned Yerushalmi to rein-in this more conservative-leaning scholar not merely because of his reliable disposition to produce the counternarrative, but because of his disposition to transgress all of the societal taboos in discussion about Islam. Yerushalmi's propensity for this kind of transgressive style was obvious, given his white-supremacist article earlier that year, "On Race," which explained why the founding fathers in their wisdom "did not give women or black slaves the right to vote" (Yerushalmi 2006). And, Yerushalmi reliably subverted the politics of truth in the academy in a transgressive syllogism. Because Muhammad was "a man who lived both a peaceful and a violent, murderous life," and whose "words and deeds are considered divinely ordained," Yerushalmi counterhegemonically reasoned, then we cannot expect Muslims to "construct a peaceful ideology or religion."

With sufficient distance from the piece, Pipes remained the subversive wizard behind the curtain, enabling Yerushalmi to explicitly conclude with a heretical statement, without any euphemization, that *"jihadism is in fact traditional Islam"* (Yerushalmi 2006). Pipes, through his Forum, then functioned as Yerushalmi's agent to get the subversive book review published at a safe distance from the Middle East Forum, in the September 9, 2006 edition of the anti-establishment and conservative *American Thinker.* Again, by quietly commissioning the counterhegemonic work and getting it published by a third-party conservative magazine, Pipes avoided sanction personally.

Conclusion

In conclusion, recall how Edward Said had charged that Daniel Pipes's productions functioned not as pure or disinterested knowledge about the Islamic threat, but as highly political knowledge that uses the topic of Islam to secure the interests of the farther-right Zionists both in Israel and in the U.S. And, recall how Said's basic paradigm for this discourse was reflected in all of the substantive literature, up through the end of the post-9/11 decade. But, this characterization enjoyed significant empirical fit with Pipes's threat writing only in his early career, which was focused on the West-Islam civilizational struggle in the 1980s, and Holy Land geopolitics in the 1990s—both juxtaposed to an ascendant, resistant, postcolonial Pan-Islamism.

But, after 9/11 and increasingly throughout the rest of the post-9/11 decade, Pipes's threat writing could no longer be forced into that mold. Early in the decade, while retaining obvious advocacy for Zionist interests, Pipes's writing related to the threat from Islam's continuum increasingly reflected a much broader conservative counterhegemonic political agenda. In other words, his threat writing functioned less to protect the West and its Holy Land from its civilizational and geopolitical competitor, "Islam," than it did as a platform for domestic, U.S. cultural struggle, against the more liberal elite, especially in the academy.

Later in the decade, with the election of Barack Obama and the ousting of the once-influential neoconservative bloc from Washington, Pipes's security productions about Islam broadly took a more blatant turn to domestic politics. It was then that he systematically positioned himself into an archetypical role of resistance ideologue in the U.S. conservative movement's domestic cultural struggle against what he derogatively referred to as "the establishment" or "officialdom"—the more progressive regime of truth housed in the dominant societal institutions of academia, government bureaucracies, and mainstream corporate media. Increasingly politically antagonistic and propaganda-like, his threat writing systematically began linking the U.S. conservative movement's newest ideological foreign enemy, Islam, to is domestic political rivals, both the more progressive regime of truth and the liberal elite more broadly, and the Democrats and the Obama administration more particularly.

By the end of the post-9/11 decade, Daniel Pipes's subversive threat writing had taken an even more marked puritanical turn. Even the name of his blog, the "Lion's Den," leveraged the semiotic elements in the iconic biblical resistance figure Daniel's uncompromising stance against illegitimate governance, refusing to defile himself by assimilating into the profane hegemonic order of his day.

5

ROBERT SPENCER

The Politically-Incorrect Guide to Islam

[T]he production of ideas about the social world is always in fact subordinated to the logic of the conquest of power…and thus can be imposed only by professionals capable of manipulating ideas and groups at one and the same time….

—Pierre Bourdieu (1991, 181)

O N July 22, 2011, the most horrific and puzzling terrorist attack on European soil in the modern era had taken place. Its perpetrator was not who many had expected—an al-Qaeda-inspired Muslim—but Anders Breivik, a 32 year-old ethnic Norwegian who saw himself as the last line of defense of Western Christendom from the enemy who was bringing about its abrupt decline. But the enemy that Breivik had in mind and the specific target of his attacks in this case was not—as we might expect—elements of Norway's 50,000 Muslim population. Instead, Breivik entered an island youth camp run by Norway's more Leftist social democratic Labour Party, where he one-by-one carefully aimed and pulled the trigger on nearly one-hundred of the mostly teenage campers, killing sixty-nine of them.

Breivik's manifesto, "2083," was code for four centuries of resistance to Islam since the year 1683, when Christian Europe defeated the Muslim Ottomans in the Battle of Vienna. 1683 is code in post-9/11 Western civilizationalist discourse for continued resistance to Islam.

Posted to the Internet the day before, Breivik's manifesto bridged the dual frames of enemies foreign and domestic—Islam and the left. It lifted segments of the Unabomber's text, where he changed Ted Kaczynski's critique of leftism by substituting the words "multiculturalism" or "cultural Marxism"—coded language, as we've seen, for Islam and the Left.

But, the main source of this deeply-disturbed young man's inspiration for bridging the enemies foreign and domestic frames was the conservative culture warrior David Horowitz's employee and founder of the wildly popular blog, *Jihad Watch*, Robert Spencer. To justify his actions, Breivik's manifesto cited Jihad Watch 116 times, and favorably cited Spencer by name 52 times. Obviously a close reader of everything Spencer had written, Breivik's manifesto reproduced many of Spencer's trademark terms for the right-wing's domestic political enemies—"useful idiots," "the leftists," and so on."[75] Recall that Robert Spencer was also the main source of inspiration for one-time GOP presidential front-runner Newt Gingrich, who borrowed Spencer's term "stealth jihadis" at his July 2010 campaign speech at the Israel lobby's American Enterprise Institute.

The use of Mr. Spencer's threat writing for political projects of all types on both sides of the Atlantic stemmed from his unique perspectives forged in an unorthodox preparation of more than twenty-five years. Spencer's academic preparation for this pivotal role in post-9/11 Western civilizationalist discourse was not—as we might imagine—a long period of analysis of security threats in respected institutions geared toward Muslim majority countries. Instead, his journey began with an unrelated master's degree in religious studies from the University of North Carolina in 1986, with a thesis emphasis in an esoteric element of Catholic history (Spencer 2008). A "non-Roman" Catholic and "Reverend Deacon" at a Melkite Greek Orthodox (Maronite) church in the US (not to be divulged here for his protection), Spencer's thesis was oriented in that faith tradition. Titled "The Monophysite in the Mirror," his thesis concerns the conversion of John Henry Newman to Catholicism in 1845 and his denunciation of the Church of England as monophysite.

Spencer then worked in obscurity for the next sixteen years in conservative think tanks such as the Free Congress Foundation (Jacobson 2010; Jihad Watch). This foundation, per its website, www.freecongress.org, states that its "main focus" is "the Culture War." It asks, "Will America return to the culture that made it great, our traditional, Judeo-Christian, Western culture? Or will we continue the long slide into the cultural and moral decay of political correctness?"

This unorthodox preparation notwithstanding, Mr. Spencer emerged as a public figure in 2002, publishing *Islam Unveiled: Disturbing Questions About the World's Fastest Growing Faith*. One of the first books set within the politically-incorrect counternarrative to the "Islam is peace" frame, the work and Spencer's bona fides as a capable conservative culture warrior at the Free Congress Foundation garnered the attention of David Horowitz. In October 2003, the two had agreed to launch Jihad Watch as a project of Horowitz's center, with Spencer as its director. Each Jihad Watch daily digest since then has contained about a dozen attention-grabbing headlines for embedded news articles that are broadly related to the threat of Islam(ization), which were sent in by faithful members of the network, and then selected for Spencer's (or one of his chosen agents) expert commentary-style analysis.

Of Levantine heritage and sufficiently proficient in Arabic, and now entirely focused on contemporary Islam in terms of its threat to the West broadly, Spencer quickly became

---

[75] See pg 647 in Breivik's manifesto, for example.

internationally known for his blunt, pessimistic, and always politically-incorrect threat assessments and commentary related to Islam as a threat.

Mr. Spencer's reliable position earned him a central interview in the widely viewed anti-Islam documentary, *Islam, What the West Needs to Know*. That film was created with the following counterhegemonic purpose:

> This documentary sets out to investigate the notion that Islam is a "religion of peace" and explore the widely circulated idea that those who commit violent acts in the name of Islam are a fanatic few. The filmmakers try to hold Islam's own sources to the light to make the controversial claim that the religion is actually driven by a violent, expansionary ideology that seeks to conquer any contradictory religion, culture, and, ultimately, government.

His interview in this provocative film cemented Spencer's text as the pole position for all national debates about the threat of Islam. On the August 13, 2006 CSPAN *Q and A*, when host Brian Lamb interviewed Ambassador Akbar Ahmed, Ibn Khaldun Chair of Islamic Studies at American University, for example, Lamb began by airing a segment of Spencer's commentary in the documentary:

> Islam is the only religion in the world that has a developed doctrine theology and legal system that mandates violence against unbelievers and mandates that Muslims must wage war in order to establish the homogeneity of the Islamic social order over the world. Now, these things are objectively verifiable facts. Anyone can look at the Koran. Anyone can look at the Muslim sources, the Muslim history, Muslim legal texts and so on and find that to be true. [76]

At this mid-point of the post-9/11 decade, Mr. Spencer's book-length analyses and his blog's shorter running commentary on selected Muslim actions worldwide had garnered the attention of the more politically-active Muslim-American leaders, who were studying and discussing his writings amongst themselves. [77] Overseas, a large percentage of Muslim leaders worldwide knew of Spencer, even though most could not access Jihad Watch due to the site being banned by their government. [78] Even Benazir Bhutto, the late prime minister of Pakistan, had singled out Spencer as the source of the increasing rift between Islam and the West. In her 2008 book, *Reconciliation: Islam, Democracy, and the West*, Bhutto accused Spencer of presenting a "skewed, one-sided, and inflammatory story that only helps to sow the seed of civilizational conflict" (Bhutto 2008, 245). To contain Spencer and Jihad Watch's influence in advancing the counternarrative on Islam, Muslim activists founded the websites Spencer Watch and Loon Watch, in which they often sarcastically countered Spencer's narratives.

Up to this point of his visibly symbolism of the politically-incorrect counternarrative, Spencer had been allowed to give briefings on the security aspects of Islam broadly at the

---

[76] Transcript from September 13, 2008 rebroadcast: http://qanda.org/Transcript/?ProgramID=1090.

[77] Author's personal experience, in Washington DC meetings with most of the more prominent Muslim-American leaders in the 2004-2008 timeframe.

[78] Author's personal experience in the interfaith movement in Washington DC, and as a security and intelligence professional with a worldwide Muslim community portfolio.

request of individual employees at official government institutions, within segments of the United States Central Command, United States Army Command and General Staff College, the U.S. Army's Asymmetric Warfare Group, the FBI, the Joint Terrorism Task Force, and the U.S. intelligence community. But, as Spencer cemented his symbolic place on polar (op)position of the Islam-is-peace narrative, the national security establishment was forced to sideline him.

Such resistance to his work and broader marginalization made little difference; Spencer would go onto author twelve books within the counternarrative, including *Islam Unveiled: Disturbing Questions About the World's Fastest Growing Faith* (Encounter); *Onward Muslim Soldiers: How Jihad Still Threatens America and the West* (Regnery); *Religion of Peace? Why Christianity Is and Islam Isn't* (Regnery), *Stealth Jihad: How Radical Islam is Subverting America without Guns or Bombs* (Regnery), and *The Complete Infidel's Guide to the Koran* (Regnery). He also wrote two *New York Times* bestsellers: *The Truth About Muhammad,* and *The Politically Incorrect Guide to Islam (and the Crusades)*—again, both published by Regnery. The back cover of the latter book begins to expose Spencer's role in the Horowitz apparatus of cultural politics:

> Everything (well, almost everything) you know about Islam and the Crusades is wrong because most textbooks and popular history books are written by left-wing academics and Islamic apologists who justify their contemporary political agendas with contrived historical "facts." But fear not: Robert Spencer (author of the bestseller *Islam Unveiled*) refutes the popular myth….

By the ten-year anniversary of 9/11, Spencer had written more and with more effect to counter the Islam-is-peace storyline than anyone. He had created 25,000 blog posts on the subject, with his signature lengthy commentary. Far surpassing the websites of other popular threat writers, such as those of Daniel Pipes, Jihad Watch achieved the rank of 45th among *all* U.S. political blogs, receiving 33 million visits between May 2006 and May 2009, for example, *before* the website became *more* popular in the "ground zero mosque" spectacle. On August 3rd, 2010, fifteen months after the blog's site meter was stopped for uncertain reasons, Spencer in a Jihad Watch post gave a verbal update on readership, stating that he thought July 2010 was "the biggest month ever for Jihad Watch, with 2,900,225 unique visitors: an average of 93,556 a day."

In the analysis that follows, we will empirically engage Mr. Spencer's threat discourse to ascertain how it functioned within the realm of domestic cultural politics.

1. Manufacturing Jihad: Producing Threat Crises as Opportunity for Politics

Recall from the introduction how about the mid-term elections in the first Obama administration there was a puzzling inward turn of U.S. conservative threat discourse— when the threat axis began to shift from the foreign threat of Islam to the wildly anti-rationalist domestic threat of Islamization.

The context surrounding this new crisis of Islamization was the broader conservative crisis of 2009. By this juncture, the U.S. conservative movement's infatuation with the new threat of Islam had largely been replaced by the "Great Recession," and the temporary rebirth of fiscal conservatism in the GOP in the form of the Tea Party movement. The threat of Islam was not mentioned anywhere on the TeaParty.org website, which lauded "true American Patriots from every race, religion, national origin, and walk of life sharing a common belief in the values which made and keep our beloved nation great," and whose stated core beliefs do not express anything related to enemies foreign as a category.[79] Director of National Intelligence Dennis Blair's February 2009 testimony before Congress seemed to reflect the mood of the Tea Party and the nation broadly. In the speech that perhaps marked the end of the post-9/11 security era and the myopic infatuation with Islam, Blair made clear that the far-and-away greatest threat to the U.S. was economic in nature (Mazzetti 2009).

The rupture in the conservative movement's master security narrative—that is, the abrupt shift from new enemies foreign to prodigal domestic economic mismanagement as the main threat to the nation—had thrown the subject position of mere jihad watchers like Spencer into crisis. The exotic news about jihad or Islam in some faraway land was no longer able to compete with the real threats within the homeland. It was in this context that the Horowitz and Spencer team seemed to have assessed that a more drastic forms of threat politics was needed. And, it was at this point that Spencer's habitus visibly shifted from a simple watcher of jihad overseas to the seemingly incoherent role of manufacturing jihad at home.

But manufacturing a new Islam-related threat crisis in the milieu of a nation gripped by economic disaster could not be business-as-usual, everyday commentary from even a blog with such high viewership as Jihad Watch. It was perhaps for this reason that Spencer's Jihad Watch posts began frequently mentioning Pamela Geller. A fiery New Yorker in her mid-fifties and of Jewish heritage, the aforementioned Geller—from our analysis of *FOX News Channel*—had been an associate publisher of the New York *Observer*, and was an intensely political blogger. Her blog *Atlas Shrugs*—an obvious take-off on Ayn Rand's famous book—was launched in February 2005, and was at that juncture ranked 16th among conservative blogs—tied with Michelle Malkin's, who, recall, was in favor of internment of Muslim-Americans, similar to that of the Japanese.

Geller was a master of grabbing attention, all the way down to her blog's photos of herself in a bikini. But her sex appeal to older men was easily matched by her political appeal to some conservatives. On Christmas Eve, 2007, frolicking in a bikini on an Israeli beach and addressing her remarks to U.S. troops deployed, she said, "I am going to endorse any candidate who can beat the anti-Christ on the Democratic ticket"—referring to Barack Obama, whom she then called "a Muslim" (Geller 2007).

It was these reliable and visceral shock statements that centered both Islam and the Left that gradually worked their designed magic—elating many conservatives, drawing

---

[79] See http://www.teaparty.org/about-us/

criticism from progressives, and drawing the attention of the media and viewers, despite the economic crisis.

Typifying this media response to Geller's more discursive form of terrorism was the October 8, 2010 *New York Times* article, "Outraged, and Outrageous," by Anne Barnard and Alan Feuer. It described Geller as waging "a form of holy war through Atlas Shrugs, a Web site that attacks Islam with rhetoric venomous enough that PayPal at one point branded it a hate site." The piece noted that Geller had "called for the removal of the Dome of the Rock from atop the Temple Mount in Jerusalem" and "suggested the State Department was run by 'Islamic supremacists'."

By the fall of 2009, Spencer and Geller had formed the *Freedom Defense Initiative* to provide some distance from Horowitz's Center and their blogs. Shortly thereafter, the new activist duo had seized the opportunity to form an American chapter of the "Stop the Islamisation of Europe" movement. Anders Gravers—the Danish leader of that movement—stated that the new Stop Islamization of America chapter "was meant to be a group that should take action, staging demonstrations, happenings and events against the Islamisation of the U.S." (Jihad Watch, 2 April 2010).

It did not matter that there was essentially no Islam in America, or that—unlike Europe's immigrants—America were largely highly traditionalist Catholic and Pentecostal Hispanics. For this bold new panic frame of the Islamization of America to advance, all that was needed was a symbol—a poster-child, so to speak. The raw material for the symbol's construction emerged the next month, on May 6th, 2010, when—following the New York City community board's unanimous vote to approve the project—Rupert Murdoch's *New York Post* carried the headline "Panel Approves 'WTC' Mosque" (Elliot 2010).

For Spencer and Geller, it was too good to be true. The heretofore little-known story went back to early 2009, when American-born, New York City imam, Feisal Abdul Rauf, along with a financier partner, proposed the Cordoba project—the renovation of 51 Park Place, an abandoned building in lower Manhattan, two blocks from the former World Trade Center, transforming it into a 13-story community center with an embedded mosque. News of the proposal broke on December 8, 2009, when the *New York Times* featured the Cordoba project on its front page. Favorable in tone, the piece cited the leading the imam's statement, "We want to push back against the extremists," and noted that the project had support among some Jewish leaders and city officials, as well as 9/11 survivors, and even vetted Rauf with a statement from an FBI spokesman regarding his cooperation with the authorities. FOX News had even taken an uncharacteristically conciliatory position on the multicultural project. On December 21, 2009, the guest-host of "The O'Reilly Factor" interviewed Imam Rauf's wife, Daisy, concluding the interview with, "I like what you're trying to do."

But, when the *New York Post* captured the story in a catchy headline "WTC Mosque," the planned Islamization of America threat narrative had its symbol, and Spencer and

Geller quickly transformed it into "the Islamic Supremacist Mega-Mosque at Ground Zero"—to use Geller's words in a post on June 14th, 2010.[80]

Geller launched the project with a post in her *Atlas Shrugs*: "Monster Mosque Pushes Ahead in Shadow of World Trade Center Islamic Death and Destruction."[81] "This is Islamic domination and expansionism," she wrote in her characteristic bombastic style. She then framed the project as an Islamic "victory mosque." "The location is no accident," she said, "just as Al-Aqsa was built on top of the Temple in Jerusalem." She was referring to Jerusalem's Dome of the Rock mosque, built atop the Jewish Temple Mount, and describing the tendency of Muslim conquerors to Islamize synagogues and churches, similar to the way Constantinople's Hagia Sophia was Islamized.

Spencer over at Jihad Watch cross-posted or commented on everything Geller was writing.

And, on May 7, 2010, Spencer and Geller's Stop the Islamization of America (SIOA) began its "Campaign Offensive: Stop the 911 Mosque!," organizing a protest against the "911 monster mosque" on May 29th, symbolically commemorating May 29, 1453, when "the Ottoman forces led by the Sultan Mehmet II broke through the Byzantine defenses against the Muslim siege of Constantinople." On May 13th, under frame and headline "Mosque Madness at Ground Zero," Geller and Spencer's negative portrayal of the project was predictably advanced by the *New York Post*.

SIOA's June 6 and September 11 anti-mosque rallies in lower Manhattan afforded the platform for more political posturing. In addition to Dutch anti-immigration leader, Geert Wilders, the rallies featured conservative apparatchiks like John Bolton and Andrew Breitbart.

The manufactured event was quickly turned into a vehicle for domestic politics, with culture warriors on both sides using it. FOX News Channel's Sean Hannity featured Geller on his radio show, and rival MSNBC's right-wing critic, Keith Olbermann gave a heartfelt monologue against SIOA's politicization of the project.

In similar vein, conservative political elite, then already actively campaigning for President, began to brandish their national security and culture warrior credentials by using the site. On July 21, 2010 for example, Newt Gingrich—in a fundamentalist speech that eerily paralleled that of Osama bin Laden—adeptly linked enemies foreign and domestic, saying that "America is experiencing an Islamist cultural-political offensive designed to undermine and destroy our civilization." He added, "sadly, too many of our elites are the willing apologists for those who would destroy them if they could" (Fisher, 2010).

With the ground zero "mega-mosque" site now fully politicized and luring in broader discourse on the topic, cultural politics was an everyday strategy. This habitus was typified by the August 24, 2010 *Jihad Watch* post that sarcastically denigrated progressive

---

[80] See http://pamelageller.com/2010/06/video-highlights-from-the-protest-against-the-islamic-supremacist-mega-mosque-at-ground-zero.html/
[81] See http://atlasshrugs2000.typepad.com/atlas_shrugs/2010/05/monster-mosque-pushes-ahead-in-shadow-of-world-trade-center-islamic-death-and-destruction.html

intellectuals: "Christopher Hitchens discovers that the Ground Zero mosque imam is not as moderate as he is cracked up to be."

And during this manufactured threat crisis, no opportunity was wasted to systematically delegitimize every part of the more progressive outside, typified by the September 27th post, "60 Minutes whitewashes Ground Zero mega-mosque leaders, smears Pamela Geller."

Much of this delegitimizing took the form of linking Islam and the Left as dual threats to the homeland. And, most of it was done in more subtle, banal but relentlessly everyday fashion, typified by his September 8th post, "McCarthy: On the Ground Zero mosque, Americans are rejecting the opinion elites," which was—also in typical fashion—a rebroadcast of McCarthy's piece at *National Review*. The piece reliably strained to link enemies foreign and domestic, Islam and the Left, by juxtaposing (without empirical evidence) the rise of sharia in the U.S. on the one hand, and new black Democratic president's use of the term "our values" on the other.

Manufacturing Islamization as the newest form of jihad from within was producing its intended returns. Jihad Watch readership surged ahead of *Daily Kos* and *Hot Air*, increasing to 2.9 million unique visitors in July 2010 and to over three million in August. On the single day of July 19th, for example, Jihad Watch garnered over 163,433 unique visitors.[82]

Even this rise in readership was opportunity for threat politics, linking enemies foreign and domestic. In a post on August 27, he wrote that "The rise in readership here at Jihad Watch indicates that there is growing dissatisfaction among the American people about the quality of reporting they're getting on jihad issues from mainstream media sources." And, when this manufactured threat crisis had run its course, with the Park 51 community center project continuing on as planned, Spencer (with Geller now a permanent fixture by his side) capitalized on the newfound fame and credentials, jointly publishing *The Post-American Presidency: The Obama Administration's War on America*—a book that had little to do with Islam (ization), but everything to do with their broader project's unstated aims.

2. Counter-Jihad as a Counter (hegemonic) Narrative

Robert Spencer's more puritanical counterhegemonic strategy of pure negation emerges not merely in form or style, but also in content—that is, in engaging the official and normative "Islam is peace" narrative, not with a more realistic *corrective*, but with the entirely pessimistic and anti-rationalist counternarrative.

Akin to the practice that Foucault (1977, 144) called "countermemory," the counternarrative rhetorical device is a form of power-knowledge; it is a discursive practice that opposes, challenges, undermines, and resists the dominant, normative memory, which itself effectively disqualifies, excludes, or silences alternative accounts of the world. It is a heretical discourse, and all such heresy is mobilized by actors who, as Castells (1997, 10)

---

82   According   to   Compete.com's   Site   Analytics;   see   http://siteanalytics.compete.com/Jihad Watch.org+hotair.com+dailykos.com/

put it, are inscribed "in positions/conditions devalued and/or stigmatized by the logic of domination."

From the conceptual framework, recall that counternarratives constitute what Bourdieu called rival "schemes of classification" (1991, 127-8), and are produced by marginalized or dominated producers who "have to resort to subversive strategies" (1986, 139). Bourdieu made frequent references to "the establishment" on the one hand, and to the challengers on the other. The challengers were positioned "outside the 'establishment', external to official culture" (1993, 2-3), who use as their weapons "subversion strategies" or "the strategies of heresy" (1993, 73). Whether it is the opposition between right and left, or orthodoxy and heterodoxy, he observed, the struggle is structurally identical, with unorthodox entrants able to challenge and even unseat the established order through cultural productions that are distinct, or distinctly unorthodox (1993, 135). In all such cultural struggle, "distinction strategies" are wielded to destroy the "ordinary order," either by severing adherence to the legitimate knowledge, or subverting that system by challenging it with "the politically unthinkable" or "taboo" (1993, 51, 115). Again, the purpose of such "heretical discourse," according to Bourdieu, is counterhegemonic, attempting to make dominant the marginalized ideology, to "produce" it as the "new common sense" (1991, 129).

In Spencer's case, especially when battling the charge of "Islamophobia," he framed his counternarrative in the more strategically advantages term—the "counter-jihad." Such framing could not mask the fact that his project's jihad watching was far less about countering the global Islamic jihad movement and much more about countering the local progressive movement. The counterhegemonic nature of his "counter-jihad" could be seen in the widespread use of political framing—in systematic, ideologically-aligned moves of selection and exclusion that served the interests of the conservative movement (Entman 1993).

Ideological Moves of Selection: Transgressing the Tabooed

Like that of Daniel Pipes's, Robert Spencer's threat writing was marked by subversion of the broader, more progressive societal norms regarding speech on Islam or other minority institutions. The notion that societal regulations place sanctions on certain objects, narratives, and perspectives, thereby relegating them to the realm of taboo, was at the root of Foucault's cynicism regarding knowledge; it was what he referred to as the "general politics of truth," or political correctness—an epistemic subculture which functions as a kind of discursive police (Foucault 1972, 224; 1980, 131, 194). In this, the conservative movement's politically incorrect discourse on Islam is a form of what Foucault called "popular justice," or a "people's court" (Foucault 1980, 1, 6).

In his book *Stealth Jihad* (2008: 238), Spencer described this politics of truth as "stifling conformism" and blamed it on "the Left" which "has been blazing an anti-American course in academic since the 1960s…," and especially after Edward Said's *Orientalism* (1978).

The first move within Spencer's counterhegemonic counterframing strategy was that of selection—selecting objects for view or commentary that deliberately transgressed societal norms or regulations. In the practice of counternarrative, objects that are regulated out of visibility by dominant norms ensconced in society's legitimizing institutions are deliberately and defiantly centered, and often constituted the entire realm of visibility. This is precisely what Spencer's counter-jihad discourse did.

As with any (counter)cultural and niche market producer, Spencer's selection of illegitimate objects of visibility—along with his selection of illegitimate perspectives or narratives on those objects which are normally visible—constitutes a site not merely of counternarrative, but counter-identity. Even the phrase "politically incorrect" is subcultural code among U.S. conservatives for *their* discourse; it denotes conservatism itself. Politically incorrect discourse is so central to conservative identity that the staunchly conservative Regnery Publishing's developed the trademarked "Politically-Incorrect Guides" series, which explains and includes Spencer's (2005) *New York Times* bestseller, *The Politically Incorrect Guide to Islam (and the Crusades)*. Understanding its market, Regnery can tout that its position is "central to the conservative movement" because—according to its website—it publishes books that "challenge the status quo." In one of the recommendations for Spencer's (and Regnery's) book, *Eurabia* author Bat Ye'or noted that it "Assails, with much erudition, the taboos imposed by the Politically Correct League."

Spencer's selection of objects for visibility—mainly, Muslims saying and doing things that countered the official and normative "religion-of-peace" storyline—was such an assault on the dominant, more progressive politics of truth. This could be seen at the height of the aforementioned "ground zero mosque" strategy, when Spencer welcomed the explosion of new readers that the website was experiencing with this statement about its main form of distinction: "Jihad Watch is a news and commentary site that brings you information about the global jihad effort that the mainstream media largely misreports or ignores altogether."

In his strategy to subvert the establishment with what in Bourdieuian terms was the politically unthinkable or taboo, Spencer selected for his entire view the very realm of objects and perspectives that the dominant "Islam is peace" storyline and its supporting discursive formation excluded from view. In other words, this first move of selection within the counternarrative was to center the narratives and objects of visibility that these popular Muslim and progressive thought leaders decentered, and vice versa. This was especially the case with the Quran and Muhammad.

In his *New York Times* best-seller *The Politically Incorrect Guide to Islam* (2005) and his *The Complete Infidel's Guide to the Koran* (2009), for example, Spencer radically centered *all* that is tabooed or negative regarding the Quran and other sacred texts and decentered or excluded everything that has been brought under the analytical lens by institutionalized scholars. And, in his 2006 bestseller, *The Truth About Muhammad: Founder of the World's Most Intolerant Religion*, Spencer radically centered all that European Muslim leader Tariq Ramadan excluded in his *In the Footsteps of the Prophet: Lessons from the Life of Muhammad*, and all that the more leftist ex-Catholic Karen Armstrong (1991, 2001, 2007) excluded in her biography of Islam's founder, *Muhammad*.

Spencer openly boasted of this strategy of subversive knowledge selection. Obviously written by him or another more Rightist polemicist, the National Review Book Service (NRBS) advertised his *Guide to Islam*, saying, "Robert Spencer reveals all the disturbing facts about Islam and its murderous hostility to the West that other books ignore, soft-pedal – or simply lie about."

The politically subversive moves of selection characteristic of Spencer's books carried over into his more banal, everyday cultural productions, especially the dozen or so daily Jihad Watch posts. For example, on January 14, 2009, one of the posts by (and typical of) the one of Spencer's trusted Jihad Watch partner bloggers, Raymond Ibrahim, was "Father Zakaria Botros on 'The perverse sexual habits of the Prophet,' Part II." The post entered the subversive realm of the unsayable or taboo by stating that "No less than 20 Islamic sources—such as the hadiths of Ahmad bin Hanbal—relay that Muhammad used to suck on the tongues of boys and girls."

This everyday counterhegemonic move of selection involved using specific statements of authoritative Muslim scholars—statements typically excluded by more progressive threat writers. When the news headline on December 19, 2009 was "Turkish PM: 'Islamophobia' is a crime against humanity," Spencer in a Jihad Watch post rhetorically asked: "does Islam include a political manifestation that teaches world domination?" and then posts examples from purportedly authoritative Islamic texts that support the counternarrative, as this excerpt from the 19 December 2009 Jihad Watch reveals:

> Don't take my word for it. Let's go to Majid Khadduri, an Iraqi scholar of Islamic law of international renown. In his book *War and Peace in the Law of Islam*, which was published in 1955 and remains one of the most lucid and illuminating works on the subject, Khadduri says this about jihad:
>
>> The state which is regarded as the instrument for universalizing a certain religion must perforce be an ever expanding state. The Islamic state, whose principal function was to put God's law into practice, sought to establish Islam as the dominant reigning ideology over the entire world....**The jihad was therefore employed as an instrument for both the universalization of religion and the establishment of an imperial world state.** (P. 51)
>
> Don't believe Khadduri? Very well. How about Imran Ahsan Khan Nyazee,

He continued by centering several statements from authoritative Muslim leaders that were obviously meant to delegitimize both the "religion of peace" and "Islamophobia" frames, and the broader more progressive societal politics of truth.

In another typical example from his website's home page, explaining "Why Jihad Watch?" Spencer transgressed the taboo and selected for heretical commentary Islam's most famous historian and scholar, Ibn Khaldun, whom the aforementioned Akbar Ahmed's chair at American University is named after. Spencer entered the realm of taboo by raising for visibility Khaldun's statements, such as the one in his *Muqaddimah* that "in the Muslim community, the holy war is a religious duty, because the universalism of the Muslim mission and (the obligation to) convert everybody to Islam either by persuasion or by force."

Spencer's posts at the beginning of the Arab Spring similarly achieved the desired countercultural distinction by selecting for his entire realm of visibility all the more pessimistic "news" that was not reported in the more idealistic, normatively-constrained reporting at the time. His February 15, 2011 Jihad Watch, for example, contained the title: "Tunisia: Muslims demonstrate in front of synagogue, chanting Islamic battle cry invoking Muhammad's massacre of Jews." In this YouTube video, Spencer brought into visibility the region's masses of undifferentiated "Muslims" who wanted to massacre Jews, evident from their shouting "Khaybar, Khaybar, O Jews, the army of Muhammad will return," in reference to Muhammad's raid on the Jewish Khaybar oasis. The piece centered this kind of information that professional and other normative discourse on Islam would deem gratuitous in terms of denigrating Muslims and their faith, and only part of the larger context and reasons for the demonstration—all of which Spencer reliably excluded.

Ideological Moves of Exclusion

Robert Spencer's second ideological move within the counterframe on Islam is the second move within framing broadly—that is, *exclusion*. We just saw how in his *New York Times* bestseller *The Politically Incorrect Guide to Islam* (2005) and his *The Complete Infidel's Guide to the Koran* (2009), for example, Spencer radically centered *all* that is tabooed or negative regarding the Quran and other sacred texts and decentered or excluded everything that has been brought under the analytical lens by institutionalized scholars.

Such ideological moves of exclusion are common to discourse; it is a feature that Foucault (1981, 52) described as "procedures of exclusion." And, so it comes as no surprise that Spencer was no exception; no small segment of conservative threat writing during the post-9/11 decade was marked by the systematic exclusion of texts and contexts that were common to professional or official security writing and academic security studies.

In this more puritanical counterhegemonic strategy, Spencer—in the production of the counternarrative on the threat of Islam broadly—systematically excluded the very crucial context that any normative security assessment would have been constrained to include. It excluded the entire and entirely relevant realms of local, pre-Islamic culture, historical and political grievances, post-colonial social structure, six decades of Western hegemonic practice, including the propping up of corrupt, inept regimes, Western-led invasions and coupes, identity insecurity, structural violence, relative and absolute deprivation, youth bulges, brain drain, human displacements or refugee migrations, regional politics, contingent events, and the strategies of self-interested elite, crony capitalism, statist economic structures, and a host other (non-U.S.) external actors—including five decades of the Saudi $100 billion proselytizing campaign to spread its radicalizing Wahhabism—to name a few. As we've already seen in several examples that showcased other features, all that was typically left in Spencer's assessment or estimates of threat of Islam was the Quran and other canonical texts, the example of the faith's prophet, Muhammad, and a highly selective—that is, exclusionary—reading of history.

Politicization was also evident in the way Mr. Spencer's counternarrative systematically excluded from view the more anthropological Islam of the literature. In the literature, much of what many newly awakened Western observers viewed as "Islam" was a much more complex set of dispositions, master narratives, discourses, and practices animated by the relatively deprived conditions or contexts in which Muslims found themselves. Anti-Americanism and anti-Semitism existed (Pew Research Center 2011) among many Muslims toward the end of the post-9/11 decade, but it paled in comparison to their resentment over the growing inequalities (or their becoming aware of them) in the neo-liberal and globalizing world order (Ahmed 2008). And, Muslim resentment of the inequalities that globalization was bringing and revealing similarly paled in comparison to resentment of local governance, which was inept in meeting the economic, political and social aspirations of its rapidly growing, urbanizing, increasingly educated and youthful demographic. And, more than any of this, the source of the most misunderstood security and political discourse in almost entirely conservative and fundamentalist Muslim-majority societies was *fear*—a profound identity insecurity emerging from the challenge that economic neo-liberalism, pluralism, secularism and globalization broadly presented to local Islamic identity or traditional patterns of life—what fundamentalist-leaning thinkers from Iran to Saudi Arabia variously described as Western cultural invasion (Susser 2010; Lapidus 2002; Crooke 2009).

In spite of Muslim discourse aimed at the perceived sources of these grievances and insecurities—together captured in the pervasive "war on Islam" narrative—the professional consensus did not support a more pessimistic identity of "Islam." But, in Spencer's (and also in Pipes's and Gabriel's) threat assessments and commentaries, no attempt was made to incorporate these elements of an interpretive, broader context-based analysis; all of it was systematically excluded.

As was the case the Daniel Pipes, in another move of pure negation, Mr. Spencer's threat assessments never cited texts and authors housed within the more progressive and dominant knowledge society of educational institutions, government bureaucracies, and the mainstream media. Instead, the entire realm of visibility of other threat analyses—his entire realm of favorable (non-critical) intertextuality—were those produced "inside the wire" of the conservative enclave.

Of course, Spencer's threat productions were marked by both framing moves—selection and exclusion. Typical was his August 13, 2011 post, "Pakistan: '800 women were victims of 'honor killings' – and 2,900 women reported raped – almost eight a day.'" Here, Spencer reliably excluded how such honor killings were similarly rampant among Hindus in India, stemming from the cultural norm that parents have a right to control who their daughter marries because caste boundaries can be preserved only by forcing women to make sure they marry within the caste. It had nothing to do with religion. Spencer—a Catholic deacon—also systematically excluded or rendered invisible a plethora of easily accessible data—data that demonstrate that femicide among Muslims is not a crisis, is less

142

than that across America, and much less than femicide in predominantly Catholic Mexico and Latin America. The most obvious question excluded from Spencer's analysis was how such a statistic in a country of 179 million compares to a country like the US, with a population of 313 million. A simple Google search of "rape statistics" quickly yields a US Department of Justice report that lists the 2010 rapes of women in the U.S. at over 233,000, equating to *638 per day*—again, compared to only 8 per day in Pakistan. Were the nature of Spencer's threat assessments not counterhegemonic, then he would not continually select for visibility the tabooed object of "Islamic honor killing," while systematically excluding the context from government reports that suggests that rape in the US is *46 times greater* than rape among the thoroughly Islamized Pakistanis.

3. Blogging Jihad: Cultural Politics via Popular Style, Political Sarcasm, Political Antagonism, Political Propagandism, and Subversive Mode of Production,

A clear signal that a discourse has become more political than informational is when it has broken with professional convention; it is when it has become what Bourdieu (1991, 185, 188-190) described as "popular," or recognized "outside the circle of professionals, or, as Bourdieu put it in different terms, discourse that is "excluded from the dictionaries of the legitimate language" (Bourdieu 1991, 91).

Given the distinctly and explicitly political features of Spencer's threat writing examined thus far, we should not be surprised to learn that they are joined by such a distinctive popular and even dissident rhetorical style and mode of production. Dissidence in both style and mode of publishing were at the heart of Spencer's leitmotiv of subversive resistance to the dominant, more progressive knowledge society. That dominant epistemic apparatus of power is housed in the government, academia, the "mainstream" media, and the more progressive societal regime of truth—all of which are part of the "enemies domestic" threat category among the farther-right social conservatives.

Popular Style

In all countercultural production, distinction is an oblique challenge to the dominant culture or field (Hebdige 1979, 16), and thus is central to the economy of production (Bourdieu 1984). Dissidence in style is perhaps the common mode, and the first thing we note in Robert Spencer's threat writing is that it is stylistically distinctive; it breaks markedly with the style of professional, apolitical security writing.

Such counterhegemonic distinction in style is evidenced in the reviews of Spencer's books on Amazon.com, for example. These reviews are vastly different from the reviews of orthodox, apolitical works related to Islam broadly by other renowned experts on the topic. Take, for example, *Global Political Islam* (2007), by George Mason University's Islamism expert, Peter Mandaville. By the end of 2012, Mandaville's superb book had received only one review on Amazon.com—a 5-star review, which made the explicit point that the book was not a polemic. Spencer's bestselling *Politically Incorrect Guide to Islam*

(2005), on the other hand, garnered a bi-polar sort of review distribution, with two-thirds being 5-stars ratings, and nearly all of the rest being 1-star, complaining that the book *was* a polemic.

But upon examination, Spencer's threat writing was far more than a mere polemic; it was performative in the role of cultural politics—functioning as a subtextual code for the conservative market that identifies with it in their daily digestion of Jihad Watch. Spencer and Horowitz's trademarked catch-phrases, such as "stealth jihad" and the "unholy alliance" of the Left and Islam, functioned as memes, or coded symbols that inscribe the boundaries of the U.S. conservative subsociety in juxtaposition to and competition with its political outside (Bourdieu 1991, 167).

This is a process of cultural production known as self-identification, or the reconstruction of the ideal Self. The process is similar to that of creating a "brand community," which is structurally related to identifying with a particular brand (Muniz and O'Guinn 2001). The goal is to get the target audience to see the brand—in this case Spencer's lexicon and frames—as part of one's identity. His distinctive style and lexicon, in other words, help reproduce a more politically dissident conservative subject position, in a process akin to that which Althusser (1971) called interpellation. Such self-identifying rhetorical strategies have been recurrent prominent features in America's everyday, popular security discourse, even in such seemingly benign or apolitical institutions like the *Reader's Digest*, as Sharp (1996) observed during the Cold War.

Spencer's strategic use of popular style to purposively subvert the regulatory structure of orthodox, legitimate, professional security writing could be seen in the September 24, 2010 post, under the title "Video surfaces of Taliban stoning woman in northwest Pakistan." Here Spencer reliably obscures from view the Pashtunwali culturally-based justice frames and cites instead "Islam" and "Islam's 'justice'" writ large, and then further distinguishes his writing from the professionals by stating this is a practice that "Muhammad approved of and participated in, according to canonical Islamic sources,". But, of course, the piece is also politically performative. Spencer then bridges the enemies foreign and domestic frames by charging that U.S. progressives, especially in academia, are the Taliban's "apologists," who are effectively aiding and abetting them in this gruesome practice.

Popular style, in Spencer's case, also entailed three more politically performative features: political sarcasm, political antagonism, and political propagandism.

Political Sarcasm

Professional security writing and academic security studies—legitimate, normative forms of threat assessment—expressly exclude sarcasm as a rhetorical device for the express reason that it *is* politically subversive. But, Spencer's popular security writing is rife with political sarcasm. But, his is not mere political sarcasm, but counterhegemonic sarcasm—that is, sarcasm directed at denigrating the establishment of more official, legitimate, professional security writing. Such counterhegemonic sarcasm, as Bourdieu

(1986, 147) observed—makes use of sarcasm, which "establishes with its audience the immediate complicity of laughter only because it has persuaded them to reject the presuppositions of the parodied discourse…." Typifying this style was his December 31st, 2009 Jihad Watch post, "Houston: Rocket launcher, jihadist writings found in apartment – no charges filed." Here, Spencer deployed the "Keystone Kops" caricature and lexicon to delegitimize "the Feds," who—as he and his readers expected—"found no ties to terrorism."

In all counterhegemonic production, words, phrases, and even quotation marks become infused with different meaning. Typical of other counterhegemonic projects, Spencer's sarcasm proceeded by taking legitimate words and phrases such as jihad and placing them in quotations, or "jihad," thereby infusing them with oppositional meaning, or transforming them into polysemes that both functioned as code within the subculture and performatively delegitimized the broader, dominant culture.

Placing the term jihad in quotations, in other words, renders it an empty shell, forcing it to function symbolically as both a self-identifying boundary, and a subversive, "politically-incorrect" stance of oppositional, counterhegemonic resistance against the legitimate frame of signifier housed in the more progressive institutions. In this sense, this signifier itself—through positioning its meaning within the cultural taboo—became a *micro-field* of struggle. From Bourdieu's (1993, 2) perspective, the massive amount of investment in such a politically-incorrect signifier could be classified within the strategy of "counterculture," or "everything that is marginal, outside the 'establishment', external to official culture," and "defined negatively by what it defines itself against."

In the piece above, sarcasm was deployed this way with the quotation marks around the word "justice" (i.e. this is Islam's 'justice'), to denote a meaning that his subcultural market will instantly recognize as opposite from that of normative discourse, or as a denigration or delegitimizing of that discourse. Spencer's sarcastic, quotation marks-laden lexicon was replete with phrases like "religion of peace," and "tiny minority of extremists" that function as code to denote the opposite meaning, and that his market also recognizes and appreciates as mocking the more progressive societal institutions.[83]

Political Antagonism

The more obvious part of style that distinguishes professional and political discourse is the presence of antagonism (Laclau and Mouffe 1985, 114). Here it is useful to distinguish between political antagonism and adversarialism. As part of the broader Horowitz advocacy for conservative causes, Spencer's threat writing about Islam (ization) was marked by constant political antagonism, as seen, for example, in the above post's phrase "which apologists will not repudiate."

It is politically antagonistic in that it entails the constant *act of the political* in the Schmittian sense; that is, the demarcation of friends and enemies. In popular threat writing

---

[83] These signifying practices, which purposively construct embattled terms to function in the broader practice of semiosis, or the performance and struggle involving signs, in order to elicit a response or achieve a goal.

among U.S. conservatives in the decade after 9/11, enemies foreign and domestic—Islam and the Left—were constantly and antagonistically objectified, as seen in the post about the "fifth column" of "dhimmi academics and dhimmi journalists" under the heading of "Why Jihad Watch" on the website's home page.

This feature of popular style was not limited to Spencer's blogging; it permeated all of his broader modes of production, as seen in his November 8, 2011 article, "Is Multiculturalism Evil?" in the counterhegemonic Catholic *Crisis Magazine*. The article functioned partly as a narration of self, re-inscribing the in-group identity by raising for visibility the superior accomplishments of Western culture and the Catholic Church. But then Spencer's act of the political abruptly shifted focus to enemy or outside identity politics. Bridging the "enemies foreign and domestic" frames, he said that "Islamic supremacists" and progressives are colluding to destroy the West through the "cult of Multiculturalism."

Spencer's predisposition to deploy this political strategy is apparently no small factor in why Horowitz sought to partner with him, and other foot-soldiers, such as Jamie Glazov, author of *United in Hate: The Left's Romance with Tyranny and Terror*. Horowitz is known for his radical political antagonism. In a March 24, 2005 *Washington Times* interview about his website DiscoverTheNetworks, Horowitz said that there "are only a couple of degrees of separation between anybody on the left and the terrorists - and that includes people in the Democratic Party." On FOX News's Glenn Beck show on September 16, 2009, he claimed that "blacks are the human shields of the Democratic Party" and on Hannity a year later on September 3, 2010, claimed that university professors are "recruiting for radical parties, terrorist supporting parties." In his book *Unholy Alliance: Radical Islam and the Radical Left*, Horowitz said that both Muslims and progressives abhor America and American values (Theel 2011).

In Spencer's case, after it was learned that he was the main inspiration for the aforementioned Norway right-wing extremist's massacre, the August 4, 2011 Jihad Watch post read: "Spencer on the Left and Islam, the Norway blame game, and more." The article discussed his interview the day before with Pat Robertson on Christian Broadcasting Network's *700 Club*. In that same August 3rd interview, Robertson asked Spencer, "Tell me what it is about the media today that is so in favor of radical Islam; why do they want to put down anyone who tells the truth about this cult?" "Well, I tell you," Spencer replied, "I think the unpleasant truth about it is that the media being essentially hard Left is essentially anti-American, and so anything that is American, that's Western, that's Christian, that's Judeo-Christian, they hate, and so they see Islam and its non-Western and non-Christian and they love it."

From such style we can gather that Spencer's strategy was not one of mere political antagonism, but—like his partner Geller— that of *agent provocateur*. It was intended not merely to inflame (rather than inform), but to create within its own very radically-antagonistic style the opportunity for more and more effective threat politics. This is evidenced in the way Spencer's productions are used by other conservative intellectuals as the raw material for their political antagonism. Even the book recommendation for

Spencer's counterhegemonic, *Religion of Peace? Why Christianity Is and Islam Isn't*, we find this strategy deployed through the words of conservative culture warrior Ann Coulter writes:

"*Religion of Peace?* is the perfect book to give liberals who fervently believe that Christianity is as dangerous – if not more dangerous – than Islam. Robert Spencer skewers the liberals' paranoid and suicidal hatred of Christianity while reminding us how they ignore the real threat: Islamic jihadists with bombs.

Political Propaganda

Studies of propaganda routinely find that repetition is the single most effective technique of persuasion. It does not matter how big the lie is, so long as it keeps being repeated (Oberschall 2000, 993). And, in the realm of cultural politics, the constitution of political identity—whether friends or enemies—occurs not through any single founding ceremony, but rather through banal, everyday ritual (Butler 1990, 1451). As master propagandists and political apparatchiks, Spencer and his boss clearly understand this. Jihad Watch's dozen or so everyday postings of short news articles strung together with Spencer's creative subversive and politically antagonistic titles, followed by an almost storyline snippet of related sarcastic, antagonistic, and otherwise politically-performative commentary, function like propaganda and imagery; it appeals less to the rational intellect than to the sub-rational, emotional and identity element of human experience. In this mode, Jihad Watch churns out a dozen such products a day on an assembly-line like planned method—akin to the "cheap biographies" that Adorno and Horkheimer (1972, 163) had termed the "culture industry." It is an assembly-line of everyday, cheap mass-produced caricatures of self and other, friend and enemy, that subtly and imperceptibly reproduce the conservative patriot in stark juxtaposition to his or her imagined opposites—enemies, foreign and domestic, religious and political.

This propaganda-like style of threat writing is a form of identity politics, and one that Spencer and Horowitz understand has special appeal, especially to social and paleoconservatives, many of whom—as previously discussed—tend to be animated by the crisis of accelerating identity pluralism and uncertainty of late-modern life. In Spencer's propaganda-like threat writing, all such uncertainty surrounding the daily global happenings around which its commentary is advanced is erased and replaced with cocksure certainty, in the absence of any curiosity. As in all propaganda, the author is positioned as the prophet—the incurious knower, but never the knowledge seeker—never treading cautiously in the presence of hybridity, but reliably reducing it, then externalizing it, then securitizing it. In this propaganda style, Spencer could never allude to even the possibility of a loyal and patriotic *pious* Muslim American, or a loyal and patriotic Christian or Jewish conservative who is critical of the Likud-led Israel's expanding occupation and control of Palestinian territory. Instead, the daily reader of Jihad Watch's short, almost image-like snippets of popular style commentary can relax at the level of their pre-cognitive predispositions, all the while nature's inherent continuum of complex identity is reduced into the parsimonious, political caricatures and political binary of the pure in-group and the defiled out-group.

Counterhegemonic Mode of Production and Authority-Building

Another counterhegemonic strategy in Mr. Spencer's toolkit enacts McLuhan's (2005) [1967] axiom, "the medium is the message." In other words, even the mode in which Spencer produced his threat assessments was politically subversive.

In legitimate security writing, an institutionalized expert on the topic of Islam as it relates to security could be considered established in the field with five to twenty articles over a decade. But Spencer boasted a publishing record an order of magnitude above that. On the home page of Jihad Watch toward the end of the post-9/11 decade, he boasted that he had authored nearly 400 articles about jihad and Islamic terrorism. But, all were produced in an unorthodox, counterhegemonic fashion. All four hundred threat assessments on Islam (ization) were produced in the "popular" realm, as Bourdieu described it—that is, produced outside the circle of professionals, and outside the legitimate knowledge society and its regulatory framework that other recognized experts on political Islam publish within. Spencer's productions appeared in the *New York Post* and the *Washington Times*, but never the *New York Times* and *Washington Post*. Or they appeared in Pipes's *Middle East Quarterly*, Horowitz's *FrontPage Magazine*, Farah's *WorldNet Daily*, *National Review Online*, *Human Events*, *PJ (formerly Pajamas) Media*, the *American Thinker*, and Catholicism's *Crisis Magazine*—all e-magazines within the alternative media, and within the aforementioned conservative knowledge society or regime of truth. But, his articles on Islam(ization) never appeared in any journal considered by security or intelligence professionals to be authoritative and apolitical. The same pattern existed in television interviews in the latter part of the post-9/11 decade, where he was invited exclusively to the enclave's evangelical *700 Club* or FOX News Channel, guest of Bill O'Reilly, Sean Hannity, Glenn Beck, and other conservative culture warriors.

Again, following McLuhan's axiom, this alternative medium of production was part of the message; it was not as much imposed upon Spencer and Horowitz as it was chosen by them. In this, their strategy was identical to that of Daniel Pipes, as we will see; it was a strategy of pure resistance that necessarily had to bypass all elements of "the establishment" in order to delegitimize them. Because Spencer designs his productions on Islam to be heretical and not submit to the regulations for authoritative production normal to society's main knowledge institutions in academia, government, and security-focused think tanks, the only place of publication remaining is the conservative institutions designed expressly for counterhegemonic struggle. Typifying this strategy was Spencer's aforementioned statement that, "we have the truth on our side…we have the alternate media—which is still very small compared to the mainstream media, but it is growing apace as the frustration of people who realize they're being lied to increases" (Jihad Watch, 9 July 2010).

This counterhegemonic feature of Spencer's mode of production was one that Bourdieu called "a movement of pure negation" (Garnham and Williams 1986, 126). And, it disallowed or proscribed security knowledge produced outside of the counter-establishment—that is, knowledge of threats produced outside of the conservative enclave. In other words, it *never* cited knowledge housed within or considered legitimate within the more normative, progressive, and authoritative societal institutions. For example, in his sarcastically-titled book, *The Complete Infidel's Guide to the Koran* (2009), Spencer was at liberty to cite for authority only fellow conservative political dissidents, such as "Islamic scholar Daniel Pipes," and never anyone in the more progressive society of security professionals.

This strategy of copiously citing each other to mutually build one another's authority or credibility is pervasive among conservative security experts. In his "The truth is spreading" post to Jihad Watch on December 17, 2011, Spencer proudly trumpeted that "some ideas that began with me or here at Jihad Watch gaining wider currency," noting that "Recently Frank Gaffney of the Center for Security Policy wrote a piece for the *Washington Times* that used the phrase 'stealth jihad' in the title," and that "Pamela Geller also makes reference to 'Islamic supremacism' and other terms I've originated."

Again, in all countercultural production, form trumps content. For this reason, Spencer's more puritanical strategy negating the more progressive outside is adhered to even when minor intertextuality could help him craft a more rigorous counternarrative. For example, in another move to deflect criticism in July 2011 when it was learned that he was perhaps the single greatest inspiration for Breivik's shooting spree in Norway, Spencer countered that Muslim terrorist attacks had since 9/11 killed 17,000—a figure produced not by any official, legitimate institution, but by the counterhegemonic, anti-Islam *TheReligionOfPeace.com*. In his move of pure negation, Spencer did not even acknowledge the existence of the U.S. State Department's *Country Reports on Terrorism*, which would have rendered the 17,000 figure much too *low*. The report's annex produced by the National Counterterrorism Center put deadly attacks at over 26,000—and not since 9/11, but since 2007, with 75 percent of these deadly attacks taking place in Muslim majority South and Near East Asia (Office of the Coordinator for Counterterrorism 2011).[84] But, as with any counterhegemonic practice—again, with form trumping content—it was more important for Spencer to delegitimize the establishment by excluding it from view, even at the expense of his argument.

In this dissident mode of production, Mr. Spencer obviously could not have included in his analysis what Harvard's Stephen Walt highlighted on the page of *Foreign Policy* only five months earlier. Walt had cited the *EU's 2010 Terrorism Situation and Trend Report,* noting that the overwhelming majority of terrorist incidents in Europe in 2009 were not Islamic in nature, and adding that "the vast majority of these incidents (237 out of 294) were conducted by indigenous European separatist groups, with another forty or so attributed to leftists and/or anarchists. According to the report, a grand total of one (1) attack was conducted by Islamists." He further noted from the report that "the number of arrests relating to Islamist terrorism (110) decreased by 41 percent compared to 2008, which continues the trend of a steady decrease since 2006" (Walt, 2011).

---

[84] See http://www.state.gov/j/ct/rls/crt/2011/195555.htm

4. Watching Jihad: Banal, Everyday Counterhegemonic Struggle

Jihad Watch's mission—according to Horowitz's website—is to "track the attempts of radical Islam to subvert Western culture." But, like Pipes's Islamist Watch and Campus Watch, Spencer's Jihad Watch is not merely a surveillance apparatus; it is a technology of power that—being discursive in nature—produced the very objects it "watched" for, and wrote about.

The notion that discourse performatively produced the world's realities was Foucault's (1981, 57). And, demonstrating his constructivist commitments, Bourdieu also viewed discourse as performative; in his words, "it contributes practically to the reality of what it announces by the fact of uttering it, or predicting it and making it pre-dicted, of making it conceivable and above all credible and thus creating the collective representation and will which contribute to its production" (Bourdieu 1991, 128). All such daily labor of representation functions to bring about its purported object (Bourdieu 1990, 92).

Of course, much of the "jihad" that Jihad Watch "watched" for had little to do with the newest enemy of Islamic jihadism. Specifically, while Jihad Watch's daily commentary produced a dozen or so instances of jihad worldwide to counter and thereby delegitimize the more progressive "Islam is peace" or "religion of peace" storyline, the puzzling, non-sequitur mass at the core of most of these had little to do with Islam—the conservative movement's newest foreign enemy born on 9/11—and much to do with the Left—its traditional domestic enemy. In other words, when you crunched through the shallow outer shell of "jihad" in many of Spencer's productions, there was this incoherent mass related to the more progressive "establishment" on the one hand—euphemized variously as the "elites," academia, government, "mainstream" media—and the Democratic party and the Obama administration more specifically on the other—topics that were politically-useful in the domestic culture war. This is not surprising, given its place in the broader Horowitz apparatus.

This feature in Spencer's technology of Jihad Watch of more banal, everyday counterhegemonic struggle under the guise of security assessments was typified in the following several blog posts produced between President Obama's first foreign policy thrusts in the spring of 2009 and his reelection in the fall of 2012.

The first strategic security initiative of the Obama Administration was, as we noted earlier, President Obama's speeches to Muslim communities worldwide to counter the dominant "war on Islam" master narrative that had captured Muslim majority communities worldwide. In early April, President Obama's speech from Turkey was reliably seized by the farther right an opportune field for cultural politics. Just as this seismic event had prompted the earlier featured counterhegemonic piece by Gaffney in the *Washington Times*, so it also prompted dozens of follow-on posts by Spencer and others in Jihad Watch. The April 13th Jihad Watch post, for example, reliably advanced the Islam(ization) threat counternarrative, but also antagonistically mocked the progressive establishment's "elites" and the President's efforts to demobilize the damaging "war on Islam" master narrative, noting that "the peoples of the West, and the rest of the Infidel world, continue to not be informed by the members of their political and media elites."

That same week, on April 19th Jihad Watch shifts from jihad to "Obama refuses to meet with Netanyahu." This piece noted that Obama had called the key Leftist figure Hugo Chavez "my friend" and that he wanted to meet with Iran's "Thug-In-Chief" and "bowed to the Saudi King."

The next week's April 27th post, "Obama wants to aid the Palestinians even with Hamas in power," typified the way in which the jihad watch technology was to function in this form of banal, counterhegemonic struggle. Its list of deadly sins of political correctness by the Obama administration began with noting how the Department of Homeland Security quietly dropped the war on terror phrase, with Janet Napolitano replacing the word "terrorism" with "man-caused disasters."

Three days later, on April 30th, the post, "Israeli intel: 'Obama wants to make friends with our worst enemies and until now the worst enemies of the United States,'" implied both the destruction of America and its Holy Land was imminent, and that the new Democrat president was more interested in appeasing its real enemies than protecting its Holy Land.

It was evident even in a quick scan of each day's dozen Jihad Watch topics that every action or statement by the new Democratic president was closely scrutinized for political opportunity. After President Obama's next speech to Muslims worldwide on June 6th— just like the earlier-featured *National Review* rebuttal article by McCarthy—the central focus or content of 17 of the 20 Jihad Watch posts that day had little to nothing to do with the threat of jihad or Islam, and much to do with domestic cultural struggle.

As the Obama administration's first year progressed, the Jihad Watch strategy of linking it to new enemies foreign became even more evident. Typical was the October 8th post, "Obama's Muslim adviser says Sharia 'misunderstood,'" which noted how the President's adviser on Muslim affairs, Dalia Mogahed, had appeared on a British television show "hosted by a member of an extremist group to talk about Sharia Law."

President Obama's first year coincided during the surge of attacks by homegrown extremists, which had been the subject of much threat commentary. In that context, even Thanksgiving Day was occasion for Spencer to mobilize for counterhegemonic struggle not only Christian apocalyptic frames, but his title was the identifying Latin phrase of St Andrews so symbolic of Western Christendom, "Dum spiro spero," noting that "the entire government and media establishment hastens to assure the world that the root cause [i.e. Islam itself] is not the root cause. And the President of the United States rushes to make more concessions to the jihadis and their sponsors and allies."

After the holidays, the February 12, 2010 post, "Obama's national defense report ignores Islamic jihad, focuses on climate change," rebroadcasted the counterhegemonic piece from *The Telegraph*, in which the title accurately conveyed the content.

Jihad Watch during President Obama's second year in office advanced the paleo-conservative master narratives of an America in abrupt cultural decline, and an Israel existentially threatened—both a consequence of the Obama administration's basic nature and policies. Typical was Spencer's July 9, 2010 article in Horowitz's *FrontPage Magazine*, "The Fear that Wilders is Right," in which he centrally advanced this non-sequitur: "As Pamela Geller and I show in our book The Post-American Presidency: The Obama Administration's War on America... [the president] is not only presiding over America's decline, but is in a very real sense the apostle of that decline."

During the 2010 mid-term campaign, the Jihad Watch post on September 16, "Obama praises Turkey as it steps toward Sharia," bolstered the counterhegemonic conspiracy narrative. And, on Christmas Eve 2010, the jihad watching industry of Spencer and Horowitz began at the first watch of 0511 AM with a post that announced a new pamphlet by Spencer and Horowitz titled "Obama and Islam," which began by noting that "no president in American history has taken a more admiring view of Islam than Barack Obama," and described his "energetic willingness to pander to the Islamic world...." "The consequence" section at the end of this post reliably delegitimizes the president who "betrayed American values," "undermined the national interest," and "abandoned staunch allies like Israel."

A month later, in the earliest stages of the Arab Spring, Jihad Watch provided threat commentaries with titles like these on February 1st: "Obama backs Muslim Brotherhood role in new Egypt government," and "Obama Administration held secret meeting with Muslim Brotherhood, planning post-Mubarak government."

The next day, on February 2, 2011, Jihad Watch continued to frame the Islamo-Leftist enemy axis and conspiracy with a post titled "Spencer: Obama's Brotherhood Moment," which advertised his article on this at his sister organization in Horowitz's apparatus, *FrontPage Magazine*. A few days later, the February 11th Jihad Watch further subverted the Obama Administration by reprinting the piece from FOX News the day before that reliably noted how "The Obama administration took the rare step Thursday of correcting its own intelligence chief after the official claimed Egypt's Muslim Brotherhood is 'largely secular'."

As news of the revolution continued to spill out of the broader Middle East and North Africa region, the banal, everyday production of the Islamo-Leftist enemy axis continued, typified by two successive posts from the February 25th Jihad Watch digest: "US State Department spends $770 million on mosques in the Middle East," and "Obama praises Algeria for lifting state of emergency that was put in place to prevent Islamic rule."

In similar vein, over the next two months, watching for "jihad" ultimately entailed watching the U.S. conservative movement's domestic political rivals, with dozens of similarly counterhegemonic posts that delegitimized the more progressive outside broadly—the culture, the media, the conservatives, academia—and especially the Obama administration. Typical titles were: "Spencer: Obama's Democracy Delusions" (March 1, 2011); "Dems at King hearings recite Muslim Brotherhood-linked group's talking points" (March 11); "Obama White House applauds Hamas-linked CAIR even as FBI cuts it off" (March 18); "Obama Administration refusing to hand over evidence, delaying trial of Fort Hood jihad murderer" (April 12); "Al-Jazeera, 'the most powerful voice of the Muslim Brotherhood,' has fans in the Obama White House" (April 17); and "DOJ source says Government's Muslim "Outreach" jeopardized active terror investigations" (April 18).

Spencer continued his practice of linking enemies foreign and domestic on April 17th in the post, "Obama's Muslim faith advisor helped craft 'perfect Islamic state' for Sharia project led by Ground Zero Mosque imam Rauf," which contained a photo of that advisor, Dalia Mogahed, with the caption, "Obama Advisor Loves Sharia."

Again, like the other years, every possible bit of "news" related to Islam in 2011 was seized as an opportunistic platform for domestic cultural struggle. President Obama's Middle East policy speech from Foggy Bottom the next month on May 19th was no exception; it provided the opportunity for nearly all of the dozen Jihad Watch posts that day—eight of which had the name "Obama" in the post title, such as "Obama calls for the destruction of Israel." The next day followed suit, with four posts with the name "Obama" in the title, including one which tacitly framed the president as Hitler, urging subscribers to "rally" against Obama's "jihad against Israel," to prevent another "Auschwitz."

The next opportunistic news event that Jihad Watch selected as a micro-site for politics was from a FOX News article the day before, on 7 December 2011, and captured in the title, "Lawmakers blast Obama's Defense Dept for classifying For Hood jihad murders as 'workplace violence'":

> Hasan was shouting "Allahu akbar" as he fired. He passed out Qur'ans on the morning of the shooting. He had earlier delivered a power point presentation that was supposed to be a lecture on psychiatry but was instead an exposition of Islam's doctrine of jihad warfare against unbelievers, and a call for Muslims to be excused from the U.S. military -- or else. He had given numerous other indications of his jihadist sentiments. And to the Obama White House his jihad murders are "workplace violence."

In this vein, Jihad Watch seized every opportunity to frame all diplomatic engagement by the Obama administration with Muslim leaders and organizations as disloyalty. In mid-December when the Department of State was discussing defamation of religion legislation with the Organization of Islamic Cooperation, for example, Spencer republished a piece from the *American Thinker* with the politically performative title, "State Department meeting with OIC to discuss free speech restrictions."

As we've seen in earlier chapters, security politics is a form of identity politics, or cultural politics, which always involves deeper cultural resources. This could be seen in the March 8, 2012 Jihad Watch post in which Spencer reliably reconstructed the Islamo-Leftist alliance by mobilizing biblical scripture and apocalyptic symbolism of the Kings of the East attacking Israel. Predictably, all of those symbolic resources were brought to bear in the counterhegemonic post, "Well done, good and faithful servant! 'Khamenei praises Obama for calming war drums.'"

5. The Self Jihad: Present Danger as the Site of Self-Narration

Political identity is always relational; the self, or political inside, is formed in juxtaposition to the other, or political outside. The other, or outside identity—the people group that is externalized—is typically also securitized, or classified as danger, the enemy, insecurity, and so on. In this way, all identity—in Campbell's (1998, 3) words—is "secured by the representation of danger." And, it is in this context that insecurity or danger—in this case jihad—as assessed through conservative threat writing—was never a threat to the U.S. conservative movement as much as it was "its condition of possibility," to use Campbell's (1998, 13) words again. In other words, the present danger from Islamic jihad as articulated by Spencer and other popular conservative threat writers in the decade after 9/11 turned out to be not just politically useful, but politically necessary; it was—along with a basket of other foreign and domestic threats—a necessary condition of the movement's identity and viability. In still other words, the cultural frame strategy of this newest foreign enemy that was being aided and abetted by the traditional domestic enemy, yielded increased vitality to the farther Right.

But, in addition to narrating or discursively identifying the political outside or other, the second crucial move of politics—which is always *identity* politics—involves "narrating the self" (Ochs and Capps 1996). And, this process of self-identification often takes place on the site of narration of threats to self. Here, as in all identity politics, we typically exaggerate the degree to which we are good, just as we typically exaggerate to the degree to which our most significant others are evil. And, as we've seen, narrating the good self in U.S. security writing typically involved two moves, or two basic strategies of action—self-aggrandizement, or reaffirming the strong self, and self-discipline, or purifying the vulnerable self.

Self-Aggrandizement: Reaffirming the Strong Self

The first move of self-identity politics in Spencer's threat writing was that of self-aggrandizement, describing the patriotic self in healthy, chauvinistic terms of self-exceptionalism or self-superiority—a move that drew from cultural antecedents in historical U.S. security writing, as we saw. Its function was politically performative in terms of self-identification; that is, it described the threat in ways that self (identity)—the U.S. conservative movement, its Holy Land, and its parent Western civilization broadly—could remain favorably positioned over that enemy, in terms of morality, power, achievements, and so forth. As such, his self-reassuring narrative functioned at the sub-rational level, like the comfort food of the old American television "Westerns," where the native Americans who resisted white settler expansionism were positioned as barbaric savages, the settlers as noble souls merely defending their land. In this way, Spencer's productions on the whole functioned politically to favorably reposition the triumphant, morally superior traditionalist self over all of its religio-political rivals.

In the Spring 2009 issue of Daniel Pipes's *Middle East Quarterly*, for example, Spencer previewed *Faith, Reason, and the War against Jihadism. A Call to Action*—a book published two years earlier by fellow Catholic and cultural warrior, George Weigel. As with all of Spencer's favorable book reviews, the work is featured *because* it is counterhegemonic, or politically subversive. Spencer reassures the conservative reader that Weigel "ably skewers numerous widely held assumptions about the conflict between the Islamic world and the

154

West," and then concludes in a self-disciplinary move, citing Weigel's "strong call for the recovery of Western cultural self-confidence…."

This notion of a crisis of confidence was a major theme in post-9/11 conservative threat writing. In his book *Stealth Jihad*, Spencer stated that "in college after college, the acolytes of multiculturalism have gained control of the faculty and administration." Speaking mainly of Europe, Spencer wrote that "university administrators and professors are unwilling and unable to halt the spread of Islamic supremacism in their own backyards" because they are "lacking confidence in their own civilization and culture" (2008, 228). In the book's concluding section, "what is to be done," the two actions that that top the list were to end Muslim immigration and take pride in our own culture—moves that appeal strongly to his paleoconservative submarket.

Self-Discipline: Purifying the Vulnerable Self

The second move within post-9/11 U.S. conservative threat discourse's category of self-narration or self-identification was that of self-discipline—a move that similarly drew from rich cultural antecedents in the security writing from earlier eras. Disciplining the self is a governmentality of "directing conduct"—to use Foucault's (2003, 284) words. The term *legitimation* has also been used to distinguish discourse which interests are advanced not merely through advocacy for particular policies, but through establishing politically-acceptable boundaries of action (Jackson 2006, ix). It is a move similar to that exercised in Christian pastoralism.

This strategy of action involves disciplining the exceptional but threatened self by diagnosing its forms of corruption, disease, weakness and other vulnerabilities. We had noted how post-9/11 threat discourse that was ostensibly about America's newest dangerous other was shot-through with frames of self and practices of self. Much more than merely a practice that identified the movement's others—its enemies foreign and domestic, religious and political, Islam and the Left—it was also what Foucault (1982, 208) described as a "*dividing practice*" that not only separated these others from the self, but also separated the healthy and diseased tissue within the body politic. This latter dividing practice functioned as a form of *self-identification*, *self-discipline*, or *self-normalization*.

This is not surprising; political blocs typically draw distinctions between subalterns who must be accommodated within the bloc, and adversaries who constitute both its threat and condition of possibility (Jones 2006, 64). Political factions work to create and sustain subcultural coherence within their ranks by imposing standards of purity on those deemed members of the group, as well as using such standards to denote heretical behavior and distinguish between those who are and are not group members (Sewell 2005, 173).

Spencer's everyday productions in Jihad Watch functioned as such a disciplinary technology to create and sustain subcultural coherence within the conservative ranks by imposing standards of purity by calling out those designated as wayward or heretical. Typical of his more banal, everyday form of pastoralism was the September 8, 2006 *Jihad Watch* post "Ralph Peters flailing in a fog of confusion," directed at the popular conservative Christian, retired military officer, and post-9/11 conflict author. Peters had just published an op-ed in the conservative *New York Post* that targeted Spencer, entitled "Islam-Haters: An Enemy Within." In it, he asserted that "a rotten core" and "really ugly" group of "right-wing extremists" is "bent on discrediting honorable conservatism" by "insisting that Islam can never reform, that the violent conquest and subjugation of unbelievers is the faith's primary agenda – and, when you read between the lines, that all Muslims are evil and subhuman." On Peters' notion that "there's nothing in the Koran as merciless as God's behavior in the Book of Joshua," Spencer politely disciplined his wayward brother, beginning with "Sure Ralph. That's why there's a global terrorist movement of Christians, committing violent acts and justifying them by quoting the Book of Joshua," and reminds him and other like-minded conservatives that "The Bible contains no open-ended, universal command to make war against and subjugate unbelievers, a la Qur'an 9: 29."

At the height of the Arab Spring, Spencer similarly exercised this more banal form of disciplinary power use the crisis as an opportunity to reproduce traditionalist Western identity. On February 7, 2011, in a cross-post from Horowitz's *FrontPageMagazine*, "Innocent as Serpents, Wise as Doves," Spencer mobilized Christian scripture in that title and went on to explore the "particular virtues of the West, and the crucial importance of defending them both on principle and in practice." He described the "post-Christian, liberal West" and then chastised Westerners, warning of the destructive nature of Islam's values and the Left's values, both of which are destroying Europe first, and now, more slowly, the US.

Another example of how Jihad Watch functions as a banal, everyday self-disciplinary technology was the December 23, 2011 post, "Cardinal McCarrick expresses "respect" for imam with ties to Muslim Brotherhood and Hamas." Here, Spencer securitized the widely-respected and loved Imam Mohamed Magid of the All Dulles Area Muslims Society (ADAMS) near Washington DC, and disciplined the Catholic leadership in the nation's capital for efforts at interfaith diplomacy.

A month later, on February 2, 2012, Spencer in a post aimed at the Catholic leadership reposted his review of Warraq's *Why the West is Best*, which he had published in the self-disciplinary and aptly named Catholic *Crisis* magazine, and in which he tacitly chastised Catholic leadership for failing to resist multiculturalism and to assert the faith's values confidently in the face of ideological, civilizational competition.

This self-disciplinary function of Jihad Watch within Horowitz's broader project of cultural politics continued through the 2012 election, typified by his lamentations-like post, "Not a dime's worth of difference" on November 7th that chastised the Republican Party for having "lost the pop culture, the educational system, and the mainstream media, all of which pump out the Democrat Party line with a fervor…."

These self-identification moves often shaded to a form of puritanism, as Spencer— who in a Saul-of-Tarsus-like subject position—zealously pursued insiders who represented more than a point of subcultural pluralism, and now constituted a threat. In the move to disambiguate, or expel ambiguity and uncertainty, Spencer systematically recategorized the complex reality in the middle into a polarized Manichean-like friend/enemy political binary. In this imaginative geography, all ambiguity and hybridity are erased; there are no good Samaritans, and no Nicodemus figures among the faction's ruling council, and so well-known conservative Muslims like Suhail Khan and Palestinian sympathizer Grover Norquist (whose wife Sanaa is of Palestinian origin) are an unstable category, and are thus reclassified into enemies practicing deception, dissimulation, or *taqiyya*. For example, on February 8, 2012, the Jihad Watch headline was "Geller: CPAC for Sissies: Self-Censoring for Sharia," where we discover that "Year in, year out, the puppetmasters, Grover Norquist and Suhail Khan, have managed to keep jihad and sharia off the CPAC schedule." In this vein, Spencer's post on October, 6 2011—"Rep. Frank Wolf calls out Grover Norquist for jihad ties; Norquist cries 'racism'"—was typical of this more puritanical form of self-discipline. In it, he states that "Norquist's influence on the Republican Party is extraordinarily damaging, as it keeps on leading so many to turn a blind eye to the stealth jihad that Norquist continues so energetically to advance."

Conclusion

In conclusion, several features of Spencer's threat writing in the decade after 9/11 suggest that the project was never intended to be anything approaching a neutral, apolitical assessment of the threat. His main and even overarching strategy of watching jihad though the surveillance technology Jihad Watch amounted to selecting from the world's happenings opportune instances of "news" related to Islam that could function politically. Each bit of news selected in Jihad Watch, or each new project of manufactured news, or each use of a tabooed signifier such as "jihad" functioned as micro sites upon which the broader strategy of cultural struggle could be incrementally enacted.

And, Spencer's practice of not merely watching jihad but manufacturing it as a site for more of this kind of threat politics was particularly telling. Instead of joining forces with a noted expert on Islam's threat, he partnered with a more extreme political conservative blogger, Pamela Geller, who had no credentials whatsoever related to the threat of Islam, but whose propensity to engage in politically-antagonistic culture war was cut from the same mold as his boss, David Horowitz. Within this overarching strategy of using Islam(ization) as a platform for cultural politics, there were four supporting moves or strategies—two of which mirrored those of Daniel Pipes.

First, Spencer's basic counternarrative on Islam was marked by more puritanical features of cultural politics. More than merely offering a Team B or pessimistic approach or corrective to the prevailing consensus regarding Islam, Spencer's project countered that consensus in a move of pure negation. It was a subversive, dissident, heretical threat assessment that opposed, challenged, undermined, and otherwise resisted the dominant, normative threat narrative housed in the dominant political outside, or establishment. Its counterhegemonic function could be seen in the counternarrative's ideological moves of selection; its entire realm of visibility was comprised of those objects that deliberately transgressed societal norms or regulations—all that was "politically incorrect." Objects that were regulated out of visibility by dominant norms ensconced in society's legitimizing institutions were deliberately and defiantly centered, and often constituted the entire realm of visibility. The corresponding move of pure negation in the counternarrative was in his ideological moves of exclusion, whereby the entire realm of visibility normative to professional security writing was excluded from view.

Second—and perhaps owing to his employment by such a long-time conservative culture warrior—much of Spencer's threat writing was marked by still more puritanical features of counterhegemonic struggle in the non-narrative realm. In addition to functioning as a subcultural identifier for his conservative market, Spencer's style of threat writing was dubiously marked by pervasive rhetorical techniques that purposively subverted the regulatory structure of orthodox professional security writing; it was replete with various forms of sarcasm, which functioned to delegitimize the going politics of truth, and was replete with political antagonism aimed at the Democrats and the Obama administration.

Spencer's threat writing was also counterhegemonic in non-narrative mode of production. Without exception, all of his nearly 400 articles about the threat of Islam (ization), for example, were published outside the circle of professionals, and outside the legitimate knowledge society and its regulatory framework that other recognized authorities whose work is at the nexus of Islam and security publish within. They appeared in the *New York Post* and the *Washington Times*, but never the *New York Times* and *Washington Post*. Or they appeared in Pipes's *Middle East Quarterly*, Horowitz's *FrontPage Magazine*, Farah's *WorldNet Daily*, *National Review Online*, *Human Events*, *PJ (formerly Pajamas) Media*, the *American Thinker*, and Catholicism's *Crisis Magazine*—all e-magazines within the alternative media, and within the aforementioned conservative knowledge society or regime of truth. But, they never appeared in any journal considered by security or intelligence professionals to be authoritative and apolitical.

Also in this vein, and like that of Pipes, Spencer's threat writing was subversive of societal norms regarding authority. In another move of pure negation, Spencer's threat assessments never cited texts and authors housed within the more progressive and dominant knowledge society of educational institutions, government bureaucracies, and the mainstream media. Instead, the entire realm of visibility of other threat analyses—his entire realm of favorable (non-critical) intertextuality—were those produced "inside the wire" of the conservative enclave.

Third, Spencer's productions typically involved delegitimizing the conservative movement's domestic political enemies. For example, Jihad Watch's everyday shallow threat commentary on the threat of Islam(ization) reliably contained a non-sequitur politically-performative segment that had little to do with the conservative movement's newest foreign enemy born on 9/11 and much to do with its traditional domestic enemy. This strategy functioned as a form of cultural politics or hegemonic struggle, in that it not only delegitimized the Democratic party and the Obama administration, but also the more progressive societal order—euphemized variously as the "establishment," the "elites," "mainstream" media, and so on.

Fourth, Spencer's threat writing was replete with the second pillar in all projects of identity politics—narrating the self, or the friend component of the political binary. And like U.S. security discourse broadly, this typically involved two sub-strategies: 1) self-aggrandizing moves, that (re)positioned the self in terms of triumphalism or exceptionalism; and 2) self-disciplinary or self-normalizing moves that disciplined the exceptional but threatened and even declining self by diagnosing its forms of corruption, disease, weakness and other vulnerabilities, identified the wolves in sheep's clothing, and that shepherded wayward elements of the flock back into the fold.

In the final assessment, Jihad Watch was far less about watching the newest foreign enemy than delegitimizing the old domestic one. In this, the knowledge it produced was not pure security knowledge, but highly performative political knowledge.

6

BRIGITTE GABRIEL

Acting for America

There is constant struggle between different classes and class fractions in society, who compete to impose the definition of social world that is best suited to their interest.

—Pierre Bourdieu (1991, 167)

AT the end of the post-9/11 decade, on November 12, 2011, a headline Nashville's premier newspaper, *The Tennessean*, was "ACT! for America founder speaks at anti-Shariah conference in Nashville." Since its readers might have wondered what the context of America and sharia in the same sentence might be, the newspaper crafted the appropriate subtitle: "Brigitte Gabriel focuses on Islamic infiltration into the American education system."

But, in what could be aptly described as the universe next door, the local Memphis Tennessee chapter of Gabriel's ACT! of America covered this news of Gabriel's speech at the anti-sharia conference with a different spin. On a web-page with links to "Muhammad's Personal Record of Jihad" in the upper left corner, and "No Room In America For Islamic Sharia Law" in the upper right, the announcement for Ms. Gabriel's speech began with the salutation: "Fellow infidels," and ended with the electronic signature of sarcastic anti-Islamization pseudonym, "burkasrugly"—which was code for far more than the literal thought that the black body-covering burkas are ugly.

In the video of the conference, Ms. Gabriel's shrill voice rang out with military cadence: "I-want-to-mobilize-the-nation." The purpose for this mobilization, she added, was "to teach Americans how the radicals are trying to brainwash the children in our country." But, while the conference—at a large Nashville church—was focused on "sharia," it quickly became apparent that "the radicals" she was talking about weren't Muslims. Instead of radical mosques—as was charged in the aforementioned article by

Yerushalmi in the *Middle East Quarterly*—the culprits behind "why we are seeing a rise in homegrown terrorism" were the radicals in "our public school system."

After all, she asked, "How did these good people—good Americans—some of them born Americans and raised as Baptists....; how can these people become so radicalized where they are hating our country so much that they are ready to die to kill Americans?" At the rest of this anti-sharia conference, Gabriel harped on about "what's happening in this country to education," and how an unnamed "they" are "trying to change our society culturally from within in order to destroy our society."

It was this army of radicals—again, the faculty at the nation's public schools and universities—that Gabriel framed as constituting "the infiltration of our country." In this discourse, the schools and universities where they work are effectively "occupied territories." In Sarah Palin fashion of dividing the nation between the "heartland" and enemy-occupied territory, Gabriel kept our eyes off of the threat of Sharia, and on the threat of the left:

> People in the heartland pinch pennies, save their money eat peanut butter and jelly sandwiches, so they can send their children to college to get an education, to have the American dream…only to find out they are sending them to the Lion's Den. Children come back home and they are completely changed; they loathe America; they do not like America….

Gabriel then bypassed the purported threat of Sharia and shifted the threat axis again to the mainstream media:

> When you look at the news and the media and the mainstream media and you think to yourself, why is the mainstream media so biased? Why can't they see what we see? The reason why is that for the last sixteen years, students graduating out of our Ivy League colleges who have been fed a steady diet of resentment against America, and against Israel, are today the bureau chiefs, the news writers, news anchors, news reporters who are reporting all these things.

They're doing exactly what Hitler did, she said, adding: "What did Hitler say; what did Hitler do. 'Give me the children; I'll change society in ten years.'" Gabriel went on, charging that we're now seeing "the results of years of the radical agenda in our public schools."

Gabriel spoke so fast and shrill that her audience never had a chance to enter the phase of cognitive reflection to realize that her talk, which was supposed to be about the invasion of the heartland by the newest foreign enemy's Trojan horse, sharia, instead dwelled almost entirely on the familiar culture war at home.

Even when Gabriel did speak of the threat from Islam, her every move was performative, or using it as an opportune platform to delegitimize the more progressive societal consensus, or the dominant politics of truth. For example, to delegitimize the broader left, Gabriel countered the more progressive "Islam-is-peace" storyline simply by saying that "the word jihad is mentioned forty times in the Qur'an—thirty-six times out of forty as a holy war against the infidels to either kill them or subjugate them."

For her final act, Gabriel continued this implicit or tacit criticism of the more progressive doxa by holding well-respected 7th grade supplementary social studies text—McDougal's (1999) *Across the Centuries*, which was obviously designed for students in multicultural nations and a globalized world to have empathy with and love for children of other faith traditions. Gabriel described a purported exercise were students are encouraged to play the script of a Muslim, imagining themselves praying the shahada. She read what she implied was part of the text: "Guide us to the straight path—the path of those whom you have favored—not of those who have incurred your wrath, which is the Jews, nor of those who have gone astray, which is the atheists and the Christians." Then she purported to read another class exercise from the textbook: "become a Muslim warrior during the Crusades or an ancient jihad; explain weapons, tactics, etc."[85]

"Excuse me?" she then railed. "This is a class exercise?!" Engaging once again the more progressive social order, Gabriel shouted to applause: "I believe political correctness needs to be thrown in the garbage…."

How can we explain the fact that a church-full of Tennessee Evangelicals would spend a couple days of their busy lives and forego the backlog of other more pressing needs to focus on the sharia-ization of the nation—something that no security professional has in the history of the country ever written about? The answer to this bizarre event begins to come into view when we see the actual subject matter of Brigitte Gabriel's statements, and the wild applause she regularly received during her rants about the threat to the cultural identity and security not from any imagined new encroachment of Islamic culture, as the conference billing suggested, but from the continuing encroachment of progressive secular culture.

We have already seen how security writing or threat discourse can function as a platform for identity or cultural politics. And, the features of Gabriel's speech and the audience's attraction to her suggests how the agents of a popular threat discourse can function in a manner distinctly different that security professionals or scholars of security studies, whose writing focuses on the same broad threat. In the analysis that follows, we will examine how her broader oeuvre of threat writing relating to Islam in the post-9/11 decade rested on the two identifiable pillars within the more fundamental act of the political—the narration of the friend/enemy distinction. This entailed primarily the narration of the self, and the narration of the enemy, with the construction of the enemy outside divided into enemies foreign and domestic, Islam and the Left.

1. Narrating the Patriotic Self

Well before Pipes began publicly criticizing him as an icon of the left, Foucault (1980, 125-126) had observed how discourse agents were not like the earlier era's more universal intellectuals, "speaking in the capacity of master of truth and justice." Instead, they were "organic" or "specific" spokesman for "specific sectors…where their own conditions of

---

[85] We say "purported" because a simple electronic word search of the readily-available and searchable text on Amazon.com cannot find any part of either phrase.

life or work situate them." Whether in the service of the state or against it, these spokespersons were necessarily "closer to the proletariat and the masses," sharing in their everyday struggles (Foucault and Rabinow 1984, 68). This built upon Gramsci's contention that the primary task of subaltern groups was to produce such personalities for the purpose of acting in history (Gramsci 2000, 59). In this vein, Gramsci had also observed that it is insufficient for organic intellectuals to remain technocrats; they also functioned in the subject position as movement leader, and thus must be cut out for and willing to participate in the struggle for hegemony—that is, to actively participate in practical, political life, "as constructor, organizer, 'permanent persuader' and not just a simple orator" (Gramsci 1971, 10).

Intellectual figures throughout history have been (self) positioned into leadership roles where they not only organize but embody or symbolize a movement's identity. They willingly fill the archetypical subject position reserved for the one who lights the path, affirms and embodies the values, and symbolizes the ideal, the true Patriot (Smith 1988, xxxv; Harré and Davies 2001). They are the movement leader, as Hoffer (1951, 114) had observed, who "personifies the certitude of the creed and the defiance and grandeur of power." They are those who Castells (1997, 361-362) called "symbol mobilizers" and "the Prophets," subverting the symbolic order "on behalf of alternative values," but also identifying the boundaries of that alternative order, embodying its values, and thus becoming a symbol of it, "so that the message is inseparable from the messenger."

The video of Gabriel's speech among Tennessee Evangelicals suggests that Gabriel played such a role. It was *because of* her distinct lack of orthodox credentials and her willingness to function as these evangelicals' *identifying* agent—their *symbol of self*, standing in defiant resistance to enemies foreign and domestic, Islam and the Left—that her audience identified with her. It was her symbolic position, or her political archetype identity that they neglected thousands of things on their "to do" list, and neglected core family needs, and registered instead attended this absurd conference on the Islamization of Tennessee, and regularly wildly applauded at her low-brow, un-informing cheerleader-like speech on the topic.

The important feature of any symbol such as the one that Ms. Gabriel embodied, is its distinctiveness or rarity—the function of the one, representing the many. For this reason, Gramsci had noted that only a minority of people function as intellectuals or leading ideologues within any given society (Jones 2006, 81-2). And, the distinctive feature of the field of popular conservative threat writers in the decade after 9/11 was that it was marked not by the many, but by the few. The field's near monopolization by a select few authorities—"rarefaction of speaking subjects," as Foucault termed the narrowing of the field's authorities to a regulated few legitimate speakers (1972, 155)—suggests its main function was not substantive but symbolic.

To U.S. cable newsmakers, there was obvious utility of such a few iconic commodity personalities who reliably sat upon the oppositional pole, embodying the (counter)narrative of one of the two main political movements. In its intensely political role, the media and especially the conservative media seemed unable to call on many nebulous subject-matter experts a few times, but were instead compelled to call on a few symbolic figures many times. What these media enterprises needed were binary logicians who reliably had *one* position on many things. Brigitte Gabriel functioned this way, as did Pipes and Spencer. These organic polemicists were called upon not because they would capably and sufficiently inform the public about the threat *du jour*, but because they functioned symbolically as those who unflinchingly represented the distinctive pure conservative subject position, and those whom the audience could personally identify with, thereby reconstituting themselves as conservative. FOX News, in this way, is much less about "news" than it is about a site where people tune into reidentify or validate their chosen identity.

Embodied ideology works this way; it causes people to read themselves into kinship with the archetypes, to make sense of the world through their semiotic acts, and to take on their storylines and narratives as natural. In this capacity—as with any symbolic figure— the crowds who were drawn to hear them, subscribe to their blogs, read their books, or watch them on Glenn Beck or FOX News, were not seeking objective information about the nation's enemies, foreign and domestic, but were identifying or interpellating themselves as conservatives through them.

Again, all political groups or movements need such identifying self-types who embody part of its master narrative set—who give material form and expression to the group's moral, philosophical, and ideological values. And, within the segment of the U.S. Evangelical community that is her principal market, it appeared that Gabriel had successfully positioned herself into this symbolic script of the self—a prophet-messenger and guardian angel who on the one hand emerged from low beginnings, suffered, and remained close to the people she saves, and on the other embodies the subculture's myths and symbols, and identifies its boundaries in juxtaposition to its religio-political rivals, Islam and the Left. It was apparently for this reason that she was named one of the fifty most influential speakers in the U.S., as claimed by her website at the time.

Her market's affinity for such a subject position is evidenced by the 15 August 2011 e-mail to her subscribers, "The Engine Behind ACT! for America's Growth." Kelly Cook, ACT!'s National Field Director, noted how that the secret to the organization's rapid growth" was simple: "Booking Brigitte Gabriel and Guy Rodgers in large events in churches." Cook continued: "For example, we recently were hosted in a large church in Minneapolis. Approximately 1500 people turned out. Out of the electricity of the evening came several stunning results, including nearly 1000 new members and 83 new chapter leader signups! In just one night!" And, in just ten months prior to her speech regarding "the end times" and "terrorism" at the 2008 Southern California Prophecy Conference, at Calvary Chapel Chino Hills, Gabriel had given two hundred similar presentations—an average of one every other day, surpassing even Spencer and Pipes at their peak.

This collective subcultural need for self-identifying agents like Gabriel was also evident in the otherwise unexplainable demand for her books. Pipes's and Spencer's books were more objective, well-written, and contained content that—when combined with that which had been excluded, and when purged of their political core—could reasonably illuminate the more textual component of Islamic extremism that professional security analyses and more anthropological works within academic security studies typically tended to deemphasize. But, we cannot begin to say anything of the sort about Gabriel's two books. Her works—much like her speeches—were far more subjective and low-brow; giving primacy to form rather than content, symbolism over substance. And, yet, Gabriel's first book's four hundred reviews averaged 4.5 stars, besting Middle East and Pulitzer Prize writer Thomas Friedman's award-winning *From Beirut to Jerusalem*—the only other story of personal journey from war-torn Lebanon to Zion. But, as was the case of Robert Spencer's books, it is the polarized nature of these reviews—353 five-star ratings, and 20 one-star ratings—and not even one rating in the two or three star categories—that reveals her threat writing's political function.

Obviously, Gabriel's power as a symbolic, identifying figure—one with the power of interpellation—was a function of cultural capital. In her case, this cultural capital was the kind accrued by life's experiences, which—as we saw in Pipes's case—have particular weight in shaping one's habitus (Bourdieu 1990, 61). In other words, to so successfully occupy this subcultural subject position, Gabriel had a form of cultural capital that Pipes and Spencer did not. Whereas they could boast either terminal or graduate degrees from Harvard or UNC, Gabriel's form of cultural capital was more symbolic: she had "street cred." Whereas Pipes and Spencer *spoke Arabic*, learning it in school and short-term immersion, Gabriel *was Arab*, living it, while growing up in the south of Lebanon. And—as we will see—she didn't merely know about violence in Islam from her infiltration of Al-Qaeda and Hezbollah chatrooms, she experienced it personally, at great cost to her family, friends, and childhood. In this regard, when challenged in 2007 on her authority with the question whether she studied Islam, Gabriel could boast:

> No, I did not study Islam; I lived Islam. I lived in the Middle East. I read the Koran in the Arabic language -- I do not need translation. There is something about living in a place and being an eyewitness and coming from a culture and blowing the whistle on that culture, and that is very different from someone majoring in Islam and living in the Middle East for two months so they can write their thesis (Elder 2007).

With an eye toward accruing this kind of symbolic capital, Gabriel's autobiographical *Because They Hate* is replete with passages like this:

> *It's 1978, I am thirteen years old. My family is in the third year of living in this bomb shelter, a tiny underground room that sits off to the side of a bombed-out pile of rubble that was once our beautiful home."* ... *"We don't talk about it, but we could die of thirst or starvation if this goes on much longer"....." I've already gone through being wounded and buried alive in rubble. A direct hit from a shell would be better."* ... *"I was born in the small town of Marjayoun, a once peaceful, idyllic Christian town in the mountains of southern Lebanon"* ... *"All that came to an end when a religious war, declared by the Muslims against the Christians, and tore my country and my life apart."* (Gabriel 2006, 1-2; italics in original for some reason).

Of course, Gabriel is not the kind of expert that would explain the new conflict as a direct result of Israel's cleansing of a half-million Palestinians—many of whom joined the resistance, the Palestinian Liberation Organization, that had fled to Southern Lebanon. Nor would she explain how Israel had invaded Southern Lebanon and shelled and bombed indiscriminately many of its villages, causing the deaths of more than 2000 people from all sects who in the fog of war often could not know who was killing them, and thereby and otherwise exacerbating the low-level tensions between the area's Shiite Muslims and the Maronite Christians and the Druze. And, nor could she explain that Lebanon's civil war was less about "Islam's" ancient hatred for Christians than it was about the way that the French had privileged Gabriel's ancestor Maronites at the expense of the Muslims, and especially the Shiite in the south.

Instead, the success of Gabriel's book, as this italicized passage suggests, was not about its insights into the facts of history, but it was about her own cultural capital and her ability to symbolize from an Arab perspective the inherent goodness of Israel—something that her audience needed to hear:

> Israel started coming in the middle of the night, between 1976 and 1978, bringing in food for the military, bringing in bomb shelters for those who did not have bomb shelters, bringing in ammunition, bringing in food for the children because the Palestinians and Muslims had cut off all food supplies. ...
>
> I remember, at the age of thirteen years old, putting on my Easter dress, my Sunday best, because I wanted to look pretty when I was dead, knowing that when they came to slaughter me, there would be no one to bury me. I remember sobbing to my parents, begging them, "I don't want to die! I'm only thirteen years old!" There was nothing my parents could say to me. I remember sitting in the corner of our bomb shelter with my father reading from Psalms. We all sat together and he started reading, "Though I walk through the valley of the shadow of death, I will fear no evil, for thou art with me." My parents told me, "When they come to slaughter us tonight, you just run towards Israel, and you never look back (Gabriel 2012).

Self-Interpellation: The Hailing of a Patriot

In the intervening years between this early part of her life that she described as "my 9/11" and the next one, she worked in Israel in her early twenties as an anchor for Middle East Television, operated Pat Robertson's Christian Broadcasting Network, and married an American co-worker. Gabriel and her husband moved to the United States in 1989 and started a film and television production company (Fichtner 2011). After 9/11, in 2002, Gabriel founded American Congress for Truth, which in June 2007 morphed into ACT! for America. But, therein we find the same puzzle that surrounded so much (if not all) of conservative threat discourse in the decade following 9/11. The founding purpose of ACT! for America was in line with the literature's characterization of this discourse as steeped in the ideology of civilizational clashism and Zionism; specifically—per the group's website—to "fearlessly speak out in defense of America, Israel and Western civilization."

But, subscribing to the ACT! For America e-mail stream suggested that an altogether different function was the real engine behind the organization's growth. Nearly all e-mails that emerged from it—several a week—had dubious content that had little if anything to do with containing what the organization dubbed "radical Islam," which was a thinly veiled euphemism for all of Islam. Instead, the e-mails always contained this dualistic non-sequitur mass—the first part related to the conservative movement's domestic enemies—

euphemized variously as "politically-correct enablers"—and the second part the conservative, patriot self, or the "modern-day 'minutemen,'" as this excerpt of Gabriel's July 3, 2012 e-mail to subscribers revealed:

> **Freedom of speech is under assault by the enablers of radical Islam, those pied pipers of political correctness who generally refuse to debate the facts and the issues, instead resorting to name calling and other propaganda techniques to suppress any and all critique of radical Islam.**
> **You who are reading this email are the modern-day "minutemen," standing in courageous opposition to the tyranny of both radical Islam and its politically correct enablers.**

As the producer of such politically-coded and symbolically-functioning text, Gabriel—as did the other organic polemicists profiled—conferred political subjectivity to her niche conservative market. Her ideologically-laden texts fixed the identity of the reader, who recognized both them and their text as symbolic of the community with which they identified (Bowman 1994).

Political ideologies work this way; they produce identities and positions for people and they are the methods through which groups legitimate a certain societal, national order, with some groups favored and others disfavored (Wetherell 2001, 286). Historically, in other forms of identity conflict, ideologues like Gabriel have created erected ideological structures that closely parallel a religion, with the nation as the deity to whom one's loyalty is due, with the nation's symbolic subject positions like patriots serving as its saviors and saints, its traitors the embodiment of evil, or demons, and its membership programs serving as self-sacrificing ritual (Kaufman 2001, 25). In this way, ACT!'s almost daily ritual of flag-colored e-mails—their red headings and special type, white space, and blue normal text—functioned as a nationalist religion, where the soteriological function was (re)constituting or interpellating the conservative "modern-day 'minutemen'" and "Patriots."

Gabriel's constant reference the "Patriot" stemmed from its central identifying function within U.S. conservative subculture, and its ability to mobilize the masses to various functions that she was offering them. She adroitly mobilized this ideational, nationalistic resource in 2011, with the launching of her "Patriot Partner" program as yet another means to hail the Patriot conservative into self-recognition through acts of token self-sacrifice. As the following excerpt from a September 24, 2012 e-mail on ACT! for America's fifth anniversary suggests, this pay-for-belonging feature had much in common with similar programs in other Christian cults, such as the Jim and Tammy Faye Bakker blessing-for-a-dollar campaign:

The entire program's underlying, basic function of self-identity politics was evident in the utter lack of content related to "radical Islam" and—in its place—language of self-identity politics, such as "your patriotism, and your love for this wonderful country," "our hopes and dreams for America," and so on.

Most often, Gabriel's "call to patriots"—as this excerpt from an October 5, 2012 e-mail just before the general election suggests—was a call to deal not with enemies foreign, but with enemies domestic, in the common euphemization of "political correctness":

America the Beautiful

Dear David,

Click on the image or link below and watch an amazing two minute rendition of America the Beautiful.

But this is more than a patriotic music video.

It's a call to patriots—and when you read the text that scrolls during the video, you'll know why!

And see if you know what the pianist is tapping out at the end.

Had enough of political correctness? Want to send a powerful, patriotic message to your friends?

Then forward this email to everyone you know!

Self-Governance

Gabriel's grassroots project had yet another feature of self-identity politics, inscribing political faction's borders through a form of self-government akin to what Foucault described as "popular justice" or a "people's court" (Foucault 1980, 1, 6). As the U.S. "patriot" movement and the hundred or more independent components of the conservative "militia" movement suggest, the nation's farther right wing is home to a wide variety of anti-government groups—self-organized citizen soldiers whose dissident political identity is captured in doing for themselves what they perceive as their government is not only unwilling to do, but working to subvert (Castells 1997, 87, 95). Gabriel's ideology was similar. Security, she wrote in her second book, "is our responsibility" and "we must not expect the government to do it for us." Civilians, she added, "must defend our families, our communities, and our nations" (2008, 207, 209).

Gabriel's e-mail on October 2nd demonstrated how ACT! was a vehicle for such self-governance, boasting how its members in this grassroots militia had done what their government was not doing, such as finding a jihadist online, and leading authorities to the point of arrest. Enacting self-security this way was fundamentally counterhegemonic, tacitly delegitimizing the more progressive institutions responsible for security.

Self-governance was also enacted in activism. For only 16 cents a day, ACT's "Patriot Partners" could participate in various forms of government policing, such as organized mass-level protests that swamp the phones of state houses and congress with phone calls and e-mails. Typical of this self-governance and patriot reconstructing function was the following ACT! e-mail to subscribers on May 29, 2012. This performative e-mail boasted how Gabriel's organization was key in advancing the aforementioned David Yerushalmi's draft anti-sharia legislation—a form of popular justice that prohibited federal and state government judges from doing what they were apparently predisposed to do—privilege Islamic law over U.S. code.

Kansas Victory: The Untold Story

Dear David,

The week of May 7th, the Kansas legislature passed, on a near-unanimous vote, the Kansas version of ALAC (American Laws for American Courts). According to a Fox News report, Gov. Sam Brownback signed the bill on May 21st.

ALAC prohibits judges from applying foreign law when doing so infringes on the constitutional rights of a party to the case. This can include sharia law.

Numerous media outlets reported the legislature's vote. But here's what happened behind the scenes that didn't get reported.

ACT! for America spearheaded a grassroots effort that produced more than 30,000 phone calls and emails to Kansas legislators.

******** 30,000 !!! ********

Another ACT! project, the "Congressional Scorecard," enabled Gabriel's modern day minutemen to not only guard the nation from its more progressive judges, but from its more progressive legislators, as she described near the end of her second book:

Another weakness of modern democratic societies is that their governments have grown so big that it's difficult for the average citizen to understand and keep track of what goes on in the national legislature. … Thus, the key to success is knowing the truth and having an organization through which to disseminate it. This is why ACT!

For America has created a 'congressional scorecard' program and a voter education project. We research bills we consider important.... We keep tabs on how each elected official votes on these bills" (Gabriel 2008, 221).

Again, such forms of self-governance—like all political action, including security and foreign policy—was a form of self-identification. Political practice works this way—positioning the actor in accordance with the nature of the act. Social action relies upon representations of identity, but it is also through the formulation and enactment of practice that identities are produced and reproduced (Hansen 2006, 1). In this way, identity is both the producer of, and the product of, all forms of social practice, including foreign policy and security discourses (Hansen 2006, 23).

The Bush administration's policy to invade Iraq, for example, offered the nation yet another opportunity for scripting the exceptional U.S. self in terms of cultural and material supremacy after the humiliation of 9/11. With regular speech acts like *"We're hunting down* the terrorists. *We're helping* Iraqis build a free nation.... *We're advancing* freedom....*We are removing* a source of violence, and so on, President Bush from the bully pulpit could point the nation to itself, repositioning it as the only actor on the global stage (Chandrasekaran 2007, 337). Gabriel's project functioned similarly, with Islam serving as the necessary prop upon which the script of conservative patriot and minuteman could be enacted. Her daily e-mails to her Patriot Partners pointed us to our own actions. We the people were doing what the more progressive government couldn't do: *keeping the nation safe.* By giving only 16 cents a day, we were "keeping tabs on how each elected official votes," producing mass-level protests that swamp the phones of state houses and congress with phone calls and e-mails, and so on.

Reconstruction of the Ideal Self

Gabriel's threat writing also functioned as a platform for self-identity politics in its self-aggrandizing component, which (re)constructed the idyllic, traditionalist, Judeo-Christian self—the extended Holy Land, Amer-Israel—and it did so in juxtaposition to its imagined religio-political opposites that threaten it—Islam and the Left. In each of her productions—books, speeches, e-mails, and so on—the good conservative self was always being produced relationally, in binary opposition to its imagined outside. In her first book, for example, the production of the Christian self always took place in juxtaposition to its civilizational opposite, Islam:

> My country of Lebanon was much like America and the West are today. It was an island of freedom in the middle of an Islamic sea of tyranny and oppression.... Our seemingly modern lifestyle progressive thinking, democratic form of government, and schools of higher learning were a thorn in the side of the backward, feuding, feudal Arab world, whose Islamic customs and religious philosophies dominated other countries of the Middle East (Gabriel 2006, 2-3).

As in many more racialized forms of identity politics, Gabriel's threat writing produced the ideal conservative self in moves that naturalized or fixed difference between the good

Judeo-Christian, Western self and its evil other, Muslims and Arabs. Naturalizing difference typically involves fixing difference biologically, through blood and not culture or circumstances, as this passage in Gabriel's first book enacts:

> My day always started with a long breakfast, usually hot milk and eggs…. For me, every day was like a party. … Lebanon is considered part of the Arab world. However, as a child, I was taught that my people, the Lebanese Christians, are the descendants of the Phoenicians….we are Arabs only by language and not by blood.

Gabriel's (2008) second *New York Times* bestseller, *They Must Be Stopped*, was similarly replete with more banal civilizationalism, with the exceptional Western self always juxtaposed in binary fashion to its imagined opposite, Islam. To explain Muslim "hatred toward the infidel West," for example, Gabriel (2008, 6) described the "envy and resentment of the West's material, intellectual, scientific, and economic superiority—in vivid contrast to "the squalor, illiteracy, and oppression that mark so much of the Muslim world."

Gabriel's civilizationalism positioned the good self as civilized, and its outside opposite, Islam, as uncivilized. "Every one of us," she said, "has been summoned to play a role in the conflict between the forces of chaos and civilization" (2008, 10-11). She added that Westerners can't understand Middle Eastern culture and its religion because we "come from a Judeo-Christian background, where the teaching of faith centers on love, tolerance and forgiveness" (2008, 13)—implying that all or most of Islamic civilization is based on the opposite urges of hatred, intolerance, and revenge.

Again, this move of reconstructing the good self through in relation to its complete opposite in Gabriel's threat writing took place not merely in her books, but also in her much more prolific speeches and e-mails. In her July 16, 2012 email, "Brutal intolerance," for example, told the story of a 16 year-old Christian girl, who had been brutalized by a Pakistani man who poured highly corrosive acid on her face and down her esophagus.

To begin, Gabriel quickly moved past the threat topic of Islam to objectify the religio-political enemy complex—the dominant Muslim-American groups, and their "politically correct enablers" on the Left. But, then the piece began the work of ideal self-construction. She told how the girl was flown to Texas by unidentified American angels, and healed through 31 surgeries by unidentified Houston, Texas doctors. The individuals involved were "unidentified" because they *were* not individuals; they were the nation—America. The final act of ideal self-identification was her description of how this brutalized young Christian woman enacted one of the supreme values and symbols of her faith: *forgiveness*.

Self-Discipline

As was the case with Spencer, Gabriel's threat writing included a substantial disciplinary element—the self-governmentality of pastoralism that defines the boundaries of self, identifies wayward elements of the flock, and shepherds them back into the fold. Gabriel's more banal, everyday form of this pastoralism would not be worth mentioning were it not for its systemic nature as part of the whole self-identification project. Typifying this pastoralism that permeated her threat writing were several statements in her second book. There, she chastises President Bush for saying "I believe that Islam is a great religion and preaches peace"; and Prime Minister Tony Blair for saying, "True Islam is immensely tolerant and open." Blair and Bush would be advised to take a course on Islam, she added, "It will serve them and freedom well" (2008, 51-52).

But, she reserved her sternest self-discipline for religious leadership: "Nothing disturbs me more," she said, "than when I see ministers, priests, and rabbis who are involved in interfaith dialogue, listening to imams say that Islam is a peaceful religion that has been hijacked by radicals." These religious leaders, she warned, "cannot imagine that someone can look them straight in the eye and lie" (2008, 77). This form of self-discipline permeated ACT! for America e-mails as well, as typified by this e-mail excerpt from December 11, 2012, titled "Interfaith naivete," wherein Gabriel gave this implicit warning of God's wrath against those "Christians who reach out to Muslims":

Dear David,

Christians who reach out to Muslims in interfaith efforts frequently do so with the best of intentions. Unfortunately, there's an old saying, "the road to hell is paved with good intentions."

Perhaps this is why Jesus warned his followers, "be wise as serpents and gentle as doves."

The story below (highlights added) illustrates the naivete that characterizes so much of Christian and Jewish interfaith outreach efforts to Muslims.

This self-disciplinary strategy of action extends to the Church broadly via Gabriel's 700 chapters nationwide. The leader of one of Gabriel's Texas ACT! for America chapters, Dorrie O'Brien of Grand Prairie, and a Tarrant County Republican Party precinct chairwoman, enacted such a self-disciplinary function when she learned that Pastor Bob Roberts Jr. of the area's Northwood Church planned an outreach to local Muslims. O'Brien said that the idea of Christians and Muslims making friends or having fun together is "repulsive and impossible."[86]

But, what this ACT! Chapter excluded in its political project was the actual reality surrounding the identity of Texas Muslims. The event produced 1,500 Muslims and 1,000 Christians. The reporter at the event wrote: "Jokes were told — one imam commented that the Dallas Cowboys needed divine intervention — and congregants stood in unison to recite the Pledge of Allegiance and Texas Pledge of Allegiance." "A young lady in a hijab sang the Star-Spangled Banner," Roberts said; and "a combined choir of Muslim and Christian kids sang You Are my Sunshine."

Toward the end, Roberts, spoke for Christians at NorthWood and other churches from the Dallas area, telling the assembled 1500 Muslims, "We love you." Then, in a stark, spontaneous reaction that would have created great dissonance within Gabriel's and ACT!

---

[86] See Northwood Church's website for a video of the event: www.northwoodchurch.org.

for America's anti-Islam master narrative, the entire Muslim audience stood and replied, "We love you too" (Evans 2011).

Self-Abiding: "Security" Writing only within the Conservative Enclave

Edward Said (1978, 23) had asserted that the unity of Orientalist texts was "due in part to the fact that they frequently refer to each other." Orientalism was, he added, "a system for citing works and authors." And, as we saw with both Pipes and Spencer, Gabriel's productions were marked by this endogamic, solipsistic practice of excluding all intertextuality with the legitimizing, more progressive societal institutions and its authorities, and by referencing only information that emerged from within the conservative knowledge society. In other words, in Gabriel's threat writing, all intertextuality was with other institutions and members of the conservative enclave, *and no others*. Her main strategy in this form of self-identity politics was sending ACT! for America e-mails that forwarded works by other vetted and symbolic movement elite, or generating ACT! events that gave them a public platform where her niche market could directly experience the conservative movement's dissident, popular security experts.

This practice of self-abiding was performative in the counterhegemonic sense through its inherent anti-intellectualism and anti-elitism, and its move of pure negation of the dominant societal politics of truth. By never quoting orthodox security professionals and other authorities across the U.S. population of over 300 million, and by quoting only a select handful of experts within the parallel conservative knowledge society, Gabriel achieved three goals of identity politics: (1) reinscribed the boundaries of the authorized self; (2) legitimized this inside; and (3) thereby subverted the more progressive political outside.

Typifying this intensely political "security" writing were Gabriel's e-mails published over the course of two months in the late summer of 2010. When the "ground zero mosque" spectacle was ascendant, ACT! for America on July 26, 2010 sent the e-mail "'Ground Zero Mosque' issue heating up." The e-mail's first task was to reinscribe the boundaries of the good self, by noting that "well-known public figures, such as Newt Gingrich and Sarah Palin, have spoken out against it," and that other Republicans like Rick Lazio (candidate for governor of New York) and NY Rep. Peter King have called for investigations of the funding for the mosque." Continuing to inscribe the conservative knowledge enclave, the e-mail then forwarded the link to a 60 second advertisement opposing the project by "our friends at [Frank Gaffney's] Center for Security Policy." Then, in a move to delegitimize domestic political rivals, the e-mail noted that public opinion was decidedly against the establishment view. In this vein, ACT! then posted a 23 July 2010 article "Behind the mosque" published in the conservative *New York Post* "by our friend and esteemed historian Andrew Bostom." Bostom is a medical doctor-turned-Islam critic who had been a close colleague of Spencer and Geller's.[87]

---

[87] Author of "The Legacy of Jihad" and "The Legacy of Islamic Antisemitism," Bostom (2010) analyzed the "ground zero" mosque founder, Imam Faisal Rauf, noting that "At least two of Imam Rauf's books, a 2000

On August 6, 2010, under the subject line of "Unbelievable Censorship!," ACT! notified its subscribers that Ground Zero Mosque news could be gained from event-leader Pamela Geller's blog AtlasShrugs. Then, citing others within this network, ACT!'s August 17th e-mail, "Secretary of State Hillary Clinton working with UN, OIC to criminalize free speech!," forwarded commentary on the topic "posted recently in Jihad Watch." On 20 September 2010, Darla from one of ACT!'s many obscure affiliates—the Patriot Action Network—a grassroots blog with over 89,000 members—posted ACT! for America's e-mail about Frank Gaffney's most recent publication under the heading "Sharia report challenges political establishment." The e-mail said this:

> A powerful new 'Team B' report on sharia law, published by the Center for Security Policy, challenges the political establishment's notions regarding the nature of the threat we are fighting. The report team included two of our speakers at the ACT! for America 2010 National Conference & Legislative Briefing, James Woolsey and Andrew McCarthy.

Further identifying the authorized inside or boundaries of the conservative subculture as it related to the topic of Islam, the ACT! e-mail added excerpts of the article from the *Washington Times* on September 14th titled: "Woolsey & McCarthy & Soysters: Second opinion needed on Shariah: Our political establishment wears blinders and ignores the threat."

ACT! events functioned similarly to reinsribe the conservative subcultural enclave and identity broadly. On March 15th, 2011, ACT! announced that Republican congressman Allen West—a notorious Islam critic—would be the keynote speaker at its annual National Conference & Legislative Briefing. It cited Newt Gingrich's statement where he said that West would be someone he would definitely consider as a vice presidential running mate. In a similar boundary making function, the e-mail affirmed the legitimacy of other speakers, such as Erick Stakelbeck, former analyst at Israel-advocate and Islam-critic Stephen Emerson's Investigative Project on Terrorism, and now host of the Christian television mogul Pat Robertson's CBN News program "Stakelbeck on Terror," which was a euphemism for Islam.

In this political twist on security writing—what we are calling security politics—knowledge of the threat or security topic is ancillary or secondary to the politically performative boundary-forming function that is advanced by citing such highly-vetted authorities who symbolically represent the identity's center—that is, those who never confuse by writing more neutrally on the topic du jour.

---

treatise on Islamic law and his 2004 "What's Right with Islam," laud "rejuvenating" Islamic religious spirit of Ibn Taymiyyah and al-Wahhab—who the NYPD report listed as the ideological foundation of Islamic extremism. Bostom concluded that "Feisal Rauf's public image as a devotee of the 'contemplative' Sufi school of Islam cannot change the fact that his writings directed at Muslims are full of praise for the most noxious and dangerous Muslim thinkers." As his final item in the case, he added that "even the classical Sufi master that Rauf extols, the 12th-century jurist Abu Hamed Muhammad ibn Muhammad al-Ghazali, issued opinions on jihad and the imposition of Islamic law on the vanquished non-Muslim populations that were as bellicose and bigoted as those of Ibn Taymiyyah."

The political utility of the project can be seen not only by the knowledge cited, but by the employees. Gabriel's assistant director, Guy Rodgers, for example, had no knowledge of Islam whatsoever, but had served as the field director for Ralph Reed's Christian Coalition, and served as presidential campaign manager for Patrick J. Buchanan in 1996, and a consultant for John McCain in 2008. In similar vein, Gabriel's previous key assistant in ACT! for America, Hal Weatherman, was formerly the Chief of Staff of Islam-critic U.S. Rep Sue Myrick (R-NC).

The political nature of Gabriel's project can be seen in the way its security writing carefully remains in the center of the conservative information ghetto. The just-mentioned Congresswoman Myrick, for example, had written the forward to the Islamization conspiracy's key text, *Muslim Mafia*, by David Gaubatz (Charlotte Observer 2011). It was Gaffney who had funded Gaubatz to write the book, and it was Joseph Farah's *WorldNetDaily* that published it, and it was Pipes in an interview with Gaffney on his website that promoted it (Pipes 2009), and it was Horowitz who further publicized it with an interview in his *FrontPageMagazine* (20 February 2009). It is such production wholly within the conservative information ghetto that characterized Gabriel's project of security politics.

2. Counter-Narrating the Foreign Enemy (Within)

As Schmitt (1932) had first theorized, the identification (and construction) of the friendly inside—the act of self-narration—is but one half of the act of the political; the other half is the identification of the enemy outside. In Gabriel's threat writing in the post-9/11 decade—as was the case with Spencer, Pipes, and many other conservative threat writers—the enemy outside was conceptualized within the schema of enemies foreign and domestic, religious and political, Islam and the Left. In the first category of narrating the foreign enemy, there were two distinctive features of Gabriel's threat writing that reveal how it functioned politically.

Radically Transgressing Societal Taboos Regarding Minorities

As was the case with Pipes and Spencer, Gabriel's threat writing did not merely produce oppositional or dissident knowledge about Islam in the context of the foreign enemy, it did so in a way that was politically performative at the level of domestic or cultural politics; that is, by systematically and more egregiously transgressing societal norms or taboos (Hall 2001, 332-3, 336).

Such transgressions of the prevailing politics of truth entailed several strategies, such as naturalizing difference, undifferentiating and dehumanization of the other, stereotyping, dividing practices, and moves of exclusion, or hiding from view all that is normative. And at the heart of every one of these tactics is the essence of identity politics—the reproduction of the self via the other.

Naturalizing Difference

Gabriel's first heretical move in assessing the threat of Islam was that racist move of *naturalizing* difference. Naturalizing difference is a key feature of all Western racialized regimes of representation, where the cultures of dark-skinned people are reduced to their internal or biological nature, instead of their more external societal environment. The political utility behind naturalizing difference is readily apparent. After all, if the differences between people with different skin color are "cultural," then immigrants or minority populations can assimilate. But if they are "natural"—as the U.S. South's slave system needed everyone to believe—then the societal order with them in their slave place is also natural (Hall 1997, 245). Just as important, by fixing difference between self and its significant others, the slide of one's own identity is halted and self-identity security is achieved.

In this strategy of naturalizing difference, Gabriel narrated the ideal conservative self via counternarrations of other. On the one hand, she represented the undifferentiated civilized Jews and Christians; on the other, she counterframed undifferentiated barbaric Muslims (of the Israeli-occupied territories of Palestine and Lebanon) and their civilization, "Islam". Gabriel's strategy of naturalizing difference within identity politics is typified even in the title of her first bestseller, *Because They Hate*—which was set in the context of Lebanon's civil war in 1975. "They"—in the book's title—was understood as the whole religion, and "Hate" was understood as that religion's and its adherents' fundamental nature, as this passage suggests:

A lot of Muslims poured in from other Muslim countries like Iran, the founder and supporter of Hezbollah, one of the leading terrorist organizations in the world today. They came from Somalia, Sudan, Syria, Jordan and Egypt. The Lebanese civil war was not between the Lebanese; it was a holy war declared on the Christians by the Muslims of the Middle East (2006, 35).

Here, unlike the threat writing of Pipes and Spencer, Gabriel was more prone to dispense with strategies of euphemization. In this book, she quickly dropped the euphemization "radical Islam" and used the term she and her audience understood as the real focus—"the Muslims of the Middle East." By using undifferentiated terms like this and telling us how undifferentiated "Muslims poured in," Gabriel was writing back against the prevailing more progressive politics of truth with the implicit message that extremism in Islam *is* Islam. In other words, the Islam of the extremists was the dominant, authoritative and historical Islam, and that instances of Muslim violence against non-Muslims are thus normative throughout the faith.

Her heretical security writing continued in this strategy of conflating and reducing all Muslims into one undifferentiated mass—with no daylight between the violent extremists and the pious. When she wrote, "They started massacring the Christians in city after city," "*they*" implied *all* of "the Muslims." On this same page she continued to dehumanize all of "the Muslims," describing how "they" "would tie one leg of the baby to the mother and one leg to the father and pull the parents apart, splitting the child in half" (2006, 35).

Purposively transgressing the societal politics of truth, she continued in this strategy of dehumanizing the other by describing her "life-changing experience" with a badly wounded Muslim woman in an Israeli hospital, of whom she said: "And for the first time in my life I saw evil." With unknown contexts surrounding the woman's worldview, Gabriel could nevertheless assert: "I realized that this Muslim couldn't love the Jews even after they saved her life." In a similarly dehumanizing sentence that followed, she added, "And when you are unable to be grateful to the people who saved your life, you have no soul."

Gabriel's threat writing often naturalized difference through such moves of dehumanization. At the radically Zionist Christians United for Israel event in 2007, she said:

> The difference, my friends, between Israel and the Arab world is the difference between civilization and barbarism. It's the difference between good and evil [applause].... this is what we're witnessing in the Arabic [sic] world, They have no SOUL!, they are dead set on killing and destruction. And in the name of something they call "Allah" which is very different from the God we believe...[applause] because our God is the God of love (Wilson 2007; Terkel 2010).

It apparently never dawned on Gabriel or the other Christians assembled that this same God of love—in the form of Jesus's first and most important Sermon on the Mount—commanded us to "love your enemy" and "pray for those who persecute you," or that the Arabic speaking Jews and Christians in places like Palestine, Syria, Lebanon, and elsewhere also us the term "Allah," which is simply Arabic for God.

And in her June 24th, 2008 speech delivered at the more rightist Intelligence Summit in Washington DC—an organization for which she served as a member of its advisory board—she said:

> America and the West are doomed to failure in this war unless they stand up and identify the real enemy: Islam... If you want to understand the nature of the enemy we face, visualize a tapestry of snakes. They slither and they hiss, and they would eat each other alive, but they will unite in a hideous mass to achieve their common goal of imposing Islam on the world.[88]

Stereotyping: "Dividing Practices"

Framing of all Muslims in such undifferentiated terms is synonymous with stereotyping. And, all such stereotyping is part of a larger binary-producing strategy that Foucault (1982, 208) described as "dividing practices"— that is, dividing the normal form the abnormal, orthodox from unorthodox, sacred from the profane, morally good from the evil, victims from the aggressors, civilized from the barbaric, with soul from the barbaric without soul, human from the non-human, and so on.

In his essay on "Stereotyping" Richard Dyer (1977) observed that without the use of types, it might be impossible to make sense of the world; we understand the world by relating its objects, people or events to their appropriate place in our cultural classification schemas (Hall 1997, 257). But, Gabriel's use of stereotypes is not merely a sense-making or

---

[88] See http://www.intelligencesummit.org/speakers/BrigitteGabriel.php

semiotic practice; it is a political practice; or practice of self, making sense of self in relation to essentialized features of the outsiders.

Thus, we are always coming full circle back to the basic act of the political. By keeping a few vivid characterizations of "the Muslims" in view, and thereby reducing all of Muslim complexity to parsimonious stereotypes that fit in neat binaries co-occupied with the opposite, traditional U.S. self in the favored half of the binary, Gabriel's threat writing concerning the other performatively functions to reposition the self. Thus, while on the one hand it is an explicit discourse about the foreign and dangerous other; on the other it is implicitly and performatively a practice of self. And, so it is with all acts of the political.

In her chapter titled, "Clash of Civilizations," Gabriel continued to subvert the academy and professional security establishment by bolstering the paradigm-forming thesis—which as we saw up front—was first set down by Bernard Lewis, and made famous by Samuel Huntington, and which security professionals almost universally tended to dismiss as overblown or misrepresentations of highly complex and different conflicts. And, Gabriel advanced this heretical thesis in a purposively subversive way—again, naturalizing difference through the civilized/barbaric binary. "It is in Jerusalem," she wrote, "that you are able to see clearly the differences between Arabic and Jewish culture as represented by the two sides of the city." Using tropes of sacred and profane, clean and unclean she wrote: "If you walk one block into the eastern side of the city, the first thing you notice is the uncleanliness."

Shifting to Islam, she wrote subversively how "Muslims" in "that part of the world" looked upon "killing both Christians and Jews as a sacred duty." In similarly politically-performative and long-tabooed racialized terms, she unreflexively continued: "While Christians and Jews learn to repair the world, love their enemy, forgive those who trespass against them, and turn the other cheek, Muslims are taught to fight the infidels, to consider them enemies of Allah" (2006, 103-105).

In her chapter, "Terrorists Among Us," Gabriel continued to transgress societal norms of linking Muslim-Americans to terror. In racialized, undifferentiated terms, she wrote that "Muslims" in the "the Arab world" have a saying: "First comes Saturday, then comes Sunday." Every Muslim in the Middle East knows exactly what this means. This is their way of saying that first they'll get the Jews (who observe Sabbath on Saturday), and then they'll get the Christians…" (2006, 124).

Gabriel's threat writing regarding Muslims is akin to racialized discourse broadly. For example, just as in U.S. racialized discourse on blacks—where a black's primitivism was a function of his biological blackness, and not his environment—so her Muslim's barbarism was a function of his or her Islamic nature, which they could change no more than a leopard could change his spots. For the black in racialized discourse, biology was destiny; for Gabriel's "the Muslims," religion is. Just as blacks were reduced to their "essential" caricatured characteristics in works like *Little Black Sambo*—thick lips, fuzzy hair, broad nose, pronounced brow, high buttocks—so her "the Muslims" are similarly reduced, by her attaching to them a standard set of stereotypical features—uncivilized, barbaric, violent, terrorist, hating, unforgiving, intolerant, unclean, and so on.

Such systematic strategies of subversion via stereotyping permeated Gabriel's more everyday form of threat writing. In an interview in 2007, for example, Larry Elder asked how Gabriel would classify the world's 1.2 billion Muslims by ideology. She replied by sweeping every Muslim into one of two close-knit categories: (1) martyrdom-seeking jihadist; or (2) jihadist supporter and suicide bomber sympathizer who hates by nature:

> Not all of them are radicals. We estimate that the radicals are between 15 and 25 percent; that translates to between 180 and 300 million people like Mohammad Atta who are willing to strap bombs to their bodies and commit martyrdom operations. Now, that is still a minority, 15 to 25 percent, but 300 million Mohammad Attas ready to unleash their blood upon the West .... Now, the rest of them . . . despise the West, they hate our westernization, they think we are morally corrupt, that we are corrupting the world, and they think we are such a bad influence on the world that we need to be stopped at any cost. They may not be willing to commit martyrdom operations themselves, but they will sit there and cheer on and rally those who are willing to kill us (Elder 2007).

Gabriel's counterhegemonic strategy to using stereotyping to subvert the more progressive societal norms surrounding the faith of the nation's Muslim minority can best be seen in her second book, *They Must Be Stopped* (2008). Here, Gabriel in several chapters— "Islam's contempt for women and minorities," "Islam and honor killings," Islam and child abuse," "Islam and sex slaves," "Slavery and Islam," "Islam and persecution of other faiths"—selected for view all that which was tabooed in the more progressive politics of truth. Her chapter titles were not merely stereotypical, but they were political in the counterhegemonic nature of that which was selected for visibility.

The text that followed was similarly heretical in that it raised to visibility all that was taboo. The section "Islam and Child Abuse," for example, begins this way:

> Mohammed was forty-nine years of age when he became betrothed to Aisha, the daughter of one of his closest friends. At the time, she was six years of age. Three years later, after she completed her first menstrual cycle, Aisha and Muhammad consummated their union. At the time, Mohammed was fifty-two, and Aisha was nine. Unfortunately, the Islamic practice of marrying a child bride of the age of nine is still practiced today (2008, 177).

Moves of Exclusion

But, transgressing or subverting societal norms of threat knowledge proceeds not merely by such moves of selection, but by moves of exclusion. Gabriel's threat writing, in other words, *always* excluded from view all that which professional security writing would be compelled to include in a threat assessment. In all of Gabriel's productions, the normative, objective facts were curiously *always* missing; there is never any news related to Islam or Muslims that might put their threat to the nation in context, or set it in its complexity. For example, her March 24, 2011 e-mail, announced "Update—The Doctrine of Abrogation: Open the Koran Day." "Our goal," she said, "is to educate the general public about a *little known* yet important doctrine called "abrogation." Yet, Gabriel reliably excluded from view the prominent Sunni Islamist sheikh Yusuf al-Qaradawi's *Fiqh of Jihad* from two years earlier, which had explicitly delegitimized the doctrine of abrogation.

In this vein, ACT! for America never once sent an e-mail that showed the threat in perspective or in its varied contexts, as did more normative works by security professionals. ACT!, for instance, never mentioned facts like, in 2011, none of America's 14,000 murders were due to Islamic extremism (Kurzman 2011). And, ACT! reliably obscured from view all problematic data; it never mentioned annual reports that showed declining Muslim violence in the U.S., or that violence by Muslims was far less per capita than violence among the broader population (Kurzman 2013).

Cultural Struggle on Micro-Fields

Gabriel's various forms of counternarrating the threat were always enacted on micro-fields of struggle —fields that were as small as more progressive constructions, such as "moderate Muslim."

Gabriel, in other words, would reliably take the struggle onto that micro-field of "the moderate Muslim" and wage war against all of the progressive discourse on which the concept was standing. Whereas the societal signifier for a "moderate Muslim," or "good Muslim" was one who was fully Muslim and fully American, both pious and patriotic— Gabriel offered a far more heretical narrative—one akin to the saying attributed to American Civil War General Philip Sheridan: "the only good Indian is a dead Indian." To her, as she explains below, the only moderate Muslim was a secular or non-practicing one— in other words, a non-Muslim:

> I call it a practicing Muslim and a non-practicing Muslim. I think it is a better description than "moderate" and "radical." A practicing Muslim goes to mosque, prays five times a day, doesn't drink, believes God gave him women to be his property - to beat, to stone to death… He believes Christians and Jews are apes and pigs because they are cursed by Allah. He believes it is his duty to declare war on the infidels because they are Allah's enemies. That is a practicing Muslim (Elder 2007).

Gabriel's counterhegemonic threat narrative on Islam regularly deployed this distinguishing device of "practicing" versus "moderate." To subvert the normative view that most practicing Muslims were moderate, she framed "practicing" Muslims who appear "moderate" as wolves in sheep's clothing, practicing dissimulation. In her 2007 lecture as part of the Islam elective at the Joint Forces Staff College (JFSC)—an arm of National Defense University in Norfolk—Gabriel fielded the question: "Should we resist Muslims who want to seek political office in this nation?" As most of the audience undoubtedly squirmed in their seats with heads bowed for fear of making eye-contact with a fellow Muslim Soldier, Marine, or Sailor, Gabriel unflinching replied: "Absolutely. If a Muslim who has—who is—a practicing Muslim, who believes the word of the Koran to be the word of Allah, who abides by Islam, who goes to mosque and prays every Friday, who prays five times a day—this practicing Muslim—who believes in the teachings of the Koran, cannot be a loyal citizen to the United States of America" (Daloglu 2007).

180

As part of her answer to this same question, Gabriel continued to frame why any practicing Muslim's oath of office is never sincere, and always dissimulation: "A Muslim is allowed to lie under any situation to make Islam, or for the benefit of Islam in the long run. A Muslim sworn to office can lay his hand on the Koran and say 'I swear that I'm telling the truth and nothing but the truth,' fully knowing that he is lying because the same Koran that he is swearing on justifies his lying in order to advance the cause of Islam" (Rodda 2008).

Gabriel's emphasis on Muslim dissimulation, of course, was grand hypocrisy, given her own propensity for the practice, as Rodda (2008) notes:

> "The next question came from a soldier who introduced himself as Muslim who has been serving in the U.S. Army for the past 19 years. He asked Gabriel if she was a member of Hasbara Fellowship. Gabriel not only answered that she was not a member, but asked, 'What's Hasbara Fellowship?' Gabriel is currently listed as a speaker on the official website of Hasbara Fellowships as a member of the organization's Speakers Bureau, and has been since 2005."

The Soldier obviously asked her that question because Hasbara Fellowships had been reportedly linked to circulating Clarion's hate-inciting film, *Obsession: Radical Islam's War Against the West*, which framed "radical Islam" as plain Islam.

"The moderate Muslim" was a signifier constructed by more progressive societal discourse over several years after 9/11 to provide a haven or safe space for the practicing Muslim who did not sympathize with the more extreme practices and beliefs that were being framed as mainstream Islam by popular security experts. Like Spencer and Pipes, Gabriel frequently advanced the culture war on this particular micro-field—"the moderate Muslim." In her second book, *They Must Be Stopped* (2008), she wrote: "We are fighting devout Muslims who drink their Islam straight," she wrote. "Radical Islamists," she added, are merely devout Muslims "following the instructions of the Koran and walking in the steps of their Prophet Mohammed…." (2008, 50). She continued, "The main driving force behind all Islamic terrorism is the Koran. What drives these passionate soldiers of Allah is Islam itself and the promises made to them by the Prophet Mohammed" (2008, 60).

In this form of counternarrative against the more progressive security discourse, Gabriel's good Muslim was something of a black swan—an idealized, but still stereotypical patriot akin to America's racialized discourse surrounding the "noble savage," the "faithful" Christian black slave, like Uncle Tom, in Harriet Beecher Stowe's pro-abolitionist novel, *Uncle Tom's Cabin* (Hall 2001, 335-6). Gabriel's Muslim "Uncle Tom"—the Muslim "good nigger" equivalent—was produced through frequent intertextual references to the heretical figure Zuhdi Jasser. Jasser, an ex-Naval officer and medical doctor, had throughout the post-9/11 decade been stalwart in his criticism of any political elements of Islamic expression. Jasser's status as Gabriel's "good Muslim" also stemmed from the fact that they both took part in the aforementioned documentary, *Obsession: Radical Islam's War Against the West*, and that Jasser also sat as one of Clarion's four-person advisory board, along with Frank Gaffney and Daniel Pipes. It was for this reason that ACT! for America e-mails regularly paraded Jasser as "a Muslim" whenever an Uncle Tom figure was deemed useful in disciplining the broader Muslim-American community, or in when these more entrepreneurial conservatives needed to deflect heat from something that was drawing criticism from their political rivals. For example, on January 4, 2011, ACT! sent the e-mail titled "A Muslim supports Rep. Peter King," thereby deflecting criticism from Democrats that King's hearings on radicalization in the Muslim-American community were politically motivated, and aimed at delegitimizing the Obama administration's policies.

3. Narrating Domestic Enemies

The third and final pillar of Gabriel's threat writing—in addition to narrating the self and counter-narrating the foreign enemy—was that of narrating the U.S. conservative movement's domestic political enemy. Similar to that of Pipes and Spencer, all of Gabriel's threat writing on the subject of the conservative movement's newest foreign enemy, Islam, and its Muslims, also contained this non-sequitur mass at the center related to their more familiar domestic enemies— that is, the Democratic Party and the administration of Barak Obama, the more progressive, the more progressive societal institutions of knowledge, and the broader, more progressive politics of truth.

We had seen how her anti-sharia conference speech in Tennessee church seemed to dwell exclusively in this part of her project, almost missing altogether the farther religious Right's newest foreign enemy—Islam and its sharia—which were, after all, the billing subject of that conference. Gabriel's threat writing over the post-9/11 decade seemed to follow this pattern, so much so that—in an interview with *der Spiegel* at the end of the decade—Gabriel described the function of ACT! For America in terms that suggested the entire project really *had little to do with the threat of Islamism*:

> Local groups are encouraged to take action against overly politically correct teachers, excessively tolerant members of Congress and local newspapers that publish "derogatory" articles about the US or Israel (Fichtner 2011).

The counterhegemonic function of this part of Gabriel's project was also evident in its prominent place in the preface to her first book:

> And yet, there are still Americans who are unable or unwilling to recognize the nature or the extent of the threat presented by radical Islam. Whether motivated by naïve wishful thinking or rigid political correctness, they assert that Islam is a "moderate," "tolerant," and "peaceful" religion that has been hijacked by "extremists." They ignore the repeated calls to jihad, Islamic holy war, emanating from the government-controlled mosques of so-called moderate Islamic countries such as Egypt, Pakistan, and Indonesia. They refuse to accept that in the Muslim world, extreme is mainstream (2006, xi).

In a similar strategy of sarcasm, Gabriel wrote: "Our leaders and politicians bend over backward to tell us how sweetly wonderful Islam is, and that most Muslims are moderate, that a few radicals have hijacked this unbelievably sweet poetry called the Koran…" (2006, 156).

Gabriel's ulterior focus on enemies domestic was manifest in her chapter titled, "The Ivy-Covered Fifth Column," where she engaged the more leftist influence in the academy. Then, in the chapter, "Societies Are Not Created Equal," Gabriel's focus was less about Islamic society than our own, and specifically about the Western governmentality of multiculturalism.[89] The following chapters—"Is Islam a Peaceful Religion," and "Political Correctness Gone Mad"—continued to center and subvert the more progressive culture and its politics of truth.

Gabriel's second book, *They Must Be Stopped*, was also marked by the dubious content that had nothing to do with the nation's newest foreign enemy, and everything to do with the religious conservatives' domestic rivals, typified by this passage:

> Because of the rise of political correctness, we have the additional burden of facing people within our own borders—government officials, academics, journalists, and others—who dismiss the threat we're up against, blame America or Israel as the cause the conflict, treat anyone who speaks out against Islamofascism as an "intolerant bigot," or treat Islamofascists as oppressed victims. These purveyors of political correctness are foolishly and dangerously aiding and abetting the rising tide of Islamofascism (2008, 208).

This counterhegemonic project continued in a more banal, everyday fashion in her ACT! for America e-mails, as we saw earlier in her co-centering of radical Islam and its "politically-correct enablers." Typical of the ACT! habitus in this strategy was her October 17th, 2009 e-mail which announced a Washington DC metro area screening of the documentary, "An American Tragedy." The documentary detailed how two reconciled fathers who had lost their sons to "Islam" in a dramatic way faced an additional nightmare: *their government.* At the screening, conservative experts on the topic of Islam—in this case, McCarthy, Pipes, Gaffney, and others—were on hand to explain what is happening to our country, and why it was that these fathers "confronted an American government that seemed in denial" and why this is "a film that Hollywood would not make," and "the media would not report." Nearly every statement was counterhegemonic in function, delegitimizing or subverting the various parts of the more progressive regime of truth.

Most ACT! e-mails functioned like Pipes's and Spencer's surveillance technologies of Jihad Watch, Islamist Watch, and Campus Watch—that is, in an everyday, banal mode of identity politics by taking advantage of emerging opportune resources from the day's news. What "news" that was selected was that which could be politicized, or rendered politically performative. Typical was the October 7th, 2011 ACT! e-mail, "Anwar al-Awlaki—bridge builder?" which started by delegitimizing the various components of the more progressive establishment:

---

[89] Spurning the dominant societal norms of politics of truth that legitimizes multiculturalism, Gabriel wrote: "believe the degraded state of Arab societies is caused by Islam," she says. "It has spawned generations of people who celebrate death over life, who glorify mass murderers, who exhibit a lack of forgiveness and instead have the drive for revenge as taught by the Koran" (2006, 189).

Dear David,

Over the past several weeks we have talked a lot about "information warfare," and how the Muslim Brotherhood and its front organizations in America have used it to successfully deceive and mislead many government officials, military leaders, members of the media, and academics.

This past September 11th, national security and terrorism correspondent Patrick Poole posted a well-researched commentary exposing how government Muslim outreach programs have frequently failed, leaving government officials with egg on their faces.

These programs often fail because too many in government fall for the disinformation they are fed. Regardless of the reason—ignorance, political correctness, gullibility, naivete', willful blindness—the fact remains that these

Then the e-mail continued in counterhegemonic fashion by delegitimizing the "establishment media":

The "establishment media" play an important role in the Muslim Brotherhood information warfare campaign. ... Here are just two of Poole's posts. Even if you don't read them, the titles tell it all.

Rewind: New York Times hailed Awlaki as "a new generation of Muslim leader"

Rewind: NPR says Awlaki can "build bridges between Islam and the West"

Anwar al-Awlaki—"bridge builder." It would be comic if it weren't so tragic.

ACT! For America's e-mails during the beginning of the election year of 2012 were similar, with Islam increasingly decentered, functioning merely as a segue for the more central content that subverted the Obama Administration and/or some other authoritative element of the more progressive society. On January 17th, 2012, for example, the ACT! e-mail was "Obama terrorism advisor distortions," citing Pipes's and Spencer's protégé, Raymond Ibrahim, who "recently posted an enlightening and troubling column on FrontPageMagazine about one of President Obama's top counter-terrorism advisors." Ibrahim's (and now Gabriel's) purpose was to subversively mock Joint Intelligence Task Force for Combating Terrorism's (and National Intelligence University adjunct military faculty) Navy Commander Youssef Aboul-Enein, and delegitimize his two-year-old book, *Militant Islamist Ideology: Understanding the Global Threat* (2010).

Also typifying this pervasive feature was the e-mail two days later, on January 19th: "Obama administration and the Muslim Brotherhood." The e-mail forwarded an article by Barry Rubin, whom—as noted in the literature review—Said (1996) had lumped together with Lewis and Pipes as pro-Israel scholars who "make sure that the [Islamic] threat is kept before our eyes." The rest of this election year's e-mails from ACT! for America followed suit. When they didn't explicitly mention Obama in the e-mail subject line, they nearly always did in the body text, or by implication. Her May 17th, 2012 e-mail, for example, derided the Pentagon leadership for ordering a review of the curricula related to Islam at its Joint Professional Military Education centers:

184

Dear David,

The Pentagon recently announced that it's reviewing its training materials to eliminate "offensive" statements.

The Obama administration has purged all references to radical Islam from its national strategic threat assessments.

Madness is on the march. Shockingly, our country's leaders are in effect allowing the Muslim Brotherhood to help determine our counterterrorism policies!

After the Republican Convention, Gabriel's e-mails more diligently framed the Islamo-Leftist alliance conspiracy to Islamize America, which, recall, Horowitz and Pipes had begun. On August 6th, 2012, the subject of Gabriel's e-mail was "The purge continues," and noted how "The Obama administration has already purged all references to radical Islam from its strategic threat assessments." Her next e-mail on August 9th, 2012, thanked ACT! patriots for the "over 20,000" email letters they sent to the U.S. House and Senate in support of the five Members of Congress who "had the courage to raise questions about Muslim Brotherhood influence in our government." ACT!'s e-mail on October 8th, 2012 seized upon the opportunity delegitimize the Obama Administration's Chairman of the Joint Chiefs.

Dear David,

Dozens of Muslim organizations, including many connected to the Muslim Brotherhood, have successfully destroyed the career of an exemplary Army officer.

Of course, they couldn't have done it without the complicity of the Chairman of the Joint Chiefs of Staff, General Martin Dempsey.

According to the Thomas More Law Center release below (highlights added), General Dempsey "publicly excoriated Lt. Col. (LTC) Matthew Dooley, a 1994 graduate of the U.S. Military Academy at West Point and a highly decorated combat veteran."

The Chairman, rather than stand up to the Muslim Brotherhood's influence in the U.S. government, Gabriel alleged, preferred to destroy the Army officer's career for telling the truth about Islam in his course at this college within his own National Defense University. Gabriel then informed us that this Army officer's case wasn't an isolated incident:

LTC Dooley's "offense" was the course he taught at the Joint Forces Staff College entitled "Islamic Radicalism." When 57 Muslim organizations objected, Gen. Dempsey fired LTC Dooley from his teaching position and ordered a negative evaluation.

This is not a unique situation. There is an ongoing purge in our national defense and law enforcement departments to remove ANY reference to Islam deemed "offensive" to the Muslim Brotherhood.

Of course, that charge is misleading; academic freedom and the ability to transgress the politics of truth in critical security analysis was always respected at both National Defense University, and National Defense Intelligence College. But, rigorous sociological hermeneutical interpretation, critical security analysis, and sound judgment were always required, and the diverse student evaluations were always the first line of appropriate oversight. To show how ludicrous Gabriel's implied message is, we might digress examine how the teaching of Islamism at these two fully accredited universities proceeds.

In 2005, when I created National Defense University's first National Security Professional accredited elective course related to Islamism, carefully titled, "Containing Al Qaedaism," the students gained a sobering view of the problematic segments of the Quran and hadith, as viewed through the lenses of many important Islamist and jihadist ideologues worldwide. But, in addition, I got to know most of the other U.S. Muslim leaders, including many of the founding and currently leading members of the Muslim Brotherhood in the U.S., and they always accepted my invitation to join the one of the seminars to engage the senior-level security professional students on Islamist ideology, or the Ikhwan's worldview. The logic of this move was axiomatic in the world of strategic-level security studies. National security professionals who would be crafting grand strategy to contain the violence from Islamist revolutionary movements of various kinds needed to meet and empathize with Islamists, who—as true believers—gave compelling reasons why they believed God gave us some specific laws to enact in the public sphere, and didn't just leave everything open to human invention. The experience usually produced the epiphany among senior security professional students that Islamism is here to stay as a powerful current in Muslim communities worldwide, and that much of it is reasonable and moderate, and that the win-lose binary that securitizes all of it and produces notion of "defeating" it is ludicrous. Does this kind of human intelligence mean that there was undue influence by the Muslim Brotherhood in the U.S. government, as Gabriel charges?

Ms. Gabriel was specifically wrong in her charge about the Ikhwan's influence in the latter part of the post-9/11 decade. Beginning in 2008, at National Defense Intelligence College and then National Intelligence University, academic freedom was similarly allowed, and was checked by the spirit of sociological scholarship and sound judgment. Thus, my course on "Islamism: Strategic Security Issues" contained much critical analysis of the Muslim Brotherhood, its de facto spiritual guide, Sheikh Yusuf Qaradawi's *Fiqh of Jihad* (2009), and other Islamist movements and Islamist ideologues worldwide. But, it always carefully disaggregated the Islamic continuum, and Muslim students within the intelligence community found the course not at all denigrating of their faith, but also highly informative in terms of actionable *strategic* intelligence—that is, how to prevent America from getting into needless and unwinnable wars, how to get us out of the ones that we're in, and how to contain strategic security threats broadly. But, within the solipsistic universe of ACT! for America, there was no desire to empirically verify these hyperbolic charges about the Muslim Brotherhood's takeover of the security establishment. After all, without such a continual conspiracy by the allegedly Leftist controlled government bureaucracies, there would be no need for ACT! Patriot campaign of remittances for the nation's salvation.

ACT! for America's series of red-white-and-blue e-mails leading up to the general election in 2012 ended on November 9th with a post-loss subject "What Now?," and subtitle "Following in the footsteps of our founding fathers." In it, Gabriel's partner, Guy Rodgers, took on one of the organization's more reflexive members who complained that ACT! e-mails were becoming "polarizing" in their focus on the Obama Administration, and wondered why the organization doesn't work *with* the Administration instead. The response was opportunity for more domestic cultural struggle:

1) Attorney General Eric Holder's exchange with House Judiciary Chairman Lamar Smith. Rep. Smith asked Holder repeatedly if "radical Islam" COULD have been a motive for many of the homegrown terrorists we had arrested. Holder literally tied himself in rhetorical knots trying to avoid answering.

2) John Brennan, President Obama's top counterterrorism advisor, has repeatedly dismissed any notion that "jihad" refers to violence against non-Muslims or that Muslims, who refer to themselves as "jihadists," should be characterized that way. Brennan's position is that jihad only refers to a personal striving to be a good Muslim. This may be appealing to Western sensibilities but it's not the way jihad is characterized in the vast majority of passages in the Qur'an and the most authoritative hadith.

3) In the 9/11 commission report, the terms "jihadist," "jihad," "Muslim," and "Islam," appeared a total of 625 times. In the Obama administration's 2009 "National Intelligence Strategy" report, those terms did not appear once. They were completely stripped out of our intelligence assessment.

4) The Pentagon report that examined the Ft. Hood massacre did not include a single reference to jihad, radical Islam, or any other related term in the body of the report. Instead, it characterized the attack as "workplace violence." This in spite of the fact that Nidal Hasan's behavior and words in the years leading up to the attack, as well as his shouting "Allahu Akbar"

And—predictably by this point—the e-mail continued on in similar fashion, with each sentence carefully mentioning the Obama administration in connection with the Islamization of America conspiracy

7) As I stated in my Wednesday email, the Obama White House has opened its doors to numerous Muslims who are leaders of or connected to Muslim Brotherhood affiliated organizations.

I could provide many other examples, the most recent of which would be the Obama administration's demonstrably false claim that an obscure film on YouTube triggered the assault on our embassy in Cairo and our consulate in Benghazi.

The course set by this administration regarding radical Islam could not be clearer. It is a dangerous course that is compromising our national security

Conclusion

In conclusion, we might be tempted to view Brigitte Gabriel's racialized, dehumanizing, conspiratorial discourse *merely* in terms of the literature, as Holy Land geopolitics, or the "new anti-Muslim racism" (Vetlesen 2005, 19). To be sure, Gabriel's threat writing in the post-9/11 decade had empirical fit with such characterizations. Ostensibly in support of Israel's expanding settlement project, it obscured from view the average Muslim in their complexity by mobilizing metonymy and synecdoche, representing the whole in terms of (and determined by) some of its parts, like other racialized regimes of representation. It was in this same way that "the Jewish problem" was solved in Germany. By removing the actual Jew in their vast complexity from view, political framers were able to construct the more abstract, archetypical, or stereotypical subject position—"the Jew."

But, without minimizing any of that, Gabriel's subversive, transgressive speech related to Islam functioned mostly in the political realm—that is, counterhegemonically, in the domestic cultural struggle, by subverting the broader more progressive order and its regime of truth. In other words, her security writing in the decade after 9/11—rather than any attempt at a professional assessment of the threat related to Islam—functioned primarily as conservative Christian identity politics. It functioned as a political act—that is, the dual and dueling identification or narration of the friendly self and the enemy other—both foreign and domestic.

First, on the narration of the "self," in addition the apparent role of Gabriel herself functioning as a self-identifying symbol or subject position for the conservative movement, her ACT! for America technology and its banal, everyday e-mails functioned far less to produce objective knowledge about the threat than to allow her market to vicariously share in her everyday struggle. Through her token, symbolic, everyday Patriot Partner giving program, banal letter-writing to members of Congress, forms of participation in self-governance or self-security like the "Congressional Scorecard," and through self-abiding, self-disciplining moves, the morally-superior, self-defined, and self-governing Patriot and minutemen were hailed into existence. Tts binary-producing moves of naturalizing difference between the Islamic other and the Judeo-Christian self functioned mainly to fix the identity of the latter.

Second, on the narration of the enemies-foreign, Gabriel's counter-narration of the Islamic threat was politically performative in two ways. It was so systematically and defiantly heretical and unorthodox in relation to normative security writing that it tacitly functioned to subvert the more progressive regime of truth's threat narrative regarding Islam, and—by extension—that more progressive establishment.

Third, on the narration of the enemies domestic, all of Gabriel's threat assessments and commentary ostensibly about America's newest foreign enemy—Islam—contained this non-sequitur mass at the center about conservative movement's traditional domestic enemies—the Left, including the government bureaucracies, mainstream media and academia, as well as the more progressive societal doxa.

7

CONCLUSIONS

Indeed, my real argument is that Orientalism is… a considerable dimension of modern political-intellectual culture, and as such has less to do with the Orient than it does with 'our' world.

—Edward Said (1978, 12)

THIS inquiry focused on a segment of U.S. public discourse on Islam and even Islamization in the decade after 9/11 that history might classify as the "Green Scare," following the historical colored convention for scares over perceived threats from the East. The specific public discourse in question was the one lodged entirely within the U.S. conservative movement, and outside the circle of professionals, or outside of government institutions, academia, mainstream media, and so on—the realm that Bourdieu called "popular." It specifically explored how the threat writing that portrayed Islam(ization) as a threat functioned politically at both the domestic and identity or cultural level, and how such political factors played a role in this discourse's expansion throughout the post-9/11 decade.

The following discussion will organize the research's conclusions and reflect upon their implications. But, first, we should review the puzzles and the associated substantive literature that seemed to warrant this project.

1. The Puzzles, the Literature, and this Project

The Puzzles

There were a few superficial features of U.S. popular security discourse on the topic of Islam that seemed to align with the prevailing characterizations of it in the literature under the paradigm of "Islamophobia"—a new variant of an apparent established xenophobic tendency among U.S. social conservatives.

First, this popular threat discourse offered not merely a more pessimistic *corrective* but an entirely opposite *counter* to the prevailing "Islam is peace" frame and the corresponding terrorist/Islam distinction maintained by security professionals, the academic community,

189

the White House, and other societal institutions where authoritative knowledge about security threats is produced. Second, while such a reaction might seem normal in the immediate and highly emotional aftermath of 9/11, this discourse that portrayed the entire religion of Islam as a threat continued to persist, and even anachronistically expanded as distance from 9/11 increased. Third, the counternarrative on Islam became gradually more irrational. As if snatched from the front pages of the tabloid press—this threat narrative claimed that the significantly Judeo-Christian and staunchly secular country of 300 million people—the vast majority of whom of whom polls confirmed admitted that they personally did not even know a Muslim—faced the present danger of its Constitution being replaced by sharia, or Islamic law, via a secretive conspiracy or "stealth jihad" by its tiny population of mostly "moderate and mainstream" Muslim-Americans, to use Pew's characterization of them. It was also maintained that this conspiratorial Muslim-American "underworld" of clandestine agents had achieved "deep penetration," had secured "sensitive positions" throughout the government, and were working to gradually install sharia.

This notion of such an Islamization of the U.S. was rendered more puzzling since it had not materialized in an authoritative professional security assessment, and since it emerged about the same time when the broader questions concerning the threat from parts of Islam's continuum had been settled—when, for example, social polling revealed that al-Qaeda had been marginalized by Muslims worldwide, and when other analyses suggested that it had been marginalized by even key segments of the more politically-aggrieved Islamist factions from which it had enjoyed at least some level of early support.

The "phobia" characterization in the literature seemed all the more safe by the time of the mid-term elections in 2010, when—for instance—conservative lawmakers in almost half of the nation's states, for instance, introduced legislation to contain sharia—a term that these elected officials themselves were at pains to even describe—and seventy percent of the Republican stronghold state of Oklahoma voted for the "Save Our State" amendment to contain the nefarious plot to Islamize their state, despite the fact that almost no one in the state had ever met a member of this minority faith community. If not an irrational fear, or phobia, then how might we classify the 2010 statement by GOP Presidential front-runner Newt Gingrich, in a major speech to the American Enterprise Institute, "I believe Shariah is a mortal threat to the survival of freedom in the United States and in the world as we know it"?

The Literature

For these reasons, the literature's predisposition to interpret this discourse in familiar terms—the latest "phobia," "new Orientalism," "new racism," "new anti-Semitism," "new McCarthyism," and so on—seemed grounded. The last two and most significant contributions to the literature that emerged in 2011 and 2012—both self-characterized under the frame of "Islamophobia"—embraced this paradigm. Their frame was not mere "phobia" related to Islam; the discourse was characterized in many of the same terms as Said's (1997, 2003)—a handmaiden to Holy Land geopolitics, or the Zionist irredentist struggle to reacquire the Jewish nation's ancient biblical homeland. The most significant and most recent work on the discourse was *The Islamophobia Industry: How the Right Manufactures Fear of Muslims* (2012), by Nathan Lean, a student of Georgetown University's authority on Western and Islamic relations, John Esposito. Lean had characterized this discourse as "the racism du jour," promoted and escalated by a few prominent right-wing Jewish and evangelical "Islamophobes" and their pro-Israel financial backers (Saif 2013). In this paradigm of hatred of Muslims/advocates for Israel, Lean stated that all of the people involved in this practice of securitizing Islam "espouse fervent anti-Muslim sentiment on the one hand, and ardent support of all things Israel on the other," and that the large portion of the discourse came from shadowy Jewish organizations "connected in some ways to the occupied territories."

This paradigm was by the end of the post-9/11 decade enjoying a broad consensus, if not an element of discursive closure. A cursory reading of the threat writing of some conservative experts on Islam, for instance, seemed to corroborate the notion that this discourse was essentially Zionist racism—a racialized regime of representation that attempted to naturalize difference between the Judeo-Christian "civilized man" inside and Muslim "savage" outside, with the obvious effect of legitimizing the Likud-led bloc's strategic expansionism into Palestinian territory. The geopolitical utility of the "savages" surrounding Israel had obvious appeal to the practice's Zionist donors, creating sufficient uncertainty regarding the identity of the people whom Israel's policies were displacing to demobilize progressive attempts at forging a reconciliation based on withdrawal. The political paralysis that ensued from this uncertainty in the U.S. allowed Israel's Zionist elite to continue to rapidly change facts on the ground with illegal settlements in the West Bank.

The literature's broad consensus in this bridged frame of hatred for Muslims— advocates for Israel notwithstanding, nearly all of the literature contained remarks—often in passing, as if "common sense"—that yet another new variant to a very old category of practice was *also* involved in its production: *domestic politics*. Ernst (2013)—for instance— described "the political angle" of "attacks on Islam, noting how they were also linked with criticism of President Obama," and especially when the enemies list is expanded to include "leftist radicals." And, CAIR (2013) found in its survey of Muslim-American leadership in 2011 that this religious and largely racial minority believed they were "being used as a political tool" and "no longer considered a community as much as a platform."

Yet—for some reason—this more domestic political factor was not incorporated into any of the literature's conclusions or any central characterization of the discourse.

This Project

This book examined this insufficiently scrutinized implication that this discourse was—in addition to any of the literature's prevailing paradigms or characterizations of it— a function of domestic politics. Specifically, it examined how this threat writing functioned politically at the domestic level, and how distinctly political structures played a role in this threat discourse's expansion throughout the post-9/11 decade.

Here, we took Edward Said's (1997) only axiom related to "all discourse on Islam"—that it "*has an interest in some authority or power*"—and extended it beyond geopolitics to domestic or cultural politics. The reasoning that undergirded this notion seemed fairly straightforward: If Jewish and Christian Zionist interests within the U.S. conservative movement had found the threat of Islam useful in the geopolitical struggle for their faith's biblical homeland, then isn't it also likely that these same elements and other parts of the U.S. conservative movement might find it similarly useful in their political struggle at home? After all, cannot we readily outline other topics of societal importance that segments of the U.S. conservative movement has politicized, or used as "wedge issues" in this post-9/11 decade alone to advance their broader cultural agenda?

To sensitize the data to this political proposition—to help us examine this discourse's political function, that is—we crafted a conceptual framework from social philosophers like Gramsci, Foucault, and Bourdieu that viewed public discourse and its agents as fundamentally political. This segment of the theoretical literature lent strong support to the notion that political interestedness was also a factor that might help explain this otherwise puzzling post-9/11 U.S. threat discourse. Then, we examined this notion in a broader interpretive paradigm that examined both the macro-level political factors involved in this discourse, as well as the micro-level political strategies deployed.

2. Conclusions at the Micro-Level: Strategies of "Security Politics"

At the micro-level—that is, at the level of discursive political strategies of the agents involved—we saw the distinct ways that this discourse and its agents functioned politically, at the domestic level, within the overarching strategy of cultural politics. The main strategy of what we will call "security politics" is that of seizing a threat topic as an opportune field for cultural struggle. In other words, like other politicized discourses—environmental politics, energy politics, and so on—security politics is a mode or vehicle of cultural struggle, or culture war that uses that topic to engage one's domestic political rivals and advance their political interests.

Analysis of this discourse suggests that this threat discourse functioned as such a strategy of security politics by the more entrepreneurial segments of the U.S. conservative movement, who—in the emotion-laden wake of 9/11 and its rupture to the nation's security master narrative—seized Islam as another opportune site to advance their ongoing project of cultural politics. In the case of the movement's iconic media institutions—from *FOX News Channel* to *The Washington Times*, to its surveillance apparatuses like Horowitz's *Jihad Watch* and Pipes's *Campus Watch* and *Islamist Watch*—we saw how every possible and even trivial bit of "news" related to the movement's newest foreign enemy was seized as an opportunistic platform upon which to engage the movement's old domestic enemies—that is, the more progressive societal institutions and culture more broadly, and the Democrats and Obama administration more narrowly.

Within this broader strategy of opportunistically seizing this new threat topic as yet another emotionally-charged field for politics, there were two supporting sub-strategies or "moves" of security politics. These two moves construct the two dyads of the political, or all projects of identity politics: 1) the political outside, others, or enemies on the one hand; and 2) the political inside, or the friendly self on the other. The second observation was that both of these moves of cultural politics were present in *virtually all* of the larger productions— books, reports, papers, documentaries, blog commentaries, and e-mails to subscribers—ostensibly on the threat of Islam or Islamization.

1st Move of Security Politics:

Use of the New Threat Topic to Delegitimize Domestic Political Opponents

The first move of security politics involved strategies to engage in discourse about the new security threat in such a way as to implicitly and explicitly delegitimize one's traditional domestic political rivals. Within this basic move of "othering"—of constructing that which is not self—there was one sub-strategy that *explicitly* delegitimized this movement's domestic political rivals, and two that more *implicitly* delegitimized them.

Counterhegemonic Narration of Domestic Political Enemies

The most obvious sub-strategy embedded in discourse about the new threat functioned to more *explicitly* delegitimize the movement's traditional domestic political rival. When we broached the thin outer shell of this segment of U.S. conservative threat assessments purportedly about the newest foreign enemy, there was at its center nearly always this non-sequitur, political mass—a segment of words, phrases, or sentences that explicitly delegitimized the more progressive "establishment" or the more progressive societal politics of truth and secular culture on the one hand—euphemized variously as the "elites," academia, government, "mainstream" media—and the Democratic party and the Obama administration more specifically on the other.

In this regard, the threat discourse's front-line organizations—Jihad Watch, Islamist Watch, Campus Watch, and ACT! for America, and others—were not mere threat surveillance apparatuses that functioned—as their names suggest—to "watch" this newest threat to the nation. On the contrary, they were political apparatuses that reliably produced little substantive analysis about the newest foreign enemy, but much about the U.S. conservative movement's old domestic rivals—the purportedly disloyal, traitorous Left, who was now said to be aiding and abetting the toppling of the U.S. Constitution via gradual sharia-ization or Islamization.

This more blatant political move of linking the conservative movement's newest foreign enemy with its traditional domestic one permeated this discourse. In the case of Jihad Watch, this practice of threat politics was to be expected, given its dubious residence in the broader David Horowitz apparatus—an apparatus created long ago and solely to advance the conservative cultural struggle.

The move of narrating the domestic enemy also functioned within this overarching strategy of self-identification. For "the patriot" subject position that figures so prominently in the U.S. conservative subculture to exist, its opposite—"the traitor"—must be prominently juxtaposed. In this regard, recall that the traitorous leftist was never a threat to the patriotic conservative, but rather a condition of his or her possibility.

Counterhegemonic Narration of the Threat

The next sub-strategy of security politics observed within this first move was the *counterhegemonic narration of the threat.* This (counter) narration was more implicit in its function within cultural politics, since it—unlike the first sub-strategy—did not directly mention the domestic political rivals, but performatively subverted their knowledge society, or the progressive politics of truth. Clearly, the early and uncompromising counternarrative—the narrative that opposed the more authoritative and institutionally dominant "religion of peace" frame—functioned this way.

A counternarrative is *always* a heretical practice—one that opposes, challenges, undermines, and resists the dominant, normative, official memory, the going orthodoxy. In this way, the more puritanical counternarrative on the threat related to Islam by a key segment of U.S. conservatives manifested much less as an apolitical description of a threat than a politically performative act aimed at unseating the going orthodoxy—described variously by its proponents as the more "liberal" "establishment." In other words, the (counter)narrative deployed to described the newest foreign enemy functioned less as a professional description of that threat than it did as a means to implicitly subvert the dominant societal threat narrative, or master security narrative, and thus delegitimize the domestic political enemy identified with that more hegemonic narrative.

As with all political framing strategies, the counternarrative's political function was marked by a lack (if not total absence) of crucial context that accompanies professional security writing, and by an abundance of *moves of selection and exclusion.* Conservative threat writers systematically selected as their *sole horizon of visibility* the set of objects about Islam that the more dominant regime of truth (i.e. professional security assessments or intelligence estimates, or even scholarly writing) typically excluded—objects that transgressed societal regulations, or had been relegated to the realm of the unsayable, taboo, or political incorrectness.

Delegitimization of the more progressive regime of truth was achieved *not by* empirically and rigorously working within the normative objects of visibility, but by *abandoning them altogether.* In other words, these farther right popular security products worked solely through an alternative, or dissident paradigm about Islam, a dissident horizon of visibility—that is, what was visible about the threat and fair game to talk about—and a dissident lexicon, with words and phrases that were tabooed in official, professional security discourse. In still more specific terms, the objects related to the threat of Islam that were typically excluded from view in professional security analysis—gratuitous selections from the Quran and other sacred texts that denigrated Muslims and their faith, for example—were deliberately and defiantly selected and centered by the popular conservative threat writers involved, often constituting their *entire realm* of visibility. The openly Catholic deacon Spencer's (2006) bestseller, *The Truth About Muhammad: Founder of the World's Most Intolerant Religion*, for example, radically centered all that the more leftist ex-Catholic Karen Armstrong (1991, 2006) felt compelled to exclude in her two biographies of Muhammad.

That counterhegemonic strategy of political incorrectness pervaded all conservative threat writing in the decade after 9/11. Even the phrase "politically incorrect" pervaded all conservative discourse on Islam and functioned politically not only as code to delegitimize the more progressive outside (via its discourse related to the threat of Islam), but to identify the U.S. conservative inside. If it was politically incorrect, it was *conservative*. The entire practice, in other words, was not merely one of subversive resistance to the going hegemony of the political enemies, but of self-identification—so much so that the staunchly conservative publishing house Regnery developed the trademarked "Politically Incorrect Guide" series, launching Robert Spencer to *New York Times* bestseller status with his *The Politically Incorrect Guide to Islam*.

Counterhegemonic Non-narrative Strategies of Threat Writing

Yet another element of this broader move of counterhegemonic threat writing involved *non* or *extra-narrative* strategies. These non-narrative strategies attempted to subvert the more progressive hegemonic order—what Daniel Pipes, for instance, derogatively and variously termed the "establishment," the "stifling consensus," "officialdom," and so on—by implicitly challenging its rules concerning authoritative knowledge. This challenge was presented by advancing the counternarrative by subversive forms of authors or authorities—those who lacked orthodox credentials— and by housing the counternarrative within similarly subversive *modes of production* and *style*—modes and style expressly forbidden in authorized or more credible security writing.

Subversive Modes of Authority

The counterhegemonic nature of this discourse could be seen in the fact that major works related to Islam by authorities celebrated within the more progressive security establishment were heretically mocked in productions by authors with no credentials in the field whatsoever. We saw, for example, the *Middle East Quarterly* and Forum's express brandishing of authors like the "sea captain and a nuclear engineer in the United States Navy," and another whose credentials were "a writer whose interests include public affairs and foreign policy," put forward as authorities on par with the more widely-celebrated authorities on Islam whose works they were criticizing. Recall, for instance, FOX News Channel's repeated commissioning of Pamela Geller to talk about events broadly related to Islam, for which she had no credentials whatsoever, and their systematic exclusion of any of the thousands of normatively credentialed scholars on the subject.

Moreover, in similar moves of pure negation, these conservative popular security experts systematically avoided any intertextuality with those authorities positioned outside of the conservative enclave, no matter how politically benign. In perhaps the oddest and most tell-tale counterhegemonic feature of this discourse, none of the central identifying institutions of the conservative movement that functioned as agents of this threat discourse, and none of the books by conservative threat writers, and none of their more everyday threat writing and commentary, ever favorably or neutrally cited texts or authors housed within the more progressive and dominant knowledge society of educational institutions, government bureaucracies, and the mainstream media—*even when it meant that not doing so rendered their counternarrative weaker.*

This mode of knowledge production and argumentation was radically contrary to the normative mode. In professional debate or courtroom litigation, for example, the disputants often work with the same realm of information, facts, or data, yet bringing it to bear in opposing ways to win the argument. That was *not* what was going on here. The conservative proponents of this discourse were so puritanical in this counterhegemonic strategy that they could not even work within the same universe of data or sources that the world outside of their narrow movement considered orthodox or authoritative.

Subverting the rules of authority, was not only counterhegemonic, but it was an important move of self-identity politics. Such subversion of the rules of authority, for instance, enacted a parallel universe, or a kind of self-imposed epistemic solipsism in which intercourse took place only within the dissident enclave. The self-identifying political utility of this move can be seen in similarly constructed dichotomizing geographies, such as dar-al-Islam and dar al-Harb of the fundamentalist Muslims, and the "inner sanctum" of the Gush Emunim; it was a move of pure negation that enabled the core/periphery distinction to be rigidly maintained, reinscribing the borders of the conservative subcultural commune. By reading only conservative experts, the readers of this discourse could live solipsistically entirely within this ghetto of the conservative self.

Subversive Modes of Production

In the publishing mode of production, we find moves of pure negation that expressly avoid any of the orthodoxy surrounding publishing of authoritative security writing. Again, it is by shunning these societal norms that these dissident forms of production are counterhegemonic, or function to tacitly delegitimizing the broader more progressive regime of truth. The erection of Pipes's *Middle East Quarterly* was an early strategic pillar in presenting a challenge to that regime of truth; its litmus test for publishing was to be able to answer "no" to the question: "Is this an article other quarterlies would publish?" Subversion in the realm of production was also seen in that the vast bulk of threat writing that could be classified within the counternarrative regarding Islam was published exclusively within the conservative knowledge enclave, and outside of any of the publishing sources considered authoritative. That politically-functioning strategy was evident in all conservative threat writing. The assessments of even Pipes and Spencer, for instance, were propagated in the *New York Post* and the *Washington Times*, but never the *New York Times* and *Washington Post*—in Farah's *WorldNet Daily*, *National Review Online*, *Human Events*, *PJ (formerly Pajamas) Media*, the *American Thinker*, Catholicism's *Crisis Magazine*, and obviously

Pipes's *Middle East Quarterly*, Horowitz's *FrontPage Magazine*, but never in any journal considered by security or intelligence professionals to be authoritative and apolitical.

Subversive Style

A clear signal that a discourse has become more political than professional is when it has broken with professional convention—that is, when it becomes "popular" in the sense that it is recognized as "theirs" by those who are outside the circle of professionals. Three stylistic features of this segment of popular conservative threat writing were politically-performative: sarcasm, political antagonism, and strategies of euphemization.

Firstly, this threat writing was replete with sarcasm, which is a common marker of popular resistance to the legitimizing identity and institutions in every society. For example, the threat writers involved took legitimate words and phrases and placed them in quotations, such as "tiny minority of extremists," thereby trademarking and infusing them with oppositional meaning, or transforming them into polysemes that functioned both as identifying code within the subculture and as a form of resistance to the broader, dominant culture.

Secondly, this discourse was also replete with political antagonism, or marked by a large sub-cultural lexicon of politically antagonistic signifiers. Recall, for example, the section in Spencer's blog, "Why Jihad Watch," where we found the tip of this politically-antagonistic lexicon, such as the "fifth column" of "dhimmi academics and dhimmi journalists."

2nd Move of Security Politics:

Use of the New Threat Topic to (Re)Construct the Self

Distinct from the politically-performative practice of narrating the political outside—the others, or enemies, both foreign and domestic—the second move of security politics observed throughout this discourse aligned with the corresponding move of all political or identity projects: *the narration of the political inside, or the self.* This second move was in no sense secondary; on the contrary, it was what the whole project seemed to be about; this segment of post-9/11 conservative threat writing was *shot through* with this feature of narrating the self. This process of self-identification typically involved two sub-strategies that enacted two basic schemas found in the security writing in earlier eras: 1) self-aggrandizing moves of reaffirming the strong, exceptional and morally superior self that was in decline; and 2) self-disciplining moves of purifying the wayward within that render the body politic vulnerable.

First, self-aggrandizement typically involved the (re)positioning the patriotic self in healthy, chauvinistic terms of triumphalism, exceptionalism, or superiority. Such self-aggrandizing framing in this discourse was always juxtaposed to the incoherent frames of civilizational declinism in the face of ascendant competing religious and political ideologies connected to U.S. social and paleo conservatives' chief rivals in both the religious and political spheres—the ascendant, globalizing and increasingly resistant, counterhegemonic Islamism on the one hand, and the dominant and widening worldview of progressivism and philosophical secularism on the other.

Second, self-discipline in this "security" discourse was similar to that exercised in the historical forms of Christian pastoralism, in that it identified and chastised its heretical forms that rendered the body politic vulnerable, or shepherded wayward elements of the flock back into the fold. This move similarly drew from rich cultural antecedents in the security writing found in earlier colonial discourse, wherein texts identifying threats outside in terms of the nation's foreign and domestic enemies were replete with identification of its critical vulnerabilities inside, almost always expressed in moral terms. The jeremiads of the Puritan era, for instance, similarly lamented the backslidden state of morality or sinfulness of society, and prophesied its downfall if meaningful repentance did not emerge. In this mode of self-identification, security discourse was deployed not merely to identify and eradicate dangers outside, but to reduce vulnerabilities inside.

The everyday productions of conservative threat writing—especially that of Spencer in Jihad Watch and Gabriel in her ACT! for America—contained these kind self-disciplinary features. They attempted to create and sustain subcultural coherence among U.S. conservatives by imposing standards of purity that both hailed their readers into scripted positions of political activism or subject positions, such as the patriot, and chastised those designated as the wayward sheep, the heretic, or the traitor.

In a final and related vein, the manufactured panic and conspiracy of "Islamization of America"—with its conspiratorial alliance of enemies foreign with domestic political rivals—served a more subtle crucial semantic and semiotic function within identity politics; it functioned as an emblematic metaphor for the aforementioned broader structural *crisis* in the conservative lebensraum and the associated self-identifying master narratives—namely, the erosion of the nation's traditional moorings by uncontrollable global flows and their progressive collaborators. But such metaphors always have a more immediate political utility. The Islamization scare, in this instance, served to condense the broader complex multichrome reality into simple terms that resonated with conservatives and catalyzed them to subscribe, give, buy books, call their members of congress, show up at rallies, and vote.

Therefore, while this discourse on the one hand was explicitly about the foreign and dangerous other—enemies foreign and domestic—on the other it was implicitly and performatively a practice of self; it was a narration of self.

These two moves or strategies of action that permeate this discourse suggest that we may classify it in terms that problematize the literatures' Islamophobia consensus. Beyond mere racism and xenophobia on the one hand, and Holy Land geopolitics on the other, it was *fundamentally political* and political mainly at the domestic level; it was part of a broader, overarching strategy of cultural struggle, identity politics to advance the farther and religious right self against the movements enemies foreign and domestic—Islam and the Left.

3. Conclusions at the Macro-Level: *The Political Apparatus and Opportunity for Security Politics*

As expected from the literature, the research demonstrated that there was much more going on in this discourse than protecting the nation from the threat of Islam—as its proponents would have us think. Yet, it also demonstrated that there was a good bit more going on here than xenophobia for purposes of Holy Land geopolitical struggle, as the critics of this discourse in the later literature argued.

Political Resources: The U.S. Conservative Apparatus for Security Politics

In the more non-discursive, social-structural realm, we discovered that there were two politically-relevant social resources that also played a significant role in this puzzling threat discourse's expansion throughout the post-9/11 decade: (1) its political-institutional base; and (2) the philanthropic base that funded its principal agents and large-scale productions.

The Political-Institutional Base

First, this discourse's social-structural base could be only tenuously categorized within the literature's prevailing characterization. The most tendentious and apparently influential parts of this threat discourse were hardly disseminated by what the prevailing literature characterized as a fringe cottage industry within the U.S. conservative movement with connections to hate groups and the Zionist movement. Rather, they were propagated by some of that political movement's more central identifying institutions—institutions that were created solely for the broader culture war, and not in a single case founded upon the basis of far right wing causes or even for struggle for the Holy Land.

Moreover, these iconic conservative institutions were not merely complicit in this discourse—as if they were aiding and abetting the key proponents—but were themselves the principal agents of this discourse. By generously publishing, and otherwise promoting those polemicists who were predisposed to use the latest "news" regarding Islam as a micro-platform to engage in domestic cultural politics, these central identifying institutions of the U.S. conservative movement not only provided these agents with necessary authority and credibility outside "the establishment," they created them and—by extension—the discourse. *National Review* and Encounter Books created Andrew McCarthy; *The Washington Times* and the Bradley Foundation and Scaife funds created Frank Gaffney and Daniel Pipes; *FOX News Channel* created Pamela Geller, and so on.

Recall, for example, how *National Review*—the foremost organ of the conservative cultural struggle since 1955—selected the unknown McCarthy to offer the politically antagonistic rebuttal to the president's rapprochement speech to Muslims worldwide, and to produce other such works as "The President Stands with Sharia." Recall how *The Washington Times* published everything and anything related to Islamization—no matter how fantastic or politically antagonistic—that Pipes and Gaffney managed to write. Each of the almost daily headlines like Gaffney's "Obama's Islamist problem," or Pipes's "Obama: My

Muslim Faith," made a weak uncontextualized reference to some purported threat related to Islam, then went on in the discussion to delegitimize the Obama administration, the Democrats, more progressive societal institutions, or progressive ideology broadly. Recall the strategy of FOX News Channel that—over the course of many separate interviews—always managed to pan its cameras across the cover of Geller's *Stop the Islamization of America* just before the cable giant interviewed her on topics broadly related to Islam, for which she had no orthodox credentials or expertise. And recall how the conservative publishing centers—Regnery and Encounter—published everything that fed the counternarrative and the Islamization conspiracy, including such works as Horowitz's *Unholy Alliance: Radical Islam and the American Left*, and McCarthy's *The Grand Jihad: How Islam and the Left Sabotage America*, and his *How Obama Embraces Islam's Sharia Agenda*.

These instances were not anomalies; nor was this strategy limited to these more iconic institutions. Thousands of such articles positioned in opposition to the Islam-is-peace frame, and attempting to propagate a panic over a sweeping Muslim-American plot to Islamize America, appeared on the pages of other more prominent if not mainstream conservative magazines, like *American Spectator* and *Human Events*, newspapers like the *New York Sun* and *New York Post*, other cable television sites like Christian Broadcasting Network, and the newer conservative e-magazines such as *WorldNetDaily*, *Pajamas* (now PJ) *Media* and *FrontPageMagazine*.

To reiterate, none of these media, publishing, or other institutions in which this threat discourse was *almost exclusively* housed were created to produce disinterested knowledge. Like *National Review*, FOX News Channel, *Washington Times*, Regnery and Encounter publishers, and the other institutions that propagated this discourse were virtually all—as seen in their history and mission statements—created as "conservative" instruments for cultural politics, or counterhegemonic struggle—for a culture war against the rival, more progressive doxa.

Thus, the literature's exclusive characterization of this post-9/11 popular threat discourse on Islam as primarily motivated by hatred for Muslims and love for Israel is problematized; clearly, this discourse was arguably much more a strategy in the broader domestic and cultural political struggle.

The Philanthropic Base

Second, our examination of this popular threat discourse's philanthropic base yields similar conclusions. We found that the support provided from mainstream conservative philanthropists—ones founded and operating exclusively in cultural struggle—played a more important role than narrower right wing or expressly Zionist philanthropic institutions.

Again, this finding ran counter to the literature. Beginning with Said and extending through the major works that emerged late in the post-9/11 decade, the literature leads us to assume that the motivations for this discourse are mainly xenophobic and Zionist geopolitical motivations. Recall Bulkin and Nevel's (2012) analysis of the discourse's political economy revealed how some of the philanthropic institutions that had funded the discourse's principal agents were lodged within the broader Zionist movement apparatus, having also funded organizations associated with the Israeli settler movement, and multiple organizations that were engaged in propaganda or hasbara initiatives designed to justify the Likud-led expansionism. But, we discovered here that pro-Zionist philanthropists were *only part* of this popular threat discourse's political-economy, and—from this perspective of actual funding provided—apparently *the smaller part*.

We found that, in the case of all of the main philanthropic organizations that funded the post-9/11 Islam(ization) threat discourse, except one—the one run by the Chernicks—their giving records, mission statements, and affiliations of their boards positioned them into one of two categories, either: (1) conservative with significant Zionist emphasis; or (2) plain conservative with no (or virtually no) Zionist interest. The largess of conservative patrons with Zionist ideological motivations notwithstanding, the largest donors to the principal framers of the Islam(ization) threat had long been the central patrons of the U.S. conservative movement broadly, with comparatively little or no Zionist sympathies in either their giving records or mission statements. The criterion for funding in the Scaife foundation—which gave the lion's share of the funding to the threat discourse's principal agents—was solidly conservative, described by the *Washington Post* with the headline "Funding Father of the Right." Similarly, the Bradley Foundation, which was described by Media Transparency as "the country's largest and most influential right-wing organization," had given the next largest amount to the threat discourse's principal agents. Yet, it similarly had little apparent Zionist interest; statements in the annual reports revealed that it intended to fund those U.S. organizations deemed by its Board to be important in the strengthening of the central institutions of the conservative movement. Together, the Scaife and Bradley foundations—with historical track records of giving tied directly to conservative cultural politics—gave *twice* as much to fund this discourse as did the patrons with Zionist interests.

In the end, our examination of the discourse's social-structure or apparatus of power offers a second tier of empirical grounding to our basic assumption regarding the fundamental political nature of this popular security discourse.

Political Opportunity Created

At the nexus of both the contingent, or eventful level and the agentic level, we added a third new dimension to the literature, revealing key elements of this discourse's political opportunity structure that were created specifically for cultural or domestic politics in mind. In this regard, the conjuncture of three elements within this category of political opportunity emerged as significant.

The Expanded Conservative Enclave of Counterhegemonic Institutions

First, in the realm of opportunities created, we found that the kind of threat politics practiced by this segment of the U.S. conservative movement in the decade after 9/11 was enabled, incentivized, and rendered credible by two related and deliberately planned transformations of the movement's apparatus of power. The first was the deliberate counterhegemonic strategy of institution-building to create a distinctly conservative knowledge enclave or parallel sub-society—a state within a state, so to speak; that is, a more traditionally conservative state within a larger and dominant more progressive state. The second opportunity seized upon was the rapid expansion of that sub-society into the alternative media during the first half of the post-9/11 decade.

For decades, many conservatives had known along that Foucault was right—that each society has its regime of truth; its general politics of truth. And, they saw that this elite or doctrinal consensus in the U.S. was more progressive and prejudiced against the conservative worldview. It was for this reason that—beginning with *National Review* in 1955, and continuing with alternative media institutions like *WorldNetDaily*, Horowitz's *Front Page Magazine*, *American Thinker*, and *Pajamas (now PJ) Media* in the largely post-9/11 era of the alternative media—the U.S. conservative movement had pursued a counterhegemonic strategy of alternative institution-building—of constructing the conservative parallel universe.

The opportunity seized to expand this media-institutional enclave presented the opening for more dissident, subversive forms of cultural politics. The reason is obvious; this dissident truth society effectively bypassed altogether the more progressive, dominant, or legitimate knowledge society. By bypassing this more progressive regime of truth, the conservative media enclave reduced its capacity for repression or sanction of its politically-resistant discourses, including this one regarding the threat of Islam. In this way, U.S. conservatives followed the pattern of other marginalized political factions—from Poland's Solidarity to Egypt's Muslim Brotherhood.

With the more progressive societal regime of truth bypassed, the conservative counterestablishment lurched farther right, and functioned more blatantly in the strategy of cultural politics. We saw how the new and powerful conservative media node, *WorldNetDaily*, for instance, seemed to print everything that the Islam(ization) threat discourse's principal agents managed to write, such as *Muslim Mafia: Inside the Secret Underworld That's Conspiring to Islamize America*, which had been funded by Frank Gaffney's Center for Security Policy; and *Stop the Islamization of America*, by Pamela Geller. As noted earlier, in this dissident media universe, opportunity for this highly anti-rationalist threat politics was readily apparent, even in the central identifying institutions such as FOX News Channel. Recall how—during the GOP primaries on May 1, 2012—FOX News's Sean Hannity did not feel compelled to challenge Geert Wilders when he wildly exaggerated the threat from Islamization, saying that Europe had become "almost half Islamic."

We found that, by the end of the decade, these more rightist alternative media-based nodes had clearly eclipsed the more centrist elements of the conservative enclave's legacy apparatus of power, and were dragging them farther right. At Andrew Breitbart's consortium of blogs, for example, all topics of news were politicized. It was here that one of the prominent conservative security experts and Islamization polemicists, Andrew McCarthy, in 2010 could say credibly (without challenge) that "Islamists" and "leftists" share totalitarian goals, "totalitarian in the sense that they want to control every aspect of the individual's life, and [are] virulently opposed to capitalism and individual liberty," adding that "even though they [Obama and Saudi King Abdullah] part company on the details of what they would transform it into, they both need to topple American constitutional republicanism in order to install their utopias."

The Alliance of Conservative Elite

Second, we discovered crucial solidarity for the threat narrative among a segment of prominent conservative political and religious elite, whose chief strategy of action in their public life—what animated their discourse and behavior—was neither xenophobia and immigration politics nor Holy Land geopolitics, but instead cultural politics, or the struggle for conservatism and against progressivism. The alignment of this loose structure of elite solidarity provided a crucial opportunity in terms of ideological cover or legitimacy for the use of Islam(ization) as a platform for security politics.

That this solidarity structure was oriented on the grounds of domestic or cultural politics— rather than how the hate-for-Islam/love-for-Israel literature would have characterized it—was manifest in several of its more peculiar features.

In the first case, recall that by the mid-point of the post-9/11 decade there were competing polarized positions regarding the characterization of Islam as a threat, and these positions were—like so many positions in Washington—based upon which political party one was affiliated with. Through various examples, we saw how it was only conservative political and religious elite, for instance, who were sympathetic to the Islam(ization) threat narrative, and this was in apparent deliberate juxtaposition to the entire swath of elite Democrats who expressly avoided identifying with either aspect of this threat discourse. For example, within this apparent strategy of *creating political opportunity* through solidarity coalitions, such solidarity for the Islam(ization) threat discourse was expressed in varying degrees among all of the front-running GOP presidential candidates *except* former Governor Romney, Congressman Ron Paul, and future potential candidate, Governor Chris Christie, and—yet—it was curiously *absent entirely* from all Democrat political figures.

In the conservative movement's central identifying "think tank," the *American Enterprise Institute*, Presidential hopeful Newt Gingrich in 2010 shifted the threat axis from the strategic crisis in American manufacturing, energy, education, structural deficit and other critical topics to the Islamization of the U.S. via "stealth jihad" by subversive elements among America's Muslims who threatened to "replace Western Civilization with a radical imposition of sharia." The same year, on the ninth anniversary of 9/11, Gingrich went as far as to produce a film, *America at Risk: The War With No Name*, in which he warned Americans about unspecified and ambiguous "radical Islamists" inside America, who were threatening "to impose an extraordinarily different system on us"—to "replace American freedom with Sharia."

Among members of the U.S. Congress, it was similarly *only* Republicans who propagated the counternarrative and related conspiracy regarding Islamization. The political nature of these loose solidarity coalitions could also be seen in the Legislative branch. When Republican New York Representative Peter King chaired House Homeland Security Committee hearings on Muslim-American radicalization, for example, it was only the Democrats who were united in their criticism of them, and only Republicans defending them, with one of King's GOP colleagues praising the hearings as a way to "end the era of political correctness." And, in addition to this strategy of solidarity among political elite, we saw how the threat discourse also enjoyed solidarity across some of the more prominent U.S. religious and cultural elite who were more readily identified as mainstream conservative cultural warriors than as apparatchiks of the farther right-wing movement or Zionism.

In the second case, it was just as dubious that Islam(ization) threat narrative's attendant practice of political frame bridging—linking the U.S. conservative movement's enemies foreign and domestic—religious and political—Islam and the Left—as revealed in Chapter 2, was prevalent throughout this loose solidarity structure of conservative political and religious elite. We saw how one prominent Islamization proponent, Minnesota Republican Congresswoman and founder of the House Tea Party caucus, Michele Bachmann, for instance, during an interview on conservative radio's popular *The Mike Gallagher Show*, asserted that the GOP's opposing domestic political party had allied with their ideological foreign enemy to destroy the nation. "It seems like there is this common cause that is occurring with the left and with radical Islam…" she said, adding that "It's frightening to think how the left in this country, just as you've correctly stated, Michael, is throwing in with common cause with these radical elements of Islamic extremism."

In the third case, the solidarity for this threat narrative among more than a few conservative elite was also marked by significant levels of anti-rationalism; that is, the systematically exclusion of inquisitiveness and critical thinking that normally attended the practice of statecraft and civic leadership—suggesting that much more was going on here than securing the nation from the threat of Islam(ization). Recall, for example, how the Republican legislators in two dozen conservative states who introduced legislation with the intent to restrict judges from consulting sharia in their rulings, did so despite the fact that state judges were already prohibited from overriding U.S. law; despite the fact that they could not even give instances of how sharia was being used in the courtroom; and despite the fact that the sharia threat reports from the main conservative security policy advocacy organizations that significantly produced this security concern were shown to be baseless if not fraudulent. Moreover, recall how, when pressed, some of the more key lawmakers introducing this anti-sharia legislation could not even explain what sharia was. Observing this anti-rationalist solidarity among many of the more prominent conservative elite, Sheila Musaji—editor of the *American Muslim*—wrote hyperbolically, in obvious exasperation, that "The GOP has declared war on American Muslims."

The Underlying Impetus for Cultural Politics: Crisis amidst U.S. Neo, Paleo, and Social Conservatives

The underlying impetus for this threat discourse's agents to politicize Islam in the decade after 9/11 was also political. The U.S. conservative movement's central and relevant constituencies in which this threat discourse was housed —neoconservatives on the one hand, and paleo and social conservatives on the other— were experiencing accentuated ideological crisis.

For U.S. paleo and social conservatives, the threat that formed the bases for their crises was the subtler threat of late modernity itself—of globalization and cosmopolitanism, and—more particularly—of multiculturalism and secularism. The conjuncture of globalization, the information and communication (ICT) revolution, with its attending new, social and alternative media, had thrown the metaphysical legitimating foundation of traditional identities in the West and worldwide into even greater crisis, with particular and progressive identities increasing relative to more singular and traditional ones. The crisis experienced by social conservatives centered on declining morality and the instability of Judeo-Christian identity as a function of secularism, and the crisis among U.S. paleoconservatives centered on the threat of diluted biological and cultural identity as a function of multiculturalism and lack of restrictions on immigration—both threats on the domestic axis.

The threat to neoconservatives up to this juncture, on the other hand, had tended to be not domestic but foreign in nature—threats to Israel, and rival universalist ideologies like "Godless Communism." But, with the demise of the rival superpower with a competing universalist ideology, and with the widening power gap between Israel and any of the two dozen Middle East regimes, the movement lacked the necessary "other" which it had been created in juxtaposition to. For its own survival—especially after its domestic political failure with regard to the invasion of Iraq—neoconservatism needed a new threat—a near-peer, hegemony-bent ideology and political rival that threatened its own universalist, hegemonic self-vision of the U.S., and that threatened Israel's existence. It is in this context that neoconservative-oriented intellectuals like Daniel Pipes, Bernard Lewis, and Frank Gaffney were able to frame Islam itself within the "clash of civilizations" paradigm.

These amalgamated crises not only caused the GOP to lurch rightward, and taking its narrative concerning the threat of Islam with it, but provided the incentive to politicize the topic of Islam as a threat. In this context, it was not surprising that this threat discourse opposed the perceived sources of the threats to Western civilizational hegemony and domestic cultural identity, which the movement ideologues identified variously as Islam and progressivism, or euphemistically, multiculturalism and secularism—or, the metaphor that captured them both: Islam(ization). The Islamization metaphor had more direct political utility; it irrationally linked the two worldviews that a politically-relevant segment of U.S. conservatives perceived to be hostile to traditional America and its Judeo-Christian identity—global Islam and the local Left—to delegitimize both rivals, and to try and advance a panic over the former to make domestic political gains against the latter.

Political Frames: U.S. Cultural Building Blocks for Security Politics

Finally, the historically-shaped and enacted mental structures that functioned as the foundation for this discourse were not merely or even mainly those that the literature had led us to anticipate. The literature led us to expect a discourse dominated by underlying frames of racism and xenophobia on the one hand, and of those of struggle for the Holy Land on the other. Yet, the subject matter and the underlying cognitive blueprints were always political, and not merely politically descriptive, but politically performative, with the conflation and delegitimization of enemies foreign and domestic on the one hand, and the reconstruction of the exceptional yet vulnerable self on the other.

And, this latest conspiracy of new foreign enemies infiltrating the homeland with the assistance of familiar domestic traitors, was incentivized and rendered credible to no small degree by the rich cultural repertory of political schemas on that general subject. The more entrepreneurial conservative political and security elites mobilized this rich resource of cultural frames and transposed them onto current contexts, with an apparent expectation of gaining political advantage.

Even with the political frames and motivation dominant, the xenophobic cognitive structure was present in no small part throughout. The "enemy within" was a culturally-fixed subject position whose genealogy could be traced from the beginning of Western Civilization, through the inquisitions, through the conspiracies over Free Masons, Illuminati, and witches, to the loyalty oaths of the American Revolution, to the life-or-death struggle with Catholicization, and so on.

But, again, the content of domestic political struggle always trumped the xenophobic element. This, too, had rich cultural master frames; the infiltrating foreign enemy was almost always tethered that of the domestic traitor, or disloyal citizen, who from their inside position functions as a crucial accomplice, aiding and abetting, or unlocking the gate, so to speak. The telltale mark of politicization within all U.S. historical threat writing was always when the more progressive, leftist, or otherwise politically-resistant elements within the population were framed as such agents of the foreign enemy. Recall, for example, how both the trade unions and women's fight for day care in the nineteenth century were similarly framed in terms of the enemy within linked to foreign elements, and, how—after World War I—the Bolsheviks turned out to be politically useful, with politicians deploying this new rhetorical resource to frame their domestic opponents as closet sympathizers with the nation's foreign enemy. And, in the discourse at hand, these frames were creatively applied to the U.S. conservative movement's domestic political enemy—the Obama administration, the Democratic Party, the progressive movement and more progressive societal institutions broadly.

Conclusion

In conclusion, much more was going on post-9/11 conservative threat writing than securing the nation from a credible, objective threat, as presented by those agents involved, or advancing a discourse of xenophobia or hatred for Muslims as cover for Zionism's geopolitical project, as was the literature critically characterized it. Islam, in this discourse—

more than pure or professional security subject matter, and more than xenophobic or Holy Land geopolitical subject matter—was significantly domestic political subject matter. And, here, it was not only *mere political* subject matter that explicitly engaged the Obama administration and Democrats for position in the upcoming election, but also *counterhegemonic* subject matter; it was a *platform* or site for more profound and implicit cultural politics or "culture war" against the more progressive multicultural and secular societal doxa and the institutions that house it. And, as in all project of identity politics, this threat discourse's main function seems to have been to serve as a platform to identify, construct, or reproduce the ideal political inside—the U.S. conservative movement itself.

In other words, in addition to any characterizations by the literature as the newest twist on the same geopolitics surrounding Israel, the newest xenophobia, or newest form of anti-immigrant racism, it was also significantly the newest opportune platform upon which the more entrepreneurial segment of U.S. neo, paleo, and social conservatives could advance their struggle against the more progressive hegemony, and—in doing so—revitalize themselves.

4. Implications for Security Professionals

From the more practical perspective, analysis of this discourse suggests that our approach to threats and other objects of security studies and international relations should proceed from a healthy dose of "realism" regarding not only the subjective, constructed nature of the world's objects, but the politics surrounding them. In addition to any objective aspect of threats to the nation, all such threats are constructed subjectively or discursively—that is, through *our discourse about them.*

There is a broad consensus comprised of prominent social philosophers such as Bourdieu and Foucault, as well as other established scholars from across the disciplinary spectrum, who have rigorously argued that all such popular discourse is significantly politically interested. From this perspective, major segments of public discourses, such as the one under scrutiny here, function not as neutral or disinterested descriptions of topics of societal importance, but as sites of power and even cultural struggle, upon which social agents advance their goals or interests.

This seems especially valid in the case of security discourses. As Foucault famously quipped, purported threats *are useful;* they "come in handy," both in the political and economic realms. In the case at hand, the notion of the threat of Islam—or, if we must, "Islamophobia"—presented significant political utility. And, for this reason, the degree to which a potential threat is a threat to the nation's interests depends entirely on the positionality or ideological commitments and affiliations of the threat writer—whether, for example, he or she is the recipient of the "Guardian of Zion" award like Daniel Pipes, or the employee of cultural warrior David Horowitz, like Robert Spencer, or the darling of Fox News, Pamela Geller.

With these realities in view, security analyses would have greater correspondence to reality if the analysts reflexively avoided the trap of false objectivity. There are several means of doing this, such as drawing upon as many sources as possible for our assessments or estimates, realizing the hazards of taking any one of them as disinterested, or for the benefit of society broadly. Of course, that healthy dose of cynicism and its attendant reflexivity would necessitate a systematic reading of productions from across the political spectrum, including those from the highly-interested threat writers profiled in this study.

The obvious "constructed" nature of the threat of Islam(ization) to America after 9/11 reveals how every so-called threat has a constructed and subjective component, and is—to a significant degree—the product of political struggle between highly interested experts, or intellectuals organic to particular political apparatuses. For this reason, purely materialist, objectivist, or "realist" accounts of the world's threats are both deluded and distorted to the extent that they are blind to this element of every threat that so powerfully shapes our master threat narratives, or what is and what isn't a threat. To the degree that we become uncritically or unreflexively trapped in our limited ontological assumptions—to the degree that we obscure the much broader and even subjective components of the threat in question—is the degree that we misapprehend the very nature and degree of that threat. The analyst who abandons such notions of objectivity in security writing—who unearths the layers of politically-interested strategies and other cultural and social structurally induced biases that shape if not distort them—will inevitably produce the elusive and much-needed corrective that enables us to see the threats and other objects of the world in all their social complexity. It is only then that we shall attain the high-ground of security assessments: *to know our enemy as our self.*

Theoretical Implications

At the more formal, theoretical level, the analysis of this discourse offers a contemporary case study that underscores the utility of a conceptual framework that views all discourse—including security writing—as political, and inherent to cultural struggle at the domestic level. Three more specific implications are offered.

Firstly, this analysis offers a pragmatic expanded interpretive framework for all inquiries into the world's discourses and other social practice; it offers methodological utility for discourse analysts who want to more examine a discourse in its greater social complexity, across its more structural non-discursive elements, such as its political apparatus, opportunity structure and resources, as well as its agent- enacted discursive strategies deployed. This is especially valuable in the analysis of security discourses, or security threats.

At the micro-level of agency, it rigorously examined the strategies of cultural politics involved. It demonstrated how counterhegemonic struggle can proceed by opportunistically seizing an object of the world—in this case, Islam—as a platform, site, or field of struggle. It also demonstrated at a more tactical level how projects of identity or cultural politics proceed; that is, via the two moves of all cultural politics, or acts of the political: the production of the enemy outside on the one hand, and the production of the friendly inside on the other.

And, at the macro-level, the study also revealed how discourses are not merely discursive or descriptive in nature, but—as Foucault, Althusser and others have pointed out—are largely a function of a significant social base or political apparatus, and therefore supported more materially or non-discursively by range of cultural, social structural, and social-psychological resources, along with favorable eventful or historical conditions. By revealing the range of structural elements that comprised this discourse's political apparatus, and how they function, this analysis adds needed strategic and contextual depth to our understanding of security politics—an understanding heretofore informed largely by Campbell's narrower internal analysis of Cold War security texts.

Secondly, the inquiry helps expand our conception of power and its relation to knowledge, especially security knowledge or the identified threats to a nation. With so much emphasis on the role of geopolitics in the production of the world's security discourses, this analysis offers us an epistemological break, underscoring the role of the distinct categorical set of politics closer to home, termed variously as cultural politics, cultural struggle, counterhegemonic struggle, and so on.

Thirdly, this analysis yields greater insight into the subtler part of the nature of security politics; that is, how *in*security is less a threat to political collectivities than it is a condition of their possibility. The study revealed many ways in which was the case. Recall, as just one example, how the rhetorical topography of "Islam" as related to "the West" after 9/11 ranged from the more progressive pole position of "religion of peace" to the stauncher conservative peripheral position of "stealth jihad." As the analysis proceeded, it became clear that these inherently opposing storylines functioned less to mark off the range of debate about a foreign enemy than they did to demarcate the domestic political factions that positioned and identified themselves by them.

Of course, there is much more that could be said with regard to theoretical implications. Suffice it to say, we have gained more appreciation for Said's earliest and core notion about Western production of knowledge about Islam broadly: that it *has less to do with that world than it does with ours*.

REFERENCES

Ackerman, Spencer. 2012. Soldier who taught 'total war' against Islam threatens to sue top military officer. *Wired*, September 21

Adatto, Kiku. 1990. Sound bite democracy: Network evening news presidential campaign coverage, 1968-1988. Harvard University Research Paper, November

Adler, Emmanuel and Vincent Pouliot, eds. 2011. *International practices.* Cambridge: Cambridge University Press

Ahmed, Akbar. 2008. *Journey into Islam: The crisis of globalization.* Washington DC: Brookings Institute Press

Ahrens, Frank. 2002. Moon speech raises old ghosts as the Times turns 20. *Washington Post*, May 23

Aleaziz Hamed. 2012. Study: Anti-Islam messages dominate media coverage. *ThinkProgress*, December 1

Alexandru about Denmark. 2007. Interview with Pia Kjaersgaard. http://alex-l.blogspot.com, November 23

Alexander, Jeffrey and Philip Smith. 1993. The discourse of American civil society: A new proposal for cultural studies. *Theory and Society* 22: 150-207

Ali, Wajahat, Eli Clifton, Matthew Duss, Lee Fang, Scott Keyes, and Faiz Shakir. 2011. *Fear, Inc: The roots of the Islamophobia network in America.* Washington DC: Center for American Progress, August

Allen, Christopher. 2005. From race to religion: The new face of discrimination. In *Muslim Britain: Communities under pressure*, ed. Tahir Abbas. London: Ashgate.

Alterman, Eric. 1999. The 'right' books and big ideas. *The Nation*, November 22

Althusser, Louis. 1971. Ideology and ideological state apparatuses. In *Lenin and Philosophy, and Other Essays*. Trans. Ben Brewster, 127-188. London: New Left Books

Alvarez, Josefina Echavarría. 2006. Re-thinking (in)security discourses from a critical perspective. **asteriskos* 1 no. 2: 61-82

American Civil Liberties Union. 2011. "Nothing to Fear: Debunking the Mythical 'Sharia Threat' to Our Judicial System." *American Civil Liberties Union*, May 20,

Anti-Defamation League. 2011. David Yerushalmi: A driving force behind anti- sharia efforts in the U.S. *The Anti-Defamation League*, March 25.

Arab News. 2011. OIC, West pledge to combat intolerance. *Arab News*, July 17

Arab News. 2012. OIC warns of exploiting Islamophobia phenomenon. Arab News, November 13.

Arkin, William. 2003. The Pentagon unleashes a holy warrior. *Los Angeles Times*, October 16.

Armbruster, Ben. 2010. Sharia hysteria comes to Oklahoma: Voters approve sharia law ban. *Think Progress.com*, November 3

Ayoob, Mohammed. 2007. *The many faces of political Islam: Religion and politics in the Muslim world*. Ann Arbor: University of Michigan Press

Babington, Charles and Darlene Superville. 2010. Obama 'Christian by choice': President responds to questioner. *AP*, September 28

Baer, Robert. 2003. *See no evil. The true story of a ground soldier in the CIA's war against terrorism*. New York: Three Rivers Press

Bakhtin, Mikhail. 1981. *The dialogic imagination*. Ed. Michael Holquist. Trans. Caryl Emerson and Michael Holquist. Austin: University of Texas Press

Baklouti, Akila. 2007. Degrees of implicitness in the expression of ideology: Freedom of expression vs. racism in the prophet cartoon controversy. *Studies in Islam & the Middle East* 4 no. 2

Balz, Daniel and Ronald Brownstein. 1996. *Storming the gates: Protest politics and the Republican revival*. Boston: Little, Brown

Bartlett, Robert. 1993. *The making of Europe*. Princeton: Princeton University Press

Bawer, Bruce. 2006. *While Europe slept: How radical Islam is destroying the West from within*. New York: Broadway.

Beecher, Lyman. 1835. *A plea for the West*. Bedford: Applewood

Beinin, Joel. 1993. Money, media and policy consensus. *Middle East Research* 23, no. 180 (January/February)

Beinin, Joel. 2004. The new American McCarthyism: Policing thought about the Middle East. *Race & Class* 46 no. 1: 101-111

Belt, David. 2009. Islamism in popular Western discourse. *Policy Perspectives*, 6 no. 2 (July-December)

Benda, Vaclav. 1991. The parallel 'polis'. In *Civic freedom in Central Europe: Voices from Czechoslovakia*, eds. H. Gordon Skilling and Paul Wilson, 35-41. New York: St. Martin's Press.

Benford, Robert. 1993. Frame disputes within the nuclear disarmament movement. *Social Forces*, 71: 677–701

Benford, Robert and David Snow. 2000. Framing processes and social movements: An overview and assessment. *Annual Review of Sociology* 26 (Aug): 611-39

Bercovitch, Sacvan. 1978. *The American jeremiad*. Madison: University of Wisconsin Press.

Berlet, Chip and Matthew Lyons. 2000. *Right-wing populism in America: Too close for comfort*. New York: The Guilford Press

Berman, William. 1998. *America's right turn: From Nixon to Clinton*. Baltimore, MD: Johns Hopkins University Press

Bhabha, Homi. 1996 [1986]. The other question: Difference, discrimination and the discourse of colonialism. In *Black British cultural studies: A reader*, eds. H. Baker, M. Diawara, R. Lindeborg, 87-106. Chicago, IL: University of Chicago Press

Bhutto, Benazir. 2008. *Reconciliation: Islam, democracy, and the West*. New York: Harper Collins

Billig, Michael. 1996. *Arguing and thinking; A rhetorical approach to social psychology*. Cambridge: Cambridge University Press.

Birkey, Andy. 2010. Bachmann: America 'cursed' by God 'if we reject Israel'. *Minnesota Independent*, February 08

Blee, Kathleen and Kimberly Creasap. 2010. Conservative and right-wing movements. *Annual Review of Sociology* 36: 269-286

Blumenthal, Max. 2006. Hell of a Times. *The Nation*, October 9

Blumenthal, Max. 2010. The great Islamophobic crusade. *Huffington Post*, December 20

Blumenthal, Max. 2011. Meet the right-wing hatemongers who inspired the Norway killer. *AlterNet*, August 3

Blumenthal, Max. 2012. The sugar mama of anti-Muslim hate. *The Nation*, July 2

Blumenthal, Sydney. 2008. The strange death of Republican America: Chronicles of a collapsing party. New York: Sterling

Bonney, Richard. 2008. *False prophets: The 'clash of civilizations' and the global war on terror*. Oxford: Peter Lang.

Boorstein, Michelle. 2010. Once considered anti-Islam, senior scholar says he's now in the middle. *Washington Post*, August 18

Boorstein, Michelle. 2010. In flap over mosque near Ground Zero, conservative bloggers gaining influence. *Washington Post*, August 19

Borum, Randy. 2011. Radicalization into violent extremism II: A review of conceptual models and empirical research. *Journal of Strategic Security* 4, no. 4: 37-62

Bosmajian, Haig. 1999. *The freedom not to speak*. New York: NYU Press

Bostom, Andrew. 2010. Behind the mosque. *New York Post*, July 23

Bourdieu, Pierre. 1977. *Outline of a theory of practice*. Cambridge: Cambridge University Press

Bourdieu, Pierre. 1977. The economics of linguistic exchanges. *Social Science Information* 16 no. 6: 645–668.

Bourdieu, Pierre. 1984 [1979]. *Distinction: A social critique of the judgment of taste*. Trans. Richard Nice. Cambridge, MA: Harvard University Press.

Bourdieu, Pierre. 1986 [1977]. *The production of belief: Contribution to an economy of symbolic goods*. Trans. Richard Nice. In *Media culture & society: A critical reader*, eds. Richard Collins, et al., 131-163. London: Sage.

Bourdieu, Pierre. 1987. What makes a social class? On the theoretical and practical existence of groups. *Berkeley Journal of Sociology* 32. 1-17

Bourdieu, Pierre. 1988 [1984]. *Homo academicus*. Trans. P. Collier. Cambridge: Polity Press

Bourdieu, Pierre. 1990. *The logic of practice*. Trans. R. Nice. Cambridge MA: Polity Press

Bourdieu, Pierre. 1990. *In other words: Essays towards a reflexive sociology*. Trans. Matthew Adamson. Stanford, CA: Stanford University Press.

Bourdieu, Pierre. 1991. *Language and symbolic power*. Ed. John B. Thompson. Trans. Gino Raymond and Matthew Adamson. Cambridge MA: Polity Press

Bourdieu, Pierre, 1993. *Sociology in question*. Trans. R. Nice. London: Sage

Bourdieu, Pierre. 1998. *Practical reason: On the theory of action*. Trans. Randall Johnson. Stanford: Stanford University Press.

Bourdieu, Pierre. 1998. *Acts of resistance. Against the tyranny of the market*. Trans. Richard Nice. New York: The New Press.

Bourdieu, Pierre. 2000 (1982). The production and reproduction of legitimate language. In *Routledge Language and Cultural Theory Reader*, eds Lucy Burke, Tony Crowley and Alan Girvin, 467-477. London: Routledge.

Bourdieu, Pierre. 2005. *The social structures of the economy*. Cambridge: Polity

Bourdieu, Pierre and Loïc Wacquant. 1989. Towards a reflexive sociology: A workshop with Pierre Bourdieu. *Sociological Theory* 7, no. 1: 26-63

Bourdieu, Pierre, and Loïc Wacquant. 1992. *An invitation to reflexive sociology*. Trans. Loïc Wacquant. Chicago: University of Chicago Press

Bourdieu, Pierre and Randall Johnson. 1993. The production of belief: Contribution to an economy of symbolic goods. In *The field of cultural production: Essays on art and literature*, ed. Randall Johnson, 74-111. Cambridge: Polity Press.

Bowman, Glenn. 1994. A country of words: Conceiving the Palestinian nation from the position of exile. In *The making of political identities*, ed. Ernesto Laclau, 138-170. London. Verso

Boyer, Paul and Stephen Nissenbaum. 1974. *Salem possessed: The social origins of witchcraft.* Cambridge, MA: Harvard University Press

Brayton, Ed. 2011. The Fraudulent Sharia in American Courts "Study." *ScienceBlogs*, June 10

Brinkley, Alan. 1994. The problem of American conservatism. *American Historical Review* 99, no 2 (April): 409–429

Buckner, Brett. 2011. "'The path': Some Americans are Trying to Ban Muslim Law without Knowing what it Means. *Anniston Star*, March 12.

Bulkin, Elly and Donna Nevel. 2012. Follow the money: From Islamophobia to Israel right or wrong. *AlterNet*, October 3

Buruma, Ian. 2009. Totally tolerant, up to a point. *New York Times*, January 29.

Butler, Judith. 1990. *Gender trouble: Feminism and the subversion of identity*. New York: Routledge

Buzan, Barry. 1991. *People, states and fear: An agenda for international security studies in the post-Cold War era.* Harlow: Pearson Education Limited.

CAIR. 2013. Legislating Fear: Islamophobia and its impact in the United States. Washington DC. Council on American-Islamic Relations.

Campbell, David. 1998. *Writing security: United States foreign policy and the politics of identity.* Rev. ed. Minneapolis: University of Minnesota

Campbell, David. 2001. Imaging the real, struggling for meaning. *911 InfoInterventions*, October 6

Campbell, David. 2001. Time is broken: The return of the past in the response to September 11, *Theory & Event,* 5 no. 4.

Cassidy, John. 2013. After Boston: A few facts about terrorism. *The New Yorker Online*, April 24

Castells, Manuel. 1997. *The power of identity*. Oxford: Blackwell Publishers Ltd

Center for Security Policy. 2011. Shariah law and American state courts: An assessment of state appellate court cases. *Center for Security Policy*, 21 June.

Center for Security Policy. 2010. *Shariah: The threat to America (An exercise in competitive analysis—report of team 'B' II).* Washington DC: Center for Security Policy.

Cesari, Jocelyn. 2011. Islamophobia in the West: A comparison between Europe and the United States. In *Islamophobia: The challenge of pluralism in the 21st Century*, eds. John Esposito and Ibrahim Kalin, 21-43. Oxford: Oxford University Press.

Chafe, William. 2003. *The unfinished journey: America since World War II*. New York: Oxford University Press

Chafe, William. 1991. *The paradox of change: American women in the 20th century*. Oxford: Oxford University Press

Chandrasekaran, Rajiv. 2007. *Imperial life in the emerald city: Inside Iraq's Green Zone*. New York: Vintage Books

Charlotte Observer. 2011. Myrick's chief of staff leaving. *Charlotte Observer*, Feb 14

Charmaz, Kathy. 2000. Grounded theory: objectivist and constructivist methods. In *Handbook of Qualitative Research*. 2nd ed., eds. Norman Denzin and Yvonna Lincoln, 509-535. London: Sage Publications.

Churchill, Winston. 1899. *The river war*, Vol. II. London: Longmans, Green & Co

Clarkson, Fred. 1987. Behind the Times: Who pulls the strings at Washington's No. 2 daily? *Fairness and Accuracy in Reporting*, August 1

Clifton, Eli. 2011. Oslo terrorist's manifesto cited many Islamophobic bloggers and pundits. *ThinkProgress*, July 25

Clifton, Eli. 2012. U.S. military taught officers: 'Islam must change or we will facilitate its self-destruction'. *Think Progress*, May 10.

Clifton, Eli and Ali Gharib. 2012. Exclusive: Class materials from military's anti-Islam class repeatedly cite Islamophobic authors. *Think Progress*, May 14

Coetzee, John. 1980. *Waiting for the barbarians*. New York: Penguin

Cohen, John and Jennifer Agiesta. 2009. Most in poll back outreach to Muslims. *MSNBC*, 5 April

Cohen, Jon. 2006. Poll: Americans skeptical of Islam and Arabs. *ABC News*, March 8

Cohen, Patricia. 2010. 'Epistemic closure'? Those are fighting words. *New York Times*, April 27

Cohen, Roger. 2011. Breivik and his enablers. *New York Times*, July 25

Cohen, Stanley. 2002 (1972). *Folk devils and moral panics: The creation of the Mods and Rockers*. 3rd ed. London and New York: Routledge

Connolly, William. 2002 [1991]. *Identity\difference: Democratic negotiations of political paradox*. Exp ed. Minneapolis: University of Minnesota Press

Cook, Deborah. 1996. *The culture industry revisited: Theodore W. Adorno on mass culture*. Lanham, MD: Rowman & Littlefield

Cook, Timothy. 2005. *Governing with the news: The news media as a political institution*. 2nd edn. Chicago: University of Chicago Press.

Corbin, Juliet. 1998. Alternative interpretations: Valid or not? *Theory & Psychology* 8, no. 1: 121-128.

Cordesman, Anthony. 2009. ABC News/Washington Post poll on U.S. views of Islam. Washington DC. CSIS, April 21

Corn, David. 2011. Did Chris Wallace really say FOX News isn't fair and balanced? *Mother Jones*, June 1

Cox, Robert. 1983. Gramsci, hegemony and international relations: An Essay in method. *Millennium: Journal of International Studies* 12 no. 2:162-175

Cox, Robert. 2002. *The political-economy of a plural world*. London: Routledge.

Croft, Stuart. 2006. Culture, crisis and America's War on Terror. Cambridge: Cambridge University Press.

Crooke, Alastair. 2006. The 'new Orientalism'. *Bitterlemons*, August 31.

Crooke, Alastair. 2009. *Resistance: The essence of the Islamist revolution*. London: Pluto

Dalby, Simon. 1988. Geopolitical discourse. The Soviet Union as other. *Alternatives* 13: 415-422.

Dalby, Simon. 1990. *Creating the second Cold War. The discourse of politics.* London: Pinter

Dalby, Simon. 2003. Calling 911: Geopolitics, security and America's new war. *Geopolitics* 8 no. 3: 61–86.

Daloglu, Tulin. 2007. US through Islamic lens. *Washington Times*, July 3

Davidson, Lawrence. 2010. Here come the true believers: The great Muslim scare. *Counterpunch*, September 16

Davidson, Lawrence. 2011. Debbi Almontaser and the problematics of paranoid politics. *Arab Studies Quarterly* 33 no. 3, 4 (Fall): 168-178

Davidson, Lawrence. 2011. Islamophobia, the Israel lobby, and American paranoia: Letter from America. *Holy Land Studies* 10 no 1: 87–95

Davis, Richard and Diana Owen. 1998. *New media and American politics*. New York: Oxford University Press

De Atkine, Norvell and Daniel Pipes. 1995. Middle Eastern studies: What went wrong? *Academic Questions*, Winter

De Atkine, Norvell and Daniel Pipes. 1997. Letters to the editor: Middle Eastern studies: What went wrong? An intifada of our very own. *Academic Questions*, Fall

Deibert, R. 1997. *Parchment, printing, and hypermedia: Communication in world order transformation.* New York: Columbia University Press

Der Derian, James, 2002. 9.11: Before, after, and in between. In *Understanding September 11*, eds. Craig J. Calhoun, Paul Price, Ashley S. Timmer, 321-335. New York: New Press

Derrida, Jacques. 1978. *Writing and difference*. London: Routledge & Kegan Paul, Ltd

Derrida, Jacques. 1981. *Positions*. Chicago IL: University of Chicago Press.

Deutsche-Welle. 2006. German mistrust of Muslims and Islam grows. *Deutsche-Well*, 05 May

Diamond, Sara. 1995. *Roads to dominion: Right-wing movements and political power in the United States*. New York: Guilford

Dickinson, Tim. 2011. How Roger Ailes built the FOX News fear factory. *Rolling Stone*, May 25

Dillon, Michael. 1996. *Politics of security: Towards a political philosophy of continental thought*. London: Routledge

Doerflinger, Janel. 2011. Whitewashing the Muslim Brotherhood, *FrontPageMagazine*, May 20

Dossa Shiraz. 1987. Political philosophy and Orientalism: The Classical origins of a discourse. *Alternatives* 12 no 3: 343-58.

Dostoevsky, Fyodor. 1933. *The Brothers Karamazov*. Trans. Constance Garnett. New York: Random House

Dreyfus, Hubert and Paul Rabinow. 1982. *Michel Foucault: Beyond structuralism and hermeneutics*. 2nd ed. Chicago: The University of Chicago Press.

Drinnon, Richard. 1997. *Facing West: The metaphysics of Indian hating and empire building*. Norman OK: University of Oklahoma Press

Duss, Matthew. 2010. Creeping sharia 'Team B' report presented to Congress. *ThinkProgress*, September 15

Eagleton, Terry. 1991. *Ideology: An introduction*. London: Verso

Edelman, Murray. 1964. *The symbolic uses of politics*. Urbana, IL: University of Illinois Press.

Edwards, Lee. 2003. The Origins of the Modern American Conservative Movement. *The Heritage Foundation*, 811 (February 21)

Ehrman J. 1995. *The rise of neoconservatism: Intellectuals and foreign affairs, 1945–1994*. New Haven, CT: Yale University Press

Elder, Larry. 2007. Because they hate. *Townhall.com*, April 12

Elliot, Justin. 2010. How the "Ground Zero Mosque" Fear-mongering began. *Salon.com*, August 16

Elliot, Justin. 2010. Mystery of who funded right-wing "radical Islam" campaign deepens. *Salon.com*, November 16

Elliot, Justin. 2011. Right-wing publisher: We run 'some misinformation'. *Salon*, 11 April

Elliott, Andrea. 2011. The man behind the anti-shariah movement. *New York Times*, July 30

Emerson, Steven. 2003. *American jihad: The terrorists living among us.* Free Press.

Emerson, Steven. 2006. *Jihad incorporated: A guide to militant Islam in the US.* Amherst NY: Prometheus

Emerson, Steven. 2009. "Moderate" Muslim Brotherhood cleric is anything but. *Family Security Matters*, February 10.

Emerson, Steven. 2009. Extremists use 'civil rights' group front to push agenda. *The Desert Sun*, March 24

Emirbayer, Mustafa and Jeff Goodwin. 1994. Network analysis, culture, and the problem of agency. *American Journal of Sociology* 99 no. 6 (May):1411-1454

Emirbayer, Mustafa and Jeff Goodwin. 1996. Symbols, positions, objects: Toward a new theory of revolutions and collective action. *History and Theory* 35, no. 3 (Oct): 358-374

Entman, Robert. 1993. Framing: Toward clarification of a fractured paradigm. *Journal of Communication* 43 no. 4 (Autumn): 51-57

Ernst, Carl. 2013. *Islamophobia in America: The anatomy of intolerance.* New York: Palgrave Macmillan

Ernst, Carl. 2012. Notes on the ideological patrons of an Islamophobe, Robert Spencer. *The American Muslim*, January 4

Esposito, John. 1992. *Islamic threat: Myth or reality.* Oxford: Oxford University Press

Esposito, John. 1994. Political Islam: Beyond the green menace. *Current History*, January

Esposito, John. 2003. Practice and theory: A response to 'Islam and the challenge of democracy'. *Boston Review*, April/May

Esposito, John. 2008. Introduction. In *Islamophobia and the challenges of pluralism in the 21st Century*, 9-17. Washington DC: Prince Alwaleed Bin Talal Center for Muslim-Christian Understanding, Georgetown University.

Esposito, John, and Ibrahim Kalin, eds. 2011. *Islamophobia: The challenge of pluralism in the 21st century.* Oxford: Oxford University Press

Esposito, John and Dalia Mogahed. 2008. *Who speaks for Islam?: What a billion Muslims really think.* New York: Gallup Press

Esposito, Richard, Mary-Rose Abraham and Rhonda Schwartz. 2009. Major Hasan: Soldier of Allah; Many ties to jihad web sites. *ABC News*, 12 November

Etzold, Thomas and John Gaddis, eds. 1978. *Containment: Documents on American policy and strategy 1945-1950.* Columbia: Columbia University Press

Evans, Terry. 2011. Keller church's event draws 1,500 Muslims, 1,000 Christians. *Star-Telegram*, September 11

Factor, Mallory. 2014. *Big tent. The story of the conservative revolution--As told by the thinkers and doers who made it happen.* New York: HarperCollins.

Fang, Lee. 2011. Allen West says new Congress should prioritize threat of 'infiltration of the sharia practice' in U.S. *ThinkProgress.org*, January 3

Fang, Lee. 2012. Hateful anti-Muslim group's efforts to bring Islamophobia into the mainstream. *Alternet*, July 23

Fars News Agency. 2010. OIC Secretary-General warns of Western plots against Islam. Fars News Agency, November 29

Fatany, Samar. 2004. Stop the attacks against Islam. *Arab News*. May 12

FBI. 2008. 2008 Crime in the United States. Washington DC: FBI Criminal Justice Services Information Division

Fekete, Liz and A. Sivanandan. 2009. *A suitable enemy: Racism, migration and Islamphobia in Europe.* London: Pluto Press.

Fichtner, Ullrich. 2011. The terrorist next door: American Muslims face growing prejudice. *Der Spiegel*, September 13.

Fischer, Max. 2010. "Guess the quote: Bin Laden or Newt Gingrich?" *The Atlantic*, August 5.

Foley, Michael. 2007. *American credo: the place of ideas in US politics.* Oxford University Press.

Foreign Economic Policy. 1977. Draft study prepared by the Policy Planning Staff, Annex VIII, NSC 68/1 "The Strategy of Freedom," November 10, 1950, in *Foreign Relations of the United States 1950, Volume I: National Security Affairs*; Washington DC: Foreign Economic Policy: 406.

Fotopoulos, T. 2007. Islamophobia: The new anti-Semitism. *International Journal of Inclusive Democracy* 3, no. 1 (January)

Foucault, Michel. 1972/2002. *The Archaeology of Knowledge, and the Discourse on Language.* 2nd ed. Abington, Oxon: Routledge.

Foucault, Michel. 1973/2003. *The birth of the clinic: An archaeology of medical perception.* Trans. A.M. Sheridan. London. Routledge.

Foucault, Michel. 1977. *Discipline and punish: The birth of the prison.* Trans. Alan. M. Sheridan. New York: Pantheon.

Foucault, Michel. 1977. *Language, counter-memory, practice: Selected essays and interviews.* Ed. Trans D. Bouchard and S. Simon. New York: Blackwell.

Foucault, Michel. 1978: *The history of sexuality, Volume I: An introduction.* Trans. Robert. Hurley. New York: Pantheon

Foucault, Michel. 1979. Truth and power: An interview with Michel Foucault. *Critique of Anthropology* 4 (January): 131-137,

Foucault, Michel. 1980. *Power/Knowledge: Selected interviews and other writings 1972-1977.* Ed. Colin Gordon. New York: Pantheon

Foucault, Michel. 1981 [1970]. The order of discourse. In *Untying the text: A post-structuralist reader.* Ed. R. Young, 48-78. London: Routledge & Kegan Paul

Foucault, Michel. 1982. The subject and power. In *Michel Foucault: Beyond structuralism and hermeneutics.* 2nd ed. Eds. Hubert L. Dreyfus and Paul Rabinow, 208-226. Chicago: The University of Chicago Press.

Foucault, Michel. 1991. Politics and the study of discourse. In *The Foucault effect: Studies in governmentality*, eds. Graham Burchell, Colin Gordon, Peter Miller, 53-72. Chicago: University of Chicago Press.

Foucault, Michel. 1994 [1970]. *The order of things: An archaeology of the human sciences.* New York: Vintage

Foucault, Michel. 1997/2003. *"Society must be defended": Lectures at the Collège de France, 1975-1976.* Trans. David Macey. New York: Picador

Foucault, Michel. 2002 [1972]. *The archaeology of knowledge, and the discourse on language*, 2nd ed. Abington, Oxon: Routledge.

Foucault, Michel and Paul Rabinow. 1984. *The Foucault reader.* New York: Pantheon Books.

FOX News Channel. 2011. Lawmakers blast administration for calling Fort Hood massacre 'workplace violence'. *FOXNews.com*, 7 Dec

Friedman, Murray. 2006. *The neoconservative revolution: Jewish intellectuals and the shaping of public policy.* New York: Cambridge University Press

Gabriel, Brigitte. 2006. *Because they hate: A survivor of Islamic terror warns America.* Macmillan.

Gabriel, Brigitte. 2007. Because they hate, Part II; Interview with Larry Elder. *Jewish World Review,* April 26

Gabriel, Brigitte. 2008. *They must be stopped: Why we must defeat radical Islam and how we can do it.* New York: Macmillan

Gabriel, Brigitte. 2012. Take AIM: Brigitte Gabriel. June 14, 2012. Interview by Roger Aronoff. *Accuracy In Media,* July 9.

Gaffney, Frank. 2010. Can this possibly be true? New Obama missile defense logo includes a crescent. *Big Government,* February 24

Gaffney, Frank. 2010. Gaffney: America's first Muslim president? *Washington Times,* 9 June

Gallup. 2011. Muslim Americans: Faith, freedom, and the future. Abu Dhabi Gallup Center (August).

Gallup Center for Muslim Studies. 2009. *Muslim-Americans: A national portrait.* Washington DC: Gallup

Gallup. 2009. The Gallup coexist index 2009: A global study of interfaith relations. Gallup & Coexist Foundation

Gamson, William and David Meyer. 1996. Framing political opportunity. In *Comparative perspectives on social movements: Political opportunities, mobilizing structures, and cultural framings*, eds. Doug McAdam, John McCarthy an Mayer Zald, 275-290. New York: Cambridge University Press

Gans, Herbert. 1979. *Deciding what's news: A study of "CBS Evening News," "NBC Nightly News," "Newsweek," and "Time."* New York: Pantheon Books.

Garnham, Nicholas and Raymond Williams. 1986. Pierre Bourdieu and the sociology of culture: An introduction, 116-130. In *Media culture & society: A critical reader*, eds Richard Collins et al. London: SAGE

Geller, Pamela. 2007. Atlas Shrugs vlogs a very Merry Christmas to our soldiers. *Atlas Shrugs*, December 24 [video no longer available].

Gergen, Kenneth. 2009. *An invitation to social construction.* 2nd ed. London: SAGE

Gerges, Fawaz. 2005. *The far enemy: Why jihad went global.* Cambridge: Cambridge University Press

Gertz, Bill. 2010. Shariah a danger to U.S., security pros say. *Washington Times*, September 15.

Getz, Leonard. 2000. Daniel Pipes: Prophet. *Lifestyles Magazine*, June

Giddens, Anthony. 1976. *New rules of sociological method: A positive critique of interpretive sociologies.* London: Hutchinson

Giddens, Anthony. 1984. *The constitution of society: Outline of the theory of structuration.* Cambridge: Polity Press.

Giddens, Anthony. 1991. *Modernity and self-identity: Self and society in the late modern age.* Stanford, CA: Stanford Univ. Press

Giddens, Anthony. 2002. *Runaway world: How globalisation is reshaping our lives.* London: Profile.

Gillette, Felix. 2008. Viewers continuing to flock to cable news networks. *The New York Observer*, October 1

Gingrich, Newt and Callista Gingrich. 2010. America at risk: The war with no name. *Human Events*, September 8

Glaser, Barney. 1992. *Basics of grounded theory analysis: Emergence vs. forcing.* Mill Valley, CA: Sociology Press.

Goldberg, Jeffrey. 2008. The Jewish extremists behind "Obsession." *The Atlantic*, October 27

Goldberg, Jeffrey. 2011. Nothing new in the idea that '67 borders should guide peace talks. *The Atlantic*, May 19

Goldberg, Jonah. 2005. Golden Days: Standing with Buckley & co. & at 50 years young. *National Review*, October 27

Goldberg, Jonah. 2007. Kill this word. Poor, abused, unrecognizable, meaningless 'neocon'. *National Review*, April 2: 18-21

Goldman, Brendan. 2010. Who're you calling a 'bigot'? Middle East studies professors attack opponents of the ground zero mosque. *American Thinker*, August 29

Goode, Stephen. 2003. Putting faith in the founding fathers: WorldNetDaily.com cofounder Joseph Farah challenges all Americans to take back their country by embracing traditional values and spurning today's MTV culture. *Insight Magazine*, March 4

Goodstein, Laurie. 2011. Drawing U.S. crowds with anti-Islam message. *New York Times*, March 7

Goodwin, Jeff and James Jasper, eds. 2004. *Rethinking social movements: Structure, meaning, and emotion.* Lanham, MD. Rowman & Littlefield

Goodwin, Matthew. 2011. Comment: The far right has the same violent intent as al-Qaeda. *The Times (London)*, July 25

Gonsalves, Chris and Kathleen Walter. 2011. Franklin Graham: World's Christians in grave danger. *Newsmax*, March 19

Gramsci, Antonio. 1971. *Selections from the prison notebooks.* Eds and trans. Quintin Hoare and Geoffrey Nowell Smith. New York: International Publishers and London: Lawrence & Wishart.

Gramsci, Antonio. 1985. *Selections from cultural writings.* London; Lawrence & Wishart.

Gramsci, Antonio. 2000. In *The Antonio Gramsci reader: Selected writings 1916–1935.* Ed. D. Forgacs. New York: New York University Press.

Gross, Doug. 2010. Survey: More Americans get news from Internet than newspapers or radio. *CNN*, March 1

Gross, Neil, Thomas Medvetz, and Rupert Russell. 2011. The Contemporary American conservative movement. *Annual Review of Sociology* 37:325–354

Guardian, 2011. PM wins row with Nick Clegg over crackdown on Muslim extremists. *Guardian*, June 4

Guardian. 2011. Far right on rise in Europe, says report. *Guardian*, 6 November.

Gurr, Ted Robert. *Why Men Rebel.* Princeton, NJ: Princeton University Press.

Hagee, John. 2007. *In defense of Israel: The Bible's mandate for supporting the Jewish state.* Rev. ed. Lake Mary, FL: Charisma House.

Hajer, Maarten. 1993. Discourse coalitions and the institutionalisation of practice: The case of acid rain in Great Britain. In *The argumentative turn in policy analysis and planning*, eds Frank Fischer and John Forester, 43-67. London: Durham

Hajer, Maarten. 1995. *The politics of environmental discourse: Ecological modernization and the policy process.* Oxford: Oxford University Press

Hajer, Maarten. 1996. Ecological modernization as cultural politics. In *Risk, environment & modernity: Towards a new ecology*, eds S. Lash, B. Szerszynski, and B. Wynne. London: Sage

Hajer, Maarten. 2005. Coalitions, practices, and meaning in environmental politics: From acid rain to BSE. In *Discourse theory in European politics: Identity, policy, governance*, eds David Howarth and Jacob Torfing, 297-315. New York: Palgrave-MacMillan

Hall, Stuart. 1971. The popular press and social change, 1935-1965. Centre for Contemporary Cultural Studies, University of Birmingham.

Hall, Stuart, Chas Critcher, Tony Jefferson, John Clarke, and Brian Roberts. 1978. *Policing the Crisis: Mugging, the State and Law and Order.* London: Macmillan Press.

Hall Stuart. 1982. The rediscovery of ideology: Return to the repressed in media studies. In *Culture, Society and the Media*, eds. M. Gurevitch, T. Bennett, J. Curon, & J. Woolacott, 56–90. New York: Methuen

Hall, Stuart. 1994. Cultural identity and diaspora. In *Colonial discourse and post-colonial theory: A reader.* Ed. Patrick Williams and Chrisma, 392-401. London: Harvester Wheatsheaf

Hall, Stuart. 1996. Who needs Identity? In *Questions of Cultural Identity*, eds. Stuart Hall and P. du Gay. London; Thousand Oaks; New Delhi: Sage Publications

Hall, Stuart, ed. 1997. *Representation: cultural representations and signifying practices.* London: Sage/Open University

Halverson, Jeffrey, H.L. Goodall Jr. and Steven Corman. 2011. *Master narratives of Islamist extremism.* New York: Palgrave Macmillan.

Hansen, Lene. 1997. A case for seduction? Evaluating the poststructuralist conceptualization of security. *Cooperation and Conflict* 34 no. 2: 369-397.

Hansen, Lene. 2006. *Security as practice. Discourse analysis and the Bosnian war.* London: Routledge

Hari, Johann. 2007. Titanic: Reshuffling the deck chairs on the National Review cruise. *The New Republic* 237 no. 1 (July 2)

Harré, Rom and Bronwyn Davies. 2001. Positioning: The discursive production of selves. In *Discourse theory and practice: A reader,* eds. Margaret Wetherell, Stephanie Taylor, Simeon Yates, 261-271. London: SAGE Publications

Hart, Jeffrey. 2005. *The making of the American conservative mind: National Review and its Times.* Wilmington, DE: ISI Books

Hebdige, Dick. 1979. *Subculture: The meaning of style.* London: Methuen.

Hefner, Robert. 2001. Public Islam and the problems of democratization. *Sociology of Religion* 62, no 4: 491–514.

Henke, Jon. 2009. The RNC responds, but will not distance itself from WorldNetDaily. The next right, September 2

Herf, Jeffrey. 1984. *Reactionary modernism: Technology, culture, and politics in Weimar and the Third Reich.* New York: Cambridge University Press

Herman, E.S. and Noam Chomsky. 2002 [1988]. *Manufacturing consent: The political economy of the mass media.* New York: Pantheon Books

Herrera-Zgaib, Miguel Ángel. 2009. Th public intellectual in critical Marxism: From the organic intellectual to the general intellect. *Pap. Polít. Bogotá* (Colombia) 14, no. 1, 143-163 (Jan-Jun)

Himmelstein, Jerome. 1983. The new right. In *The new Christian right: Mobilisation and legitimization,* eds. Robert C. Liebman and Robert Wuthnow. Hawthorne, N. Y.: Aldine Publishing Co.

Hiscott, William. 2005. 'Parallel societies': A neologism gone bad. *Multicultural Center Prague,* July

Hoar, Jennifer. 2006. Poll: Sinking perceptions of Islam. *CBS News,* April 12

Hoffer, Eric. 1951. The true believer: Thoughts on the nature of mass movements. New York: Perennial/HarperCollins

Hofstadter, Richard. 1964. *The paranoid style in American politics: and other essays.* New York: Knopf.

Hoodbhoy, Pervez. 2005. "Afghanistan and the Genesis of Global Jihad," *Peace Research* 37 no. 1 (May).

Hook, Janet and Tom Hamburger. 2010. "New York Mosque Debate Splits GOP." *The Los Angeles Times,* August 17.

Howarth, David. 2000. *Discourse.* Buckingham: Open University Press.

Howarth, David and Yannis Stavrakakis. 2000. Introducing discourse theory and political analysis. In *Discourse theory and political analysis: Identities, hegemonies and social change,* eds. David. Howarth, A. Norval and Y. Stavrakakis, 1-24. Manchester and New York: Manchester University Press.

Howarth, David., Aletta Norval and Yannis Stavrakakis, eds. 2000. *Discourse theory and political analysis: Identities, hegemonies and social change.* Manchester and New York: Manchester University Press.

Hoyt, Clark. 2008. A radical Islamophobe? *New York Times*, August.

Hunter, James. 1991. *Culture wars: The struggle to define America.* New York: Basic Books

Huntington, Samuel. 1993. Clash of civilizations? *Foreign Affairs* 72 no. 3 (Summer): 22-49

Huntington, Samuel. 1996. *The clash of civilizations and the remaking of the world order.* New York: Touchstone.

Huntington, Samuel. 1999. Robust nationalism. *National Interest*, 20 January

Huntington, Samuel. 1999. The lonely superpower. *Foreign Affairs*, March/April

Huntington, Samuel. 2004. *Who are we?* New York: Simon & Schuster.

Ingersoll, Julie. 2011. "The Left" and Islamists to bring down Judeo-Christian America. *Religion Dispatches (RD) Magazine*, June 27

IPT. 2009. John Esposito: Defending radical Islam. IPT investigative report #304. Investigative Project on Terrorism, October 4 (updated)

Israel Project. 2010. By 10-1 Margin Americans want U.S. to support Israel in conflict with Palestinians. *Israel Project*, March 21

Jackson, Richard. 2005. *Writing the war on terrorism: Language, politics and counter-terrorism.* Manchester: Manchester University Press.

Jackson, Thaddeus. 2006. *Civilizing the enemy: German reconstruction and the invention of the West.* University of Michigan Press.

Jacobson, Mark. 2010. Muhammad comes to Manhattan. *New York*, August 22

Jamieson, Kathleen Hall and Joseph Cappella. 2008. *Echo chamber: Rush Limbaugh and the conservative media establishment.* New York: Oxford University Press.

Jan, Abid Ullah. 2002. *War on Islam?: What does the "War on Terror" mean for the Muslim and non-Muslim world?* Maktabah Al Ansaar

Jenkins, Brian. 2011. Stray dogs and virtual armies: Radicalization and recruitment to jihadist terrorism in the United States since 9/11. Arlington, VA: RAND Corp

Jenkins, Brian. 2010. Would-be warriors: Incidents of Jihadist terrorist radicalization in the United States since September 11, 2001. Santa Monica, CA: Rand.

Jesson, Jill. 2011. *Doing your literature review: Traditional and systematic techniques.* London: SAGE.

Jihad Watch. 2011. Spencer discusses Muslim Brotherhood on FOX News. Jihad Watch, February 1

Jilani, Zaid. 2012. Romney and Ryan court leaders of anti-Muslim hate fest. *AlterNet*, September 16

Johnson, Charles. 2012. FOX News commenters react to Afghan killings: 'A dead Muslim is a good Muslim'. *LittleGreenFootballs.com*, March 11

Johnson, Charles. 2012. Breitbart editor John Nolte calls for Right Wing 'Twitter War'. *Little Green Footballs*, May 16

Johnson, Charles. 2012. Gates of Vienna hateblogger Ned May speaks at European parliament, whines about LGF. *LittleGreenFootballs*, 11 July

Johnson, Charles. 2012. Hate Group Leader Robert Spencer Now Featured Writer at PJ Media: The Backstory. *Little Green Footballs*, June 12

Jones, Jeffrey. 2012. FOX News and the performance of ideology. *Cinema Journal* 51 no. 4 (Summer): 178-185.

Jones, Jeffrey. 2014. FOX & Friends' fear factor: Performing ideology in morning talk. In *How to Watch Television: Media Criticism in Practice*, eds. Ethan Thompson and Jason Mittell. New York: New York University Press.

Jones, M, and E. Jones. 1999. *Mass Media*. London: Macmillan Press

Jones, Steve. 2006. *Antonio Gramsci, Routledge Critical Thinkers*. London and New York. Routledge.

Jørgensen, Marianne, and Louise Phillips. 2002. Discourse analysis as theory and method. London: SAGE Publications

Kabaservice, Geoffrey. 2012. *Rule and ruin: The downfall of moderation and the destruction of the Republican Party*. New York: Oxford University Press

Kagen, Robert. 2008. Neocon nation: Neoconservatism, c. 1776. *World Affairs*, Spring

Kaiser, Robert and Ira Chinoy. 1999. Scaife: Funding Father of the Right. *Washington Post*, May 2: A1

Kampleman M. 1984. Introduction to the Committee on the Present Danger. In *Alerting America: The papers of the Committee on the Present Danger*, ed. C. Tyroler. New York: Pergamon Brassey

Kane, Alex. 2012. Top 5 Islam-bashing Republicans to watch in 2013. *AlterNet*, December 29

Kaplan, Fred. 2004. Can the CIA be saved? *Slate*, July 9

Kaplan, Thomas. 2011. Hearing on terror includes heated debate on Islam. *New York Times* (City Room), April 8

Kaufman, Stuart. 2001. *Modern hatreds: The symbolic politics of ethnic war*. Ithaca NY: Cornell University Press

Kearns, Gerry. 2003. Imperial geopolitics. In *A Companion to Political Geography*, eds. M. Agnew, K. Mitchell, and G. Toal, 173-187. Blackwell, Oxford.

Keck, M. and K. Sikkink. 1998. *Activists beyond borders: Advocacy networks in international politics*. Cornell University Press.

Kedar, Mordechai and David Yerushalmi. 2011. Shari'a and violence in American mosques. Middle East Quarterly, Summer 2011

Kern, Soeren. 2011. European Concerns Over Muslim Immigration Go Mainstream, Hudson, NY, August 15

Kershner, Isabel. 2008. Radical settlers take on Israel. *New York Times*, September 25

Kessler, Ronald. 2007. Podhoretz: World war IV is here. *Newsmax*, September 10

Keyes, Scott. 2011. "EXCLUSIVE: Herman Cain Tells ThinkProgress 'I Will Not' Appoint A Muslim In My Administration." *ThinkProgress*, March 26, http://thinkprogress.org/politics/2011/03/26/153625/herman-cain-muslims/

Khalaji, Mehdi 2012. The clerics vs. modernity. *The Majallah*, May 23

Khaneman, Daniel. 2011. *Thinking fast and slow*. New York: Farrar, Straus and Giroux

Kindy, Kimberly. 2008. Group swamps swing states with movie on radical Islam. *Washington Post*, October 26

Kirk, Russell. 1953. *The conservative mind: From Burke to Eliot*. 7th ed. Washington DC: Regnery Publishing

Koopmans, Ruud. 2003. Political. Opportunity. Structure: Some splitting to balance the lumping, In *Rethinking social movements: Structure, meaning, and emotion*, eds Goodwin and Jasper, 61-73. Lanham, MD: Rowman&Littlefield

Kovel, Joel. 1994. *Red hunting in the promised land*. New York: Basic Books

Krehely J, M. House and E Kernan. 2004. *Axis of ideology: Conservative foundations and public policy*. Washington, DC: National. Committee for Responsive Philanthropy

Krepel, Terry. 2009. Conservatives seek to boycott WorldNetDaily supporters (like the RNC?). *Media Matters*, August 31.

Kumar, Deepa. 2012. *Islamophobia and the politics of empire*. Chicago: Haymarket.

Kumar, Deepa. 2012. Islamophobia: A bipartisan project. *The Nation*, July 2

Kumar, Krishan. 1993. Civil society: An inquiry into the usefulness of an historical term. *British Journal of Sociology* 44, no 3 (September)

Kurth, James. 2009. Samuel Huntington (1927-2008): Ideas have consequences. *Foreign Policy Research Institute*, January 28

Kurzman, Charles. 2011. Muslim-American terrorism since 9/11: An accounting. Triangle Center for Terrorism and Homeland Security, February 2

Kurzman, Charles. 2013. *Muslim-American terrorism: Declining further.* Triangle Center on Terrorism and Homeland Security, February 1

Laclau, Ernesto, ed. 1990. *New reflections on the revolutions of our time.* London: Verso

Laclau, Ernesto, ed. 1994. *The making of political identities.* London: Verso

Laclau, Ernesto. 1996. *Emancipation(s).* London: Verso.

Laclau, Ernesto. 1996. The death and resurrection of the theory of ideology. *Journal of Political Ideologies* 1 no 3: 201-220.

Laclau, Ernesto. 2000. Forward. In *Discourse theory and political analysis*, eds. David Howarth, Aletta Norval, Yannis Stavrakakis, x-xi. Manchester and New York: University of Manchester Press.

Laclau, Ernesto and Chantal Mouffe. 1985/2001. *Hegemony and socialist strategy.* 2nd ed. London: Verso.

Lafferty, Andrea. 2011. Islamic radicalism deserves our focus. Freedom Federation, March 10

Lagos, Taso, Ted Coopman, and Jonathan Tomhave. 2007. Parallel polis: Towards a theoretical framework of the modern public sphere and the structural advantages of the internet to foster parallel institutions. Paper presented at the Western States Communication Association convention, Seattle, WA, February.

Langer, Gary. 2009. Most back outreach to Muslim nations, but suspicion and unfamiliarity persist: ABC News/Washington Post poll: 48 percent hold unfavorable opinion of Islam. *ABC News*, April 5.

Lapidus, Ira. 2002. Egypt: secularism and Islamic society. In *A history of Islamic societies.* 2nd ed. 529-534. Cambridge: Cambridge University Press

Lately, Thomas. 1973. *When even angels wept: The Senator Joseph McCarthy affair—a story without a hero.* Now York: Morrow.

Lean, Nathan. 2012. *The Islamophobia industry: How the right manufactures fear of Muslims.* London: Pluto

Lean, Nathan. 2012. The Islamophobia industry strikes in Kansas. *Huffington Post.com*, June 1

Lean, Nathan. 2012. Book event. Georgetown University: The Islamophobia industry. *Nathan Lean.com*, November 27.

Leffler, Melvyn. 1994. *The specter of Communism.* New York: Hill and Wang

Le Monde. 2011. 42 percent of French people are afraid of Islam. *Le Monde*, 5 January

Lee, Melvin. 2008. The fallacy of grievance-based terrorism. *Middle East Quarterly*, Winter

Levy, Leonard. 1963. *Jefferson and civil liberties: The dark side*. Cambridge, MA: Harvard University Press

Library of Congress. 2014. Japanese-American internment.

Lin, Joy. 2012. "Gingrich to Church: 'Apologists' and 'Elites' Imposing Will on Citizens." FoxNews.com, February 26, http://www.foxnews.com/politics/2012/02/26/gingrich-to-church-apologists-and-elites-imposing-will-on-citizens/

Lind, William. 2007. Who stole our culture? *WorldNetDaily*, May 24

Lobe, Jim. 2011. New report identifies organizational nexus of Islamophobia. *Washington Report on Middle East Affairs* 30 no. 1 (Nov): 18-19.

Lunsing, Wim. 2003. Islam versus homosexuality? Some reflection on the assassination of Pim Fortuyn. *Anthropology Today* 19 no 2: 19–21.

Lynch, Marc. 2010. Veiled truths: The rise of political Islam in the West. *Foreign Affairs* (July, August)

Lyons, Jonathan. 2011. *Islam through Western eyes: From the Crusades to the War on Terrorism*. New York: Columbia University Press

MacDougall, C. 1968. *Interpretive reporting*. New York: Macmillan

Mackinder, Halford J. 1902. *Britain and the British seas*. New York: D. Appleton

MacLeans. 2011. Majority of Canadians see "irreconcilable" rift between Islam and the West. *MacLeans*, September 12

Mansur, Salim. 2008. Immigration and Muslim extremists in the post-9/11 World. *Fraser Institute*, 5 May.

Mantyla, Kyle. 2007. The most objective name in news. *RightWingWatch*, May 18

Mantyla, Kyle. 2010. AFA's Fischer calls for an end to Muslim immigration and the deportation of all Muslims in the US. *Right Wing Watch*, April 8

Mantyla, Kyle. 2010. Boykin: Islam "should not be protected under the First Amendment. *RightWingWatch*, December 6, http://www.rightwingwatch.org/content/boykin-islam-should-not-be-protected-under-first-amendment

Mantyla, Kyle. 2011. Dobson and Boykin expose the Muslim conspiracy to take over the world. *RightWingWatch*, February 17

Mantyla, Kyle. 2011. Boykin terrifies Dobson with dire warnings of America's pending Islamification. *RightWingWatch*, February 18

Mantyla, Kyle. 2011. Video: Gingrich with Hagee, warning US becoming "secular atheist country dominated by radical Islamists." *Right Wing Watch*, April 25, http://www.rightwingwatch.org/content/video-gingrich-hagee-warning-us-becoming-secular-atheist-country-dominated-radical-islamists

Mantyla. Kyle. 2012. Boykin: Go to Dearborn, Michigan and "you would think you were in Beirut or Damascus." *RightWingWatch*, 26 June

Marr, Kendra. 2011. Newt Gingrich: President Obama won't confront radical Islam. *Politico*, March 25

Martin, Frankie. 2010. My take: New portrait of Muslim America shows community on edge. *CNN Belief Blog*, 11 June.

Martin, Richard and Abbas Barzegar, eds. 2010. *Islamism: Contested perspectives on political Islam*. Stanford: Stanford University Press

Marty, Martin and R. Scott Appleby, eds. 1991. *Fundamentalisms observed*. Chicago: University of Chicago Press.

Marty, Martin and R. Scott Appleby, eds. 1993. *Fundamentalisms and the state: Remaking polities, economies, and militance*. Chicago: University of Chicago Press.

Marty, Martin and R. Scott Appleby, eds. 2004. *Fundamentalisms comprehended* (The Fundamentalism Project). Chicago: University Of Chicago Press

Marx, Karl. 1979. Eighteenth brumaire of Louis Bonaparte. In *Karl Marx, Frederick Engels: collected Works* 11. London: Lawrence and Wishart.

Mazzetti, Mark. 2009. "Global Economy Top Threat to U.S., Spy Chief Says," *New York Times*, February 12

McAdam, Doug. 1996. The framing function of movement tactics: Strategic dramaturgy in the American civil rights movement. In *Comparative perspectives on social movements: Political opportunities, mobilizing structures, and cultural framings*, eds. D. McAdam, J. McCarthy, & M. Zald, 338–355. New York: Cambridge University Press

McAdam, Doug, John McCarthy and Mayer Zald, eds. 1996. *Comparative perspectives on social movements: Political opportunities, mobilizing structures, and cultural framings*. New York: Cambridge University Press

McAdam, Doug, Clarance Tarrow and Charles Tilly. 1997. Toward an integrated perspective on social movements and revolution. In *Comparative politics: Rationality, culture and structure*, eds. Mark Lichback and Alan Zuckerman, 142-173. Cambridge: Cambridge University Press.

McAdam, Doug, Clarence Tarrow and Charles Tilly. 2001. *Dynamics of contention*. Cambridge: Cambridge University Press.

McAdam, Doug and William Sewell. 2001. It's about time: Temporality in the study of social movements and revolutions. In *Silence and voice in the study of contentious politics*, eds

Ron Aminzade, Jack Goldstone, Doug McAdam, Eizabeth Perry, William Sewell, Sidney Tarrow, and Charles Tilly. Cambridge: Cambridge University Press.

McCarthy, Andrew. 2009. Making Believe: Obama's speech was deep in fable, short on fact. *NationalReviewOnline*, June 5

McCarthy, Andrew. 2010. The president stands with sharia. *National Review Online*, August 14

McCarthy, Andrew. 2011. The coordinates of radicalism: Sharia compliance correlates with violent attitudes among American Muslims. *National Review*, June 8

McGann, James with Richard Sabatini. 2011. *Global think tanks: Policy networks and governance*. London: Routledge

McLuhan, Marshall, Quinten Fiore, Shepard Fairey. 2005 [1967]. *The medium is the message: An inventory of effects*. Ginko Press

McLuhan, Marshall. 1994[1964]. *Understanding media: The extensions of man*. MIT Press

Mearsheimer, John and Stephen Walt. 2006. "The Israel Lobby," in *London Review of Books* 28 no. 6 (March 23).

Mearsheimer, John and Stephen Walt. 2007. *The Israel lobby and U.S. foreign policy*. New York: Farrar, Straus and Giroux

MediaMatters. 2006. Robertson labeled Islam a "bloody, brutal type of religion." *MediaMatters*, May 1

MediaMatters. 2007. Savage accused Rep. Hinchey of being "in cahoots with al-Qaeda. *MediaMatters*, May 11

MediaMatters. 2010. Report: FOX provides megaphone to New York City mosque opponents. *MediaMatters*, August 13

MediaMatters. 2012. FOX guest Pamela Geller: Obama Is "sanctioning these murderous rages that these Muslim mobs have been going on." *MediaMatters*, September 15

MediaMatters. 2013. FOX guest Pam Geller: Obama "is consistently on the side of jihadic Islamic supremacist regimes." *MediaMatters* July 1

Medvetz, Thomas. 2012. *Think tanks in America: Power, politics, and the new forms of intellectual engagement*. Chicago: University of Chicago Press.

Meyer, David and Debra Minkoff. 2004. Conceptualizing political opportunity. *Social Forces* 82 no. 4 (June)

Meyer, David. 2004. Protest and political opportunities. *Annual Review of Sociology* 30: 125-145

Meyrowitz, Joshua. 2008. Medium theory. In *The international encyclopedia of communication*, ed. Wolfgang Donsbach. Blackwell Publishing/Blackwell Reference Online

Middle East Forum. 2010. Efraim Karsh appointed Middle East Quarterly editor. *Middle East Forum*, July 1

Middle East Forum. 2011. Islamic civilization is dying: A briefing by David P. Goldman. *Middle East Forum*, November 15

Middle East Online. 2010. UN rights body passes Islamophobia resolution. *Middle East Online*, March 25.

Middle East Quarterly, 2009. Editors' note: On peer review. *Middle East Quarterly* 16, no. 1 (Winter)

Miller, David, et al. 2011. The cold war on British Muslims: Conservative think-tanks help fuel a culture of fear, allowing far-right groups to prosper. *Al-Jazeera English*, August 5

Miller John. 2006. *A gift of freedom: How the John M. Olin foundation changed America*. San Francisco: Encounter Books

Miller, Lisa. 2010. The misinformants: What 'stealth jihad' doesn't mean. *Newsweek*, August 28.

Mills, Jane, Ann Bonner and Karen Francis. 2006. The development of constructivist grounded theory. *International Journal of Qualitative Methods* 5, no.1 (March): article 3

Mirkinson, Jack. 2011. Glenn Beck stands by Egypt caliphate conspiracy theory: 'I'm not wrong." *Huffington Post*, February 4

Mitzner, Dennis and Ariel Solomon. 2010. Daniel Pipes: 'Israel has no policy'. *Pajamas Media*, December 10.

MN Progressive Project. 2010. Bachmann: Left in common cause with Islamic extremism. *MN Progressive Project*, June 4

Moghaddam, Fathali and Anthony Marsella, eds. 2003. *Understanding terrorism: Psychosocial Roots, consequences and interventions*. Washington, DC: American Psychological Association

Moore, Malcom. 2006. Muslims outraged by new cartoon of prophet in Hell (Italy). *The Telegraph*, April 1

Morse, Samuel. 1835. *Foreign conspiracy against the liberties of the United States: The numbers of Brutus*. New York: Leavett, Lord & Co.

Moss, Kenneth. 2000. Europe, the Mediterranean, and the Middle East. *Middle East Review of International Affairs* 4 no 1 (March)

Mouffe, Chantal. 2005. *On the political: Thinking in action*. London: Routledge

Mouffe Chantal. 2008. Critique as counter-hegemonic intervention. Transversal multilingualwebjournal. Vienna: European Institute for Progressive Cultural Policies.

Muniz, Albert Jr and Thomas O'Guinn. 2001. Brand community. *Journal of Consumer Research* 27 no. 4 (March)

Muravchik, Joshua. 2007. The past, present, and future of neoconservatism. *Commentary*, October 1

Murphy, Tim. 2011. "Breaking: Anti-sharia Bill Sponsors are Kind of Clueless." *Mother Jones*, April 22

Musaji, Sheila. 2012. "Is Congressional Christian Brotherhood Group Behind GOP Islamophobia?" *The American Muslim*, July 20

Musaji, Shiela. 2011. The GOP has declared war on American Muslims. *The American Muslim*, 23 November.

Nawara, Wael, 2013. Was Morsi's ouster a coup or new Egyptian revolution? *Al-Monitor*, July 4

Newport, Frank. 2007. One-third of Americans believe the Bible is literally true. Gallup.com, May 25

Newport, Frank. 2011. Republicans and Democrats Disagree on Muslim Hearings. Gallup.com, 9 March

NewsMax. 2012. Rev. Franklin Graham: Obama helps Islamists, ignores Christian persecution. *NewsMax*, 21 Feb

Newsweek. 2010. Newsweek poll: Obama/Muslims: Princeton Survey Research Associates International. *Newsweek*, 27 August

Norris, Pippa, Montague. Kern, and Marion Just. 2003. *Framing terrorism: The news media, the government, and the public.* New York: Routledge

Norval, Aletta. 1994. Social ambiguity and the crisis of apartheid. In *The making of political identities*, ed. Ernesto Laclau, 115-137. London. Verso

O' Connor, Alice. 2008. Financing the counterrevolution. In *Rightward bound: Making America conservative in the 1970s*, eds. Bruce Schulman and Julian E. Zelizer, 148–68. Cambridge MA: Harvard University Press

O'Connor, Larry. 2012. Romney campaign: Drudge, Breitbart leading rise of center-Right media. *Breitbart.com*, 29 Jun

Ó Tuathail, Gearóid. 1992. 'Pearl Harbor without bombs': a critical geopolitics of the US-Japan 'FSX' debate. *Environment and Planning A* 24.

Ó Tuathail, Gearóid. 1993. Japan as threat: geo-economic discourse on the USA-Japan relationship in US civil society, 1987-91. In *The political geography of the new world order*, ed. Colin H. Williams. Belhaven Press: London.

Ó Tuathail, Gearóid. 1996. *Critical geopolitics.* London: Routledge

Ó Tuathail, Gearóid. 2003. Just out looking for a fight: American affect and the invasion of Iraq. *Antipode* 35 no. 5 (November): 856-870

Ó Tuathail, Gearóid, and John Agnew. 1992. Geopolitics and discourse: Practical geopolitical reasoning in American foreign policy. *Political Geography* 11 no 2 (March): 190-204.

Oberschall, Anthony. 2000. The manipulation of ethnicity: From ethnic cooperation to violence and war in Yugoslavia. *Ethnic and Racial Studies* 23, no. 6 (November): 982-1001

Ochs, Elinor and Lisa Capps. 1996. Narrating the self. *Annual Review of Anthropology* 25 (October): 19-43

Office of the Coordinator for Counterterrorism. 2011. National Counterterrorism Center: Annex of Statistical Information. In *Country reports on terrorism 2010*. Washington DC: US. Department of State, August. http://www.state.gov/s/ct/rls/crt/2010/170266.htm

O'Hagan, Jacinta. 2002. *Conceptualizing the West in international relations: From Spengler to Said.* New York: Palgrave.

O'Hagan, Jacinta. 2004. 'The power and the passion': Civilizational identity and alterity in the wake of September 11. In *Identity and global politics: Theoretical and empirical elaborations*, eds. Patricia Goff and Kevin Dun, 27-45. New York: Palgrave-Macmillan

Open Society Institute. 2010. Muslims in Europe: A Report on 11 EU Cities. Budapest, London: Open Society Institute

Packer, George. 2005. *The assassins' gate: America in Iraq*. New York: Farrar, Straus and Giroux

Pajamas Media. 2005. Pajamas Media closes $3.5 million venture round (Press release). *Pajamas Media*, November 14

Pareen, Alex. 2011. And boy, WorldNetDaily sure is upset at us. *Salon*, April 14

Parry, Nigel and Ali Abunimah. 2002. Campus Watch: Middle East McCarthyism? *The Electronic Intifida*, September 25

Patten, David. 2010. Palin warns of 'Armageddon,' 'Third World War' in exclusive Newsmax broadcast. *Newsmax*, 11 October.

PBS Newshour. 2001. President Bush. *PBS*, September 17

Peck, James. 2006. *Washington's China: The national security world, the Cold War, and the origins of globalism.* Amherst: University of Massachusetts Press

Persaud, Trevor. 2011. "Q & A: Herman Cain on Faith, Calling, and Presidential Aspirations." *Christianity Today*, March 21

Petersen, Roger. 2002. *Understanding Ethnic Violence: Fear, Hatred, and Resentment in Twentieth-Century Eastern Europe*. Cambridge: Cambridge University Press.

Pew Research Center. 2013. After Boston, little change in views of Islam and violence. Pew Research Center, May 7

Pew Research Center. 2012. Most who know Romney's religion are comfortable: Half identify Obama as a Christian. Pew Research Center, 26 July

Pew Research Center. 2012. Beliefs and practices of U.S. Muslims differ from Muslims abroad. Pew Research Center, August 14

Pew Research Center. 2012. U.S. religious landscape survey. Pew Research Center, 30 July

Pew Research Center. 2011. Common concerns about Islamic extremism: Muslim-Western tensions persist. *Pew Research Center*, July 21

Pew Research Center. 2011. *The Future of the Global Muslim Population: Projections for 2010 to 2030*. Washington DC: Pew Research Center, January. http://www.pewforum.org/files/2011/01/FutureGlobalMuslimPopulation-WebPDF-Feb10.pdf

Pew Research Center. 2010. *Growing number of Americans say Obama is a Muslim*. Pew Research Center, August 18.

Pew Research Center. 2009. No decline in belief that Obama is a Muslim. Washington DC: Pew Research Center, 1 April

Pew Research Center for the People and the Press. 2009. FOX News viewed as most ideological network. Pew Research Center, October 29

Pew Research Center. 2008. Key news audiences now blend online and traditional sources. Pew Research Center, August 17

Pew Research Center. 2007. *Muslim-Americans: Middle class and mostly mainstream*. Pew Research Center, May 22

Pew Research Center. 2007. Public knowledge of current affairs little changed by news and information revolutions: What Americans know: 1989-2007. Pew Research Center, April 15

Phillips, Louise and Marianne Jorgensen. 2002. *Discourse analysis as theory and method*. London: Sage.

Pierson Paul and Theda Skocpol, eds. 2007. *The transformation of American politics: Activist government and the rise of conservatism*. Princeton, NJ: Princeton Univ. Press

Pipes, Daniel and Khalid Durán. 2002. Backgrounder: Muslim immigrants in the United States. Center for Immigration Studies, August

Pipes, Daniel and Jonathan Schanzer. 2002. Extremists on campus. *New York Post*, June 25

Pipes, Daniel and Sharon Chadha. 2006. CAIR: Islamists fooling the establishment. *Middle East Quarterly* (Spring): 3-20

Pipes, Daniel. 1989. *The long shadow: Culture and politics in the Middle East.* New Brunswick, NJ: Transaction Publishers

Pipes, Daniel. 1995. There are no moderates: Dealing with fundamentalist Islam. *National Interest*, Fall

Pipes, Daniel. 1997. *Conspiracy: How the paranoid style flourishes and where it comes from.* New York: Simon & Schuster

Pipes, Daniel. 2002. [Beltway snipers]: Converts to violence? *New York Post* October 25

Pipes, Daniel. 2002. CAIR: 'Moderate' friends of terror. *New York Post*, April 22

Pipes, Daniel. 2002. *Militant Islam reaches America.* New York: W.W. Norton

Pipes, Daniel. 2003 [1990]. *The Rushdie affair: The novel, the ayatollah, and the West.* New Brunswick, NJ: Transaction.

Pipes, Daniel. 2003. Someone named Daniel Pipes. DanielPipes.org, June 20

Pipes, Daniel. 2004. [Samuel Huntington and] American purposes in Iraq. *New York Sun*, April 27

Pipes, Daniel. 2004. In the Mideast, Bush dared to be different. *Philadelphia Inquirer*, October 24.

Pipes, Daniel. 2004. *Miniatures: Views of Islamic and Middle Eastern Politics.* New Brunswick: Transaction

Pipes, Daniel. 2004. The U.S. Institute of Peace stumbles. *New York Sun*, March 23

Pipes, Daniel. 2004. Why the Japanese internment still matters. *New York Sun*, December 28

Pipes, Daniel. 2005. Good News could end in Mideast. *New York Sun*, March 8

Pipes, Daniel. 2007. Bolstering moderate Muslims. *FrontPageMagazine.com*, April 18

Pipes, Daniel. 2007. Five years of Campus Watch. *Jerusalem Post*, September 20

Pipes, Daniel. 2008. The allied menace. *National Review*, July 14

Pipes, Daniel. 2008. Interview by Iivi Anna Masso, Helsinki: TundraTabloidSextra, June 22,

Pipes, Daniel. 2008. Interview by *NPR: Talk of the Nation.* May 15

Pipes, Daniel. 2008. Obama wins, Muslims divided. *Philadelphia Bulletin*, November 12

Pipes, Daniel. 2009. CAIR's inner workings exposed. *WorldNetDaily.com*, October 15

Pipes, Daniel. 2009. Islamism 2.0. *Jerusalem Post*, November 25

Pipes, Daniel. 2009. Resistance to Islamization. *Jerusalem Post*, December 9

Pipes, Daniel. 2009. The system "worked really very, very smoothly" in detroit? *FrontPageMagazine*, December 28

Pipes, Daniel. 2010. "PIPES: 'Rushdie rules' reach Florida. *Washington Times*, September 20

Pipes, Daniel. 2010. In Europe, remorse has turned to masochism. *National Review Online*, April 27

Pipes, Daniel. 2010. Interview with the Friends of Israel Gospel Ministry. Interview by Elwood McQuaid. *Israel My Glory Magazine*, July/August

Pipes, Daniel. 2010. Looking back on DanielPipes.org's first decade. *DanielPipes.org*, December 31

Pipes, Daniel. 2010. Obama, Israel & American Jews: The challenge. *Commentary*, June

Pipes, Daniel. 2010. Why I stand with Geert Wilders. *National Review*, January 19

Pipes, Daniel. 2011. Are we safer? *Center for Security Policy*, September 8

Pipes, Daniel. 2012. Israel's Arabs, living a paradox. *The Washington Times*, March 22

Pipes, Richard. 2004. *Vixi: Memoirs of a non-belonger*. *New Haven and London*: Yale University Press.

Piraneo, Lisa. 2011. Round 2: House Homeland Security Committee hearing on the threat of Muslim-American radicalization in U.S. prisons. *ACT! For America*, June 15

Podhoretz, Norman. 2007. *World war IV: The long struggle against Islamofascism*. New York: Doubleday

Posen, Barry. 1993. The security dilemma and ethnic conflict. *Survival* 35, no. 1 (Spring): 27-38.

Posner, Sarah. 2011. Sharia threat bandwagon just keeps rolling on. *The Guardian*, March 16

Posner, Sarah. 2011. Welcome to the shari'ah conspiracy theory industry. *AlterNet*, April 1

Pötzl, Norbert. 2008. Muslims in Germany: Life in a parallel society. *Spiegel Online International*, April 16

Press and Guide. 2011. Dearborn cited in effort to pass anti-Sharia law in Texas. *Press and Guide*, April 12

PRRI. 2011. Majority day congressional hearings on alleged extremism in American Muslim community 'good idea'. Public Religion Research Institute, February 16

PRRI. 2011. Survey: What it means to be American: Attitudes towards increasing diversity in America ten years after 9/11. Public Religion Research Institute, September 6

PRRI. 2012. Survey: Evangelical voters strongly support Romney despite religious differences. *Public Religion Research Institute*, May 10

Public Policy Polling. 2014. FOX News once again most and least trusted name in news. *PPP*, January 30

Public Policy Polling. 2013. FOX News' credibility ceclines. PPP, February 6

Public Policy Polling. 2013. Republicans and Democrats differ on conspiracy theory beliefs. PPP, Raleigh, NC. April, 2

Public Policy Polling. 2012. Very close race in both Alabama and Mississippi. PPP, March 12

Public Religion Research and The Brookings Institute. 2011. What it means to be American: Attitudes in increasingly diverse America after 9/11. September

Q & A. 2006. Robert Spencer Jihad Watch, Director. Q & A/C-SPAN. August 20

Quilliam Foundation. 2010. *Radicalisation on British university campuses: A case study*. London: Quilliam Foundation, October: 2-26

Rand, Ayn. 1993. *The new left: The anti-industrial revolution*. Rev ed. New York: Plume.

Rasmussen Reports. 2005. 63% believe Bible literally true. *Rasmussen Reports*, 23 April

Reclaim Democracy. 2014. The Powell memo (also known as the Powell Manifesto). *ReclaimDemocracy.org*

Reeves, Thomas. 1997. *The life and Times of Joe McCarthy: A biography*. Madison Books

Reeves, Minou and P. J. Stewart. 2000. *Muhammad in Europe*. Reaves, UK: Garnet Publishing

Reger, Jo, Daniel Myers, Rachel Einwhoner, eds. 2008. *Identity work in social movements*. Minneapolis: University of Minneapolis Press

Reuters. 2009. Anniversary of Rushdie book fatwa. *Reuters*, February 14

Rayfield, Jillian. 2011. Social conservative Bryan Fischer: Muslims are stupid because of inbreeding. *Right Wing Watch*, May 13. http://talkingpointsmemo.com/muckraker/social-conservative-bryan-fischer-muslims-are-stupid-because-of-inbreeding

RightWing Watch. 2011. Robertson: Fighting Muslims is just like fighting Nazis. *Right-wing Watch*, June 1

Roberts, Michael. 2011. David Harsanyi thinks Glenn Beck's The Blaze will "do better" in future than Denver Post. DenverWestword.com, May 3

Robison, John. 1798 [1797]. *Proofs of a Conspiracy against all the Religions and Governments of Europe, carried on in the Secret Meetings of the Free Masons, Illuminati, and Reading Societies*. 3rd edn. Philadelphia: T. Dobson

Rodda, Chris. 2008. Obsession "stars" have lectured at U.S. military colleges; U.S. Navy uses film. *Huffington Post*, September 25

Romano, David. 2006. *The Kurdish nationalist movement: Opportunity, mobilization, and identity*. Cambridge: Cambridge University Press

Rowe, John Carlos. 2012. *The cultural politics of the new American studies*. Michigan Publishing

Rozen, Laura. 2010. The Park 51 money trail. *Politico*, September 4

Runnymede Trust. 1997. *Islamophobia: A challenge for us all*. London. Runnymede Trust

Rupert, G.G. 1911. *The Yellow Peril or Orient vs Occident*. Choctaw OK: Union Publishing Co.

Rusher, William. 2002. Toward a history of the conservative movement. *Journal of Policy History* 14, no. 3: 321-330

Rushing, Josh. 2012. US military under fire for 'anti-Islam class'. *Al-Jazeera*, May 12

Rusin, David. 2009. Government's Fort Hood follies. *IslamistWatch*, November 30

Safi, Omid. 2009. Who put hate in my Sunday paper? Uncovering the Israeli-Republican-evangelical networks behind the "Obsession" DVD. *American Journal of Islamic Social Sciences* 26, no. 1(Winter)

Said, Edward. 1985. Orientalism reconsidered. *Race & Class* 27 no. 2: 1-15

Said, Edward. 1995. Afterward. In *Orientalism*, 329-344. London: Penguin.

Said, Edward. 1997/1981. *Covering Islam: How the media and the experts determine how we see the rest of the world*. Rev ed. New York: Vintage Books

Said, Edward. 2001. The Clash of Ignorance. *The Nation*, October 22

Said, Edward. 2003 [1978]. *Orientalism*. 25th anniversary edn. New York: Vintage Books

Said, Edward and David Barsamian. 2003. *Culture and resistance: Conversations with Edward W. Said*. London: Pluto Press

Saif, Hamzah. 2013. Exposing America's Islamophobes. *The Washington Report on Middle East Affairs* 32 no. 2 (Mar): 59-60.

Sandbrook, Dominic. 2011. *Mad as hell: The crisis of the 1970s and the rise of the populist right*. New York: Alfred A Knopf.

Santorum, Rick. 2007. Speech to second national Academic Freedom Conference. Students for Academic Freedom, March 3, http://www.studentsforacademicfreedom.org/news/2472/speech-by-senator-rick-santorum

Sapsted, David. 2010. UK poll finds profound anti-Muslim sentiment. *The National* (UAE, January 14

Saunders, Doug. 2012. *The myth of the Muslim tide: Do immigrants threaten the West?* New York: Vintage

Sanders, Jerry. 1983. *Peddlers of Crisis: The Committee on the Present Danger and the Politics of Containment.* South End Press.

Schewel, Ben. 2011. Islam and Hegel's philosophy: The hidden link in spirit's history. *Academia.edu*

Schmitt, Carl. 1996 [1932]. *The concept of the political.* Exp ed. Trans. George Schwab. Chicago: University of Chicago Press.

Schubiner, Prerna. 2006. Deconstructing security discourse in past national security strategies. Social Science Research Network, May 6

Schwartz, Stephen. 2010. Islamophobia: America's new fear industry. Phi Kappa Phi Forum (Fall)

Scott, John and Gordon Marshall, eds. 2009. *Oxford dictionary of sociology.* 3rd ed. Rev. Oxford: Oxford University Press

Seitz-Wald, Alex. 2011. FOX News watchers consistently more likely to have negative views of Muslims. *Think Progress.org*, February 16

Seitz-Wald, Alex. 2012. Bachmann defends her witch hunt. *Salon*, July 19

Sen, Amartya. 2006. *Identity and violence: The illusion of destiny.* New York: W. W. Norton

Sewell, William. 2005. *Logics of history: Social theory and social transformation.* Chicago: University of Chicago Press.

Shane, Scott. 2011. Killings in Norway spotlight anti-Muslim thought in U.S. *New York Times*, July 24

Shane, Scott. 2011. In Islamic Law, Gingrich Sees a Mortal Threat to U.S. *New York Times*, December 21

Shapiro, Michael. 1988. *The politics of representation: Writing practices in biography, photography, and policy analysis.* Madison, WI: Wisconsin University Press.

Sharp, Joanne. 1996. Hegemony, popular culture and geopolitics: The Reader's Digest and the construction of danger. *Political Geography* 15 (July-September): 557-570.

Sheehi, Stephen. 2011 *Islamophobia: The Ideological Campaign Against Muslims.* Atlanta: Clarity Press

Shi-xu, ed. 2007. *Discourse as cultural struggle.* Aberdeen, Hong Kong: Hong Kong University Press

Shryock, Andrew. 2013. Attack of the Islamophobes: Religious war (and peace) in Arab/Muslim Detroit. In *Islamophobia in America: The anatomy of intolerance*, ed. Carl Ernst, 145-174. New York: Palgrave-Macmillan.

Shuy, Roger. 1997. Discourse clues to coded language in an impeachment hearing. In *Towards a social science of language: Social interaction and discourse structures Vol II*, ed. Gregory Guy et al., 122-137. Philadelphia, PA: John Benjamins Publishing Co.

Skocpol, Theda and Vanessa Williamson. 2012. *The Tea Party and the remaking of Republican conservatism.* Oxford: Oxford University Press.

Slotkin, Richard. 1973. *Regeneration through violence: The mythology of the American frontier, 1600-1800.* Middletown Connecticut: Wesleyan University Press

Smith, Paul. 1988. *Discerning the subject.* Minneapolis: University of Minnesota Press

Smith, Thomas. 2010. Islam's primary objective is conquest. *Human Events*, August 3

Smith, Tierney. 2011. House panel approves resolution calling on Turkey to return confiscated Christian churches. *CNSNews.com*, August 5

Snow, David and Robert Benford. 1988. Ideology, frame resonance, and participant mobilization. *International Social Movement Research* 1:197–218

Snow, David and Robert Benford. 1992. Master frames and cycles of protest. In *Frontiers in social movement theory*, eds Aldon Morris and Carol Mueller, 133-55. New Haven, CT: Yale Univ. Press

Snow, David and Doug McAdam. 2000. Identity work processes in the construction of social movements: Clarifying the identity/movement nexus. In *Self, identity, and social movements*, eds S Stryker, T.J. Owens, and R.W. White, 47-67. Minneapolis: University of Minnesota Press.

Somanader, Tanya. 2011. "Texas GOP Rep. Introduces Sharia Ban Because He Heard Sharia Is A Threat On The Radio, Asks 'Isn't That True?'" ThinkProgress.org, April 13, http://thinkprogress.org/politics/2011/04/13/158256/texas-sharia-ban/

Southern, R.W. 1962. *Western views of Islam in the Middle Ages.* Cambridge, MA: Harvard University Press

Southern Poverty Law Center. 2012. The year in hate and extremism 2011. *Intelligence Report* 145 (Spring).

Southern Poverty Law Center. 2013. FBI: Bias crimes against Muslims remain at high levels. *Intelligence Report* 149 (Spring)

Spencer, Robert. 2007. *The truth about Muhammad: Founder of the world's most intolerant religion.* Washington DC: Regnery.

Spencer, Robert. 2008. *Stealth jihad: How radical Islam is subverting America without guns or bombs.* Washington DC: Regnery

Spencer, Robert. 2008. Wikipedia and Robert Spencer. *Jihad Watch*, March 6

Spencer, Robert. 2009. Selectivity and spin? An open request to critics. *Jihad Watch*, July 13

Spencer, Robert. 2009. Spencer on the Fred Thompson Show: Interview from November 6. *Jihad Watch*, November 19

Spencer, Robert. 2009. *The complete infidel's guide to the Koran*. Washington DC: Regnery.

Spencer, Robert. 2010. Symposium: The fear that wilders is right. *FrontPageMagazine*, July 9

Spencer, Robert. 2011. The five easy steps to end Islamophobia. *FrontPageMagazine*, December 30

Spencer, Robert. 2012. Good for Gingrich, who dares to disavow sharia. *HumanEvents*, January 24, http://humanevents.com/2012/01/24/good-for-gingrich-who-dares-to-disavow-sharia/

Speckhard, Anne. 2012. *Talking to terrorists: Understanding the psycho-social motivations of militant jihadi terrorists, mass hostage takers, suicide bombers & 'martyrs.'* (McClean VA, Advances Press)

Stauffer, Vernon. 1918. *New England and the Bavarian Illuminati*. PhD diss. Columbia University

Stefancic, Jean, and Richard Delgado. 1996. *No mercy: How conservative think tanks and foundations changed America's social agenda*. Philadelphia, PA: Temple Univ. Press

Stein, Sam. 2010. Poll: Majority of GOP believes Obama sympathizes with Islamic fundamentalism, wants worldwide Islamic law. *Huffington Post*, August 30

Steinert, Heinz. 2003. Unspeakable September 11th: Taken-for-granted assumptions, selective reality construction and populist politics. *International Journal of Urban and Regional Research* 27 no. 3: 651-665

Stern, Eliyahu. 2011. Don't fear Islamic law in America. *New York Times*, September 2

Stern, Jessica. 2001. How terrorists hijacked Islam. *USA Today*, October 1

Stevenson, Richard. 2003. Aftereffects: Washington memo; for Muslims, a mixture of White House signals. *New York Times*, April 28

Steyn, Mark. 2008. *America alone: The end of the World as we know it*. Washington DC: Regnery

Stillwell, Cinnamon. 2009. Mogahed's excuses don't add up. *FrontPageMagazine.com*, October 30

Strauss, Anselm and Juliet Corbin. 1998. *Basics of qualitative research: techniques and procedures for developing grounded theory*. 2nd ed. Thousand Oaks, CA: Sage

Sullivan, Amy. 2011. Column: The sharia myth sweeps America. *USA Today*, June 14

Summers, Juana. 2011. GOP litmus test: Sharia opposition. *Politico*, May 10.

Susser, Asher. 2010. The rise of Hamas in Palestine and the crisis of secularism in the Arab world. Crown Essays (Crown Center for Middle East Studies, Brandeis), February: 1-40

Swedberg, Richard. 2003. Bourdieu's advocacy of the concept of interest and its role in economic sociology. *Economic Sociology* 4, no. 2 (March)

Swidler, Ann. 1986. Culture in action: Symbols and strategies. *American Sociological Review* 51 no. 2 (April): 273-86

Tarrow, Sidney. 1994. *Power in movement: Social movements, collective action and politics.* Cambridge: Cambridge University Press

Tashman, Brian. 2010. Meet Allen West: Fanatical opponent of Muslims, immigrants, progressives & obama. *RightWingWatch*, November 9

Tashman, Brian. 2011. Boykin: Obama administration has shown 'support for the infiltration of the Muslim Brotherhood into our government'. *RightWingWatch*, July 6

Tashman, Brian. 2012. Bachmann says Obama 'spit at the constitution'; warns the Muslim Brotherhood 'penetrated' government. *RightWingWatch*, June 22.

Tassel, Janet. 2005. Militant about "Islamism": Daniel Pipes wages "hand-to-hand combat" with a "totalitarian ideology." *Harvard*, Jan-Feb.

Terkel, Amanda. 2010. Florida Tea Party to host 'radical Islamophobe' who said Muslims shouldn't hold political office. *AlterNet*, July 18

Theel, Shauna. 2011. Beck turns to the fringe to validate his "crazy conspiracy theory." *MediaMatters,* March 5

ThinkProgress. 2011. Texas GOP rep. introduces sharia ban because he heard Sharia is a threat on the radio, asks "isn't that true?" *ThinkProgress*, April 14

Thompson, John. 1990. *Ideology and modern culture: Critical social theory in the era of mass communication.* Stanford, CA: Stanford University Press

Thompson, John. 1991. Editor's introduction. In *Language & symbolic power*, by Pierre Bourdieu. Ed. John B. Thompson. Trans. Gino Raymond and Matthew Adamson, 1-31. Cambridge MA: Polity Press

Tilly, Charles. 1978. *From mobilization to revolution.* Reading: Addison-Wesley

Time Magazine. 1933. Foreign news: Again, Yellow Peril. *Time Magazine*, September 11

Toal, Gerard 1989. Critical geopolitics: The social construction of place and space in the practice of statecraft. PhD Diss. Syracuse University

Torfing, Jacob. 2005. Discourse theory: Achievements, arguments and challenges. In *European politics: Identity, policy and governance*, eds. David Howarth and Jacob Torfing, 1-30. Basingstoke: Palgrave-Macmillan

Trivedi, Rita. 2004. Creating opportunities, opening doors: The American woman suffrage movement 1850-1919. Paper presented at the annual meeting of the American Sociological Association, San Francisco, CA, August 14

UC Berkeley-CAIR. 2011. Same hate, new target: Islamophobia and its impact in the United States, January 2009-December 2010.

United Nations Population Fund. 2000. Ending violence against women and girls. In *State of the world population 2000*. New York: United Nations Population Fund. Chapter 3

U.S. Congress. 1967. House Un-American Activities Committee (HUAC). Subversive influences in riots, looting, and burning. Washington DC: Government Printing Office

U.S. Congress. 1951. Senator Joseph McCarthy. The history of George Catlett Marshall. In The Congressional Record: Proceedings and Debates of the 82nd Congress, First Session, Vol. 97, Part 5 (May 28, 1951-June 27, 1951): 6556-6603.

U.S. Department of Justice. 2008. *Criminal victimization in the United States, 2006: Statistical tables*. US Department of Justice, August.

USHistory.org. 2014. Japanese-American internment. *U.S. History Online Textbook*

Van Dijk, Teun. 1993. Principles of critical discourse analysis. *Discourse & Society* 4 no. 2: 249-283

Van Dijk, Teun. 2006. Ideology and discourse analysis. *Journal of Political Ideologies* 11 no. 2 (June): 115-140

Van Stekelenburg, Jacquelien and Bert Klandermans. 2010. The social psychology of protest. *Sociopedia-ISA*

Vest, Jason. 2002. Coming soon: "Total war" on the Middle East. *The Nation*, August 28

Vetlesen, Arne. 2005. *Evil and human agency: Understanding collective evildoing*. New York: Cambridge University Press

Viorst, Milton. 2006. *Storm from the East: The struggle between the Arab world and the Christian West*. Random House

Vitello, Paul. 2011. Amid rift, imam's role in Islam center is sharply cut. *New York Times*, January 14

Vogel, Kenneth and Giovanni Russonello. 2010. Latest mosque issue: The money trail. *Politico*,
September 4

Wacquant, Loïc. 2013. Symbolic power and group-making: On Pierre Bourdieu's reframing of class. *Journal of Classical Sociology* 0 no 0: 1-18

Waever, Ole. 1993. Identity, migration and the new security agenda in Europe. London: Pinter.

Wæver, Ole.1995. Securitization and desecuritization.' In *On security*, ed. R. Lipschutz, 46–86. New York: Columbia University Press.

Walshe, Sushannah. 2012. Santorum says quality 'doesn't come from Islam' but from 'God of Abraham, Isaac & Jacob'. *ABC News*, January 20

Walt, Stephen. 1991. The renaissance of security studies. *International Studies Quarterly* 35 no. 2 (June): 211-239

Washington Post. 1985. U.S. may still strike back, Reagan hints. *Washington Post*, June 29

Washington Times. 2007. "Times Challenges Worldview of Elites," *Washington Times*, May 16. http://www.washingtontimes.com/news/2007/may/16/20070516-040557-5645r/?page=all

Washington Times. 2007. CAIR membership falls 90% since 9/11. *Washington Times*, June 12

Washington Times. 2009. Gaffney: America's first Muslim president? *Washington Times*, June 9

Washington Times. 2010. Pipes: 'Rushdie rules' reach Florida: Obama endorses privileged status for Islam. *Washington Times*, September 20.

Weber, Max. 1946. *From Max Weber: Essays in sociology*. Eds. H.H. Gerth and C. Wright Mills. New York: Oxford University Press

Webb, Lee. 2009. Army Gen.: Ft Hood worst terrorism since 9/11. CBN, November 16

Weigel, George. 2008. Remembering Bill Buckley. *Catholic Exchange*, April 14

White House. 2001. "Islam is Peace" says President: Remarks by the President at Islamic Center of Washington, D.C. Washington, D.C.: White House, September 17

Wickham, Carrie. 2002. *Mobilizing Islam*. New York: Columbia University Press

Widmaier, Wesley. 2007. Constructing foreign policy crises: Interpretive leadership in the Cold War and war on terrorism. *International Studies Quarterly* 51 no. 4: 779–794.

Wike, Richard & Brian Grim. 2010. Western views toward Muslims: Evidence from a 2006 cross-national survey. *International Journal of Public Opinion Research* 22 no. 1: 4-25

Wiktorowicz, Quintan. 2005. A genealogy of radical Islam. *Studies in Conflict and Terrorism* 28: 75-97.

Williams, Juan. 2011. *Muzzled: The assault on honest debate*. New York: Crown.

Williams, Michael. 2003. Words, images, enemies: Securitization and international politics. *International Studies Quarterly* 47: 511–531

Wilson, Bruce. 2007. McCain and Lieberman frolic at CUFI's festival of hate. *Talk to Action*, August 15

Winter, T.J. 2004. The poverty of fanaticism. In *Islam, fundamentalism, and the betrayal of tradition*, ed. Joseph E. B. Lumbard, 283-296. Bloomington, IN: World Wisdom

Wittgenstein, Ludwig. 1969. *On certainty*, eds G. Anscombe and G. von Wright. New York: Harper & Row

Wolf, Z. Byron. 2011. Director of National Intelligence James Clapper: Muslim Brotherhood "largely secular." *ABC News*, February 10

Woods, Jeff. 2004. Black struggle; Red Scare; Segregation and anti-Communism in the South, 1948-1968. Baton Rouge: Louisiana State University

World Economic Forum. 2008. *Islam and the West: Annual report on the state of dialogue.* World Economic Forum, January

World Public Opinion and Knowledge Networks. 2010. *Misinformation and the 2010 election: A study of the US electorate.* World Public Opinion and Knowledge Networks, December 10

Wren, K. 2001. Cultural racism: something rotten in the state of Denmark? *Social & Cultural Geography* 2 no. 2

X (George Kennan). 1947. The sources of Soviet conduct. *Foreign Affairs*, July

Yeh, Becky. 2010. Islam and immigration. *OneNewsNow.com*, August 3

Ye'or, Bat. 2005. *Eurabia: The Euro-Arab axis.* Fairleigh Dickinson University Press

Yerushalmi, David. 2006. On race: A tentative decision. *The McAdam Report* 585 (May 12)

Yildirim, Seval. 2007. Discussing Islam in the post-9/11 epistemological terrain. *Pace International Law Review* 19 no. 2 (Fall): 223-231

YouGov. 2010. Press release: Major campaign to challenge misperceptions of Islam. YouGov, June 7 [republished by Quilliam Foundation]

Zafar, Walid. 2011. Rep. Gohmert suggests Obama's allegiances are to "Islamic states." *Political Correction*, June 17

Zinn, Howard. 1980. *A people's history of the United States: 1942-present.* New York: Harper-Collins

Zogby, James. 2008. *The way we'll be: The Zogby report on the transformation of the American dreams.* New York: Random House

www.ingramcontent.com/pod-product-compliance
Lightning Source LLC
Chambersburg PA
CBHW081147270326
41930CB00014B/3065